Congress and Its Members

Congress and Its Members

THIRD EDITION

Roger H. Davidson
University of Maryland

Walter J. Oleszek
Congressional Research Service

CQ
PRESS

A Division of Congressional Quarterly Inc.
1414 22nd Street N.W., Washington, D.C. 20037

Printed in the United States of America

Photo Credits: 2, Architect of the Capitol; 12, Library of Congress; 46, Wide World Photos; 82, Campaigns and Elections; 158, Architect of the Capitol; 171, Wide World Photos; 179, *Washington Post;* 226, Wide World Photos; 256, George Tames; 306, Architect of the Capitol; 336, Warren Leffler; 364, Steve Karafyllakis, Congressional Quarterly; 392, Marty LaVor 1989; 416, Ken Heinen.

Library of Congress Cataloging-in-Publication Data

Davidson, Roger H.
    Congress and its members / Roger H. Davidson, Walter J. Oleszek. -
- 3d ed.
        p.   cm.
    Bibliography: p.
    Includes index.
    ISBN 0-87187-491-1 (pbk.)
    ISBN 0-87187-536-5
    1. United States. Congress. 2. Legislators--United States.
I. Oleszek, Walter J.   II. Title.
JK1061.D29   1990
328.73--dc20   89-9814
                                                       CIP

For Nancy, Douglas, and Christopher
R.H.D.

Janet, Mark, and Eric
W.J.O.

Contents

Tables, Figures, and Boxes

Tables

Figures

Boxes

Preface

The U.S. Congress is an institution that mirrors its political surroundings and adapts and adjusts to events and trends. As our first edition went to press in 1981, the Reagan era had just begun. It was one of those rare moments—only the fourth in this century—when the undeniable momentum of presidential leadership, backed by popular support, swept aside roadblocks to effect far-reaching shifts in the political agenda, public debate, and national priorities.

By 1985, when the second edition appeared, the Reagan revolution had slowed perceptibly. The era of divided government was marked by sharp ideological cleavages in both domestic and foreign affairs. Hurt by the Iran-contra revelations and lacking fresh ideas, the Reagan administration loosened its hold on the political agenda. This political vacuum was soon filled by the Democrats, frustrated and impatient after six years of Reagan in the White House. Emboldened by their recapture of the Senate and continued domination of the House in the 100th Congress (1987-1989), the Democrats gathered their forces (with some bipartisan help) to pass an ambitious legislative program, override key presidential vetoes, redirect Central American policy, help frame U.S.-Soviet arms agreements, and reject a Supreme Court nominee, Robert H. Bork.

As Congress and the presidency enter the post-Reagan era, this third edition attempts to provide a new portrait of our fast-moving target. Congress, in certain crucial respects, is a very different institution than it was in 1981. Nearly half the members of the House and Senate have been elected to their present positions since then (this despite low electoral turnover that has critics worried). Most committee chairmen and virtually all party leaders assumed their posts after 1981. And while there have been few formal alterations in structures or procedures, Congress's legislative workload and its techniques for handling that workload are vastly different than they were just a few years ago.

Because of the continued urgency of fiscal issues, we added a new chapter on the budget and domestic policy making. Another new chapter, on national security, consolidates our treatment of foreign policy and also discusses issues such as military "pork barreling" and the war powers. Structural shifts in the legislative workload are described—for example, the increased use of a few "mega-bills" and a large number of uncontroversial "commemorative" bills. Changes in leadership (particularly in the Speaker of the House) and impressive levels of party voting are analyzed, along with changes in the balance of power between authorizing and appropriating committees. George Bush's early encounters with Congress are evaluated in detail.

Trends in Congress's political environment also are highlighted. Intensified concern about congressional recruitment (especially for House seats) is reflected in an expanded discussion of the quality of challengers. We attempt to explain not only why incumbents are so formidable but also why serious challengers are in short supply. Our analysis of gerrymandering is more thorough in light of the Supreme Court's noteworthy—though we think misguided—ruling in an Indiana case, *Davis et al. v. Bandemer et al.* (1986), which raised more questions than it answered.

Amid all these legal, political, and institutional changes, there are underlying constants in Congress's character and behavior. Most important is the dual nature of Congress as a collection of career-maximizing politicians and an arena for shaping and refining national policy. In this edition we use the "two Congresses" theme even more extensively to explain the myriad details of congressional life as well as scholarly findings about legislators' behavior. Colorful personalities and practical examples are presented to enliven the enduring topics essential for understanding Capitol Hill. We strive to describe recent facts and trends precisely and perceptively; more than that, we try to place these developments in the broader historical and conceptual contexts necessary for full comprehension. Moreover, in writing this edition we have kept in mind general readers seeking an introduction to the modern Congress as well as college or university students taking courses on the legislative process and national policy making.

As with most interpretive texts, this is a collaborative work. Professors Jerry Calvert of Montana State University, Linda L. Fowler of Syracuse University, and Jean Torcom of California State University, Sacramento, were kind enough to review the second edition of our book and to offer many thoughtful recommendations. To them, as well as to those who contributed to the first two editions, we offer heartfelt thanks. We also would like to thank our readers, including students and teachers at the more than 300 colleges and universities here and abroad where our book has been adopted.

Our colleagues and fellow scholars have provided encouragement and assistance at many specific junctures. Among them we acknowledge especially Joe Cantor, Royce Crocker, Edward M. Davis III, Paul Dwyer, Louis Fisher, David Huckabee, Robert Keith, Johnny Killian, Ronald Moe, Ilona Nickels, John Pontius, Sula P. Richardson, and Richard Sachs.

The staff at CQ Press deserves special thanks. Director Joanne Daniels has given us enthusiastic support. Our editor for this edition, Barbara de Boinville, is one of the best in the business; she has been unfailingly a tough yet cheerful critic. Kerry Kern, the production editor for this volume, juggled balky software and insistent authors with diplomatic aplomb. And for their valuable production help and photo research we thank Nancy Kervin and Jamie Holland.

Our deep appreciation for our families, their love and support, cannot be fully encompassed by words. As a measure of our affection, this edition is dedicated to them.

Roger H. Davidson
Walter J. Oleszek
Washington, D.C.
June 1989

PART ONE

In Search of the Two Congresses

A good government implies two things: first, fidelity to the object of government, which is the happiness of the people, secondly, a knowledge of the means by which that object can be best attained.

The Federalist, No. 62 (1788)

Legislatures are really two objects: a collectivity and an institution. As a collectivity, individual representatives act as receptors, reflecting the needs and wants of constituents. As an institution, the Legislature has to make laws, arriving at some conclusions about what ought to be done about public problems.

Charles O. Jones
"From the Suffrage of the People: An Essay of Support and Worry for Legislatures" (1974)

These two statements—one by the authors of *The Federalist,* the other by a modern scholar—express our thesis. As the words suggest, the idea that representative assemblies contain an inherent tension between representation and lawmaking, between individual and institution, is neither new nor novel. This dualism is embedded in the Constitution, manifested in history, and validated by scholars' findings.

In elaborating the "two Congresses" notion, this book is organized into four parts, each with a brief explanatory introduction. In this part the two Congresses theme is outlined, and the historical development of the institution and its members is briefly traced.

Two at a time, flags are raised and lowered on a special flagpole for constituents requesting a "flag flown over the Capitol."

CHAPTER ONE

The Two Congresses

In California's 19th Congressional District a battle royal was raging. It was a rarity in congressional politics: a close-fought election contest between an eight-term U.S. representative and a well-financed challenger, a veteran state legislator.

Just beyond the northern outposts of metropolitan Los Angeles, the 19th district runs North and South from Santa Barbara along the Pacific Ocean. Despite its idyllic beaches, neat Spanish-style homes, and orchards of lemons and avocadoes, the 19th is a battleground in more ways than one. Issues of growth and the environment generate intense political pressures and divide the citizenry. At the northern and southern edges of the district, including the working-class cities of Santa Maria and Ventura, industry and growth are welcomed. But in Santa Barbara, where 60 percent of the voters reside and where costly homes overlook a phalanx of offshore oil platforms in the Santa Barbara Channel, environmental protection issues rally support.

The home of Ronald Reagan's mountain-top Rancho Cielo, the district has voted Republican in recent national elections. But the 19th "has enough Democrats to keep it from being a safely Republican district," and it has sent Democrats to the state legislature in Sacramento.[1] One of these was state senator Gary K. Hart (no relation of the one-time Colorado senator and presidential contender). Growing impatient, Hart at last decided to challenge veteran representative Robert J. Lagomarsino in 1988. Lagomarsino had built his congressional career, begun in 1974, out of a deft combination of attentive constituent service and a reputation for being something of an environmentalist on the House Interior Committee. Overall, his voting record was quite conservative, and his main enthusiasm on Capitol Hill seemed to be unflagging loyalty to the cause of the Nicaraguan contras as a senior member of the House Foreign Affairs Committee.

Hart's well-financed campaign tried to convince the district that the incumbent was a right-winger out of step with the area's moderate voters. He charged that Lagomarsino had lagged in protecting the Santa Barbara Channel from oil exploitation and that Lagomarsino's frequent forays to

Nicaragua detracted from his effectiveness in district politics. (In the end the challenger came close to victory but fell short, 49 percent to 51 percent. Like most incumbents, Lagomarsino was able to parlay his constituency outreach and superior fund raising into victory, albeit a narrow one.)

Three thousand miles away on the East Coast, the 100th Congress lurched toward its conclusion. The smouldering warfare between the Democratically controlled Congress and the Reagan administration prolonged the legislative deliberations. Carefully laying their groundwork for the 1988 campaign, Democrats passed a series of popular measures—including welfare reform, catastrophic health insurance, and drought aid—and forced the lame-duck president's hand on issues such as required worker notification of plant closings.

The Dual Nature of Congress

Both the partisan debates on Capitol Hill and the intense struggle in the California 19th point up the character of the U.S. Congress. Both scenes, in fact, describe integral aspects of Congress—as a lawmaking body and a representative assembly. But how can we reconcile these disparate elements?

The answer is that there are really two Congresses, not just one. Often these two Congresses are widely separated; the tightly knit, complex world of Capitol Hill is a long way from California's 19th Congressional District—not only in miles, but in perspective and outlook as well. Moreover, the two Congresses are analytically distinct: studies indicate that public officials and citizens view the twin functions of elected assemblies—lawmaking and representing—as separate, definable tasks.

And yet these two Congresses are closely bound together. What affects one sooner or later affects the other. Representative Lagomarsino's behavior in Washington was shaped by his district and its character—slightly right-of-center yet environmentally aware. By the same token, the image he projected back home to his constituents reflected what he accomplished on Capitol Hill as secretary of the Republican Conference and as a senior member of two important committees. For his challenger, Hart, the interdependencies were no less important. His Democratic party had compiled an attractive legislative record for what was hoped would be "a good year for Democrats"; his job was to persuade voters that the incumbent was not in tune with the district and its needs.

One of these two entities, Congress as a lawmaking institution, is the Congress of textbooks, of "how-a-bill-becomes-a-law." It is Congress acting as a collegial body, performing constitutional duties and handling legislative issues. And it is an intriguing subject. To tourists no less than veteran Congress-watchers, Capitol Hill is a fascinating arena where converge many of the forces of American political life—ambitious politicians, White House and executive officials, lobbies both powerful and weak, not to mention intricate congressional structures and procedures that organize the legislative struggle. The issues aired on Capitol Hill, to invoke a time-worn sentiment, affect the well-being of all of us.

Yet there is a second Congress, every bit as important as the Congress of the textbooks. This is the representative assemblage of 540 individual senators, representatives, and delegates. They are men and women of diverse ages, backgrounds, and routes to office. Their electoral fortunes depend, not upon what Congress produces as an institution, but upon the support and goodwill of voters hundreds or thousands of miles away. Journalist Richard Rovere once compared members of Congress with tribesmen whose chief concern while in Washington was what was going on around the council fires back home. This may be an exaggeration, but it contains an important truth: by no means does all congressional activity take place in Capitol Hill chambers or committee rooms.

The Historical Basis

The dual character of Congress is rooted in history. Congress's mandate to write the nation's laws is found in Article I of the Constitution, which details the powers of government as set forth by the Founders in 1787. It was no accident that the Constitution's drafters devoted the first article to the legislature nor that here were enumerated most of the government's powers. Familiar with the British Parliament's prolonged struggles with the Crown, the Constitution's authors assumed the legislature would be the chief policy-making body and the bulwark against arbitrary executives. ("In republican government, the legislative authority necessarily predominates," observed James Madison in *The Federalist Papers*.[2]) Although in the ensuing years, initiative shifted many times between the legislative and executive branches, the U.S. Congress remains virtually the only national assembly in the world that actually tries to write the laws it passes, rather than simply ratifying measures prepared by the government in power.

At the very same time, Congress as a representative body must respond to the heavy demands of voters and constituents. Although not specifically mentioned in the Constitution, these duties flow from its provisions for electing representatives and senators.

The House of Representatives is, and was intended to be, the most representative part of our government. Representatives are elected directly by the people for two-year terms to ensure that they do not stray too far from popular opinion. As Madison explained, the House should have "an immediate dependence on, and an intimate sympathy with, the people." [3] For most members of the House, this means nonstop campaigning, visiting, looking after constituents, and errand running. For some others the job is simpler; yet no elected official is totally immune to electoral defeat.

The Senate originally was intended to be one step removed from popular voting to temper the popular sentiments of the House. But the Founders were ultimately overruled. The people were assured a voice in 1913 by ratification of the Seventeenth Amendment, which provided for direct election of senators. Even though elected for six-year terms, senators typically are servants of their constituents; most have transformed their office staffs into veritable cottage industries for generating publicity and handling constituents' inquiries.

Thus, the Constitution and subsequent historical developments affirm Congress's dual functions of *lawmaker* and *representative assembly*. Although the roles are tightly bound together, they nonetheless impose separate duties and functions.

Legislators' Tasks

This dualism between institutional and individual duties surfaces in legislators' role orientations and daily activities. As Speaker Sam Rayburn, D-Texas, once remarked:

> A congressman has two constituencies—he has his constituents at home, and his colleagues here in the House. To serve his constituents at home, he must also serve his colleagues here in the House.[4]

Like most of us, senators and representatives suffer from a lack of time to accomplish what is expected of them. No problem vexes members more than that of juggling constituency and legislative tasks. Despite scheduled recesses for constituency business (called "district work periods" by the House, "nonlegislative periods" by the Senate), the pull of constituency business is relentless. The average representative spends 120 days a year in the home constituency, the average senator 80 days.[5] Even in Washington, legislative and constituency demands constantly intrude; according to one study, less than 40 percent of a representative's Washington time is allotted to lawmaking duties on the floor of the House or in committee.[6]

Members of Congress themselves, when asked to describe the functions they should perform in office, stress the twin roles of legislator and representative. Naturally, legislators differ in the weight they assign these roles, not to mention the time and resources they devote to them. With their longer terms, senators can follow a more cyclical attention span, stressing voter outreach and fence mending during the year or so before reelection, but focusing on legislative activities at other times. Yet senatorial contests are normally more competitive than House races, and many senators now run flat out for reelection all the time—like most of their House colleagues.[7]

Legislators often must choose between the demands of these two roles. A House-sponsored survey once asked members about differences between how they *actually* spent their time and what they would like to do *ideally* as a member of Congress. By far the most frequent complaint, voiced by half of the representatives, was that constituent demands interfered with lawmaking and other Hill activity.[8]

Congress's dual nature—the unresolved dichotomy between its lawmaking and representative functions—is dictated by the Constitution, validated by historical experience, and reinforced by the inclinations of voters and legislators alike. And yet Congress is literally one body, not two. The same members who shape bills in committee and vote on the floor must rush to catch planes back to their districts where they are plunged into a different world, one of local problems and personalities. And the same candidates who must sell themselves at shopping center rallies must, in Washington, focus on baffling issues such as inflation rates or military weapons systems. The unique character of Congress flows directly from its dual role as a representative assembly and a lawmaking body.

Popular Images

The two Congresses notion also conforms with the perceptions of the average person. Opinion studies reveal that citizens view the Congress in Washington through different lenses than they do their individual senators and representatives. Congress as an institution is seen primarily as a lawmaking body. It is judged mainly on the basis of citizens' overall attitudes about politics, policies, and the state of the union. Do people like the way things are going, or do they not? Are they optimistic or pessimistic about the nation's future? Do they subscribe to Mark Twain's harsh, cynical view that Congress is a "distinctly native criminal class"?

By contrast, citizens view their own legislators as agents of local interests. They measure these legislators by yardsticks such as service to the district, communication with constituents, and "home style"—that is, the way the officeholder deals with the home folks.

In judging their senators or representative, voters are likely to ponder questions such as: Do I trust the legislator? Does the legislator communicate well with the state (or district) by answering mail promptly and offering timely help to constituents? Does the legislator listen to the state (or district) and its concerns?[9]

The public's divergent expectations of Congress and its members often send conflicting signals to senators and representatives. Congress as a whole is judged by policies and results, however vaguely these are perceived by voters; individual legislators are elected, and returned to office, mainly because of personal qualifications and constituent service. To many legislators, this dictates a strategy of putting as much distance as possible between themselves and "those other politicians" back in Washington—including their party's leaders. Many candidates and incumbents run *for* Congress by running *against* Congress.[10]

Back to Burke

On November 3, 1774, in Bristol, England, the British statesman and philosopher Edmund Burke set forth for his constituents the dual character of a national legislature. The constituent-oriented Parliament, or Congress, he described as

> a Congress of ambassadors from different and hostile interests, which interests each must maintain, as an agent and advocate, against other agents and advocates.

The Parliament of substantive lawmaking he portrayed in different terms:

> a deliberative assembly of one nation, with one interest, that of the whole—where not local purposes, not local prejudices, ought to guide, but the general good, resulting from the general reason of the whole.[11]

From Burke we have chosen the titles for Part Two, A Congress of Ambassadors, and Part Three, A Deliberative Assembly of One Nation. Burke himself preferred the second concept and did not hesitate to let his voters know it; he would give local opinion a hearing, but his judgment and conscience would prevail in all cases. "Your faithful friend, your devoted servant, I shall be to the end of my life," he declared; "flatterer you do not wish for." [12]

Burke's Bristol speech is an enduring statement of the dilemma confronting members of representative assemblies. Burke was an inspired lawmaker. (He even sympathized with the cause of the American colonists.) But his candor earned him no thanks from his constituents, who turned him out of office at the first opportunity.

Today we might say Burke suffered from an inept "home style." Yet he posed the tension between the two Congresses so vividly that we have adopted his language to describe the conceptual distinction that forms the crux of this book. Every legislator must sooner or later come to terms with Burke's question; as citizens and voters, you will have to form your own answers.

Divergent Views of Congress

In describing and analyzing the two Congresses we will draw upon a wide variety of materials. Congress has been the subject of a bewildering array of books, monographs, and articles. Many of its features make Congress such a favorite object of scholarly scrutiny. It is open and accessible. Its work can be measured by statistical indicators (floor votes, for example) that permit elaborate comparative analyses. And Congress is, above all, a fascinating place—a strategic site from which to view the varied actors in the American political drama.

Many of these same features attract journalists and interpretive reporters to Congress. Although Congress does not enjoy the media attention lavished on the president and his entourage, it is extensively covered. Some of the nation's most perceptive commentators have written incisive, provocative analyses of Congress and the politicians who inhabit it. In short, interested observers can draw upon a large body of information about Congress.

Writers of an interpretive book on the U.S. Congress are thus faced with an embarrassment of riches. Studies of Congress constitute perhaps the richest body of political literature. This is a mixed blessing because we have to integrate this information into something resembling a coherent whole. Moreover, much of the writing is highly specialized, technical, or theoretical; we have tried to put such material into perspective, make it understandable to interested nonspecialists, and use illustrative examples wherever possible.

Another body of information about Congress, less accessible to the average citizen, is Capitol Hill history, precedents, and lore. Some of it is recorded in public documents, but most of it is stored in the memories of legislators, their staffs, and the lobbyists and executive officials who deal with them. By and large, this information focuses on the day-to-day "real world" of Capitol Hill—its events, its personalities, and its rules and habits.

A gap sometimes exists between those who write about Congress and those who actually live and work on Capitol Hill. Legislators and their aides are often suspicious of "those professors," who (they say) spin theories of little practical value.[13] And they are equally wary of journalists, who are as potentially dangerous to a politician's career as they are essential to it. Outside commentators often dismiss Capitol Hill wisdom. Professors tend to regard the "insider" view as unsystematic, anecdotal, or mere gossip. Journalists suspect the insider view is self-serving (which it often is), designed to obscure the public's view. These conflicting perspectives naturally spring from varying motives and divergent premises.

Is this book, then, an "insider" or an "outsider" view of Congress? Both, we hope. While it would be presumptuous to claim that we can fully integrate these two viewpoints, our own careers have enabled us to see Congress from both perspectives—as academic political scientists and as congressional staff members. We understand the wide gap between observing Congress as a scholar or commentator and having direct responsibilities for advising members of Congress.

Intimate knowledge of an institution helps one interpret it to others, but being too close can invite distortion. We believe we know our subject well enough to appreciate its foibles and understand why it works the way it does. Yet we try to maintain a degree of professional—and scholarly—distance from it. It is hard enough to describe how and why an institution functions; it is even more challenging to analyze its strengths and defects and to propose how it might operate differently. No one can be entirely sanguine about the future of Congress or indeed of representative government, and we invite students and colleagues to join us in contemplating what alternatives lie before us.

Notes

1. Alan Ehrenhalt, *Politics in America: The 100th Congress* (Washington, D.C.: Congressional Quarterly, 1987), 148.
2. James Madison, *The Federalist,* No. 51, ed. Edward Mead Earle (New York: Modern Library, n.d.), 338.
3. Ibid., 343.
4. Sam Rayburn, *Speak, Mr. Speaker,* ed. H. G. Dulaney and Edward Hake Phillips (Bonham, Texas: Sam Rayburn Foundation, 1978), 263-264.
5. Glenn R. Parker, *Homeward Bound: Explaining Changes in Congressional Behavior* (Pittsburgh: University of Pittsburgh Press, 1986), 18.
6. House Commission on Administrative Review, *Administrative Reorganization and Legislative Management,* 2 vols., H. Doc. 95-232, 95th Cong., 1st sess., September 28, 1977, 2:18-19.
7. Alan Abramowitz, "A Comparison of Voting for U.S. Senator and Representative in 1978," *American Political Science Review* 74 (September 1980): 633-640; and Richard F. Fenno, Jr., *The United States Senate: A Bicameral Perspective* (Washington, D.C.: American Enterprise Institute, 1982), 29ff.
8. House Commission on Administrative Review, *Final Report,* 2 vols., H. Doc. 95-272, 95th Cong., 1st sess., December 31, 1977, 2:875.
9. Glenn R. Parker and Roger H. Davidson, "Why Do Americans Love Their Congressmen So Much More Than Their Congress?" *Legislative Studies Quarterly* 4 (February 1979): 53-61.
10. Richard F. Fenno, Jr., *Home Style: House Members in Their Districts* (Boston: Little, Brown, 1978), 168.
11. Edmund Burke, "Speech to Electors at Bristol," in *Burke's Politics,* ed. Ross J. S. Hoffman and Paul Levack (New York: Alfred A. Knopf, 1949), 116.
12. Ibid.
13. Fenno, *Home Style,* 294.

Three pioneer women representatives—Alice M. Robertson, R-Okla., Mae E. Nolan, R-Calif., and Winnifred S. M. Huck, R-Ill.—on the Capitol steps.

CHAPTER TWO

Evolution of the Modern Congress

The very first Congress met in New York City, the seat of government, in the spring of 1789. Business was delayed until a majority of members arrived to make a quorum. On April 1, the thirtieth of the fifty-nine elected representatives reached New York; Frederick A. C. Muhlenberg of Pennsylvania promptly was chosen Speaker of the House. Five days later the Senate achieved its quorum, although its presiding officer, Vice President John Adams, did not arrive for another two weeks.

New York City was then a bustling port on the southern tip of Manhattan Island. Congress met in Federal Hall at the corner of Broad and Wall streets. The House occupied a large chamber on the first floor and the Senate a more intimate chamber upstairs. The new chief executive, George Washington, was still en route from his home at Mount Vernon, his trip having quickly turned into a triumphal procession with crowds and celebrations at every stop. To most of his countrymen, Washington—austere, dignified, the epitome of propriety—embodied a government that was otherwise little more than a plan on paper.

The two houses of Congress, headstrong even then, did not wait for Washington's arrival. The House began debating tariffs, a perennially popular legislative topic. Upstairs in the Senate, Vice President Adams, a brilliant but self-important man, needled his colleagues to decide upon proper titles for addressing the president and himself. (Adams was dubbed "His Rotundity" by a colleague who thought the whole discussion absurd.)

On inaugural day, April 30, Adams was still worrying about how to address the president. The issue was discarded when the representatives, led by Speaker Muhlenberg, burst into the Senate chamber and seated themselves. Meanwhile, a special committee was dispatched to escort Washington to the chamber for the ceremony. The actual swearing-in was conducted on an outside balcony in front of thousands of assembled citizens. The nervous Washington haltingly read his speech. Then everyone adjourned to St. Paul's Chapel for a special prayer service. Thus, the U.S. Congress became part of a functioning government.[1]

Antecedents of Congress

The legislative branch of the new government was untried and unknown, groping for procedures and precedents. And yet it grew out of more than 500 years of historical development. If the architects of the Constitution of 1787 were unsure exactly how their design would work, they had strong ideas about what they intended.

The English Heritage

From the time of the English king Edward the Confessor in the eleventh century, the central problem of political theory and practice was the relationship of the Crown to its subjects. Out of prolonged struggles, a strong, representative parliament emerged that rivaled and eventually eclipsed the power of the Crown.

The evolution of representative institutions on a national scale began in medieval Europe. Monarchs gained power over large territories where inhabitants were divided into social classes, groupings, and communities. The monarchs called together representatives of these groupings, or estates, not to create representative government, but to fill the royal coffers. As Charles A. Beard and John Lewis observed, "Even the most despotic medieval monarch could not tax and exploit his subjects without limits; as a matter of expediency, he had also to consider ways and means." [2]

These groups—*parliaments*, they came to be called—evolved over the centuries into the representative assemblies we know today. Four distinct stages of their development have been identified. At first the parliament, representing estates of the realm (nobility, clergy, landed gentry, town officials), met to vote taxes for the royal treasury, engaging in very little discussion. Next the tax-voting body turned into a lawmaking body that presented grievances to the king for redress. Third, by a gradual process culminating in the seventeenth century revolutions, Parliament wrested lawmaking and tax-voting power from the king, turning itself into a sovereign body. In the nineteenth century, finally, parliamentary representation extended beyond the older privileged groups to embrace the masses, eventually every man and woman. [3]

By the time the New World colonies were founded in the 1600s, the struggle for parliamentary rights was well advanced into the third stage, at least in England. Bloody conflicts, culminating in the beheading of Charles I in 1649 and the dethroning of James II in 1688 (the so-called "Glorious Revolution"), established parliamentary influence over the Crown. Out of such struggles flowed a remarkable body of political and philosophic writings. By the eighteenth century, works by James Harrington (1611-1677), John Locke (1632-1704), and others were the common heritage of educated people—including the leaders of the American Revolution.

The Colonial Experience

This tradition of representative government migrated to the New World. As early as 1619, the thousand or so Virginia colonists elected twenty-two delegates, or burgesses, to a General Assembly. In 1630 the Massachusetts Bay Company established itself as the governing body for the Bay Colony, subject to annual elections. The other colonies, some of them virtually self-governing, followed suit.

Representative government took firm root in the colonies. The broad expanse of ocean shielding America fostered self-reliance and autonomy on the part of colonial assemblies. Claiming prerogatives similar to those of the British House of Commons, these assemblies exercised the full range of lawmaking powers—levying taxes, issuing money, and providing for colonial defense. Legislation could be vetoed by colonial governors (appointed by the Crown in the eight royal colonies), but the governors, cut off from the home government and depending on local assemblies for revenues and even for their own salaries, usually preferred to reach agreement with the locals. Royal vetoes could emanate from London, but these, too, were sparing.[4]

Other factors nourished the tree of liberty. Many of the colonists were free spirits, dissidents set on resisting all authority, especially the Crown's. Readily available land, harsh frontier life, and—by the eighteenth century—a prosperous economy fed the colonists' self-confidence. The town meeting form of government in New England and the Separatists' church assemblies helped cultivate habits of self-government. And newspapers, unfettered by royal licenses or government taxes, stimulated exchange of opinions.

When England decided in the 1760s to tighten its rein upon the American colonies, it was met, not surprisingly, with stubborn opposition. Did not the colonists enjoy the same rights as Englishmen? Were not the colonial assemblies the legitimate government, deriving their authority from popular elections? As parliamentary enactments grew increasingly unpopular, along with the governors who tried to enforce them, the locally based colonial legislatures took up the cause of their constituents.

Especially resented by the colonists were the Stamp Act of 1765 (later repealed) and the import duties imposed in 1767. From these inflated customs receipts the home government began paying the salaries of royal governors and other officials, thus freeing them from the hold of colonial assemblies. The crisis worsened in the winter of 1773-1774 when, to protest the Tea Act, a group of colonists staged the Boston Tea Party. In retaliation, the House of Commons closed the port of Boston and passed a series of "Intolerable Acts" further strengthening royal control.

On September 5, 1774, the First Continental Congress convened in Philadelphia, marking the birthdate of national representative assemblies in America. Every colony except Georgia sent delegates, a varied group that included peaceable loyalists, moderates like John Dickinson, and radicals like

Samuel Adams and Paul Revere. Gradually anti-British sentiment congealed, and the Congress passed a series of declarations and resolutions (each colony casting one vote) amounting to a declaration of war against the mother country.[5] After the Congress adjourned on October 22, King George III declared that the colonies were "now in a state of rebellion; blows must decide whether they are to be subject to this country or independent." [6]

If the First Continental Congress gave colonists a taste of collective decision making, the Second Continental Congress proclaimed their independence from Britain. When this body convened on May 10, 1775, many still thought war might be avoided. A petition to King George asking for "happy and permanent reconciliation" was even approved. The British responded by proclaiming a state of rebellion and launching efforts to crush it. Sentiment in the colonies swung increasingly toward independence, and by the middle of 1776 the Congress was debating Thomas Jefferson's draft resolution proposing that "these United Colonies are, and of right ought to be, free and independent states." [7]

The two Continental Congresses gave birth to national politics in this country. Riding the wave of patriotism unleashed by the British indignities of 1773-1774, the Congresses succeeded in pushing the opinion of leaders and the general public toward confrontation and away from accommodation with the mother country. They did so by defining issues one by one and by reaching compromises acceptable to both moderates and radicals—no small accomplishment. Shared legislative experience, in other words, moved the delegates to the threshold of independence. Their achievement was all the more remarkable in light of what Jack Rakove describes as the "peculiar status" of the Continental Congress, "an extra-legal body whose authority would obviously depend on its ability to maintain a broad range of support." [8]

More than five years of bloody conflict ensued before the colonies won their independence. Meanwhile, the colonies hastened to form new governments and draft constitutions. Unlike the English constitution, these charters were written documents. All of them included some sort of bill of rights and all paid tribute to the doctrine of separating powers among legislative, executive, and judicial branches of government. *Equal* branches of government were not created, however. Nearly all the constitutions gave the bulk of powers to their legislatures. Earlier conflicts with the Crown and the royal governors had instilled in the colonists a fear of executive authority. "In actual operation," a historian wrote, "these first state constitutions produced what was tantamount to legislative omnipotence." [9]

At the national level, legislative dominance was even more complete. Strictly speaking, no national executive existed between 1776 and 1789—the years of the revolutionary war and the Articles of Confederation. The Congress struggled on its own to direct the war effort, often with haphazard results. As the war progressed and legislative direction proved unwieldy, the Congress tended to delegate authority to its own committees and to permanent (executive) agencies. The government's frailty under the Articles, adopted in 1781, proved the weakness of government by legislature alone. The Congress was paramount; a vigorous, independent executive was sorely needed.

The inability of all-powerful legislative bodies, state and national, to deal with postwar problems spurred demands for change. At the state level, newly rewritten constitutions reinstated the notion of a strong executive. At the Confederation level, it became apparent that a more "energetic" government was needed—one that could implement laws, control currency, dispose of war debts, and, if necessary, put down rebellion. In this spirit delegates from the states convened in Philadelphia on May 25, 1787, intending to strengthen the Articles of Confederation. Instead they drew up an entirely new governmental charter.

Congress in the Constitution

The structure and powers of Congress formed the very core of the Constitutional Convention's deliberations. On these questions, the fifty-five delegates at the Philadelphia convention were divided, and more than three months passed before they completed their work. A tripartite governmental system was outlined, with Congress named first in the Constitution. The plan, agreed upon and signed September 17, 1787, represented a compromise. Nationalist and states' rights interests, large states and small ones, northern states and southern had to be placated. The result was a singular blend of national and federal features based on republican principles of representation and limited government. The Constitution served the nationalists' goal of energetic central government that could function independently of the states. It also conceded the states' rights principle of limited powers shared by the various branches.

Powers of Congress

The federal government's powers are shared by three branches—legislative, executive, and judicial. Although considered one of the Constitution's most innovative features, "separation of powers" flowed naturally from English and colonial experience, which argued for dispersing governmental functions. It was advocated by philosophers Harrington, Locke, and Baron de Montesquieu. And many Americans regarded as a mistake the failure of the Articles of Confederation to separate these functions.

Legislators are accorded latitude in performing their duties. To prevent intimidation, they cannot be arrested during sessions or while traveling to and from sessions (except for treason, felony, or breach of the peace). In speech and debate, "they shall not be questioned in any other place" (Article I, Section 6). They have unfettered authority to organize the chambers as they see fit.

Familiar with the Parliament's long-term struggles with the Crown, the

Founders viewed the legislature as the chief repository of governmental powers. Locke had observed that "the legislative is not only the supreme power, but is sacred and unalterable in the hands where the community have placed it." [10] Locke's doctrine found expression in Article I, Section 8, which enumerates Congress's breathtaking array of powers. Indeed, virtually the entire scope of governmental authority as the eighteenth century Founders understood it is spelled out. No one reading this portion of the Constitution can fail to be impressed with the Founders' vision of a vigorous legislature as a keystone of energetic government.

Raising and spending money for governmental purposes lies at the heart of Congress's prerogatives. The "power of the purse" was the lever by which parliaments historically gained bargaining advantages over kings and queens. The Constitution's authors, well aware of this, gave Congress full power of the purse. There are two components of this power: *taxing* and *spending*.

Financing the government is carried out under a broad mandate in Article I, Section 8: "The Congress shall have power to lay and collect taxes, duties, imposts and excises, to pay the debts and provide for the common defense and general welfare of the United States." Although this wording covered all known forms of taxing, there were limitations: taxes had to be uniform throughout the country; duties were prohibited on goods traveling between states; and "capitation . . . or other direct" taxes were prohibited, unless levied according to population (Article I, Section 9). This last provision proved troublesome, especially when the Supreme Court held in 1895 (*Pollock v. Farmers' Loan and Trust Co.*) that it applied to taxes on incomes. To overcome this confusion, the Sixteenth Amendment, ratified eighteen years later, explicitly conferred the power to levy income taxes.

Congressional power over government spending is no less sweeping than revenue power. Congress is to provide for the "common defense and general welfare" of the country (Article I, Section 8). Furthermore, "No money shall be drawn from the Treasury, but in consequence of appropriations made by law" (Article I, Section 9). This is one of the legislature's most potent weapons in overseeing the executive branch.

Although the three branches are presumably coequal, the legislature takes the lead in formulating the structure and duties of the other two branches. The Constitution mentions executive departments and officers, but it does not specify their structure or duties, aside from those of the president. Thus, the design of the executive branch, including cabinet departments and other agencies, is spelled out in laws passed by Congress and signed by the president. The judiciary, too, is largely a creation of statutes. It consists of a Supreme Court and "such inferior courts as the Congress may from time to time ordain and establish" (Article III, Section 1). And while the courts' jurisdiction is delineated, the Supreme Court's appellate jurisdiction is subject to "such exceptions" and "such regulations as the Congress shall make" (Article III, Section 2).

Congress possesses potentially broad powers over the nation's economic well-being and political security. It may coin money, incur debts, regulate commerce, establish post offices, build post roads, issue patents and copyrights, provide for a militia, and call it forth to repel invasions or suppress rebellions.

Congress also plays a role in foreign relations with its powers to declare war, ratify treaties, raise and support armies, provide and maintain a navy, and make rules governing the military forces. Finally, Congress is vested with the power "to make laws which shall be necessary and proper for carrying into execution the foregoing powers" (Article I, Section 8). This so-called "elastic clause" probably was added to give Congress the means to implement the enumerated powers. Later this provision triggered far-reaching debates over the scope of governmental powers.

Limits on Legislative Power

Congress's enumerated powers—those "herein granted"—are not boundless. The very act of listing the powers was intended to limit government, for by implication those powers that are not listed are prohibited. The Tenth Amendment reserves to the states or to the people all those powers neither explicitly delegated nor prohibited by the Constitution.

Eight specific limitations on Congress's powers are noted in Article I, Section 9. The most important bans are against *bills of attainder*, which pronounce a particular individual guilty of a crime without trial or conviction and impose a sentence, and *ex post facto laws*, which make an action a crime after it has been committed or otherwise alter the legal consequences of some past action. Bills of attainder and ex post facto laws are traditional tools of authoritarian regimes. Congress's enumerated powers are also limited in matters such as the slave trade, taxation, appropriations, and titles of nobility.

The original Constitution contained no bill of rights or list of guarantees for citizens or states. Pressed by opponents during the ratification debate, supporters of the Constitution promised early enactment of amendments to remedy this omission. The resulting ten amendments, drawn up by the first Congress and ratified December 15, 1791, are a basic charter of liberties that limits the reach of government. The First Amendment prohibits Congress from establishing a national religion, preventing the free exercise of religion, or abridging the freedoms of speech, press, peaceable assembly, and petition. Other amendments secure the rights of personal property and fair trial and prohibit arbitrary arrest, questioning, or punishment.

Rights not enumerated in the Bill of Rights are not necessarily denied. In fact, subsequent amendments, legislative enactments, and judicial rulings have enlarged citizens' rights to include the rights of citizenship, of privacy, of voting, and of "equal protection of the laws." Initially, the Bill of Rights was held to limit only the national government, but the Fourteenth Amendment, ratified in 1868, prohibited states from impairing citizens' "privileges and immunities," depriving them of life, liberty, or property without "due process of law," and denying anyone the "equal protection of the laws." At first courts held that these clauses covered mainly economic rights. Beginning in 1925 (*Gitlow v. New York*), however, the Supreme Court began to incorporate Bill of Rights guarantees under the "due process" clause. Today almost every portion of the Bill of Rights applies to the states as well as to the federal government.

Separate Branches, Shared Powers

The Constitution not only delineates Congress's powers but distinguishes them from those of the other two branches. For all practical purposes, senators and representatives, while in office, are prohibited from serving in other federal posts; those who serve in such posts are in turn forbidden from serving in Congress (Article I, Section 6). This prevents any form of cabinet government in which key executive officials also sit in legislative chambers.

Because the branches are separated, some people contend that the powers they exert should also be isolated, like so many bottles of inert chemicals on a shelf. Former chief justice Warren Burger, an exponent of this view, declared in *Immigration and Naturalization Service v. Chadha* (1983) that

> the Constitution sought to divide the delegated powers of the new Federal Government into three defined categories, Legislative, Executive, and Judicial, to assure, as nearly as possible, that each branch of government would confine itself to its assigned responsibility. The hydraulic pressure inherent within each of the separate Branches to exceed the outer limits of its power, even to accomplish desirable objectives, must be resisted.[11]

In *Bowsher v. Synar* (1986), the decision striking down the original Gramm-Rudman-Hollings budget law, the Court (again speaking through Burger) seemed to say that once an act was passed by Congress and signed by the president, the legislative branch had no further role to play in it.[12]

In fact, governmental powers are interwoven, even if the branches are separate. The Constitution vests Congress with "all legislative powers," but these powers cannot be exercised without involvement by the president and the courts. The same interdependency applies to executive and judicial powers. Madison observed that the Constitution created, not a system of separate institutions performing separate functions, but separate institutions that *share* functions so that "these departments be so far connected and blended as to give each a constitutional control over the others." The Constitution did not erect "parchment barriers" against interbranch collaboration, Madison claimed. Instead, the powers of one should not be "directly or completely administered by either of the other departments," and none should wield "an overruling influence" over the others.[13]

Even in lawmaking, Congress does not act alone. According to Article II, the president can convene one or both houses of Congress in special session.

Although unable to introduce legislation directly, the president "shall from time to time give to the Congress information on the state of the Union, and recommend to their consideration such measures as he shall judge necessary and expedient." The president also has the power to veto congressional enactments. Within ten days (excluding Sundays) after a bill or resolution has passed both houses of Congress, the president must sign or return it. To overrule a presidential veto, a two-thirds vote is required in each house.

Implementing laws is the duty of the president, who is enjoined by the Constitution to take care that they are faithfully executed. The president is the head of the executive branch and has the power to appoint "officers of the United States," with the Senate's advice and consent. While Congress sets up the executive departments and agencies, outlining their missions by statute, chief executives and their appointees set the character and pace of executive activity. Moreover, Congress has power to impeach or remove civil officers for treason, bribery, or "other high crimes and misdemeanors."

In diplomacy and national defense, traditional bastions of royal prerogative, the Constitution apportions powers between the executive and legislative branches. Following tradition, presidents are given wide discretion in such matters: they appoint ambassadors and other envoys, they negotiate treaties, and they command the country's armed forces.

Yet here, too, functions are intermeshed. Like other high-ranking presidential appointees, ambassadors and envoys must be approved by the Senate. Treaties do not become the law of the land until they are ratified by the Senate. Although the president may dispatch troops, only Congress has the power of formally declaring war. Reacting to the Vietnam War experience, Congress in 1973 passed the War Powers Resolution, a reminder to the president of congressional war-making powers.

Historically, presidents and Congresses (and courts) have reached accommodations in order to exercise powers they share. As Justice Joseph Story once wrote, the authors of the Constitution sought to "prove that rigid adherence to [separation of powers] in all cases would be subversive to the efficiency of government and result in the destruction of the public liberties." Justice Robert Jackson wisely noted in 1952 that "while the Constitution diffuses power the better to secure liberty, it also contemplates that practice will integrate the dispersed powers into a workable government." [14]

One of Justice Jackson's former law clerks, Chief Justice William Rehnquist, reasserted the Madisonian view of separation of powers in *Morrison v. Olson* (1988). By a 7-1 margin the Court upheld the Ethics in Government Act of 1978, under which the Justice Department can appoint independent counsel to investigate charges of wrongdoing within the executive branch.

The question at issue was whether this act represented legislative (or judicial) invasion of executive prerogatives. Invoking a series of tests for breaches in the separation of powers doctrine, Rehnquist concluded that independent counsel were permissible. The law was not "an attempt by Congress to increase its own powers at the expense of the executive branch." Neither did it represent any "judicial usurpation of properly executive functions" or "impermissibly undermine" executive powers. Finally, it did not disrupt the proper balance between the branches by "preventing the executive branch from accomplishing its constitutional assigned functions." These tests add up to a rough measure of what is required by separation of powers. "We have never held," Rehnquist claimed, "that the Constitution requires that the three branches of Government 'operate with absolute independence.' " [15]

Judicial Review

The third of the separated branches, the judiciary, has assumed a leading role in interpreting laws and determining their constitutionality. Whether the Founders actually anticipated this function of "judicial review" is open to question. Perhaps each branch was expected to reach its own judgments on constitutional questions, especially those pertaining to its own powers.

Whatever the original intent, Chief Justice John Marshall soon pre-empted the other two branches with his assertion of judicial review in *Marbury v. Madison* (1803). Judicial review involves both interpretation and judgment. First, "it is emphatically the province and duty of the judicial department to say what the law is." Second, the Supreme Court has the duty of comparing laws with the Constitution, the "supreme law of the land," and invalidating those that are inconsistent—in this case a minor provision of the Judiciary Act of 1789. Yet Congress, not the Court, remained the main forum for weighty constitutional debates throughout the nineteenth century. Until the Civil War only one other law, the Missouri Compromise, was declared unconstitutional by the Court (*Dred Scott v. Sandford*, 1857). Since the Civil War, however, the Court has evidenced no shyness in interpreting and judging congressional handiwork.

For the record, the Supreme Court has invalidated a total of 124 congressional statutes, in whole or in part, from *Marbury* in 1803 through 1988.[16] This count does not include lower court holdings that have not been reviewed by the Supreme Court. Nor does it cover laws whose validity has been impaired because another, similar law was struck down. For example, in the 1983 case of *INS v. Chadha,* the Court invalidated many forms of the so-called legislative veto, which authorized administrators or agencies to take certain actions subject to congressional approval or veto. Although only one law was at issue, more than 120 other laws containing one or more such provisions were called into question by the ruling (see Chapter 9).

When the courts speak on an issue, Congress tends to accept the decision. Yet that is not necessarily the last word on the matter. A judicial holding may prod Congress to enact statutes that meet the court's objections or achieve the same goal by different means. Occasionally, Congress responds to court holdings by trying to nullify, thwart, modify, or simply ignore them. Despite *Chadha*, legislative veto provisions continue to be enacted; political prudence usually leads administrators to honor such provisions. Nonetheless, the courts play the primary role in interpreting laws and the regulations emanating from them. When Congress passes a law, the policy-making process has just begun. Courts and administrative agencies then take over the task of refining the policy, always under Congress's watchful eye.

Bicameralism

Although we talk about "the Congress" as if it were a single entity, Congress is divided internally into two very different, virtually autonomous chambers. Following the pattern initiated by Parliament and imitated by most of the colonies, the Constitution outlines a bicameral legislature. If tradition recommended the two-house formula, the politics of the era commanded it. The larger states preferred the "nationalist" principle of popularly based representation, while the smaller states insisted on a "federal" principle ensuring representation by states.

The first branch—as the House was termed by Madison and Gouverneur Morris, among others—rests on the nationalist idea that the legislature should answer to people rather than to states. As George Mason, the Virginia statesman, put it, the House "was to be the grand depository of the democratic principles of the government." [17] Many years later the Supreme Court ruled in *Wesberry v. Sanders* (1964) that these principles demanded that congressional districts within each state be essentially equal in population.

In contrast, the Senate embodied the federal idea: not only did each state have two seats, but senators were to be chosen by the state legislatures rather than by popular vote. The Senate was to provide a brake on the excesses of popular government. "The use of the Senate," explained Madison, "is to consist in its proceeding with more coolness, with more system, and with more wisdom, than the popular branch." [18]

Historical evolution overtook the Founders' intentions. In most cases, to be sure, senators tended to voice dominant economic interests and shun the general public. British commentator Lord Bryce once remarked that the Senate seemed to care more for its "collective self-esteem" than it did for public opinion.[19] Yet state legislators frequently "instructed" their senators how to vote on key issues. In other states, legislative elections turned into statewide "canvasses" focusing on senatorial candidates. Such was the famous 1858 Illinois contest between Sen. Stephen A. Douglas and challenger Abraham Lincoln. The Democrats captured the legislature and sent Douglas back to Washington, but Lincoln's eloquent arguments against extending slavery to the territories west of the Mississippi River vaulted him into national prominence.

Direct election of senators came with the Seventeenth Amendment, ratified in 1913. A byproduct of the Progressive movement, it was designed to broaden citizens' participation and blunt the power of shadowy special interests, such as party bosses and business trusts. Thus, the Senate became directly subject to popular will.

Because states vary widely in population, the Senate is the one legislative body in the nation where "one person, one vote" emphatically does not apply. Article V assures each state of equal Senate representation and guarantees that no state will be deprived of this without its consent. Because no state is apt to give such consent, Senate representation is for all practical purposes an unamendable provision of the Constitution.

Bicameralism is the most conspicuous organizational feature of the U.S. Congress. Each chamber has a distinct process for considering legislation. According to the Constitution, each house determines its own rules, keeps a journal of its proceedings, and serves as final judge of its members' elections and qualifications. In addition, the Constitution assigns unique duties to the two chambers. The Senate ratifies treaties and approves presidential appointments. The House must originate all revenue measures; by tradition, it originates appropriations bills as well. In impeachments, the House prepares and tries the case, and the Senate serves as the court.

The two houses jealously guard their prerogatives and resist intrusions by "the other body." Despite claims that one or that the other chamber is more important—for instance, that the Senate has more prestige or the House pays more attention to legislative details—the two houses staunchly defend their equal places.

Institutional Evolution

Written constitutions, even those as farsighted as the 1787 one, go only a short way in explaining real-life governmental institutions. On many questions such documents are inevitably silent or ambiguous; issues that lie between the lines must be resolved in the course of later events.

In adapting to demands far removed from those of eighteenth century America, Congress has evolved dramatically. Many of these changes can be subsumed under the term *institutionalization*—the process whereby structures and procedures take shape and become regularized. Rather than being unformed and unpredictable, the institution becomes structured and routinized, following established traditions and widely held expectations about how it should perform. We will see how institutionalization has shaped the two Congresses—Congress-as-deliberative-body and Congress-as-individual-representatives.

The Size of Congress

Looking at the government of 1789 through modern lenses, one is struck by the relatively small circles of people involved. The House of Representatives, that "impetuous council," was composed of sixty-five members—when all of them showed up. The aristocratic Senate boasted only twenty-six members, two from each of the thirteen original states.

Article I, Section 2, of the Constitution sets forth the method of apportioning House members—a decennial census. When the first census was taken in 1790, the nation's population was fewer than 4 million—smaller than that of an average state today. The historical growth of the two houses can be seen from Table 2-1. There were thirty-two senators in 1800, sixty-two in 1850, and ninety in 1900. Since 1912, only the states of Alaska and Hawaii have been added, and the House has stabilized at 435.

In addition to its 435 full-fledged members, the House has one resident commissioner and four delegates. While they cannot vote on the House floor, these individuals sit on committees and enjoy other House privileges. Their posts are created by statute. Puerto Rico in 1900 was granted the right to elect a commissioner. More recently, nonvoting delegates were approved for the District of Columbia (1971), Guam (1972), the Virgin Islands (1972), and American Samoa (1980).

The House's size is fixed by law. Enlarging the House is suggested periodically—especially by representatives from states losing seats after a census. However, many concur with Speaker Sam Rayburn of Texas, who served from 1913 to 1961, that the House is already at or above its optimum size.

Size profoundly affects an organization's work. Growth compelled the House to develop strong leaders, to rely heavily on its committees, to impose strict limits on floor debate, and to devise elaborate ways of channeling the flow of floor business. It is no accident that strong leaders emerged during the House's rapid growth periods. After the initial growth spurt in the first two decades of the Republic, vigorous leadership appeared in the person of Henry Clay, whose Speakership (1811-1814, 1815-1820, and 1823-1825) demonstrated the potentialities of that office. Similarly, post-Civil War growth was accompanied by an era of strong Speakers lasting from the 1870s until 1910. Size is not the only impetus for strong leadership, but it tends to centralize procedural control.

In the smaller and more intimate Senate, vigorous leadership has been the exception rather than the rule. The relative informality of Senate procedures, not to mention the long-cherished right of unlimited debate, testify to looser reins of leadership. Compared with the House's complex rules and voluminous precedents, the Senate's rules are relatively brief and simple. Informal negotiations among senators interested in a given measure prevail, and debate is typically governed by unanimous consent agreements—agreed upon ways of proceeding, brokered by the parties' floor leaders. Although too large for its members to draw their chairs around the fireplace on a chilly winter morning—as they used to do in the early years—the Senate today retains a clubby atmosphere that the House lacks.

Electoral units, too, have grown very large. Congressional constituen-

Table 2-1   Growth in Size of House and Its Constituents, 1790-1990 Census

Year of census	Congress	Population base[a] (1,000s)	Number of states	Number of repre- sentatives[b]	Apportionment population per representative
	1st-2d	—	13	65	30,000[c]
1790	3d-7th	3,616	15	105	34,438
1800	8th-12th	4,880	16	141	34,609
1810	13th-17th	6,584	17	181	36,377
1820	18th-22d	8,972	24	213	42,124
1830	23d-27th	11,931	24	240	49,712
1840	28th-32d	15,908	26	223	71,338
1850	33d-37th	21,767	31	234	93,020
1860	38th-42d	29,550	34	241	122,614
1870	43d-47th	38,116	37	292	130,533
1880	48th-52d	49,371	38	325	151,912
1890	53d-57th	61,909	44	356	173,901
1900	58th-62d	74,563	45	386	193,167
1910	63d-66th	91,604	46	435	210,583
1920[d]	67th-72th	105,711	48	435	243,013
1930	73d-77th	122,093	48	435	280,675
1940	78th-82d	131,006	48	435	301,164
1950	83d-87th	149,895	48	435	334,587
1960	88th-92d	178,559	50	435	410,481
1970	93d-97th	204,053[e]	50	435	469,088
1980	98th-102th	226,505	50	435	520,701
1990 est.	103d-107th	250,000	50	435	573,394

Sources: U.S. Department of Commerce, Bureau of the Census, *Historical Statistics of the United States, Colonial Times to 1970,* Part 2 (Washington, D.C.: Government Printing Office, 1975), 1084; 1980 Census figures released by Commerce Department, December 31, 1980; 1990 estimate from Bureau of the Census, *U.S. Department of Commerce News,* April 1, 1988, 1.

[a] Excludes the population of the District of Columbia, the population of outlying areas, the number of Indians not taxed, and (prior to 1870) two-fifths of the slave population.
[b] Actual number of representatives apportioned at the beginning of the decade.
[c] The minimum ratio of population to representatives stated in Article 1, Section 2, of the Constitution.
[d] No apportionment was made after the census of 1920.
[e] Includes 1,575,000 in population abroad.

cies—states and districts—are among the most populous electoral units in the world. The mean congressional district now numbers more than half a million people, the average state more than 4 million. This affects the bonds between citizens and their elected representatives. Whereas old-time legislators spent a great deal of each year in their home districts, working at their normal trades or professions and mingling with townspeople, today's legislators keep in touch by frequent visits, radio and television appearances, press releases, staff contacts, WATS lines, and computerized mailings.

The congressional establishment itself has changed in scale. Staffs were added gradually. In 1891 a grand total of 142 clerks, 62 for the House and 80 for the Senate, were on hand to serve members of Congress. Many senators and all representatives handled their own correspondence; keeping records and counting votes were the duties of committee clerks. Around the turn of this century, House and Senate members, their clerks, and their committees moved into two ornate office buildings, one for each house. Today individual members and committees are served by more than 18,000 staff members, not to mention employees in several supporting agencies (see Figure 2-1). Housed in more than a dozen Capitol Hill buildings, they include experts in virtually every area of government policy and comprise a distinct Washington subculture.

The Legislative Workload

During the Republic's early days, the government at Washington was "at a distance and out of sight." [20] Lawmaking was a part-time occupation. As President John F. Kennedy was fond of remarking, the Clays, Calhouns, and Websters of the nineteenth century could afford to devote a whole generation or more to debating and refining the few great controversies at hand. Rep. Joseph W. Martin, R-Mass., who entered the House in 1925 and went on to become Speaker (1947-1948, 1953-1954), described the leisurely atmosphere of earlier days and the workload changes during his service:

> From one end of a session to another Congress would scarcely have three or four issues of consequence besides appropriations bills. And the issues themselves were fundamentally simpler than those that surge in upon us today in such a torrent that the individual member cannot analyze all of them adequately before he is compelled to vote. In my early years in Congress the main issues were few enough so that almost any conscientious member could with application make himself a quasi-expert at least. In the complexity and volume of today's legislation, however, most members have to trust somebody else's word or the recommendation of a committee. Nowadays bills, which thirty years ago would have been thrashed out for hours or days, go through in ten minutes.[21]

The most pressing issue considered by the Foreign Affairs Committee during one session, Martin related, was a $20,000 authorization for an international poultry show in Tulsa.

Figure 2-1   Member and Committee Staffs, 1891-1986

Number of employees

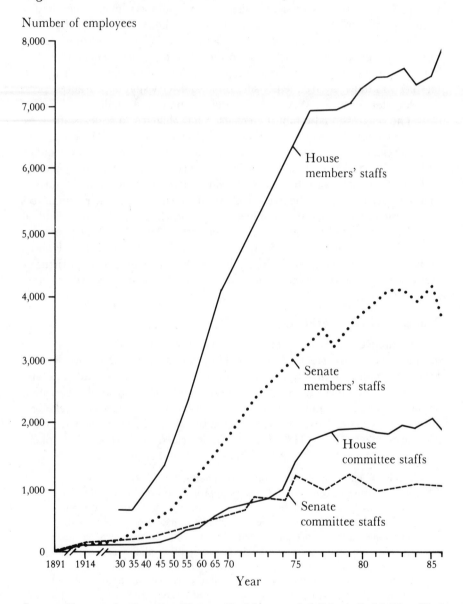

Year

Source: Norman J. Ornstein, Thomas E. Mann, and Michael J. Malbin, *Vital Statistics on Congress, 1987-1988* (Washington, D.C.: Congressional Quarterly, 1987), 143.

Even in the 1950s, the legislative schedule was quite manageable, as indicated in the following summary of a representative's day offered by former Speaker Rayburn:

> The average member will come down to the office around eight or eight-thirty. He spends his time with visitors until around ten o'clock, then he goes to a committee meeting, and when the committee adjourns he comes to the House of Representatives, or should, and stays around the House chamber and listens.[22]

Needless to say, the days of a single morning committee meeting and time to witness an entire afternoon's floor proceedings have gone the way of the Edsel. Conflicting committee sessions, snatches of floor deliberation, and repeated roll calls are now the order of the day.

Congress's workload—once limited in scope, small in volume, and simple in content—has grown to huge proportions. The data in Table 2-2 show the soaring numbers of measures introduced and enacted by Congress since 1789. The number of hours Congress is in session also has increased, as Figure 2-2 illustrates. By most measures—hours in session, committee meetings, floor votes—the congressional workload has just about doubled since the 1950s. Recent downturns in some workload figures, like numbers of laws enacted, reflect not so much a slackened workload as a changed workload: for example, the tendency to enact lengthier "mega-bills" on basic matters and to spend more time overseeing the executive branch.

Legislative business has expanded in scope and complexity as well as sheer volume. Today's Congress copes with many issues that once were left to state or local government or were considered entirely outside the purview of governmental activity. Moreover, legislation tends to be more complex than it used to be.[23]

For most of its history, Congress was a part-time institution. Well into the twentieth century, Congress remained in session only nine months out of each twenty-four, the members spending the remainder of their time at home attending to private business. In recent decades legislative business has kept the House and Senate in almost perpetual session—punctuated by constituency work periods. During the average two-year Congress, the House is in session about 275 eight-hour days. The average senator or representative works an eleven-hour day when Congress is in session.[24]

Structures and Procedures

A mature institution is marked not only by the professionalism of its members but also by the number and complexity of its structures and procedures. By that measure, today's House and Senate are mature institutions indeed.

No trait illustrates Congress's institutional growth more dramatically than division of labor through the committee system. Although fashioned gradually and seemingly inexorably, the committee system rests on precedents drawn from the British House of Commons, the colonial assemblies, and the

Table 2-2 Measures Introduced and Enacted, Selected Congresses, 1789-1988

Years	Congress	Measures introduced			Measures enacted		
		Total	Bills	Joint resolutions	Total	Public	Private
1789-1791	1st	144	144	—	118	108	10
1795-1797	4th	132	132	—	85	75	10
1803-1805	8th	217	217	—	111	93	18
1811-1813	12th	406	406	—	209	170	39
1819-1821	16th	480	480	—	208	117	91
1827-1829	20th	632	612	20	235	134	101
1835-1837	24th	1,107	1,055	52	459	144	315
1843-1845	28th	1,085	979	106	279	142	137
1851-1853	32nd	1,167	1,011	156	306	137	169
1859-1861	36th	1,746	1,595	151	370	157	213
1867-1869	40th	3,723	3,003	720	765	354	411
1875-1877	44th	6,230	6,001	229	580	278	302
1883-1885	48th	11,443	10,961	482	969	284	685
1891-1893	52nd	14,893	14,518	375	722	398	324
1899-1901	56th	20,893	20,409	484	1,942	443	1,499
1907-1909	60th	38,388	37,981	407	646	411	235
1915-1917	64th	30,052	29,438	614	684	458	226
1923-1925	68th	17,462	16,884	578	996	707	289
1931-1933	72nd	21,382	20,501	881	843	516	327
1939-1941	76th	16,105	15,174	931	1,662	1,005	657
1947-1949	80th	10,797	10,108	689	1,363	906	458
1955-1957	84th	17,687	16,782	905	1,921	1,028	893
1963-1965	88th	17,480	16,079	1,401	1,026	666	360
1971-1973	92nd	22,969	21,363	1,606	768	607	161
1979-1981	96th	12,583	11,722	861	736	613	123
1987-1989	100th	11,272	8,505	1,073	480	464	16

Sources: U.S. Department of Commerce, Bureau of the Census, *Historical Statistics of the United States: Colonial Times to 1970,* Part 2 (Washington, D.C.: Government Printing Office, 1975), 1081-1082; Bureau of the Census, *Statistical Abstract of the United States, 1980* (Washington, D.C.: Government Printing Office, 1980), 509; and Roger H. Davidson and Carol Hardy, *Indicators of House of Representatives Workload and Activity and Indicators of Senate Activity and Workload* (Washington, D.C.: Congressional Research Service, 1987).

Note: Measures introduced and enacted exclude simple and concurrent resolutions.

Figure 2-2 Hours in Session, House of Representatives, Selected Congresses, 1955-1988

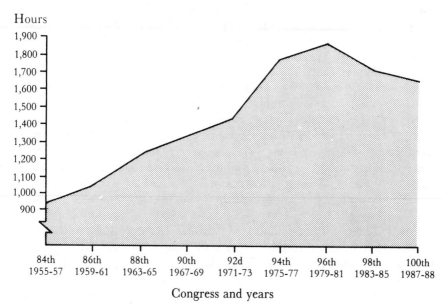

Hours

Congress and years

Source: House Commission on Administrative Review, *Administrative Reorganization and Legislative Management,* 2 vols., H. Doc. 95-232, 95th Cong., 1st sess., September 28, 1977, 2:21. Recent calculations by the authors.

Continental Congresses.[25] The first House standing committee (Elections) was created in 1789, but initially legislative business in both houses was handled mainly by temporary committees or on the floor. By the third decade of the nineteenth century, however, the standing committee system was well established.

The creation and, in infrequent instances, abolition of committees parallel important historical events and shifting perceptions of public problems.[26] As novel political problems arose, new committees were added. The House, for example, established Commerce and Manufactures in 1795, Public Lands in 1805, Freedmen's Affairs in 1866, Roads in 1913, Science and Astronautics in 1958, Standards of Official Conduct in 1967, and Small Business in 1975. Numerous committees have existed at one time or another—as many as sixty-one in the House and seventy-four in the Senate.

Today there are sixteen standing committees in the Senate and twenty-two in the House (see Chapter 7, Table 7-1). However, this is only the tip of the iceberg. Although standing committees have been trimmed, subcommittees have proliferated. House committees have nearly 150 subcommittees. The House also has five select committees with twelve subcommittees. In the

Senate there are about eighty-five subcommittees of standing committees and four select or special committees. In addition, there are four joint House-Senate committees with eight subcommittees. This is more than 300 workgroups—not counting party groups, voting blocs, informal caucuses, and the like. By any measure, the House and Senate are complex organizations with many internal partitions.

The number of formal and informal leaders in Congress has grown as a function of proliferating work groups. Every committee and subcommittee has a chairman and a ranking minority member. The formal party leaders help organize the two chambers, assign members to committees, schedule business, and devise parliamentary strategy. Strong party leadership in the House dates from the era of Speaker Henry Clay in the early nineteenth century. Senate party leaders emerged much later, probably in response to activist presidents such as Woodrow Wilson and Franklin D. Roosevelt.[27]

Supplementing formal leadership posts in Congress are a host of informal leaders who represent factions, regions, industries, or simply issue positions. The result is a complicated network of give-and-take relationships in which less informed members seek cues from better-informed colleagues, issue by issue (see Chapter 12). Today's Congress, in other words, abounds in leaders of various types.

In the early days, proceedings at the Capitol were disorderly, especially in the crowded, noisy, and badly ventilated chambers. One House historian noted that "debate has been rough and tumble, no holds barred, bruising, taunting, raucous, sometimes brutal. The floor of the House has been no place for the timid or the craven." [28] Prior to the Civil War, duels between quarreling legislators were not uncommon. One celebrated incident occurred in 1856, when Rep. Preston Brooks, a southern Democrat, coldly stalked Sen. Charles Sumner, a Republican from Massachusetts, and beat him senseless with a cane on the Senate floor for his views on slavery in the new territories.

As Congress matured, decorum replaced chaos, and strict rules of order began to govern the proceedings. Today there are formidable rules and precedents as well as numerous informal norms and traditions. When, for example, a lawmaker appeared on the House floor without his coat and tie one steamy summer day in 1979, Speaker Thomas P. O'Neill, D-Mass., pronounced him out of order and refused to recognize him until he reappeared in more formal garb. Meanwhile, the House sweltered because thermostats had been turned up to conserve energy. But the vast majority of O'Neill's colleagues seemed to support his effort to preserve decorum.

Altering House or Senate rules is no casual matter. (The House adopts its rules anew with each new Congress; as a continuing body, the Senate has ongoing rules.) Most rules changes result from concerted effort by the leadership, party caucuses, or the respective rules committees. When major rules changes or committee realignments are considered, select committees may be established to make recommendations. Since World War II there have been no less than eight reorganization committees or study commissions. Although rules and procedural shifts do occur, time-honored ways of doing things are staunchly defended, and changes must be broached cautiously.

In short, Congress is no longer an informal institution. It bristles with norms and traditions, rules and procedures, committees and subcommittees. The modern Congress, in other words, is highly *institutionalized*. How different from the first Congress, personified by fussy John Adams worrying about what forms of address to use! The institutional complexity of today's Congress enables it to cope with a staggering workload and to contain political conflict. However, institutional complexity carries its own costs—in rigidity and the cumbersome administrative apparatus needed to keep the system afloat.

Evolution of the Legislator's Job

What is it like to be a member of Congress? The legislator's job, like the institution of Congress, has evolved since 1789. During the first Congress, being a senator or representative was a part-time occupation. Few members regarded congressional service as a career, and from most accounts the rewards were slim. Since then the lawmakers' exposure to constituents' demands, their expectations, and their factional loyalties have changed dramatically.

Constituency Demands

Constituency demands are many: making personal appearances in the district or state, communicating through newsletters and electronic media, explaining stands on legislative issues, assisting constituents with problems (so-called "constituency casework"), and corresponding with constituents. Of course, American legislators have always been expected to remain close to their voters. From the very first, representatives reported to their constituents through circularized letters.[29]

In an era of limited government, however, there was little constituent errand running. "It was a pretty nice job that a member of Congress had in those days," recalled Rep. Robert Ramspeck, D-Ga. (1929-1945), describing the Washington of 1911 when he came to take a staff job:

> At that time the government affected the people directly in only a minor way. . . . It was an entirely different job from the job we have to do today. It was primarily a legislative job, as the Constitution intended it to be.[30]

In those days a member's mail was confined mainly to awarding rural mail routes, arranging for Spanish War pensions, sending out free seed, and only occasionally explaining legislation. At most, a single clerk was required to handle correspondence.

This unhurried pace has long since vanished. Reflecting on his forty years on Capitol Hill, Representative Martin remarked on the dramatic upsurge of constituent awareness:

> Today the federal government is far more complex, as is every phase of national life. People have to turn to their Representative for aid. I used to think ten letters a day was a big batch; now I get several hundred a day. In earlier times, constituents didn't know their Congressman's views. With better communications, their knowledge has increased along with their expectations of what he must know.[31]

Even Martin, who left the House in 1967, would be astonished at the volume of constituency work now handled by House and Senate offices. In 1988 the House Post Office logged more than 200 million pieces of incoming mail— four times the 1970 figure; the Senate logged 50 million. Not only are constituents more numerous than ever before; they are better educated and served by faster communication and transportation. Public opinion surveys show that voters expect legislators to "bring home the bacon" in terms of federal services and to communicate frequently with the home folks. There is little reason to suppose these demands will fade in the future.

The Congressional Career

Careerism, or prolonged service, is a key ingredient of any human organization. It engenders loyalty, helps define an institution's place in its social and political environment, and lends stability by ensuring the presence of experienced members. On the other hand, high careerism usually means low turnover, curbing the vitality and creativity that new members provide. This is especially critical for legislative bodies, which need to be responsive as well as stable.

Levels of careerism have fluctuated throughout Congress's history. During its early years, Congress was an institution composed of transients. The nation's capital was an unsightly place; its culture was provincial, and its summers humid and mosquito-ridden. Members remained in Washington only a few months, spending their unpleasant sojourns in boardinghouses. "While there were a few for whom the Hill was more than a way station in the pursuit of a career," James S. Young observes, "affiliation with the congressional community tended to be brief."[32]

The early Congresses failed to command the loyalty needed to keep members in office. Congressional service was regarded as an odious duty, not as rewarding work. "My dear friend," wrote a North Carolina representative to his constituents in 1796, "there is nothing in this service, exclusive of the confidence and gratitude of my constituents, worth the sacrifice.... Having secured this, I could freely give place to any fellow citizen, that others too might obtain the consolation due to faithful service."[33] Of the ninety-four senators who served between 1789 and 1801, thirty-three resigned before completing their terms, and only six left to take other federal posts.[34] In the House almost 6 percent of all early nineteenth century members resigned during each Congress. "Citizen legislators" characterize this era.

Careerism mounted after the Civil War. As late as the 1870s, more than half the House members at any given time were freshmen, and the mean length of service for members was barely two terms. By the end of the century, however, the proportion of newcomers fell to 30 percent, and average House tenure reached three terms or six years. About the same time senators' mean term of service topped six years or one full term.[35] Figure 2-3 shows changes since 1791 in the percentage of new members and the mean number of years served by incumbents.

Rising careerism had a number of causes. For one thing, proliferating one-party states and districts following the Civil War made possible repeated reelection of a dominant party's candidates: Democrats in the core cities and the South, Republicans in the Midwest and the rural Northeast. Militant state and local party organizations dominated the recruitment process and tended to select party careerists.[36]

At the same time, the power of the legislative branch—epitomized in Woodrow Wilson's phrase, "congressional government"—made federal service more attractive and rewarding. The government's subsequent growth enhanced the excitement and glamour of the national political scene, especially compared with state or local politics. Moreover, the physical environment of the nation's capital improved steadily over the years. As Representative Martin related:

> The installation of air conditioning in the 1930s did more, I believe, than cool the Capitol: it prolonged the session. The members were no longer in such a hurry to flee Washington in July. The southerners especially had no place else to go that was half as comfortable.[37]

As members stayed longer, they needed rewards for lengthy service. When few senior members were available, presiding officers looked more to party loyalty than to seniority in naming committees or chairmen. But as careerism increased, greater respect was paid to seniority in distributing favored committee posts. In the Senate, the seniority "rule" has been largely unchallenged since 1877.[38]

In the House, seniority gained a foothold more gradually.[39] Strong post-Civil War Speakers, struggling to control the unruly chamber, sometimes ignored seniority to appoint loyal lieutenants to key committees. But in 1910, when Speaker Joseph G. Cannon (1903-1911) passed over senior members in making assignments and in general acted arbitrarily, the House revolted, removing committee assignment power from the Speaker.[40] Since then seniority has been generally inviolable as a measure for selecting committee chairmen.

The seniority principle fostered career patterns within the two houses. New members found themselves at the bottom of internal career ladders that they could ascend only through continued service. Although the committee

Figure 2-3   Turnover and Seniority in Congress, 1791-1988

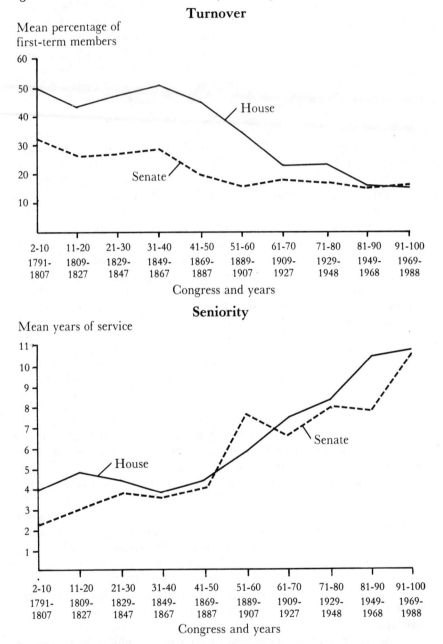

Sources: Nelson W. Polsby, "The Institutionalization of the U.S. House of Representatives," *American Political Science Review* (March 1968): 146-147; and Randall B. Ripley, *Congress: Process and Policy*, 4th ed. (New York: W. W. Norton, 1988), 53-54. Calculations for recent Congresses by the authors.

reforms of the 1970s multiplied the number of career ladders, seniority is still a prerequisite for top leadership posts. In the past generation, however, many junior members grew restless with the long waiting periods or apprenticeships required for those posts. As their ranks swelled, junior members lobbied for broader and more equitable assignments—which opened leadership posts to more members earlier in their careers.

Parties and Factions

Political parties had no place in the constitutional blueprint, which was deliberately fashioned to divide and dilute factional interests. With the unveiling of Treasury Secretary Alexander Hamilton's financial program in 1790, however, a genuine partisan spirit infused Capitol Hill. The Federalists, with Hamilton as their intellectual leader, espoused "energetic government" with forceful national action on public problems. The rival Republicans, who looked to Thomas Jefferson and James Madison for leadership, attracted opponents of Federalist policies and championed local autonomy, weaker national government, and programs favoring lower class or debtor interests.

When war broke out in Europe between revolutionary France and a coalition of old regimes, the Federalists sided with the dependable (and commercially profitable) British, while the Republicans tended to admire "French principles." As early as 1794, Sen. John Taylor of Virginia could write:

> The existence of two parties in Congress is apparent. The fact is disclosed almost upon every important question. Whether the subject be foreign or domestic—relative to war or peace—navigation or commerce—the magnetism of opposite views draws them wide as the poles asunder.[41]

In this country Speakers have always been political officers, and so they quickly came to reflect partisan divisions in wielding their powers. The other partisan institution in those early days was the congressional nominating caucus that selected a faction's presidential candidates. Not all members professed clear-cut partisan or factional affiliations, however. During the so-called "Era of Good Feeling" (roughly 1815-1825), party voting was the exception rather than the rule. With the conspicuous exception of the nominating caucuses, no formal party apparatus existed. Between the quadrennial caucuses, Young explains, "the party had no officers, even of figurehead importance, for the guidance or management of legislative processes."[42] The nominating caucus collapsed after 1824, and the Jacksonians laid the foundation for something approaching a stable party system based on grass-roots support.

Parties flourished in the years following the Civil War. Regional conflicts, along with economic upheavals produced by rapid industrialization, nurtured partisan differences. The Civil War and World War I mark the boundaries of the era of strongest partisanship on Capitol Hill and in the country at large.

From his study of the House in the McKinley period (1897-1901), David Brady concluded that "the two major parties were spatially more distinct on the urban-rural and industrial-agricultural continuum than are the two parties today." [43] This period of vigorous partisanship was characterized by the "strong Speakership" in the House. At the grass-roots level, the parties were differentiated to a degree unheard of in the twentieth century, and party organizations were militant by American standards. By comparison, today's parties, while organizationally and procedurally powerful, are diffuse in representing issues or ideologies.

Since World War I, the parties have weakened but by no means have disappeared. After 1910 party caucuses or committees assumed responsibility for assigning members to committees and even sometimes for formulating policy. During the 1965-1975 period, party caucuses on both sides of Capitol Hill were vehicles for reform efforts. The parties' formal apparatus is extensive. There are policy committees, campaign committees, research committees, and elaborate whip systems. About 125 staff aides are employed by party leaders and perhaps an equal number by assorted party groups. [44] Party-oriented voting-bloc groups (such as the Democratic Study Group or the Republicans' Wednesday Group—both liberal House groups), "class clubs" (such as the House Democrats' New Members Caucus), and social groups complement and reinforce partisan ties.

Despite the widely proclaimed "death" of traditional political parties, partisanship and factionalism are very much alive on Capitol Hill. The first thing a visitor to the House or Senate chamber notices is that the seats or desks are divided along partisan lines, Democrats to the left facing the dais, Republicans to the right. Seating arrangements betoken the parties' role in organizing the legislative branch. By means of party mechanisms, leaders are selected, committee assignments made, and floor debates scheduled. Parties also supply members with voting cues. Indeed, party-line voting reached modern-day highs in the 1980s.

Today in Washington, D.C., party institutions are visible and ubiquitous—from the luxurious headquarters buildings of national associations and the lobbyists who crowd Capitol Hill offices and meeting rooms to the parties' staffs and research groups and the mushrooming issue and voting-bloc groups. Signs of institutionalized partisanship are everywhere, even if they don't always carry traditional Republican or Democratic labels.

Conclusion

At its birth, the U.S. Congress was an unstructured body. Although the Founders knew the guiding principles of representative assemblies, especially from reflecting upon the British experience, they could not have realized exactly what sort of institution they had created. They wrote into the Constitution the powers of the legislature as they understood them and left the details to future generations. During its rich and eventful history, Congress developed into a mature organization with highly articulated structures, procedures, routines, and traditions. In a word, it became institutionalized.

This fact must be taken into account by anyone who seeks to understand Congress. Newcomers to the Capitol encounter not an undeveloped, pliable organization, but a traditional one that must be accepted on its own terms. This has a number of important consequences, some good and some bad.

Institutionalization enables Congress to cope with its contemporary workload. Division of labor, primarily through standing committees, permits the two houses to process a wide variety of issues at the same time. In tandem with staff resources, this specialization allows Congress to compete with the executive branch in assembling information and applying expertise to given problems. Division of labor also serves the personal and political diversity of Congress. At the same time, careerism encourages legislators to develop skills and expertise in specific issues. Procedures and traditions can contain conflict and channel the political energies that converge upon the lawmaking process.

The drawback of institutionalization is that it can lead to organizational rigidity that produces paralysis. Institutions that are too brittle can frustrate policy making, especially in periods of rapid social or political change. Structures that are too complex can tie people in knots, producing delays and confusion. Such organizational tie-ups often produce agitation for change or reform. Even with its size and complexity, the contemporary Congress has undergone periodic waves of change or reformism. Events of the last two decades show that congressional evolution has by no means run its full course.

Notes

1. Alvin M. Josephy, Jr., *On the Hill: A History of the American Congress* (New York: Simon & Schuster, 1980), 41-48.
2. Charles A. Beard and John P. Lewis, "Representative Government in Evolution," *American Political Science Review* (April 1932): 223-240.
3. Ibid.
4. Jock P. Green, ed., *Great Britain and the American Colonies, 1606-1763* (New York: Harper Torchbooks, 1970), xxxix.
5. Edmund C. Burnett, *Continental Congress* (New York: W. W. Norton, 1964).
6. *Congressional Quarterly's Guide to Congress,* 3d ed. (Washington, D.C.: Congressional Quarterly, 1982), 13.
7. Burnett, *Continental Congress,* 171.

8. Jack N. Rakove, *The Beginnings of National Politics: An Interpretive History of the Continental Congress* (New York: Alfred A. Knopf, 1979), 43.

9. Charles C. Thach, Jr., *The Creation of the Presidency, 1775-1789: A Study in Constitutional History* (Baltimore: Johns Hopkins University Press, 1969), 34.

10. John Locke, *Two Tracts on Government*, ed. Philip Abrams (New York: Cambridge University Press, 1967), 374.

11. *Immigration and Naturalization Service v. Chadha,* 462 U.S. 919, 952 (1983).

12. *Bowsher v. Synar,* 478 U.S. 714 (1986).

13. James Madison, *The Federalist,* No. 48, ed. Edward Mead Earle (New York: Modern Library, n.d.), 321.

14. Joseph Story, *Commentaries on the Constitution of the United States,* 5th ed. (Boston: Little, Brown, 1905), 1:396; for Jackson's comments, see *Youngstown Sheet and Tube Co. v. Sawyer,* 343 U.S. 579, 635 (1952).

15. *Morrison v. Olson,* 108 S.Ct. 2597 (1988).

16. *The Constitution of the United States of America: Analysis and Interpretation,* S. Doc. 92-80, 92d Cong., 2d sess., 1973, 1597-1619. Recent figures courtesy of Johnny H. Killian, Congressional Research Service.

17. Charles Warren, *The Making of the Constitution* (Boston: Little, Brown, 1928), 162.

18. Charles Warren, *The Supreme Court in United States History* (Boston: Little, Brown, 1919), 195.

19. Lindsay Rogers, *The American Senate* (New York: Alfred A. Knopf, 1926), 21.

20. Alexander Hamilton, *The Federalist,* No. 27, ed. Edward Mead Earle (New York: Modern Library, n.d.), 168.

21. Joe Martin, *My First Fifty Years in Politics,* as told to Robert J. Donovan (New York: McGraw-Hill, 1960), 49-50.

22. Sam Rayburn, *Speak, Mister Speaker,* ed. H. G. Dulaney and Edward Hake Phillips (Bonham, Texas: Sam Rayburn Foundation, 1978), 466.

23. Allen Schick, "Complex Policymaking in the United States Senate," in *Policy Analysis on Major Issues,* Senate Commission on the Operation of the Senate, 94th Cong., 2d sess., 1977 committee print, 5-6.

24. House Commission on Administrative Review, *Administrative Reorganization and Legislative Management,* 2 vols., H. Doc. 95-232, 95th Cong., 1st sess., September 28, 1977, 2:17; Senate Commission on the Operation of the Senate, *Senators: Offices, Ethics, and Pressures,* 94th Cong., 2d sess., 1977 committee print, xi.

25. See *Jefferson's Manual,* Section XI; House, *Rules of the House of Representatives,* H. Doc. 97-271, 97th Cong., 2d sess., 1983, 136-139.

26. George B. Galloway, *History of the House of Representatives* (New York: Thomas Y. Crowell, 1961), 67.

27. See David J. Rothman, *Politics and Power: The United States Senate, 1869-1901* (Cambridge, Mass.: Harvard University Press, 1966); Margaret Munk, "Origin and Development of the Party Floor Leadership in the United States Senate," *Capitol Studies* (Winter 1974): 23-41.

28. Neil MacNeil, *Forge of Democracy: The House of Representatives* (New

York: David McKay, 1963), 306.

29. Noble Cunningham, Jr., ed., *Circular Letters of Congressmen, 1789-1839,* 3 vols. (Chapel Hill: University of North Carolina Press, 1978).
30. Galloway, *History of the House,* 122.
31. Martin, *My First Fifty Years,* 101.
32. James S. Young, *The Washington Community, 1800-1828* (New York: Columbia University Press, 1966), 89.
33. Cunningham, *Circular Letters,* 57.
34. Roy Swanstrom, *The United States Senate, 1787-1801,* S. Doc. 64, 87th Cong., 1st sess., 1962, 80.
35. Nelson W. Polsby, "The Institutionalization of the House of Representatives," *American Political Science Review* 68 (March 1968): 146-147; Randall B. Ripley, *Power in the Senate* (New York: St. Martin's Press, 1969), 42-43.
36. Peter Swenson, "The Influence of Recruitment on the Structure of Power in the U.S. House, 1870-1940," *Legislative Studies Quarterly* 7 (February 1982): 7-36.
37. Martin, *My First Fifty Years,* 49.
38. Ripley, *Power in the Senate,* 43-44.
39. See Samuel Kernell, "Toward Understanding 19th Century Congressional Career Patterns: Ambition, Competition, and Rotation," *American Journal of Political Science* 21 (November 1977): 669-693.
40. Nelson W. Polsby, Miriam Gallagher, and Barry S. Rundquist, "The Growth of the Seniority System in the U.S. House of Representatives," *American Political Science Review* 63 (September 1969): 794.
41. Swanstrom, *The United States Senate,* 283.
42. Young, *The Washington Community,* 126-127.
43. David W. Brady, *Congressional Voting in a Partisan Era* (Lawrence: University Press of Kansas, 1973), 190.
44. House Select Committee on Committees, *Final Report,* H. Rept. 96-866, 96th Cong., 2d sess., April 1, 1980, appendix 1.

PART TWO

A Congress
of Ambassadors

Democratic senator Sam Nunn is a powerful figure in Washington and probably the most influential person in Georgia. Chairman of the Senate Armed Services Committee, he is a leading voice on military budgets, arms control, war powers, and reform of the Pentagon. He reportedly was offered, and declined, the post of secretary of defense in the Bush administration. So why is Senator Nunn, recently reelected, visiting a pasture in Calhoun, Georgia, where a local poultry farmer is demonstrating his method of converting chicken droppings into electricity?

> Arriving a few minutes late, Nunn steps from his car wearing a banker's pin-striped suit and buckled leather shoes. He pumps a few hands and embarks on a walking tour of the fetid farm, striding briskly ahead like a man who takes his chicken manure seriously.
> "Are you going to show us where you collect the waste?" Nunn inquires impatiently at one point.
> "We can, yes. It's around back," his guide replies.
> "Good." Nunn pauses. "I'm used to that smell." [1]

National security and chicken droppings. This bizarre contrast lies at the very heart of the two Congresses. As legislators, senators and representatives must apply their judgment to thorny policy questions; as members of a representative assembly, "a Congress of ambassadors," they must capture and hold the support of voters in their states or electoral districts.[2] Often this means contacting constituents in far from glamorous settings. No matter how valuable or esteemed a member's contribution to policy making, it is only as durable as his or her ability to stay in office.

The pull of local interests is seen in members' paths to office. Winning candidates usually forge close ties with their states or districts long before they arrive at Capitol Hill. Their campaign appeals must be framed in terms congenial to local voters. While national trends impinge, most congressional elections are decided by local personalities or local issues. In Chapters 3 and 4 we will describe the electoral game senators and representatives must play to win office.

Once in office, members of Congress quickly learn that reelection hinges upon the continued support of their constituents. Legislators "represent" voters to win support, it is customarily said. One way to represent people is to resemble them; by this standard, Congress is not very representative in certain key ways. Another way of representing is to work and vote for policies and laws that the people favor—or that they would favor if they had the knowledge and expertise to evaluate them. Still another is to attend to constituents' problems and gain credit for resolving them. Another is by communicating with constituents to establish an agreeable personality or style—more a matter of presenting oneself than of representing issues. Such activities devour legislators' time and energies, as we will see in Chapter 5.

Part Two, A Congress of Ambassadors, reveals Congress as a collectivity of 540 members pursuing individual careers. To comprehend our national legislature, we need to study the men and women who compose it.

Notes

1. Steve Coll, "Sam Nunn, Insider from the Deep Southland," *Washington Post,* February 18, 1986, B1.
2. Edmund Burke, "Speech to Electors at Bristol," in *Burke's Politics,* ed. J. S. Hoffman and Paul Levack (New York: Alfred A. Knopf, 1949), 116.

Rep. Tom Tauke, R-Iowa, and his young son make a campaign appearance in a Tipton, Iowa, Fourth of July parade.

CHAPTER THREE

Going for It:
Recruitment Roulette

It's their first day on the job. A former banker, government professor, U.S. district judge, cattle rancher, and owner of the Milwaukee Brewers baseball team wait expectantly for their names to be called. They come from Cape Coral, Florida; Pindars Corners, New York; South Portland, Maine; Big Horn, Wyoming; and Milwaukee, Wisconsin. The sergeant at arms calls them forward alphabetically in groups of four. Colleagues from their states escort them to the front of the Senate chamber, where the vice president, the Senate's constitutionally designated presiding officer, administers the oath of office. Newly elected or reelected, the senators are now officially members of "the world's greatest deliberative body," as the Senate likes to call itself. Over in the House chamber, 440 elected or reelected members have just been sworn in as well.

How did these people get to Congress? There is no single answer to that question. In the broadest sense all incumbent legislators are products of *recruitment*—the social and political process through which people achieve leadership posts. Social analysts agree that recruitment is a key to the effective functioning of all institutions, including legislatures. The first great book about politics, Plato's *Republic*, addressed the question of fitting the ablest people into leadership positions. Conservatives, following Plato, believe that societies should be ruled by the most talented people—in John Adams's phrase, the "rich and the wise and the well-born." Marxists believe recruitment reflects a society's class structure, with the most privileged people landing in the ranks of leadership. Modern political scientists, regardless of ideology, eagerly chart the paths individuals travel to posts in the White House, Congress, and the courts.

Any recruitment process has both formal and informal elements. In the case of the Congress, formal elements include the constitutional framework and state and federal laws governing nominations and elections. Equally important are informal, often unwritten, "rules of the game." Some people are more ambitious than others for elective office; skills and attributes make some aspirants more "eligible" than others; and certain attitudes persuade citizens to vote for some aspirants and against others. Taken together, such elements comprise a screening process through which some individuals pass more easily than others. The recruitment process and its "biases," both overt and hidden, affect the day-to-day operation of the House and Senate, not to mention the quality of representation and decision making.

Formal Rules of the Game

The constitutional requirements for holding congressional office are few and simple. They include *age* (twenty-five years of age for the House, thirty for the Senate); *citizenship* (seven years for the House, nine years for the Senate); and *residency* in the state from which the officeholder is elected. Thus, the constitutional gateways to congressional officeholding are fairly wide.

Even these minimal requirements, however, sometimes arouse controversy. During the 1960s and 1970s, when people of the post-World War II "baby boom" reached maturity and the Twenty-sixth Amendment, permitting eighteen-year-olds to vote, was ratified, an unsuccessful effort was made to lower the eligible age for senators and representatives.

Because of Americans' geographic mobility, residency sometimes is an issue. Voters normally prefer candidates with longstanding ties to their states or districts and shun "carpetbaggers." Defending his Senate seat in 1988 against Pete Dawkins, Frank R. Lautenberg, D-N.J., unleashed a campaign portraying Dawkins as a celebrity candidate (Heisman Trophy winner, Rhodes scholar, army general, Wall Street banker) who had shopped around for a state in which to run. The harshest TV slogan was, "Pete Dawkins: He'll move anywhere, say anything to get elected."[1] Candidates can sometimes overcome such barriers, especially in fast-growing areas. Sen. John McCain, R-Ariz., a career navy officer, war hero, and six-year prisoner in North Vietnam, beat three established politicians for a congressional nomination barely a year after he settled in the state. He stifled carpetbagging charges by explaining that as a navy officer and the son of one, he had never been able to put down roots: "The longest place I ever lived was Hanoi."

Senate Apportionment

In the Senate the "one person, one vote" rule does not apply. Article V of the Constitution assures each state, regardless of population, two Senate seats and guarantees that this equal representation cannot be taken away without the state's consent. The Senate was intended to add stability, wisdom, and forbearance to the actions of the popularly elected House. Thus, the Founders stipulated that senators be chosen by their respective state legislatures rather than by the voters themselves. This distinction between the two houses was eroded by the Seventeenth Amendment, which in 1913 provided for the direct popular election of senators.

Today's senators tend to approach their tasks from a generalist's or nationwide perspective, not because of long terms or indirect selection, but because their constituencies are so large and diverse. When senators were selected indirectly and states were less populous, the Senate tended to be a collection of spokesmen for dominant regional interests such as cotton, rails, or tobacco. Today, however, most states boast highly developed economies and reasonably competitive politics. Statewide electorates display ethnic, racial, and social diversity; many are microcosms of the whole nation. Senate seats are, in fact, more competitive than House seats—a state of affairs that would surely confound the Framers.

So although the Senate is malapportioned by design, it is not *necessarily* unrepresentative. During the 1945-1964 post-World War II era, the Senate probably reflected national demographic trends more faithfully than did the unredistricted House.[2] More recently, the GOP's hold on less populous western states gave it control of the Senate between 1981 and 1987, even though Republican candidates garnered only a minority of the major-party votes cast.

House Apportionment

The 435 House seats are apportioned among the states by population. In addition, there are four nonvoting delegates (District of Columbia, Guam, Virgin Islands, and Samoa) and one resident commissioner (Puerto Rico). Once the population figures from the decennial census are gathered, apportionment is derived by a mathematical formula called the Method of Equal Proportions.[3] The idea is that proportional differences in the number of persons per representative for any pair of states should be kept to a minimum. The first fifty seats are fixed because each state is guaranteed by the Constitution at least one representative. The question then becomes: which state deserves the fifty-first seat, the fifty-second, and so forth? The mathematical formula yields a priority value for each seat, up to any desired number.

As the nation's population shifts, states gain or lose congressional representation. This is especially true today, when the more or less fixed size of the House means that one state's gain is another's loss. For several decades rural areas and core cities have been losing seats to the suburbs; older industrial states of the Northeast and Midwest are yielding ground to fast-growing states of the South and West—the declining "Rust Belt" versus the booming "Sun Belt." [4]

The 1980 census confirmed these trends and showed what a difference ten years can make: one Florida district had amassed almost four times as many people (nearly 890,000) as one district in the desolated South Bronx. The resulting reapportionment shifted seventeen seats among states. Figure 3-1 shows the 1980 apportionment and projected gains and losses of House seats after the 1990 census.[5]

The national census is used to allocate not only House seats but

Figure 3-1 Congressional Apportionment in 1980 and Projected Seat Changes after 1990 Census

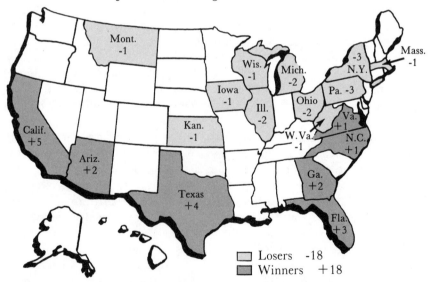

Congressional Apportionment, 1980
(Representation in the House for the 98th-102d Congresses)

Projected Seat Changes after 1990 Census

Losers -18
Winners +18

Source: David C. Huckabee, "House Apportionment: Preliminary Projections," Congressional Research Service Report 88-567, Washington, D.C., August 31, 1988.

Note: The projected seat changes are based on recent Census Bureau estimates of current population and its projections of the likely 1990 population.

legislative seats within states as well. Furthermore, data collected by the census (numbers of poor, city dwellers, ethnic groups, and so forth) are used by the federal government to distribute aid to states, cities, counties, and towns. No wonder that many lawmakers and other public officials are wary of undercounting by census-takers—who may miss the homeless, transients, illegal aliens, and other hard-to-count groupings. In short, political power and federal funds hinge upon the once-a-decade count.

Reapportionment does not yield exactly equal districts because of disparities between states. South Dakota, reduced to a single House seat, began the 1980s as the nation's largest single district, with more than 690,000 people. Least crowded was Montana's 2d Congressional District, with fewer than 380,000 people. Concerned about losing a seat in the 1990s, Montana leaders urged people to move into the state.

Districting in the House

Once congressional seats are apportioned, the states must draw district lines. (A 1967 congressional statute prohibits *at-large elections* in states with more than one representative.) Redistricting is a fiercely political process involving intensely interested parties—state legislators, the governor, incumbent House members, and national party officials. If these political actors become deadlocked on redistricting, judges may step in to finish the job—sometimes conferring victory on parties that lost out in the earlier political fracas.

Because congressional seats are political prizes, it is not surprising that districting is an instrument of partisan, factional, or even personal advantage. Two historical districting anomalies are malapportionment and gerrymandering.

Malapportionment

Prior to 1964, districts of grossly unequal population often existed side by side. Within a single state, districts varied by as much as eight to one. Rural regions tended to dominate growing urban areas in the state legislatures, where district population disparities were even greater than among congressional districts. Sometimes malapportionment resulted from explicit actions; more often legislators simply failed to redistrict, letting population movements and demographic trends do the job for them. This was called the "silent gerrymander."

Preferring a posture of judicial restraint, the courts were slow to venture into the political thicket of districting. By the 1960s, however, the problem of unequal representation cried out for resolution. Although metropolitan areas had grown in population and political clout, their representation still lagged in state legislatures and in Congress. Meanwhile, a new spirit of judicial activism had taken hold. In 1961 a group of Tennessee city-dwellers challenged the state's legislative districting, which had not been altered since 1901. In 1962 the Supreme Court held that federal courts had a right to review legislative districting under the Fourteenth Amendment's equal protection clause (*Baker v. Carr*, 1962). Two years later the Court was ready to strike down state districting schemes that failed to meet standards of equality (*Reynolds v. Sims*, 1964). Chief Justice Earl Warren declared that state legislative seats, even under bicameral arrangements, must be apportioned "substantially on population."

That same year the principle of "one person, one vote" was extended to the U.S. House of Representatives. An Atlantan who served in the Georgia Senate, James P. Wesberry, Jr., charged that the state's congressional districting violated equal protection of the laws, and the Supreme Court upheld his challenge (*Wesberry v. Sanders*, 1964). The decision was based on Article I, Section 2, of the Constitution, which directs that representatives be apportioned among the states according to their respective numbers and be chosen by the people of the several states. This language, argued Justice Hugo Black, means that "as nearly as is practicable, one man's vote in a congressional election is to be worth as much as another's." But how much equality of population is "practicable" within the states? As states struggled to comply with the *Wesberry* mandate, this question inevitably came up.

Increasingly, the Supreme Court has adopted rigid mathematical equality as the underlying standard. In a 1983 case (*Karcher v. Daggett*), a 5-to-4 majority voided a New Jersey plan in which districts varied by no more than one-seventh of one percent. "Adopting any standard other than population equality would subtly erode the Constitution's ideal of equal representation," wrote Justice William J. Brennan for the majority. This doctrine guarantees the federal courts an active role in redistricting. The dissenting judges, speaking through Justice Byron R. White, contended that the majority opinion would ensure "extensive intrusion of the judiciary into legislative business." They also maintained it was an "unreasonable insistence on an unattainable perfection" that would encourage gerrymandering by making mathematics more important than geographic or political boundaries. The Court invited states to defend districting plans that deviate from equality—for example, to make districts compact, follow municipal boundaries, preserve the cores of prior districts, or avoid contests between incumbent representatives. Yet such considerations had been summarily rejected in a 1969 Missouri case (*Kirkpatrick v. Preisler*).

Population equality has thus been achieved at the expense of other goals. Parity in numbers of residents makes it hard to respect political divisions such as county lines. It also makes it hard to follow economic, social, or geographic boundaries. The congressional district, therefore, tends to be an artificial creation with little relationship to real communities of interest—economic or geographic or political. This heightens the congressional district's isolation, forcing candidates to forge their own unique factions and alliances. It also aids incumbents, who have ways of reaching voters without relying on commercial communications media.

Gerrymandering

"All districting is gerrymandering" in the sense that single-member districts, with a winner-take-all feature, normally favor the majority party. The term is usually reserved, however, for conscious line drawing to maximize partisan advantage. The gerrymander takes its name from Gov. Elbridge Gerry of Massachusetts, who in 1812 created a peculiar salamander-shaped district north of Boston to benefit his Democratic party. Actually, gerrymandering can be used not only to provide partisan advantage but also to protect incumbents, help state legislators' political ambitions, punish political mavericks, and help or hinder racial or ethnic groups.

Packing and *cracking* are two gerrymandering techniques. Packing a district is drawing the lines to embrace as many of one party's voters as possible to make the district "safe." Needless to say, incumbents prefer safe districts to stave off defeat. In cracking, an area of partisan strength is split among two or more districts to minimize that party's voting leverage. Following the Voting Rights Act of 1965, law enforcement officials moved to restrain states from "cracking" minority votes, while backing selective efforts to "pack" them to elect minority officeholders. After the 1980 census, the Justice Department rejected a North Carolina plan for drawing a fishhook around Durham County, where blacks have voting strength, to accommodate an incumbent (who later decided to retire). It sent back a Texas plan because it diluted Hispanic voting strength in the Rio Grande Valley. It blocked a Georgia plan for splitting black votes in the Atlanta area. Meanwhile, a federal court drew up a plan giving black voters in Mississippi's 2d Congressional District a 53 percent majority. In short, when gerrymandering affects minority voters, the law insists that its impact be benign.

The effects of gerrymanders are not easily measured. Marginal or competitive districts (those where the winner gains less than 55 percent of the votes) are tougher for a party to capture and hold, but they have the advantage of yielding legislative seats with a modest number of voters (that is, a minimal winning coalition). Safe districts, while naturally preferred by incumbents, waste the majority party's votes by furnishing outsized victories.

Gerrymandering is said to tilt elections in incumbents' favor by creating more safe districts. For this reason it is mentioned as a possible contributor to the rising success of incumbents since the late 1960s. The evidence, however, does not point in that direction.[6] Incumbents are reelected just as frequently in unredistricted areas as in redistricted ones. In short, while gerrymandering can alter the results in specific cases, its larger impact upon legislative representation is at best unclear.

Partisan gerrymandering usually occurs in states where one political party clearly controls the process. In California a 1981 Democratic plan masterminded by the late representative Phillip Burton decimated several incumbent Republicans, bolstered threatened Democrats, and created districts for friendly state legislators. (A GOP lawmaker called it the "mine-shaft plan": Democrats could say, "I got mine," and Republicans could say, "I got the shaft." [7]) The plan netted five Democratic seats in 1982, surviving court challenges and a statewide referendum.

Bipartisan gerrymandering tends to flow from divided party control—within the legislature or between the legislature and the governor. A bargain is struck between the parties to protect each other's incumbents, often shutting off competition for the state's congressional seats. This occurred in Ohio, which lost two seats after the 1980 count. Legislators threw two Cleveland Democrats into one district and eliminated a district held by a Republican running for the Senate.

Districting tailored to protect incumbents of one or both parties results from political deadlock. In some cases, federal courts intervene; in others, a disgruntled party brings suit.

Such political cunning is not always rewarded; like all other political actions, gerrymandering may fall prey to the "law of unanticipated consequences." Consider the case of the Indiana Republicans, who in 1981 controlled the governor's office, both chambers of the General Assembly, and a $250,000 war chest (more than the state Democratic party's entire annual budget). Money was poured into sophisticated computer technology to redraw the state's congressional district lines, yet by the end of the 1980s, Democrats held six of the ten seats—more than when the decade began.[8]

In states slated to gain or lose seats, parties and incumbents work feverishly behind the scenes to affect districting. Today they are aided by the latest computer technology. Sophisticated data bases and computer programs provide instant analysis of how shifts in boundaries will affect district composition—racial, ethnic, and economic characteristics and the numbers of Republicans and Democrats. "The potential, high-tech gerrymandering of the next decade is frightening to consider," declared Rep. Guy Vander Jagt of Michigan, who as head of the National Republican Congressional Committee was enmeshed in the phenomenon.[9]

The Court Enters the Quagmire.   Congressional reapportionment laws from the mid-nineteenth to the early twentieth century usually required that districts be equal in population and contiguous in territory. A 1911 law specifying "contiguous and compact territory" lapsed, however, and it was not replaced, despite several attempts to enact congressional districting standards. For most of its history, Congress regarded gerrymandering as part of the spoils of partisan control. And the Supreme Court, for most of its history, also was quite content to leave gerrymandering alone.

Then, in the 1960s, the Court declared certain forms of gerrymandering unconstitutional. It repeatedly ruled against districts drawn deliberately to disadvantage a racial or ethnic group. The 1960 case of *Gomillion v. Lightfoot* declared unconstitutional the "obscene, 28-sided" boundaries in Tuskegee, Alabama, that disfranchised blacks by excluding them from the city. The Voting Rights Act of 1965 prohibited districting intended to dilute the voting power of minorities. In 1975 Congress amended the act to cover "language minorities." A further amendment in 1982 (upheld by the Supreme Court in 1984) outlawed districting that produced discriminatory results, regardless of intent.

These rulings dealt with racially motivated districting, but it was not until 1986 in the case of *Davis et al. v. Bandemer et al.* that the Supreme Court faced head-on the question of partisan gerrymandering—that is, districting designed to promote or hinder a political party.[10] A group of Indiana Democrats challenged the legality of the district boundaries drawn by the Republican-controlled state legislature in 1981. As one Republican leader admitted, "The name of the game is to keep us in power." Although Democrats won almost 52 percent of the statewide vote in 1982, they gained only 43 of 100 seats in the state House.

The Supreme Court handed down three opinions in this important case: a majority opinion by Justice Byron R. White, a separate concurring opinion by Justice Lewis Powell, and a minority opinion by Justice Sandra Day O'Connor. White declared that gerrymandering was a justiciable issue. If the gerrymandering was substantial, longstanding, and truly harmful to the political minority, it would violate the Constitution's equal protection clause, but the Indiana gerrymander did not meet that test, in White's opinion.

Justice Powell agreed with White that gerrymandering could be unconstitutional, and he was ready to strike down the Indiana gerrymander. He enumerated various proofs of its adverse effects upon the minority.

Justice O'Connor rejected outright the challenge to gerrymandering. She recited the pitfalls of trying to use party voting as an indicator of voters' permanent loyalties. The majority opinion provided "no clear stopping point to prevent the gradual evolution of a requirement of roughly proportional representation for every cohesive political group."

Davis v. Bandemer raised more questions than it answered. Perhaps it will lead analysts to develop accurate measures of partisan gerrymandering. Perhaps Justice Powell's multiple tests for denial of equal protection will prove workable, although only if the Court relaxes its standards of population equality among districts. More likely, Justice O'Connor is right: the task of defining and assessing partisan gerrymandering lies beyond the courts' ability to identify wrongs and fashion practical remedies. (In early 1989 the Supreme Court declined, by a vote of 6 to 3, to review a lower court's ruling on California's redistricting scheme; the lower court had declared that the districts did not amount to unconstitutionally partisan gerrymandering.) So while the Court has invited legal challenges to districting schemes, it has yet to grapple with the problem of measuring inequities. Redistricting following the 1990 census is likely to face careful judicial scrutiny. As an important formal element in the recruitment process, districting will receive greater attention from political strategists, legislatures, and courts.

The "Matthew Effect." Gerrymandering underscores a basic recruitment effect of our single-member district representation. The party winning the most votes captures a disproportionately large share of legislative seats, if districts are equally competitive. This is the so-called "Matthew effect," named for a biblical aphorism (Matthew 13:12): "For whosoever hath, to him shall be given, and he shall have more abundance; but whosoever hath not, from him shall be taken away even that he hath."

Political analysts and critics of gerrymandering point to the *votes-seats gap*—that is, the discrepancy between a party's votes and the seats it receives. Democrats' share of U.S. House seats has exceeded their share of the popular vote in all but two elections since 1942; their average "bonus" of seats has been 5.8 percent. In 1988, for example, Democrats captured nearly 60 percent of the House seats with about 55 percent of the two-party vote nationwide—a typical spread for recent elections. Republican strategists claim this gap is caused by partisan gerrymandering in the states, which turned the Democrats' expected losses in the 1980s redistricting into slight gains.

Numerous factors distort the ratio of seats to votes, however. In winner-take-all contests, winners receive a "bonus" while losers receive nothing, no matter how close the outcome. In theory, a party could capture *all* the seats by winning every contest by a bare majority, a highly improbable outcome. Generally, though, the larger the margin of votes garnered by the majority party, the larger the excess of seats over votes.

Many lucky candidates run without opposition. In 1988 there were seventy-nine uncontested House seats, 18 percent of the total; three-quarters of these were Democratic. Votes are cast in some of these districts but not in others. Either way, nationwide vote tallies are distorted. The dominant party in such noncontests (mainly Democratic) may actually "lose" if votes are unrecorded or if their supporters neglect to vote when the outcome is assured. One can only speculate on the party margins, had real contests taken place.

Equally serious problems confront efforts to calculate a normal or equitable party share of state or district votes. How many Republicans are there in a given area? Party registration figures are unreliable. Not all states have them, many voters register as independents, and voters sometimes register with a party other than their own (for example, to take part in a dominant party's primaries in a one-party area). American voters are notoriously fickle about party labels, and they are becoming ever more so. As many as half of them tend to split their tickets between the parties in any given election. Past voting records are decent guides (the architects of gerrymanders use them), but they are by no means infallible (think of the Indiana GOP, whose House gerrymander went awry).

Another complication: turnout varies greatly among districts. Economically affluent areas tend to have higher vote totals than do economically deprived areas, which usually helps the Republicans. For example, in 1988 nearly a quarter million votes were cast in California's 12th Congressional District ("Silicon Valley"), where Republican Tom Campbell narrowly edged the Democrat, Anna Eshoo. Meanwhile, Democrat Augustus F. Hawkins won 86 percent of the vote in his South-Central Los Angeles district, four-fifths of which is black or Hispanic and which cast fewer than 100,000 votes overall. Raw vote totals, even within a single state, ignore these demographic variations.

Gaps between raw votes and House seats, then, prove neither the presence of gerrymandering nor the disadvantaged status of the minority. Thus, some critics of gerrymanders, like Justice Powell, suggest more traditional tests. Are the districts compact? Are traditional political boundaries respected? Are odd shapes avoided in drawing the lines? Yet following these guidelines may be at odds with the Court's "one person, one vote" rule.

To escape these problems, some political scientists suggest looking at the "swing ratio," which Richard Niemi defines as "the change in the proportion of seats won by a party that occurs when there is a one-percent change in the votes won by that party." [11] In other words, will seats change hands as votes change? Yet political scientists disagree about what a "normal" swing ratio might be. And the swing ratio is subject to many of the same objections raised against using raw vote totals.

In sum, the use of single-member districts with winner-take-all voting is one of the most fundamental rules of the recruitment game. This principle affects not only the shape and character of electoral constituencies, but also the overall membership of the House and Senate. Prodded by the *Davis v. Bandemer* ruling, political scientists are beginning to study what constitutes fairness in drawing district lines.[12] More research, debate—and litigation— can be expected.

Becoming a Candidate

Obviously, not all who are eligible actually run for Congress. It is not enough to meet the legal qualifications; one must decide—based on a blend of considerations, some personal and emotional, others practical and rational—to enter a given race. Candidacy decisions are often the pivotal moments in the recruitment process, although students of politics have only recently given them the attention they deserve. "The decision to run obviously structures everything else that goes on in the primary process," writes Sandy Maisel. "Who runs, who does not run, how many candidates run. These questions set the stage for the campaigns themselves." [13]

Called or Chosen?

Some candidates are recruited and sponsored by locally influential individuals or groups; others are self-starters who pull their own bandwagons. Parties once acted as recruiters or screeners. They sought out suitable candidates and assured them support. Although less common today, party or group sponsorship survives in areas of strong political organizations or clubs.[14]

If candidate recruitment is handled more gingerly than in the past, it nonetheless figures prominently in party leaders' activities. According to a recent survey, seven out of ten local parties took part in finding candidates, and about half of the state parties reported doing so. Of 251 candidates surveyed after the 1978 races, about 40 percent had consulted with political leaders in deciding whether to enter the race.[15]

The two parties' House and Senate campaign committees, while trying to avoid clashes with state and district leaders, work actively to recruit and sponsor winning candidates. The majority of today's candidates, however, launch their own careers, lining up supporters and financial backing. Once common in suburbs and other areas usually lacking strong party organizations, this self-promotion has spread to most areas. None of the American Enterprise Institute's panel of House freshmen from the "class of 1978" felt party organizations had been critical in recruiting them; several ran against the party leaders' choice to win their primaries. As one summarized,

> You can look around the floor of the House and see a handful—twenty years ago, you saw a lot of them—today, you can see just a handful of hacks that were put there by the party organization, and there are very, very few of them left. It is just mostly people who went out and took the election.[16]

Incumbents, Challengers, and Open Seats

How do would-be candidates, whether they are self-starters or handpicked by party leaders, make up their minds to run? A serious contender is a *strategic politician*—that is, someone who rationally weighs the pros and cons of launching a campaign. Do the rewards exceed the drawbacks of the office, especially compared with what I am doing now? What are the chances of success, and what will it cost to succeed? If there is an incumbent, what are his or her weaknesses? And as a candidate, what would I bring to the contest? What are my strengths and weaknesses in campaigning, voter appeal, and fund raising? The circle of people pondering these questions—the *challenger pool*—may be large or small, depending on the office and the circumstances.[17]

Of all the inducements to launch a candidacy, the likelihood of winning probably stands at the top. A seat that is clearly winnable seldom lacks for candidates eager to capture it. Where the odds are slim, few contenders will step forward; party leaders may have to beat the bushes to find a sacrificial lamb, although even the most hopeless races usually attract someone yearning for publicity.

So it was that Orvas E. Beers, longtime Republican chairman of Allen County, Indiana, was hunting for someone to run against the incumbent Democratic representative, J. Edward Roush, in 1976. A Fort Wayne newspaper editor suggested a young lawyer and newspaperman, Dan Quayle, as "bright, articulate, really fast on his feet."

> Beers met Quayle at a luncheon in the Chamber of Commerce and liked what he saw. On the way out, Beers recalled: "I said, 'Danny, how would you like to run for Congress?' "
>
> "You mean now?" Quayle asked.
>
> "Yes."
>
> "I'll have to check with my dad," said the young man.... (Quayle Senior owned the newspaper at which his son was general manager.) [18]

"Go ahead, you won't win," Quayle's father told him. But win he did. In 1980 he successfully challenged incumbent senator Birch Bayh, and in 1988 Quayle was elected vice president. Quayle benefited from lucky timing and his state's Republican leanings. But his father, weighing the odds, was right to be skeptical: Dan Quayle had to knock off seemingly invincible incumbents to gain his House and Senate seats—an extremely rare occurrence.

In nine out of ten House contests, incumbents will be running, and most of them will be reelected. As Gary C. Jacobson writes, "nearly everything pertaining to candidates and campaigns for the House of Representatives is profoundly influenced by whether the candidate is an incumbent, challenging an incumbent, or pursuing an open seat." [19] With only slightly less force, the same could be said of the Senate.

Anyone contemplating a congressional race would do well to study Table 3-1 with care. Since World War II, on the average 92 percent of all incumbent representatives and 75 percent of incumbent senators running for reelection have been returned to office. Higher than normal casualty rates occur periodically: for example, the post-World War II generational shift (1946-1948), a midterm recession (1958), the Goldwater debacle (1964), the Watergate fallout (1974), and a combination of generational shift and conservative realignment (1978-1980). Otherwise, reelection rates have been high and involuntary turnover low.

Nowadays it is nearly impossible to topple a House incumbent, short of a major scandal or misstep. This is a relatively recent phenomenon. Although incumbents have been fattening their margins of victory for some time, through the 1970s they were just as vulnerable to defeat as they had been earlier. That is, incumbents were on average winning by wider margins, when they did win, but they were just as likely to lose any given election as before.[20] By the 1980s, however, incumbents had erected such imposing barriers against defeat that competition for their House seats dropped to exceedingly low levels.

Table 3-1 The Advantage of Incumbency in the House and Senate, 1946-1988

Year	House		Defeated			Senate		Defeated		
	Seeking reelection	No opponent	Primary	General	Percent reelected	Seeking reelection	No opponent	Primary	General	Percent reelected
1946	398	81	18	52	82.4	30	1	6	7	56.7
1948	400	83	15	68	79.2	25	5	2	8	60.0
1950	400	99	6	32	90.5	32	3	5	5	68.8
1952	389	93	9	26	91.0	31	3	2	9	64.5
1954	407	86	6	22	93.1	32	6	2	6	75.0
1956	411	73	6	16	94.6	29	5	0	4	86.2
1958	396	94	3	37	89.9	28	1	0	10	64.3
1960	405	78	5	25	92.6	29	3	0	1	96.6
1962	402	58	12	22	91.5	35	1	1	5	82.9
1964	397	42	8	45	86.6	33	1	1	4	84.8
1966	411	56	8	41	88.1	32	3	3	1	87.5
1968	409	46	4	9	96.8	28	2	4	4	71.4
1970	401	59	10	12	94.5	31	0	1	6	77.4
1972	390	54	12	13	93.6	27	2	2	5	74.1
1974	391	59	8	40	87.7	27	2	2	2	85.2
1976	384	52	3	13	95.8	25	2	0	9	64.0
1978	382	69	5	19	93.7	25	1	3	7	60.0
1980	398	53	6	31	90.7	29	1	4	9	55.2
1982	396	53	8	29	90.6	30	0	0	2	93.3
1984	410	60	3	17	95.1	29	1	0	3	89.7
1986	393	71	2	6	98.0	28	0	0	6	75.0
1988	410	79	1	6	98.3	27	0	0	4	85.2
Average	399	68.1	7.2	26.4	91.6	29.2	0	1.7	5.3	75.4

Sources: *Congressional Quarterly Weekly Report*, April 5, 1980, 908; November 8, 1980, 3302, 3320-3321; July 31, 1982, 1870; November 6, 1982, 2781; November 10, 1984, 2897, 2901; November 12, 1988, 3264, 3270.

Note: Percent reelected includes both primary and general election defeats.

Challengers for Senate seats have a better chance of unseating incumbents, but there are important qualifications. Senate elections, it appears, have become somewhat more competitive *overall* in the past two decades—in striking contrast to House races. This is due mainly to the dramatic transformation of the South from a Democratic bastion to a two-party region—a development at the statewide level that has spread more selectively into House districts. In nonsouthern states it appears that, if anything, Senate contests are increasingly less competitive. Four out of five incumbents win the contests they enter; the proportion of "marginal" elections (candidates winning by 55 or 60 percent or more) has dropped. Winning candidates receive more than 60 percent of the vote in almost half of today's nonsouthern Senate elections.[21]

Why are incumbents so formidable? Political scientists have launched a veritable cottage industry to answer this question. It is no secret that incumbents have built-in methods of promoting support—through speeches, press coverage, newsletters, staff assistance, and constituent service. The average House member enjoys perquisites valued at well over a million dollars in a two-year term; with six-year terms, senators have resources between $4 million and $7 million (box, page 141).

Everyone concedes the value of incumbents' perquisites, but scholars differ sharply on exactly how they affect electoral success. One view is that incumbents exploit their resources to ensure reelection, seizing upon their ability to assist constituents in dealing with the bureaucracy to build electoral credit. Others counter that legislators are simply responding to constituent demands and available technology. Still others question whether incumbents' resources are directly translatable into votes. However these questions are resolved (we discuss them further in Chapters 4 and 5), incumbents spend much of their time and effort forging links with their voters, and most of them succeed in doing so.[22]

Incumbents typically win their elections far in advance by scaring off potential candidates. As Jacobson observes, "the incumbent's most effective electoral strategy is to discourage serious opposition."[23] Some are totally successful: an average of sixty-eight representatives and two senators in each electoral cycle face no opponents at all. Impressive victory margins are beneficial; any drop may invite opponents the next time around. That is why wise incumbents try to sustain wide electoral margins, show unbroken strength, keep up constituency ties, and build giant war chests of funds. Failing this, there is always the option of retiring more or less gracefully.

Thus, the quality of challengers and the vigor of their campaigns are critical factors in many battles for congressional seats.[24] Often the races turn on bids that are *not* made. For example, despite rumblings about his remoteness and inattention to constituent affairs, Sen. Daniel Patrick Moynihan, D-N.Y., crushed a relatively obscure opponent in 1988 by more than 2 million votes. More than a dozen prominent Republicans were mentioned as challengers, but the hapless, disorganized state party could convince none of them to make the race.[25]

The all-important recruiting season takes place many months before the final balloting. At this time the two parties' leaders and campaign committees "reach out across the country in search of political talent. Like college football coaching staffs in hot pursuit of high-school prospects, they are . . . putting together the lineups of the future." [26] Filing deadlines must be met, backers lined up, and financing sought out. Because estimates of candidate strength must be made so far in advance, previous margins of victory count heavily, along with early (and unreliable) polls. Also magnified are nationwide conditions during the recruiting season. The Democrats' success in finding attractive candidates for the 1988 House and Senate elections was attributed to favorable signs more than a year before the elections—the Reagan administration's low ebb, including the 1986 loss of the Senate and the Iran-contra scandal and subsequent White House shakeup.

Where Are the "Quality Challengers"?

When they beat the bushes for "quality challengers," what do party recruiters look for? Broadly speaking, quality challengers are people who are *attractive* to voters and *skilled* in presenting themselves as candidates.[27] Usually, to be attractive is to be experienced in public office, which implies visibility among, and credibility with, the voters. Alternatively, fame or notoriety may overcome lack of prior background or experience. Attributes include physical appearance and personality, talent for organizing or motivating others, and the ability to raise money to mount an effective campaign.

All too often candidates of such caliber prefer to remain in the bushes. The road to public office can be arduous and costly, and the odds are often long, especially against a dominant party or an entrenched incumbent. Therefore, quality challengers are scarce, particularly for House races. Two researchers recently studied the 312 House races in 1978 and ranked in eight categories the quality of the challengers. Fewer than one in ten that year were truly blue-ribbon contenders—widely known veterans of elective office with other attractive traits (top two categories). More than half the challengers (161 out of 312) had never held elective office and had few other traits likely to attract voters (lowest two categories).[28] Needless to say, low-quality challengers (by these definitions) raise less money and are less successful than the handful of blue-ribbon contenders. Occasionally a Dan Quayle can beat the odds, but the majority of contenders end up nearly as obscure as when they began.

Open seats—those where incumbents have died or retired—especially attract contenders. Given the looseness of party ties, shifts in party control are quite common in races lacking an incumbent candidate. Party strategies pinpoint these districts.

Failing an open seat, an inattentive or vulnerable incumbent may provide an opening. Any sign of weakness in the incumbent may bring on challengers who smell a chance of success. For others, a long-shot bid is the only way of becoming a candidate: they run because "it was something they knew they were going to do sometime and for whatever reasons [it] appeared to be the right time." [29] Others run to air their views on particular issues, to present an alternative, or to lay the groundwork for later attempts.

Most successful candidates are professional politicians long before they run for Congress. Many elective offices such as mayor, district attorney, or state legislator are springboards to candidacy for the House. Governors, lieutenant governors, and attorneys general are leading contenders for the Senate because they have already won a statewide election. House members—especially from small states—are also in a strategic spot: thirty-eight senators in the 101st Congress had moved from the House.

Ever since Lyndon Johnson came to Washington in 1932 as a representative's aide, ambitious politicians have seen staff jobs as stepping stones to elective office. In the 99th Congress fifty-five representatives and six senators had worked in some capacity for a legislator, congressional committee, or other Hill agency. But even a favorably located official may need added thrust to contend for a House or Senate seat. In populous states with multiple media markets, it is virtually impossible for local officials and House members—indeed, anyone aside from the governor or attorney general—to gain the statewide visibility needed for the U.S. Senate. Moynihan's successful run for the Democratic Senate nomination in 1976 would hardly have been possible without his highly publicized stint the year before as U.S. ambassador to the United Nations. The New York media gave heavy coverage to his spirited attacks on the Soviets and his defense of Israel against its many U.N. detractors. His celebrity status helped Democrats forget that he had been a professor, a neoconservative, and an out-of-stater. "He spoke up for America," one of his ads said, "He'd speak up for New York."

Some nonpolitical careers can position a person for candidacy. Astronauts, war heroes, and athletes are in big demand as candidates. So are local or statewide television personalities. Several of these, including Sen. Jesse Helms, R-N.C., and Rep. Al Swift, D-Wash., converted their media visibility into successful candidacies. Rudy Boschwitz, R-Minn., began appearing in television ads for his plywood business years before he picked the right time—1978—to make his Senate bid. Sen. Herbert Kohl, D-Wis., was well known throughout the state from his family's food stores long before he wrote an $18.5 million check to keep the Milwaukee Bucks basketball team from moving elsewhere—not a bad advertisement for a would-be senator.

The Personal Equation

Personal attributes also determine who is urged to run, and who decides to run, for Congress. Stamina, background, personal style, and physical appearance influence whether someone has "the right stuff" for campaigning. Ambition and a keen desire for public life and congressional perquisites lead people to become candidates and help them to succeed.[30]

Many potential candidates—no one knows how many—disqualify themselves because they are physically or mentally unprepared for the rigors of campaigning. Few are able to knock on doors, greet people, attend meetings, raise money, and travel constantly—all the time appearing to enjoy it. Former Florida governor Reubin Askew, an odds-on favorite to capture an open Senate seat in 1988, quit the race when estimated expenses escalated from $3.2 million to $5.7 million. "Frankly, I underestimated the time and effort [fund raising] would take and how it would limit my ability to have more direct contact with the voters," Askew confessed. "Something is seriously wrong with our system when many candidates for Senate need to spend 75 percent of their time raising money." [31]

Other candidates reject campaigns because of the cost to their personal lives, incomes, and families. From the number of successful politicians who complain about such sacrifices, however, one can only conclude that few count the costs accurately before taking the plunge. Many simply miscalculate or indulge in self-delusion. Sandy Maisel, a political scientist who wrote candidly of his unsuccessful 1978 congressional primary campaign, described politicians' "incredible ability to delude themselves about their own chances. If I could honestly think that a young, liberal Jewish college professor from Buffalo could win a primary and then beat a popular incumbent in Downeast Maine, any level of delusion is possible." [32]

Not a few candidates—again, no one knows how many—enter races not to win but to advance themselves. Some hope their national party will take notice and appoint them to a job. Others see running as a way of advertising their business or professional careers—in law, real estate, insurance, and the like. Still others find self-advertisement its own reward: a chance to get in the papers, on TV, and into the record books.

The Money Factor

"Money is the mother's milk of politics," declared California's legendary boss, Jess Unruh. To be sure, money isn't everything in politics, but many campaigns falter for lack of it, and many others squander valuable time and energy struggling to get it. Money attracts backers (who in turn give more money), it can frighten away rivals, and it can augment or lessen the gap between incumbents and challengers.

The High Cost of Running

Campaigns in the United States are very costly. In 1988 about half a billion dollars were poured into House and Senate races. And the price of admission to Congress has soared. Winning House members of the class of 1974 spent

Table 3-2 Average House and Senate Campaign Contributions, 1974-1986

	1974	1976	1978	1980	1982	1984	1986
House Elections							
Average total contribution	$ 61,084	$ 79,421	$111,232	$ 148,268	$ 222,620	$ 249,755	$ 289,753
Percentage from							
Individuals	73	59	61	67	63	58	60
Parties	4	8	5	4	6	7	4
PACs	17	23	25	29	31	36	37
Candidates[a]	6	9	9	—	—	—	—
Senate Elections							
Average total contribution	$455,515	$624,094	$951,390	$1,079,346	$1,771,167	$2,319,118	$2,936,765
Percentage from							
Individuals	76	69	76	78	81	75	70
Parties	6	4	2	2	1	7	8
PACs	11	15	14	21	18	18	23
Candidates[a]	1	12	8	—	—	—	—
Source not known	6	—	—	—	—	—	—

Sources: Data for 1974-1982, Gary C. Jacobson, "Money in the 1980 and 1982 Congressional Elections," in *Money and Politics in the United States*, ed. Michael J. Malbin (Chatham, N.J.: Chatham House Publishers, 1984), 39; for 1984 and 1986, Norman J. Ornstein, Thomas E. Mann, and Michael J. Malbin, *Vital Statistics on Congress, 1987-1988* (Washington, D.C.: Congressional Quarterly, 1987), 95-98.

Note: Includes all major-party candidates in general election contests.

[a] Includes candidates' contributions to their own campaigns, loans, transfers, and other items.

an average of $106,000. Freshmen elected twelve years later spent nearly $534,000 on average. The average Senate race in a competitive state costs more than $4 million; House contests can cost half a million or more (Table 3-2). Even controlling for inflation, expenditures for congressional campaigns more than doubled in the 1972-1988 period.[33]

Hotly contested races are especially costly. California's 1986 Senate contest between incumbent Democrat Alan Cranston and Republican representative Ed Zschau cost nearly $24 million. Two years later, in the same state, Republican House incumbent Robert J. Lagomarsino edged out Democratic challenger Gary K. Hart in an evenly matched contest that cost $2.3 million.

No mystery surrounds these skyrocketing costs. Inflation, population growth, and an expanded potential electorate account for the increase. Moreover, television ads and computerized mailings are expensive. Opening up the campaign process and relying on nonparty campaigners are other trends that have escalated costs. An old-style campaign with a caucus or convention nomination and legions of partisans to canvass voters costs less than a modern campaign with a primary nomination and voter appeals via electronic media. In short, reaching voters today is an expensive proposition.

Campaign price tags also depend on the kind of district and the level of competition. In 1984, in marginal districts (where the winner received less than 60 percent of the vote), the winner's campaign cost averaged $590,000— more than the national average of $324,000.[34] Often in such elections, one or both candidates face fierce primary fights extending over many months. Many of these races are fought over open seats, where incumbency is not a factor and where the average combined cost for general election candidates far exceeds the national average. "Candidates for open seats tend to raise and spend the most money because when neither candidate enjoys the benefits of incumbency, both parties normally field strong candidates, and the election is usually close." [35]

The district's demography also affects campaign costs. One study showed that suburban districts had the most expensive campaigns and urban districts the least expensive, with rural districts somewhere in between.[36] In the suburbs, partisan loyalties are notoriously weak and contests volatile. Lacking stable party organizations, candidates must advertise via electronic media. In cities, candidates shun media contests because of the huge cost and wasted impact upon adjoining districts. Here, too, party organizations are strongest. In rural districts, wide open spaces keep costs high: candidates must travel farther and advertise in many media markets to get their message across.

The Haves and Have Nots

Although incumbents need less money than nonincumbent challengers, they receive more—a double-barreled financial advantage (Figure 3-2). Because they are better known and have government-subsidized ways of communicat-

Figure 3-2 Average Congressional Campaign Expenditures for Incumbents, Challengers, and Open-Seat Candidates, 1972-1986

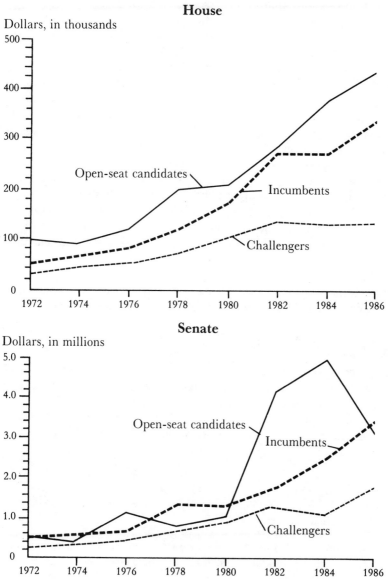

Sources: Congressional Research Service papers by Joseph E. Cantor, "Cost of Congressional Elections, 1972-1982: Statistics on Total and Average Campaign Spending," August 6, 1984; David C. Huckabee, Joseph E. Cantor, and Roger Walke, "Senate Campaign Expenditures, Receipts, and Sources of Funds: 1980-1986," March 5, 1987, 6; and "House Campaign Expenditures: 1980-1986," May 20, 1987, 6.

ing with constituents, they usually can get their message across less expensively. Hardly any officeholders are as tightfisted, though, as Sen. William Proxmire, D-Wis., who spent $145.10—postage and filing fees—on his final campaign in 1982. (Proxmire's successor, Democrat Herbert Kohl, spent more than $4 million, much of it his own money, to gain the seat.)

Incumbents usually attract more money than challengers because contributors see them as better "investments." As Jacobson points out, "Incumbents can raise whatever they think they need. They are very likely to win, and even when they lose, it is almost always in a close contest." [37] Incumbents captured nine out of every ten dollars given by political action committees (PACs) to congressional candidates in 1988; every incumbent received PAC support (whether through direct contributions or independent PAC spending), while 104 challengers received no PAC money.[38] In recent elections incumbents have spent several times as much as challengers. In 1988 nineteen incumbents out of every twenty outspent their challengers. In fact, most incumbents finish their campaigns with a surplus: after the 1987-1988 electoral cycle, the average returning House member had more than $154,000 on hand.[39] This money can be hoarded for future races, dispensed to needier candidates, or even (for members in office before January 8, 1980) converted to private use upon retirement.

In House races the incumbency advantage has worked to the benefit of Democrats, who have more incumbents than Republicans do. This factor aside, however, Republicans tend to be more generously funded than Democrats.

Shaking the Money Tree

Raising money preoccupies all candidates. Incumbents need it to scare off opponents; challengers need it to gain visibility; and contenders for open seats need it to gain an edge. Fund raising is time consuming, odious, and demeaning. Sen. Tom Daschle, D-S.D., who spent much of the 1985-1986 election cycle raising $3.5 million to defeat an incumbent, reflected on the process:

> You're with people you have nothing in common with. You have a cosmetic conversation. You paint the best face on their issues and feel uncomfortable through the whole thing. You sheepishly accept their check and leave feeling not very good about it.[40]

Funding sources fall into several categories: donations from individuals (including those from candidates and their families), party committees, and PACs.

Individuals.   About two-thirds of the money raised by House candidates and more than three-quarters of the money raised by Senate candidates are from individuals. Individuals may lawfully contribute up to $1,000 per candidate for primaries and $1,000 per candidate in the general elections, totaling no more than $5,000 in any given year. Primary, runoff, and general contests are regarded as separate elections. Individuals may contribute up to $20,000 a year to a political party and may spend an unlimited amount independently to promote parties, causes, or candidates. (One California businessman mounted a $1-million-plus ad campaign against Sen. Charles Percy, R-Ill., in 1984, apparently out of personal pique over some Middle East votes.) Expenditures greater than $250 must be reported, and the individual must declare that the money was not spent in collusion with the candidate. (Individuals may give up to $1,000 for a candidate and $2,000 for a party in volunteer expenses—housing, food, personal travel—without reporting it.)

There are no restrictions on how much congressional candidates or their supporters may spend, nor on how much candidates may contribute to their own cause. (This includes donations or loans from family members.) In long-shot races, a candidate's ability to shoulder the financial burden may attract support from party or group leaders. In other cases, heavy candidate spending may help pad a frontrunner's margin of victory or boost an underdog's chances of winning. Sen. John D. Rockefeller IV, D-W.Va., spent about $10 million of his fortune to win his Senate seat in 1984—more than $27 for every vote he received.

Federal law requires strict accounting by candidates and political committees. All contributions of $50 or more must be recorded; donors of more than $100 must be identified. Accounting of funds must be made by a single committee for each candidate, and receipts and expenditures must be reported regularly.

Party Committees. National or state party committees may contribute $10,000 to each House candidate ($15,000 if there is a runoff primary) and $17,500 to each Senate candidate. State party committees may contribute an additional $10,000. Even with contributions from several such committees, these sums do not begin to cover the cost of today's campaigns. Direct party contributions in 1986 amounted to only 4 percent in the average House race and 8 percent in Senate races.

Far more important are *coordinated expenditures* that the law permits. These are funds a party pays out for services (polling, ad production, or buying media time) requested by a candidate who has a say in how they are spent. For Senate races, party committees may spend two cents (adjusted for inflation) for every voting-age person. In 1988 these figures ranged from $40,400 to $752,410 (in California). For House races, committees may spend no more than $18,440 in coordinated funds. Such funds are used in general elections but not in primaries.

Since embarking on a rebuilding effort following Watergate, Republicans have had spectacular success in raising money—much of it through modest contributions solicited by targeted mail and phone efforts. Democrats have tried to catch up but lag far behind. In 1988 GOP committees granted congressional candidates more than twice as much money as Democratic groups provided their candidates (Figure 3-3). Especially in Senate contests, the GOP can pump in huge sums of money. This comes about through cooperative arrangements among state committees and several national committees.[41]

Over and above money that flows according to legally prescribed limits is so-called *soft money*—individual, corporate, or union gifts to party entities that can be used for grass-roots party-building activities but not for individual campaigns. The bulk of this money goes to presidential campaigns (boosting 1988 spending to twice the legal limits, for example). But activities fueled by soft money, such as generic advertisements, voter registration, and get-out-the-vote drives, indirectly help the party's candidates. In the 1980 campaign, the GOP spent $9.6 million on a nationwide television blitz urging voters to "Vote Republican. For a Change." [42] Six different spots highlighted Democratic "failures": the most talked-about one featured an actor who looked like Speaker Tip O'Neill. One GOP leader observed that the effort gave them two national campaigns when the Democrats had only one. Two years later the GOP mounted an $11-million campaign urging voters to "stay the course."

Needless to add, the parties do more for candidates than give money. They help identify promising candidates, brief candidates on issues, and give advice on everything from raising funds to giving TV interviews. Here again, Republican groups are ahead of Democrats.

Funding patterns affect candidates' strategies and, on occasion, electoral outcomes. The GOP's fund-raising success, some have argued, helped swell their 1978 and 1980 victories and minimize 1982 losses.[43] Incumbents' funding advantages, however, have helped Democrats offset the GOP's national fund-raising superiority. With so many incumbents, House Democrats were able to fend off Republican assaults and even add slightly to their ranks in the late 1980s. Incumbents' war chests, however, don't necessarily buoy challengers or open-seat candidates. In 1982—a good year for Democrats—House gains were limited because the party lacked a way of rechanneling incumbents' surpluses to challengers who needed the money.

PACs. Labor unions, corporations, and membership organizations may recommend to their stockholders, personnel, or members the election or defeat of a candidate. Such expenditures are unlimited although amounts over $2,000 must be reported. The groups must declare, under penalty of perjury, that the expenditure was not made in collusion with the candidate. Unions and corporations also may spend unlimited amounts for "nonpartisan" registration or voter participation drives directed at their members, stockholders, or employees.

Under existing law, corporations and labor unions may not contribute

Figure 3-3 Party Committees' Giving to Congressional Candidates, 1976-1988

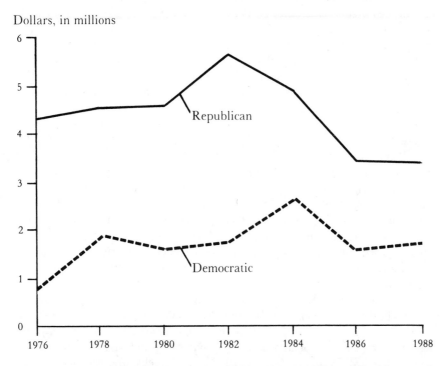

Dollars, in millions

Sources: Authors' calculations from Norman J. Ornstein, Thomas E. Mann, and Michael J. Malbin, *Vital Statistics on Congress, 1987-1988* (Washington, D.C.: Congressional Quarterly, 1987), 99-101; figures for 1988 from Federal Election Commission, press release, March 27, 1989, 3.

Note: Figures represent contributions to federal candidates by party committees at all levels.

funds directly to candidates, but they may underwrite administrative or fund-raising costs of political action committees. For some years PACs have been a popular method of channeling corporate or union energies into campaign war chests. Corporate executives contribute to PACs with names such as the "Good Government Club"; most unions have PACs, the best known of which is the AFL-CIO's Committee on Political Education (COPE). Ostensibly such groups are voluntary; however, it does not take a confirmed cynic to assume that subtle coercion and social pressure help keep money in the coffers.

Other types of groups are embraced by the finance law. Multicandidate committees may give no more than $5,000 per election to a candidate. These committees must have more than fifty members and must support five or more candidates. Such committees also may give up to $15,000 per year to a political party.

Political action committees are thriving, partly because the 1976 law encourages them. At the end of 1974 there were 608 PACs; by 1988 there were 4,200. All types of PACs grew in numbers, but corporate PACs grew most of all—from 89 in 1974 to more than 1,800 in 1988 (see Chapter 10, Table 10-1). The growth of PACs has changed the way campaigns are run. Candidates are forced to make the rounds of PACs to beg for funds. For incumbents, this may mean finding a lucrative committee assignment and compiling a good voting "report card." For nonincumbents, it means knocking on doors, filling out forms, and undergoing interviews.[44]

PACs also have grown in financial clout. In 1972 they contributed $8.5 million to House and Senate candidates; in 1988 this figure was nearly twenty times greater. PAC donations are more significant in House races than Senate races. In 1987-1988 PAC donations accounted for 34 percent of House campaign receipts but only 23 percent of Senate campaign receipts.

More than most interested parties, PACs favor incumbents and shun all but the most promising nonincumbents. Consider the case of Ronald K. Machtley, a forty-year-old lawyer who in 1988 challenged Fernand J. St Germain, D-R.I., a twenty-eight-year House veteran and chairman of the Banking Committee. Early that year, Machtley attended a PAC reception for GOP challengers sponsored by the National Republican Congressional Committee. "I would go up to [PAC representatives] and introduce myself," Machtley recalled, "and they'd read my name tag and say, 'You're running against Fred St Germain? Good Luck!' " Four weeks after the election, at a reception thrown for GOP victors, the tables were turned. Machtley, who scored an upset win, thus described what happened:

> My wife and I literally stood in one place, and people kept coming up to me for two hours. It was like a receiving line. They'd say, "I'm from XYZ PAC. It's super that you won. I can't tell you how happy we are. Do you have any debt from the campaign? We'd like to help you." [45]

"Do you have a card?" responded the new representative, who had $149,000 in unpaid bills. He left the affair with a two-inch stack of business cards— many from PACs that had given generously to his opponent.

Among incumbents, PACs stick with those in a position to promote their policy aims and those who loyally vote for these aims. The Seafarers International Union's 80,000 members poured $1.3 million into 1983-1984 congressional campaigns. Thirty-six of the forty members of the House Merchant Marine and Fisheries Committee benefited, half of whom got $5,000 or more. A Seafarers' PAC representative explained: "We support, unashamedly and with no denials, those people who will help us." [46]

Committee members aren't the only incumbents targeted by PACs.

Votes and vote indexes are employed to pinpoint friends and enemies (see Chapter 10). In 1986 the National Rifle Association gave more than $1 million—an average of $3,652 each—to the 292 House members who voted for final passage of a weak gun-control bill favored by the group; in contrast, it gave the bill's 130 opponents a total of only $11,614.[47] Pressure flows both ways, of course. PAC officers complain that they are dogged by incumbents, many of whom don't need the contributions, and that members of Congress keep mental accounts of contributors. "I've had congressmen open up the door and look down a list to see if we have contributed," one of them said. "And I've had them say, 'Well, I like your organization but you haven't given me a contribution.' "[48]

Overall, Democrats have benefited more than Republicans from PAC funding—because there are so many Democratic incumbents and because PACs expect Democratic control of the House and usually the Senate. In the 1987-1988 campaign cycle, Democrats claimed almost two-thirds of all PAC contributions. Ninety-two percent of labor PAC money went to Democrats; corporate PACs gave nearly a million dollars more to Democratic candidates than to Republicans. While corporate PACs might be expected to lean Republican, they tend to back any incumbent who can serve their interests. This situation was embarrassing enough that a group of GOP senators, led by Minority Leader Bob Dole of Kansas, summoned seventy officials of conservative and business PACs to a meeting to complain that they ought to give more to the party's candidates. "We are suitably irked," said Rudy Boschwitz of Minnesota, chairman of the Senate campaign committee. "We're doing all the heavy lifting and all they're doing is buying a bunch of access and playing the damn thing like a horse race. They don't do it philosophically. They do it on who's going to win."[49]

In addition to outright donations, PACs can indulge in so-called *independent spending*—efforts for or against candidates but without the candidates' cooperation or consent. According to the Federal Election Commission (FEC), $2.3 million was spent this way for and against candidates in 1979-1980. Eight years later, $6.0 million was spent in efforts involving 625 congressional candidates.

A portion of the dollars spent independently by PACs goes to *negative campaigns* to discredit a candidate, usually an incumbent. For instance, the National Association of Realtors unleashed $49,000 of TV ads late in the 1984 campaign to persuade voters to elect Baltimore Republican Helen Delich Bentley over ten-term Democratic incumbent Clarence D. Long. "The realtors felt Long had a very bad, antibusiness record," explained a grateful Bentley aide. Although Bentley had no control over the association's activity, in effect NAR added about 11 percent to her campaign funds and probably helped her unseat Long.[50] Although negative campaigning was prevalent in earlier election cycles, the FEC reported that it accounted for only 14 percent of independent spending in 1987-1988.

Candidate Funding: A Regulated Industry?

Financial inequalities in campaigning—between incumbents and nonincumbents, and between wealthy and poor donors—inevitably lead to demands for legal controls. Campaign finance laws are urged not only to "clean up" campaigns but to shift political influence from those who rely on financial contributions to those who depend on other resources. Several techniques have been employed to control campaign spending. The primary ones are disclosure of campaign contributions and expenditures; limits on campaign contributions; limits on campaign expenditures; free radio and television time for candidates; and public financing of campaigns.

In the wake of several campaign financing scandals of the early 1970s, Congress decided to amend the Federal Election Campaign Act of 1971. On October 15, 1974, President Gerald Ford signed into law a broad-gauged campaign finance law, the Federal Election Campaign Act Amendments of 1974. Two years later the Supreme Court upheld certain portions of the statute and voided others (*Buckley v. Valeo*, 1976). To end the confusion and meet the Court's constitutional objections, Congress quickly passed a revised act reconciling the Court's rulings with the original congressional intent. The 1976 act was amended three years later to simplify paperwork requirements and remove some restrictions on party assistance to federal candidates and volunteer activities. Major features of the Federal Election Campaign Act as amended embrace limits on individual contributions, limits on party and nonparty group contributions, and controls on campaign spending.

Now that political campaigning is a regulated industry, there is an official regulator: a six-member Federal Election Commission, appointed by the president and confirmed by the Senate. The commission may issue regulations and advisory opinions, conduct investigations, and prosecute violations of the law.

The campaign funding laws of the 1970s have failed to reduce inequalities between incumbents and challengers. The changes may even help incumbents and make it harder for challengers to raise the money they need to win.[51] Campaign financing laws also have failed to limit the influence of "big money" in politics. Big money is alive and well in American elections, although now it flows through more issue and candidate groups than in the past. Moreover, many of the best-funded PACs depend on large numbers of mail-solicited donations rather than a few from fat cats. Finally, the "reforms" have blurred the distinction between interest groups and political parties. Concerned groups (labor unions, business and industry associations, consumer and environmental organizations, ideological movements, and a host of special-issue groups) play conspicuous roles in the electoral arena as never before, boosting or hindering candidates in their quest for favorable treatment on Capitol Hill.

Campaign finance laws are so riddled with loopholes that money flows freely into congressional elections. Tax-exempt foundations are used by parties and PACs to take donations in excess of legal limits. Creative accounting and "independent spending" on behalf of candidates are used to skirt legal limits on what PACs can give directly to candidates. Bankers and other monied people can lend money or extend credit to candidates under loose rules. And money is moving underground, thwarting federal enforcement and disclosure efforts. "You can do just about anything, as long as you take care," said one party official.[52]

Some critics advocate public funding of Senate and House campaigns. Although the 1974 act included an optional public financing scheme for presidential races—used by most major presidential contenders—Congress declined to extend public financing to its own elections. Instead, the 1974 act set spending limits for House and Senate candidates, limits well below the level normally required by challengers to unseat incumbents. Reviewing the law, the Supreme Court held that overall spending limits were unconstitutional in the absence of a public financing plan. The effect has been to leave congressional elections open to unlimited financing while imposing limits on publicly funded presidential campaigns.

Those who thrive under existing rules can be counted on to resist change. Both Democrats and Republicans tout campaign funding reform, but both want it on terms favorable to them. As for contribution limits, the Democrats, especially in the House, are eager to preserve their PAC advantage; Republicans want to protect their party's superior fund-raising capabilities. Independent spending will remain uncontrolled as long as the Supreme Court sees fit to equate political spending with free expression. Public funding runs afoul of public antipathy and federal budget deficit concerns. Perhaps the most promising way to level the playing field, at least for incumbents and challengers, would be to provide the latter with subsidized mailings and free radio and TV time. (This last, predictably, is fiercely opposed by broadcasters.)

Nominating Politics

Nominating procedures, set forth in state laws and conditioned by party customs, help shape the potential pool of candidates. Historically, they have spread to ever-wider circles of participants—a development that has diminished party leaders' power and thrust more initiative upon the candidates themselves. In most states the *direct primary* is the formal mechanism for nominating congressional candidates. Some Republican parties in southern states use conventions, and several states combine conventions with primaries. But for virtually all members of Congress, the direct primary is the gateway to nomination.

Who should be permitted to vote in a party's primary? The states have adopted varying answers. The *closed primary*, found in thirty-eight states, requires voters to declare party affiliation to vote on their parties' nominees. This affiliation is considered permanent until the voter follows procedures to change it. In the so-called *open primary*, conducted in nine states, voters can vote in the primary of either party (but not both) simply by requesting the party's ballot at the polling place. Alaska, Louisiana, and Washington use the *blanket* or *nonpartisan primary*, with a single multiparty ballot that permits voters to cross party lines to vote for one candidate for each office. Party leaders naturally favor strict rules of participation, which reward party loyalty and simplify the leaders' task of influencing the outcome. Therefore, states with strong party traditions typically have closed primaries.[53]

Not all primaries are competitive races since incumbents are normally renominated. In recent years no more than 2 percent of incumbent representatives have been denied renomination, and less than 10 percent of Senate incumbents fail to be renominated. A fair number of representatives face no challenge at all for renomination.

When a veteran senator or representative retires, a contest for the seat usually ensues. The level of competition depends on the party's prospects in the general election. One landmark study of primaries showed a strong tie between a party's success in general elections and its number of contested primaries.[54] In one-party areas, where a party's nomination virtually ensured election, a primary contest was almost certain; contests also were likely in two-party competitive areas.

The direct primary was one of the reforms adopted early in the twentieth century to overcome corrupt, boss-dominated conventions. Certainly it has permitted more participation in selecting candidates. Yet primaries normally attract a narrower segment of voters than do general elections (except in some one-party states, where primaries dictate the outcomes). Less publicized than general elections, primaries tend to attract voters who are somewhat older, wealthier, better educated, more politically aware, and more ideologically committed than the electorate as a whole.[55]

Primaries also have hastened the decay of political parties by encouraging would-be officeholders to appeal directly to the public and construct support networks apart from party leaders. Primaries are thus a costly way of choosing candidates: unless they begin with overwhelming advantages (such as incumbency), candidates must mount virtually the same kind of campaign in the primary that they must later repeat in the general election.

Summary

In this chapter we have considered the "rules of the game" that narrow the potential field of congressional contenders. Think of these as a series of gates, each narrower than the one before. Out of the millions of people who qualify for congressional office, these gates limit "real" contenders into ever smaller groups of people.

First are the constitutional qualifications for holding office. Then there are complex rules of apportionment and districting. Beyond these are nominating procedures (usually, though not always, primaries) and the availability of financial resources. These rules of the game cut down sharply those who are likely congressional candidates.

Most important, individuals must decide to become candidates for the House or Senate. As we have seen, such choices embrace a range of considerations—many personal and emotional, but all based on some estimate of likely benefits and costs of candidacy. This presents voters with a limited choice on election day—two, rarely more, preselected candidates. From this restricted circle, senators and representatives are chosen—as we explain in the next chapter.

Notes

1. Howard Kurz, "Dawkins Switches Tactics in Caustic Jersey Race," *Washington Post,* November 2, 1988, A24.
2. Lewis A. Froman, *Congressmen and Their Constituencies* (Chicago: Rand McNally, 1963).
3. *Congressional Districts in the 1980s* (Washington, D.C.: Congressional Quarterly, 1983), 616.
4. Larry M. Schwab, "The Impact of the 1980 Reapportionment in the United States," *Political Geography Quarterly* 4 (April 1985): 141-158.
5. Robert G. Dixon, Jr., *Democratic Representation* (New York: Oxford University Press, 1968), 462-463.
6. David C. Saffell, "1980s Congressional Redistricting: Looks Like Politics as Usual," *National Civic Review* (July-August 1983): 364. See also Q. Whitfield Ayres and David Whiteman, "Congressional Reapportionment in the 1980s: Types and Determinants of Policy Outcomes," *Political Science Quarterly* 99 (Summer 1984): 303ff.
7. Dennis Farney, "Phil Burton Has Cut Many Political Deals: Is It One Too Many?" *Wall Street Journal,* September 28, 1982, 1.
8. Edward Walsh, "GOP Plays Chess with Indiana Hill Democrats," *Washington Post,* May 11, 1981, A4.
9. Guy Vander Jagt, "Drawing Up Fair Districts," *Washington Times,* May 1, 1989, D4.
10. *Davis et al. v. Bandemer et al.,* 106 S. Ct. 2797 (1986).
11. Richard G. Niemi, "The Relationship Between Votes and Seats: The Ultimate Question in Political Gerrymandering," *UCLA Law Review* 33 (October 1985): 195.
12. See the essays in Bernard Grofman, ed., *Toward Fair and Effective Representation* (New York: Agathon Press, 1988).
13. Louis Sandy Maisel, *From Obscurity to Oblivion: Running in the Congres-*

sional Primary (Knoxville: University of Tennessee Press, 1982), 34.

14. Leo M. Snowiss, "Congressional Recruitment and Representation," *American Political Science Review* 60 (September 1966): 627-639.

15. John F. Bibby, Cornelius P. Cotter, James L. Gibson, and Robert L. Huckshorn, "Parties in State Politics," in *Politics in the American States,* 4th ed., ed. Virginia Gray, Herbert Jacob, and Kenneth N. Vines (Boston: Little, Brown, 1983), 80-81; and Maisel, *From Obscurity to Oblivion,* 21-22.

16. John F. Bibby, ed., *Congress Off the Record* (Washington, D.C.: American Enterprise Institute, 1983), 43.

17. The seminal work on strategic politician theory is Gary C. Jacobson and Samuel Kernell, *Strategy and Choice in Congressional Elections,* 2d ed. (New Haven, Conn.: Yale University Press, 1983).

18. George Lardner, Jr., and Dan Morgan, "Quayle Drew on Energy, Affability in Political Rise," *Washington Post,* October 2, 1988, A1, A26. A somewhat different version is found in Richard F. Fenno, Jr., *The Making of a Senator: Dan Quayle* (Washington, D.C.: CQ Press, 1989), 3-4.

19. Gary C. Jacobson, *The Politics of Congressional Elections,* 2d ed. (Boston: Little, Brown, 1987), 26.

20. Gary C. Jacobson, "The Marginals Never Vanished: Incumbency and Competition in Elections to the U.S. House of Representatives, 1952-1982," *American Journal of Political Science* 31 (February 1987): 126-141.

21. Donald Gross and David Breaux, "Historical Trends in U.S. Senate Elections: 1912-1988" (Paper presented at the annual meeting of the Midwest Political Science Association, April 13-15, 1989), 13.

22. On the first view mentioned in this paragraph, see Morris P. Fiorina, *Congress: Keystone of the Washington Establishment* (New Haven, Conn.: Yale University Press, 1977); and Bruce Cain, John Ferejohn, and Morris Fiorina, *The Personal Vote: Constituency Service and Electoral Independence* (Cambridge, Mass.: Harvard University Press, 1987), esp. chaps. 6-7. For more on the second view, see Glenn R. Parker and Roger H. Davidson, "Why Do Americans Love Their Congressmen So Much More than Their Congress?" *Legislative Studies Quarterly* 4 (February 1979): 53-61. On the question of whether incumbents' resources are directly tied to votes, see John R. Johannes, *To Serve the People: Congress and Constituency Service* (Lincoln: University of Nebraska Press, 1984), esp. chap. 8.

23. Jacobson, *The Politics of Congressional Elections,* 26.

24. Jacobson and Kernell, *Strategy and Choice,* chap. 3.

25. Clifford D. May, "A Shaky GOP Hunts in Vain for Rival to Moynihan in Race," *New York Times,* March 22, 1988, B1.

26. Edward Walsh, "To Every Campaign, There Is a Recruiting Season," *Washington Post,* November 12, 1985, A1.

27. Donald Philip Green and Jonathan S. Krasno, "Salvation for the Spendthrift Incumbent: Reestimating the Effects of Campaign Spending in House Elections," *American Journal of Political Science* 32 (November 1988): 887.

28. Ibid., 889.

29. Maisel, *From Obscurity to Oblivion,* 23.

30. Linda L. Fowler and Robert D. McClure, *Political Ambition: Who Decides to Run for Congress* (New Haven, Conn.: Yale University Press, 1989).

31. Ike Flores, "Askew Quits Senate Race Despite Lead in Polls," *Washington Post,* May 8, 1988, A-16; and Dexter Filkins, "For Senate Candidates the Only Issue Is Money," *Washington Post,* May 25, 1988, A19.
32. Maisel, *From Obscurity to Oblivion,* 23.
33. Joseph E. Cantor, "Cost of Congressional Elections, 1972-1982: Statistics on Total and Average Campaign Spending," Congressional Research Service, Washington, D.C., August 6, 1984.
34. Authors' calculations from Norman J. Ornstein, Thomas E. Mann, and Michael J. Malbin, *Vital Statistics on Congress, 1987-1988* (Washington, D.C.: Congressional Quarterly, 1987), 79-80.
35. Gary C. Jacobson, "Money in the 1980 and 1982 Congressional Elections," in *Money and Politics in the United States,* ed. Michael J. Malbin (Chatham, N.J.: Chatham House Publishers, 1984), 58.
36. Christopher Buchanan, "Candidates' Campaign Costs for Congressional Contests Have Gone Up at a Fast Pace," *Congressional Quarterly Weekly Report,* September 29, 1979, 2154-2155.
37. Jacobson, in *Money and Politics,* 57.
38. "PAC Support Scoreboard: The House," *Washington Post,* May 10, 1989, A-17; May 11, 1989, A21.
39. Public Citizen, *House Insurance: How the Permanent Congress Hoards Campaign Cash* (Washington, D.C.: Public Citizen, 1989).
40. Andy Plattner, "The High Cost of Holding—and Keeping—Public Office," *U.S. News and World Report,* June 22, 1987, 30.
41. Jacobson, in *Money and Politics,* 46-50.
42. David Adamany, "Political Parties in the 1980s," in *Money and Politics,* ed. Michael J. Malbin, 82.
43. Jacobson, in *Money and Politics,* 58-59.
44. Veteran political reporter James M. Perry wrote an intriguing series focusing on the workings of the Realtors Political Action Committee (RPAC). See, for example, "How Realtors' PAC Rewards Office Seekers Helpful to the Industry," *Wall Street Journal,* August 2, 1982, 1.
45. Dale Russakoff, "The Fickle Affections of PACs," *Washington Post,* January 5, 1989, A23.
46. Howard Kurtz, "Industry Factions Protect Their Turf," *Washington Post,* July 18, 1985, A16.
47. Thomas Edsall, "How Gun Lobby Filled Friendly House Holsters," *Washington Post,* April 17, 1986, A17. The article reported on a Common Cause study.
48. Richard L. Berke, "Problems of the PAC System; Study Measures Frustration," *New York Times,* February 14, 1988, 32.
49. Richard L. Berke, "Dole Leads GOP on PAC Complaints," *New York Times,* September 26, 1988, A20. See also David S. Cloud, "Feud Between GOP, PACs Stings Candidates," *Congressional Quarterly Weekly Report,* September 9, 1988, 2447-2542.
50. Cited in Peter Grier, "Lobbying in Washington," *Christian Science Monitor,* December 6, 1984, 32.
51. Gary C. Jacobson, *Money in the Congressional Elections* (New Haven, Conn.: Yale University Press, 1980).

52. Brooks Jackson, "Loopholes Allow Flood of Campaign Giving by Business, Fat Cats," *Wall Street Journal,* July 5, 1984, 1.
53. Malcolm E. Jewell and David M. Olson, *American State Political Parties and Elections,* 3d ed. (Homewood, Ill.: Dorsey Press, 1988), 87-88.
54. V. O. Key, Jr., *Parties, Politics and Pressure Groups,* 5th ed. (New York: Thomas Y. Crowell, 1964), 438, 447.
55. Austin Ranney, "Parties in State Politics," in *Politics in the American States,* ed. Herbert Jacob and Kenneth Vines (Boston: Little, Brown, 1976), 61-99.

This TV ad shows Sen. Patrick Leahy, D-Vt., in a diner. Rebutting the liberalism charge, the narrator concludes: "Big spender? C'mon. The man is *cheap*!"

CHAPTER FOUR

Making It:
The Electoral Game

At first television viewers saw only a pair of running legs, clad in jogging shorts. The camera then pulled back to reveal California's senior senator, Alan Cranston—a lifelong runner whose ads began six months before the voters had to decide whether to grant him a fourth term or send Republican challenger Ed Zschau to Washington.

"Always ahead of the pack," began the voice of Lloyd Bridges, known to "baby boomers" as star of the 1960s television show "Sea Hunt." "Sometimes it's lonely to be out front, but that's where he's been—to stop the war in Vietnam, to save our coastline from offshore drilling." [1] Another Cranston TV ad featured breathtaking photos of California by the late Ansel Adams, who was heard declaring "Alan Cranston is a great leader." Another compared Cranston to a pantheon of California heroes, among them Theodore Roosevelt, Earl Warren, Robert F. Kennedy, and even Ronald Reagan.

Cranston, an awesome figure in California politics (he once scared off a potential challenge to his seat from Reagan), entered the 1986 reelection race with some definite liabilities. He was a certifiable liberal in Reagan's home state—a fact all too apparent during Cranston's short-lived presidential run in 1984. And although at age seventy-one he was younger than Reagan, he had to prove his vigor and fresh ideas to hordes of new voters.

Cranston won reelection the new-fashioned way: a television campaign fueled by buckets of money. Cheaper traditional methods simply won't work in this mega-state of 26 million people. With fourteen major media markets, seventy-five major commercial stations, and more than 17 million television sets, California can be spanned only by video. Face-to-face campaigning is time consuming and ineffective. In the words of Robert Shrum, Cranston's campaign consultant: "A political rally in California consists of three people around a television set."

Cranston was good at setting his reelection campaign agenda and even better at raising the money to finance it. In 1986 he spent $10.8 million (his well-financed opponent spent $1 million more). Today an estimated thirty-four cents of every campaign dollar goes to television. And the size of California's media market boosts the price tag. According to media analysts, the average voter should see a single TV ad five times for it to have an impact; in California this costs $300,000 to $400,000. A thirty-second spot on "The Cosby Show" would cost $1,000 in Fargo, North Dakota, but $30,000 on one Los Angeles station.[2] No wonder Cranston's free time was spent contacting donors, not voters. And the senator has few equals in tapping potential contributors, typically by personal phone calls made during spare moments at airports or between Senate votes. "Cranston is the man with the pocketful of dimes," remarked one admiring California politician. "He's always on the phone." [3]

This is the modern-style congressional campaign. Traditional party organizations have largely been supplanted by candidate-centered efforts directed by costly pollsters, direct-mail specialists, fund raisers, advertising agencies, and media buyers. Face-to-face campaigning survives, of course, in some races. In this chapter we consider the conditions under which the "new politics" thrives and those under which the "old politics" persists. The topic is the politics of elections: the structure of campaigns and the calculus of voter choice.

Campaign Strategies

Campaigns are volatile mixtures of personal contacts, fund raising, speech making, advertising, and symbolic appeals. As acts of communication, campaigns are designed to convey messages to potential voters. The goal is to ensure a plurality of those who cast ballots on election day.

Asking the Right Questions

Candidates and their advisers strive to set the basic tone or thrust of the campaign. This all-important decision determines the allocation of money, time, and personnel. In mapping out a successful strategy, candidates ask themselves: What sort of constituency do I have? Are my name, face, and career familiar to voters or am I relatively unknown? What resources—money, group support, volunteers—am I likely to attract? What leaders and groups are pivotal to a winning campaign? What issues or moods are uppermost in the minds of potential voters? What are the easiest and cheapest means of reaching voters with my message? When should my campaign begin and how should it be paced? And what are my chances for victory? The answers to such questions determine the campaign strategy.

The type of constituency broadly dictates campaign plans. Mounting statewide campaigns, Senate candidates must deal with heterogeneous economic and social groups, scattered over wide areas and typically in multiple media markets. Few Senate candidates can know their states as intimately as House candidates know their districts. Most House districts are narrower entities than states, often paralleling no other natural geographic, community, media-market, or political dividing lines. They are more homogeneous, but have fewer automatic forums or media outlets for candidates, not to mention ready-made partisan hierarchies.[4] Would-be representatives are very much "on their own" to piece together a network of supporters.

Incumbency is a prime consideration that colors the entire electoral process because incumbents are extraordinarily hard to beat. Also important is the partisan affiliation of the electorate, although it is difficult to assess these days because of rampant split-ticket voting. Majority candidates in one-party areas are virtually assured election. Their campaigns, which stress party loyalty, concentrate on voter registration drives because high voter turnout usually aids their cause. Minority party campaigns try to obscure partisan differences, stress personalities, or exploit factional splits within the majority party.

The perceptions and attitudes of voters are also major factors in campaign planning. Through informal "pulse taking" or formal surveys, strategists try to grasp what is on voters' minds and what, if anything, they think about the candidate. What is the candidate's "name recognition" level? If the candidate is well known, what "profile"—positive or negative—is conjured up by his or her name? Candidates who are well known try to capitalize on their visibility; lesser known candidates take out ads that repeat their names over and over again. Candidates known for openness and friendliness will highlight those qualities in ads; those who are less voluble will stress experience and competence, at the same time displaying photos or film clips reminding voters that they, too, are human. Candidates who have made tough, unpopular decisions are touted as persons of courage. And so it goes.

As popular moods change, so do the self-images candidates seek to project. In crises, voters prefer experience, competence, and reassurance; in the wake of scandals, honesty and openness are the virtues most cherished by voters. Candidates' speeches, appearances, advertising, and appeals are designed to exploit such voter preferences. Many Democratic legislators gained office in the 1960s and 1970s by championing government activism in solving problems; then, when running for office in the 1980s, they shifted to advocating balanced budgets and lower taxes. By the same token, conservatives who run on a platform of downsizing government learn, once they are in office, that constituents who bought the rhetoric nonetheless count on government services and assistance.

Choosing a Theme

A candidate's strategy is usually distilled into a single theme or slogan that is repeated in radio and TV spots, billboards, and campaign literature. Campaign strategists use those themes to define the nature of the contest in terms favorable to their candidate. Incumbents advertise their experience, seniority, and service—with the implication that they can do more than their competitor for the state or district. "Burdick's clout is North Dakota's," proclaimed the campaign for eighty-year-old Quentin N. Burdick, a Democrat running for his sixth Senate term. Rep. Edward F. Feighan, D-Ohio, showed commercials with the slogan, "He's All Work." Connecticut Democrat Bruce Morrison, another member of the House, ran testimonials from New Haven voters, all of which ended cheerily, "Thanks a lot, Bruce."

Going for the Jugular

Incumbency can be hazardous, however. Given citizens' doubts about the efficacy or honesty of the federal government, protracted public service can sometimes turn into a liability. To avoid being dragged down by unpopular features of the government in Washington, many incumbents take pains to distance themselves from "the Washington crowd." As Sen. Howard M. Metzenbaum, D-Ohio, once quipped: "You tell me somebody who does not run against Congress—instead of for Congress—and I will have his name put in 'Believe It or Not.' " [5]

Moreover, an extensive public record gives enterprising opponents many potential opportunities to exploit. Votes or positions may be highlighted, and sometimes twisted, to discredit the incumbent. Controversial actions provide a field day. When Sen. Slade Gorton, R-Wash., revealed that he had swapped his vote on a questionable judicial appointment for White House approval of another judicial candidate he was supporting, the home state press went wild. One Seattle paper tagged him "Slippery Slade." His Democratic opponent, Brock Adams, took up the theme and unseated Gorton, who returned to the Senate two years later only after apologizing and recasting his public image.[6] Sen. David K. Karnes, R-Neb., turned a close contest into a walkaway for his opponent, Democrat Bob Kerrey, when he told a crowd at the Nebraska State Fair, "We need fewer farmers."

An incumbent's flaws or weaknesses are seized upon by aggressive challengers. Incumbents may be accused of laziness, inattention to local needs, or simply "Potomac fever." They may be shackled to unpopular issues like nuclear waste dumps or cuts in Social Security benefits. Age, failing health, or scandals—personal or official—are normally fair game. "We need a fresh start" was the well-chosen theme of a challenger to Rep. Fernand J. St Germain, D-R.I., defeated in 1988 after a grand jury probe charged "serious and sustained misconduct" in his dealings with financial industry lobbyists.

Campaign Resources

Campaigns require resources to play out the strategy that has been devised. The cleverest strategy in the world is of no avail without the wherewithal to bring its message to voters. Beyond the resources inherent in a specific contest—type of state or district, incumbency status, candidate visibility, and party margin—are two types of resources essential to all candidates and their managers: *money* and *organization*.

Allocating Money

The importance of money in campaigns, as already noted, cannot be overemphasized. Virtually any kind of campaign can be mounted with enough money; while there are cut-rate alternatives like door-to-door canvassing or volunteer organizations, these eat up time that might be used reaching larger numbers of voters.

Especially useful is "early money." Available at the outset of the campaign, these funds not only scare off challengers but also buy up advertising and radio-TV time. With ongoing campaign and fund-raising efforts, incumbents have a running start in stockpiling this early money. Candidates with tough contests in both primary and general elections face an especially vexing dilemma: should they ration their outflow of funds and risk losing the primary, or should they wage an expensive primary campaign and risk running out of money later on?

Incumbents not only raise more money but also spend more on their campaigns than challengers. Because incumbents are already better known than challengers, their spending often has strategic purposes. *Preemptive spending* involves constant fund raising that, along with surpluses from previous campaigns, can dissuade serious opponents. Veteran Florida Democratic representative Sam Gibbons engaged in preemptive tactics after his 1984 reelection, when he was caught off guard by a little-known opponent and saw his winning tally dip just below 60 percent, his worst-ever showing. "When you get down in the 50s," explained his son and adviser, "you don't have to move too many figures before you are in real trouble." Gibbons' offensive included new fund-raising efforts, extensive polling, a nationally known media consultant, and a final price tag of more than $550,000.[7] The result: no opponent filed against Gibbons in the 1986 and 1988 elections.

In case a strong, well-financed challenger surfaces, incumbents can pursue *reactive spending*—efforts to raise and send more money to stave off defeat. The close escape by Rep. Robert J. Lagomarsino, R-Calif., from the well-financed challenge of Democratic state senator Gary K. Hart was attributed by PAC managers to Lagomarsino's ability to outspend his opponent. A last-minute effort by the Republican incumbent brought in nearly $150,000.[8] Spending makes a difference for incumbents; they "are able to defend themselves quite effectively through campaign spending." [9]

New incumbents tend to invest heavily in preemptive and reactive spending for they are more apt than longtime veterans to face vigorous challenge. Members with more seniority raise and spend less, especially in the early campaign stages (before July). Incumbents who are sure-fire vote getters over the long haul—five or more terms—may establish such a commanding position that they rarely have serious challenges.

Sometimes established incumbents deliberately overspend for reasons apart from the race at hand. They may want a decisive victory to establish a claim to higher office—representatives with their eye on the Senate or senators looking to be presidential contenders. They may wish to impress colleagues or interest groups with their electoral prowess. They may bid for freedom to concentrate on Capitol Hill business or other pursuits. Or they may distribute some of their receipts to more needy colleagues, perhaps expecting, in return, support for career advancement.

Challengers, for their part, spend all the money they can raise to make their names and faces known to voters. And because they normally start so far behind, their campaigning dollars tend to be more cost effective (see Figure 4-1). As Gary C. Jacobson has demonstrated, the more a challenger spends, the more votes he or she is likely to attract.[10] The November 1986 senatorial elections, which returned the Senate to Democratic control, demonstrated the ability of well-financed challengers to defeat incumbents.

Where do campaign dollars go? As exercises in communication, campaigns are shaped, and their budgets driven, by the need to reach the largest number of voters at the lowest cost. Because political organizations and media markets differ greatly, campaign costs vary widely between the House and Senate, among congressional districts, and among states.

As a rule, statewide Senate races are mass media contests whose messages are conveyed mainly through radio and television. According to figures compiled for the National Association of Broadcasters, candidates in the 1985-1986 electoral cycle spent about $97.3 million on broadcast advertising time, or 24.3 percent of their total expenditures. The bulk of the money came from Senate candidates, who spent 34 percent of their campaign funds on radio and TV. House candidates spent less than 16 percent of their money in this way.[11] In mega-states such as California, Texas, or Florida— with many media markets to reach huge, mobile populations—media costs are far higher. The 1986 Cranston-Zschau battle in California, the second costliest Senate battle in history, is a case in point. Cranston, the incumbent and eventual winner, spent 57 percent of his campaign budget of $10.8 million on television time and production costs. His opponent spent more than half his campaign's total budget on broadcast time alone. Costs of this magnitude permeate other aspects of the campaign (for example, fund raising to finance paid commercials and efforts aimed at winning free radio and TV coverage).

Despite the astronomic costs, television advertising is popular because candidates find it cost effective, and they believe it works. They may be right. Political scientist Thomas Patterson estimated that it cost about one-half cent to get to a single television viewer in the 1980s, compared to one and a half cents to reach a newspaper reader and twenty-five cents to reach a direct-mail recipient.[12]

Figure 4-1   Campaign Spending and Public Recognition of
Candidates

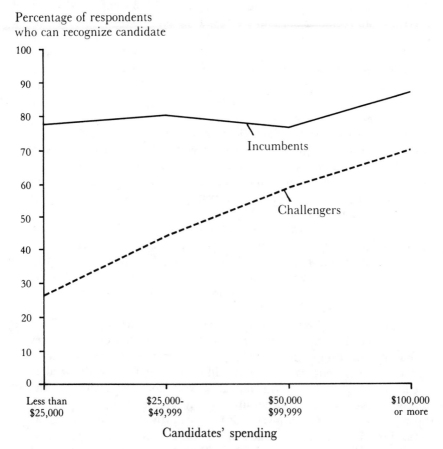

Percentage of respondents
who can recognize candidate

Candidates' spending

Source: Edie N. Goldenberg and Michael W. Traugott, *Campaigning for Congress* (Washington, D.C.: CQ Press, 1984), 138.

Note: Data drawn from surveys of respondents in 108 congressional districts selected by the American National Election Study, Center for Political Studies, University of Michigan.

Not all states feature such high-tech campaigns. Residents in smaller states usually prefer personal appearances by the candidates at festivals, parades, or annual county fairs; politicians are expected to show up. "If you ain't seen at the county fair, you're preached about on Sunday," remarked an Oklahoma politician as he led his party's Senate candidate around the hog and sheep barns in Ada, Oklahoma.[13] In his two Senate races Steve Symms, R-Idaho, a former apple grower, toured his state's back roads from top to bottom in a bus caravan called "The Apple Corps Express." Old-fashioned politics, in other words, can still be found even in Senate races.

House races, though less dependent upon mass media, manifest varying patterns of media use. According to a survey of 1978 campaigns, nearly 60 percent of all spending fell into the broad category of advertising and media (see Figure 4-2). In four House races selected by *National Journal*, however, a majority of the funds went to organization, which included salaries, office supplies, printing, and telephones. Spending for advertising (newspaper ads and radio and TV commercials) ranged from 13 to 36 percent, depending on whether the electoral district could be covered efficiently by television. In Oregon's 5th Congressional District, the winner spent the bulk of his advertising budget on television because local stations reached most of the district's voters. New Jersey's 9th Congressional District, however, is in the New York City media market, which includes millions of people not eligible to vote in the district. There, the winning candidate spent 86 percent of his media budget on radio, which is less expensive and allows candidates to target their messages more precisely.[14]

The character of candidates and their party organizations also affects media mix and budgeting. Confident incumbents tend to channel their money into newspaper ads that target their messages to activists, partisans, and supporters. Lesser known candidates must turn to broad-scale media, such as television or outdoor advertising, to promote name recognition.[15]

Uncertainty looms over the spending decisions of candidates and their managers. No one knows exactly what works in reaching and influencing voters (although many high-priced consultants swear they do), nor can events throughout the campaign be predicted with certainty. So money tends to be spread widely among various items (billboards, bumper stickers, media, and the like) in the hope of covering all bases. No doubt much money is "wasted" this way. Nor are all expenditures clearly aimed at the campaign itself. Spending reports reveal a myriad of unusual activities, such as organizing a softball team or purchasing tickets to sporting events, on the ground that they are connected to members' reelection efforts.[16]

Organizing the Campaign

Implementing the campaign strategy is the job of the candidate and the candidate's organization. The elements of an organization vary, but usually include opinion surveyors, issue specialists, speechwriters, advertising writers and producers, media buyers, advance people, fund raisers, and district and precinct workers. In the past, contenders depended upon the ongoing party apparatus to wage campaign battles, and in some places this is still done. But today most party organizations have neither the permanent workers nor the financial wherewithal to carry out effective campaigns. Citizen or interest group activists and hired campaign consultants have replaced the old party pros. In short, many candidates create their own personal party organizations in their states or districts.

Figure 4-2   Where Does the Campaign Dollar Go?

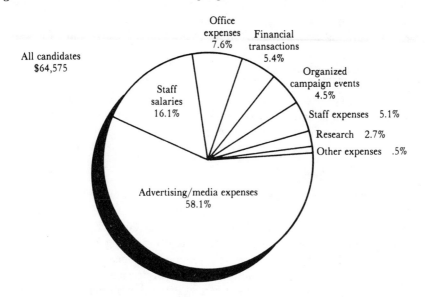

Source: Edie N. Goldenberg and Michael W. Traugott, *Campaigning for Congress* (Washington, D.C.: CQ Press, 1984), 88.

As long as they can pay the price, today's candidates can procure campaign services from political consulting firms. Some companies offer a wide array of services; others specialize in survey research, direct-mail appeals, advertising, coordinating volunteer efforts, or financial management and accounting.

Enjoying greater resources, incumbents are more likely to have experienced, professional managers. Edie Goldenberg and Michael Traugott explain that incumbents' campaigns

> tend to be managed by people who are experienced and earn their living by doing this kind of work. Overall, their campaign staffs are relatively large, heterogeneous teams possessing a wide variety of skills necessary to cope with a campaign environment that is becoming more complex, broader in scope, and increasingly reliant upon technology.[17]

Experienced aides on the office payroll help build support throughout the legislator's term of office. As one scholar described it:

> The incumbent's staff, in short, allows him to attract and retain the nucleus of his personal political organization.... The incumbent fields a publicly paid team of experienced veterans to do a task they have succeeded in before, perhaps many times before, and which differs very little from their everyday jobs.[18]

Congressional aides are supposed to refrain from actual reelection activities during their official hours of work, but in practice the distinction is hard to draw. The normal duties of a member's office staff—especially constituent errand running and outreach—have inescapable electoral consequences.

Campaign Techniques

Campaigns are designed to convey the candidate's message to people who will support the candidate and vote in the election. Campaigns are not necessarily directed at *all* voters; often narrower groups are targeted. Indeed, campaign techniques are distinguished by the breadth and kind of audiences they reach.

Pressing the Flesh

Every campaign features direct voter appeals through personal appearances—at shopping centers, factory gates, or even front doors. In his first Senate campaign in 1948, Lyndon Johnson swooped out of the sky in a helicopter to visit small Texas towns, grandly pitching his Stetson hat from the chopper for a bold entrance. (An aide was assigned to retrieve the hat for use at the next stop.)[19] Other candidates, preferring to stay closer to the ground, stage walking tours to attract attention. In strong party areas, voter contact is the job of ward, precinct, and block captains. Some candidates still dispense "walking-around money" to encourage local captains to get out the vote and provide small-scale financial rewards for voting.

Few neighborhoods today boast tight party organizations. Candidates and their advisers must recruit workers—usually volunteers—to make sure constituents are registered, distribute campaign leaflets, produce crowds at rallies, and win the vote on election day. Campaign workers operate sophisticated telephone banks in central headquarters and trudge door to door to drum up support.

Personal contact is a potent campaign technique, especially in House districts and small states. (Nearly a quarter of the citizens questioned in national surveys claim to have met their incumbent representatives personally.) Not all candidates are as dedicated to or as enthusiastic about this technique as was crowd-pleaser Johnson, but few elected officials get by without doing a great deal of what is inelegantly called "pressing the flesh."

Playing to the Cameras

Candidates to some extent can bypass face-to-face voter appeals by running advertisements and making televised appearances. Especially in statewide elections, media efforts are the only way of getting a candidate's message to the mass of voters. Television is the "broadest-spectrum" medium and also the most effective. If skillfully done, TV ads can be artful as well as effective in bringing home the candidate's themes.

A case in point is the now-classic "bloodhound" ad devised by media slickster Roger Ailes for Republican Mitch McConnell, a Louisville judge and executive who began his 1984 Senate campaign trailing incumbent Democrat Walter "Dee" Huddleston by some fifty points. In the ad a detective follows a pack of bloodhounds sniffing around the U.S. Capitol grounds and other locales in search of Huddleston, who allegedly was impossible to find because he was away giving speeches for personal gain. "Where's Dee?" the announcer intoned at each locale. It was a masterpiece of negative advertising, and it enabled McConnell to win by 5,269 votes. Four years later the missing-person theme turned up in Connecticut Democrat Joseph I. Lieberman's "bear cartoons" challenging Senate Republican Lowell P. Weicker, Jr. The ads portrayed Weicker as a bear sleeping through important votes; the tag line was "Where Was Lowell?" Such ads prompted incumbents to "inoculate" themselves against such attacks: Huddleston's colleague, Sen. Wendell H. Ford, D-Ky., was determined not to fall prey to the "bloodhound treatment" in his reelection campaign two years later. His ads portrayed him burning the midnight oil in his Capitol office—accompanied by his own faithful dog!

Successful media ads bring home the candidate's themes. Millionaire senator Herb Kohl, D-Wis., seeking in 1988 to succeed retiring senator William Proxmire, conveyed the subtle message that his personal wealth could enable him to match Proxmire's independence and integrity. His theme: "Nobody's senator but your own." Taking note of the money Kohl was pouring into his campaign, his opponent had bumper stickers reading, "Make Herb Spend It All."

In the more costly races, voters' opinions are tracked throughout the campaign and damaging opposition tactics countered at once. More than one politician has been defeated by hesitating to counter opponents' thrusts. Sen. Jesse Helms, R-N.C., whose TV ads began running eighteen months before his 1984 reelection, aired a series staking out his own position and challenging his opponent, Gov. James B. Hunt, Jr., with the question, "Where do you stand, Jim?" Hunt's slowness to respond to these damaging ads was widely considered a prime factor in Helms's narrow victory.[20]

Researchers Lynda Kaid and Dorothy Davidson have compared Senate incumbent and challenger "videostyles," defined as "the presentation of self through political advertising."[21] Incumbents used longer commercials, relied more heavily on testimonials, stressed more positive themes, dressed more formally, used other people's narration more often, and emphasized competence. Challengers were more apt to use negative arguments, to dress casually, to show the candidate head-on, to use their own voice in narration, and to stress the themes of trustworthiness and closeness to the voters.

Media efforts are further distinguished by the degree to which their preparation and distribution are controlled by the candidate. Paradoxically, some of the most effective appeals—news coverage and endorsements, for example—are controlled by news organizations and not by the candidate. By contrast, the appeals controlled wholly by the candidate—newsletters, media ads, and direct mail—may be less credible because they are seen as promotional devices.

Yet, campaign coverage by the news media is sketchy, especially in House races.[22] So most candidates are left to their own devices in reaching voters. Herein is a major difference between House and Senate races: the former are covered less than the latter by the news media. But, while Senate contenders gain wider publicity, they have less control over it than do House candidates.

How Voters Decide

Although Congress is supposed to be the people's branch of government, fewer than half of voting-age citizens take part in House elections in presidential years and less than 40 percent in off years. As Figure 4-3 indicates, voting participation in national elections has declined since 1960.

Political analysts disagree over the reasons for the embarrassingly low voting levels in the United States, the lowest among all the Western democracies. Four types of explanations have been suggested. One is *demographic:* an expanded electorate now embraces segments of the populace with traditionally low voting rates—young voters, blacks, and Hispanics. Yet the one factor most closely linked with voting participation—educational level—has been on the rise among the population.[23] A second explanation stresses *barriers to voting:* difficulties encountered by citizens in registering and getting to the polling places for our often-held elections. Yet many barriers to registering and voting have been lowered over the past generation. A third explanation is *citizen disaffection:* supposedly the poor quality of candidates and campaigns has dissuaded people from voting. Fourth, citizens may be abandoning voting for *other forms of participation* in politics, including membership in political groups and activism on issues. Especially when many congressional races are a foregone conclusion, citizens may seek more meaningful participation elsewhere. All of these explanations probably contain elements of truth.

Many analysts, it should be noted, dispute this view of the low levels of voting in the United States. They point out that other Western democracies compute voter turnout based on the number who have registered. Turnout in the United States, by contrast, is calculated on the basis of the total number of voting-age people. If similar methods of computation were used, our turnout levels would be more comparable to those in other Western nations.

Turnout varies according to whether the election is held in a presidential or midterm year. Midterm races often lack the intense publicity and stimulus to vote provided by presidential contests. Since the 1930s, turnout in midterm congressional elections has averaged about 12 percent below that of the preceding presidential election. Midterm electorates include proportionately

Figure 4-3 Turnout in Presidential and House Elections, 1932-1988

Percentage of
adult population voting

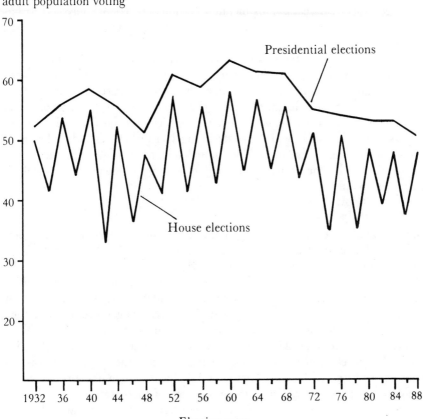

Election year

Sources: U.S. Bureau of the Census, *Statistical Abstract of the United States, 1982,* 104th ed. (Washington, D.C.: Government Printing Office, 1983), Table 439; U.S. Bureau of the Census, *Statistical Abstract of the United States, 1988,* 108th ed. (Washington, D.C.: Government Printing Office, 1987), Table 419; and Richard L. Berke, "50.16% Voter Turnout Was Lowest Since 1924," *New York Times,* December 18, 1988, 36.

more people who are interested in politics and, incidentally, who are more affluent and better educated.[24] Turnout also varies according to region. Less than 20 percent of the voters turn out in certain one-party areas, especially in the South; in competitive states, turnout well above 50 percent is not uncommon.

What induces voters to cast their ballots for one candidate and not another in congressional elections? Scholars don't know as much as they would like about this question because most voting studies have focused on presidential races. In 1978, however, the University of Michigan's Center for Political Research launched a congressional election survey that has been repeated every two years. This biennial National Election Study (NES) has greatly advanced our understanding of voters' behavior in congressional contests.

When they enter the polling booth, America's voters do not, in general, carry a lot of ideological or even issue-specific baggage. In other words, they do not usually make detailed calculations about which party actually controls Congress, which party ought to control Congress, or which party favors what policies. As a general rule, voters reach their decisions on the basis of three factors: party loyalties, which are declining in saliency; candidate loyalties, growing in saliency and heavily weighted toward incumbents; and overall judgments about the state of the nation and its economy. Each will be discussed in turn.

Party Loyalties

Political analysts traditionally have found party identification the single most powerful factor in determining voters' choices. In his exhaustive study of House elections between 1920 and 1964, Milton Cummings, Jr., weighed the effect of party strength in a given constituency, "presidential tides," third parties, special local factors, and individual candidate appeals.[25] Party was far more powerful than candidate appeals in determining outcomes, although incumbency exerted an independent impact. Charles O. Jones's work yielded similar results: although House incumbents were advantaged, party affiliation was a key to election results.[26] For example, when the incumbent was not running (that is, had died, retired, or been defeated in the primary), the incumbent's party prevailed in three-quarters of the cases.

Insofar as party loyalty controls citizens' voting choices, we would expect election results to coincide roughly with party divisions in the electorate. As Figure 4-4 suggests, a plurality of adult Americans identify themselves as Democrats. The overall ratio is about 57-43 in the Democrats' favor, leaving aside independents (that is, assuming they split similarly). Not all party identifiers actually vote, however, and proportionately fewer Democrats than Republicans vote because low-participating demographic groups are over-represented in the Democratic party (see Chapter 3). Therefore, we must adjust party loyalties by participation rates to arrive at the parties' expected nationwide share of the vote, called the *normal vote* by political scientists.[27] Barring other factors, this "normal" split would result in a vote about 52-54 percent Democratic and 46-48 percent Republican. Electoral outcomes that depart from the normal vote may be due to many factors—for example, partisan defections or movement by independents. Nonetheless, it is remarkable that the national House vote still hovers around the normal vote; the Senate vote is not far afield. Even more striking is the persistence of this Democratic advantage in the face of GOP successes at the presidential level.

Party Decline. The importance of party identification has declined over the past three decades (see Figure 4-4). Majorities of party identifiers still cast their votes for candidates of their party. However, party loyalties have weakened. Increasing proportions of citizens consider themselves independents. Of those who continue to profess partisan leanings, fewer regard themselves as strong partisans. Finally, because of weakened partisan identification, rising proportions of congressional voters defect from their party (see Figure 4-5). In 1956, only 9 percent of the voters (as indicated by a national sample survey) identified with one party but voted for the congressional candidate of another party. By 1978, in contrast, 22 percent of the voters were in that category; throughout the 1980s the proportion of "defectors" remained substantial.[28]

Even more widespread is *ticket splitting,* voting for different parties' candidates for president and Congress or for House and Senate. In surveys between 1952 and 1980, the proportion of voters who reported that they split their ticket between presidential and House candidates increased from 12 to 34 percent. Those who split their ballots between different parties' House and Senate candidates grew from 9 to 31 percent.[29] The number of House districts

Figure 4-4   Political Party Identication of the Electorate, 1952-1988

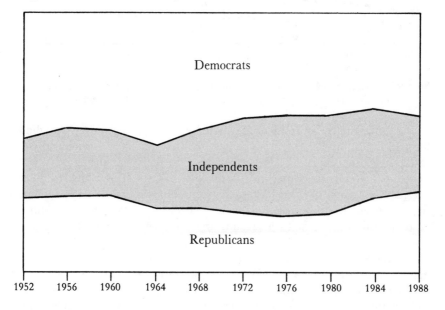

Source: American National Election Study, Center for Political Studies, University of Michigan.

Figure 4-5   Party-Line Voters, Defectors, and Independents in House
Elections, 1956-1980

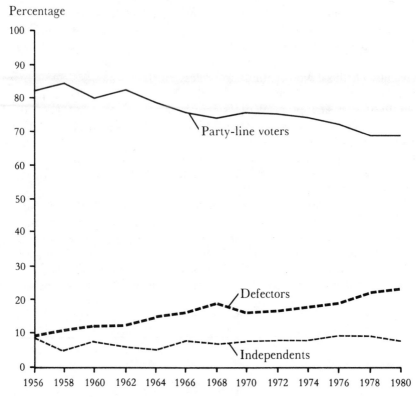

Source: Thomas E. Mann and Raymond E. Wolfinger, "Candidates and Parties in
Congressional Elections," *American Political Science Review* 74 (September 1980): 620.

voting for one party's presidential candidate and the other party's candidate
for the House of Representatives has grown even more dramatically. In
1920 only 3 percent of all House districts split their vote in this way; until
1948 no more than 15 percent of the districts split their tickets in any
presidential year. But from 1920 to 1984 one-quarter of the districts fell into
this category. In the Reagan landslide victory of 1984, no less than 45
percent of all districts had split results, most of them returning Democrats to
Capitol Hill.[30]

  Some analysts argue that voters deliberately split their ballots in order to
maintain ideological balance between the two branches or make sure that the
two branches check one another. While a majority of the electorate seems to
endorse the idea of divided government, it seems improbable that the average
voter would engage in such a logical exercise to ensure divided partisan
control.

More plausible is the argument that voters, seeking different attributes in presidents and lawmakers, naturally turn to different parties to find those attributes. Americans harbor inconsistent desires about cutbacks in government services or protections. Republican presidents provide the rhetoric of limited government, while Democratic lawmakers supply the advocacy of government services that voters favor.[31] This theory, too, may exaggerate the cunning of the average voter, but it provides an intriguing explanation for the increased incidence of "divided government."

Historically, partisan forces have operated rather differently in presidential and midterm years. Until about 1960, presidential-year races displayed a high correlation between voting for president and voting for House members on a district-by-district basis. Since then the correlation has declined as ticket splitting has become more common.

Politicians used to talk about "coattails"—the ability of popular presidential candidates to attract votes for other candidates of the same party. Coattail effects are still found, but they are less pronounced and can run upward as well as downward on the ticket. A popular presidential nominee may boost congressional candidates: Reagan, for example, boosted his party's congressional votes by 2 to 3 percent in 1980 and 4 to 5 percent in 1984.[32] Conversely, presidential candidates can gain from their party's local strength. In either case, spillovers from one contest to another are less frequent than they once were. Democratic candidates' success in 1988 despite George Bush's victory was only the latest reminder of the prevalence of ticket splitting and of the power of localism and incumbency in congressional elections. As Rep. Patricia Schroeder, D-Colo., quipped, "Bush had no coattails; he had a bikini!"

Midterm Elections. What happens in midterm contests, when presidential candidates are not on the ballot? As already noted, the midterm electorate is both smaller than and different from the presidential-year electorate. Moreover, midterm elections normally result in losses for the party that captured the White House two years earlier (see Table 4-1). In midterm elections during this century, the presidential party has lost an average of thirty-one House seats and four Senate seats.

The so-called surge and decline theory holds that shrinkage of the electorate in midterm years explains the falloff in the presidential party's votes. That is, a presidential surge, swollen by less motivated voters attracted by presidential campaigns, is followed two years later by a decline as these voters drop out of the electorate. But other studies indicate that midterm voters are no more or less partisan than those in presidential years and in fact share most of their demographic characteristics.[33]

As the link between presidential and congressional voting has loosened, other theories have been advanced to help explain midterm losses. First, midterm elections may serve in part as a referendum on the president's

Table 4-1   Midterm Fortunes of Presidential Parties, 1934-1986

Year	President	House	Senate
1934	Roosevelt (D)	+9	+10
1938	Roosevelt (D)	−71	−6
1942	Roosevelt (D)	−50	−8
1946	Roosevelt-Truman (D)	−54	−11
1950	Truman (D)	−29	−5
1954	Eisenhower (R)	−18	−1
1958	Eisenhower (R)	−47	−13
1962	Kennedy (D)	−4	+4
1966	Johnson (D)	−47	−3
1970	Nixon (R)	−12	+3
1974	Nixon-Ford (R)	−47	−5
1978	Carter (D)	−3	−12
1982	Reagan (R)	−26	0
1986	Reagan (R)	−6	−8

Source: Compiled by the authors.

popularity and performance in office during the previous two years.[34] This is a plausible explanation and the only one that accounts for phenomena such as the Democrats' 1974 post-Watergate bonus of forty-three representatives and five senators, and their 1982 recession harvest of twenty-six House seats. And yet the referendum aspect of midterm elections is hard to discern in some years. In 1978, for example, Alan Abramowitz concluded that "voters' evaluations of the performance of the Carter administration apparently had little or no bearing on how they cast their ballots for Senator or Representative." [35]

A second explanation for midterm losses lies in the impact of economic conditions upon congressional elections. Votes shift toward the president's party when per capita income rises; they shift away from the president's party when income falls.[36] Voters may hold the president's party responsible for their personal economic well-being (called "pocketbook voting"). More likely, voters assess the president's party on the basis of their impression of overall economic health ("sociotropic voting").

Several political analysts have devised formulas for predicting the midyear performance of the president's party. One of them, by Edward R. Tufte, employs the president's public approval rating a month before the election and changes in real per capita disposable income. Another relies on voters' notions of which party is best able to cope with the nation's most pressing problems.[37] Still others factor in the calculations of strategic politicians, which are based on economic trends and which in turn raise or lower the caliber of congressional candidates.

While these and similar models offer plausible explanations, they can be thrown awry by outside variables. In 1982 the models tracked the economic recession and overestimated Republican losses; the GOP's wealth and superior organization cushioned the expected referendum effect. In 1986 the predictions were closer to the mark. Such models, however, are in their infancy, and some vigorously dispute the economic linkage altogether.[38]

The Appeal of Candidates, Especially Incumbents

After partisan loyalties, the appeal of given candidates is the strongest force in congressional voting. Not surprisingly, candidate appeal normally tilts toward incumbents. When voters abandon their party to vote for House or Senate candidates, they usually do so to vote for incumbents.

The incumbency factor has grown over the past generation to the point where it rivals and often eclipses partisanship. One estimate fixed the incumbency advantage in House races at about 2 percent of the vote totals during the 1954-1960 period. After about 1966, according to follow-up studies, this advantage grew to 6 percent.[39] In 1978, according to a nationwide election survey, incumbents captured nine votes out of every ten cast by party defectors. Two decades earlier the incumbents' share of party defectors' votes was only 57 percent, or little better than an even break.

Although more pronounced in House elections, "incumbency now serves . . . as an important alternate voting cue to party" in Senate contests.[40] Senate elections are relatively hard-fought and well covered by the media, especially compared with House contests, but incumbency looms as a voting cue in many Senate races. Statewide contests can be quite lively, especially in those southern states that have developed vigorous two-party competition over the past generation; yet in nonsouthern states competition for Senate seats has actually declined since 1958. So while Senate seats are more hotly contested than House seats, "a substantial proportion of Senate races are low-key affairs that attract scant notice: media coverage is limited, spending by the challenger is relatively low, and the outcome is often a foregone conclusion." [41]

Taken together, party and incumbency are an almost unbeatable combination.[42] In 1978 House elections covered by the Michigan survey, 95 percent of those voters identifying with the incumbent's party voted for the incumbent. Among independents, 79 percent voted for the incumbent. Even among members of the challenger's party, the split was 54 to 46 percent in the incumbent's favor. An incumbent senator's edge, although less, is nonetheless substantial. Senators running for reelection attracted 89 percent of their own party's voters and 64 percent of the independents' votes. Even among the opposition party's voters, senators captured almost a third of the ballots.

Incumbents are better known than their opponents. Even if voters can't recall officeholders' names in an interview, they can identify and express opinions about them when the names are presented to them—as in the voting booth. In the NES survey, nearly all respondents were able to recognize and rate Senate and House incumbents running for reelection (96 and 93 percent, respectively). Senate challengers were recognized and rated by 86 percent of the respondents, House challengers by only 44 percent. Open-seat candidates fell somewhere between incumbents and challengers in visibility. Thus, most voters can recognize and express views about congressional candidates, except for House challengers. These opinions exert a powerful impact on voting decisions, and indeed in the eyes of some analysts are the most potent influences on congressional voting.[43]

In evaluating candidates, voters tend to favor incumbents over nonincumbents. Of voters' comments about incumbents in the NES survey, four out of five were favorable. In contrast, only 57 percent of the comments about challengers were positive. Most of the comments centered on job performance or personal characteristics; relatively few dealt with issues. Voters evaluated House incumbents largely on the basis of personal characteristics and such noncontroversial activities as casework and constituent outreach. Even on the issues, references to incumbents were overwhelmingly positive. Only one voter in ten claimed to know how his or her representative had voted on a piece of legislation during the preceding two years, but more than two-thirds of those voters claimed to have agreed with their legislator's vote.

Incumbents' popularity stems partly from their ability to shape information that constituents receive about them and their performance—through advertising, credit claiming, and position taking.[44] Not surprisingly, high levels of contact are reported with House and Senate incumbents; the more contact voters have with their legislators, the more positive their evaluations are likely to be. In the NES survey, only 10 percent of all voters denied having exposure of any kind to their representative; only 6 percent reported no exposure to their senator. Table 4-2 sets forth the various types of contact voters report having with incumbents, challengers, and open-seat candidates. Many representatives' constituents receive mail from them or read about them in newspapers; almost a quarter have met the representative face to face. For senators, the major point of voter contact is TV appearances or newspaper and magazine coverage.

The "visibility gap" between incumbents and challengers is wider in House races than in Senate races. Whereas nine voters out of every ten report some form of contact with their representative, fewer than half that proportion have been exposed to challengers. Senate voters are more apt to be reached by *both* incumbent and challenger. Of those questioned in 1978, 82 percent reported contact with nonincumbent Senate candidates in their state compared to 94 percent reporting contact with incumbent senators. In open seats the gap is narrower. Candidates for seats with no incumbent are able to reach nearly three-quarters of their potential House voters and 90 percent of potential senatorial voters.

Table 4-2   Voter Contact with House and Senate Candidates
(in percentages)

Forms of contact	House			Senate		
	Incum-bents	Chal lengers	Open seats	Incum-bents	Chal lengers	Open seats
Any type	90	44	73	94	82	88
Read about in news-paper, magazine	71	32	57	73	63	78
Received mail	71	16	43	53	32	47
Saw on TV	50	24	48	80	70	78
Family or friend had contact	39	11	26	—	—	—
Heard on radio	34	15	28	45	37	49
Met personally	23	4	14	9	5	9
Saw at meeting	20	3	13	10	5	13
Talked to staff	12	2	13	6	4	9
(*N*)	(756)	(756)	(121)	(409)	(409)	(158)

Source: American National Election Study, Center for Political Studies, University of Michigan, 1978. Cited in Thomas E. Mann and Raymond E. Wolfinger, "Candidates and Parties in Congressional Elections," *American Political Science Review* 74 (September 1980): 627.

These figures suggest why senators are more vulnerable at the polls than their House counterparts. Surveys indicate that representatives are viewed more favorably than senators—probably because they are judged primarily on noncontroversial acts such as personal contact or constituent service, whereas senators are more closely linked to divisive national issues. Second, Senate challengers are far more visible than House challengers. Senate contests are more widely reported by the media, and challengers can gain almost as much exposure as incumbents. Media coverage of House races is more fragmentary, throwing more weight to incumbents' techniques of contacting voters. Third, senators cannot manipulate voter contacts as much as representatives do. Voters largely get their information about senators through organized media that senators do not control; representatives gain exposure through diverse means—personal appearances, mailings, and newsletters—that they fashion to their own advantage. "Somewhat ironically," observes Michael Robinson, "powerful senators are less able to control their images than 'invisible' House members."[45] Finally, senatorial elections are simply harder fought than House elections. There are fewer one-party states than one-party congressional districts.

"Most incumbents face obscure, politically inexperienced opponents whose resources fall far short of what is necessary to mount a formidable campaign," Jacobson observes.[46] But nonincumbents can win with luck and attention to certain basic principles: run for an open seat or for one where the incumbent's support is slipping. Be a credible, forceful candidate. Be prepared to spend money to erase the incumbent's visibility advantage. Blame the incumbent for "the mess in Washington." It's risky strategy. Yet every election year a handful of challengers win this way; and that's enough to keep incumbents on their guard.[47]

Issue Voting

According to conventional wisdom, issues and ideologies play a relatively minor role in voting, especially in congressional races. In their 1962 study of House elections, Warren Miller and Donald Stokes found that voters knew next to nothing about the performance of either the parties or individual members of Congress.[48]

A 1986 voter survey offers a more mixed picture of the bases for choice in House elections (see Table 4-3). A plurality of voters claimed that they would vote on their assessment of the candidates' personal qualities, not on any specific issues. Yet 31 percent said their vote would hinge on national issues; foreign policy and the economy were most often cited. Another 19 percent mentioned state and local matters, such as unemployment or farm problems. But when pressed, many of those who claimed they would vote on issues could not name one. Scarcely any respondents mentioned political party as a basis for choice, although party ties no doubt lie hidden in other responses, such as national issues.

As usual, we must distinguish between House and Senate voting. House incumbents and challengers can more easily sidestep divisive national issues and stress personal qualities and district service. Senators, on the other hand, are more closely identified with issues. One study comparing incumbents' ratings by Americans for Democratic Action with voters' self-classifications on a seven-point liberal-conservative scale found that ideology had "no discernible impact on evaluations of House candidates." [49] Contact was the prime influence on evaluations of House candidates; ideology and party identification were more important in evaluating Senate candidates. Another study, based on 1982 exit polls, found that "policy issues play an important role" in the Senate elections, where "policy effects are substantial and systematic." [50]

Such generalized findings perhaps should be taken with a grain of salt. Regardless of what nationwide surveys may show, legislators and their advisers are highly sensitive to voters' anticipated reactions to issue stands. Much energy is devoted to framing positions, communicating them (sometimes in deliberately obscure words), and assessing their impact. Moreover, every professional politician can relate instances where issues tilted an election one way or another. Frequently cited are the so-called "single interest" groups. Some citizens vote according to a single issue they regard as

Table 4-3 How People Explained Their Vote in 1986 House Races (in percentages)

Main basis for choice	Republican	Democrat	Independent	All voters
Personal qualities	41	32	40	37
National issues	34	29	29	31
Local/state issues	12	22	21	19
Other/combination[a]	4	6	1	2
No opinion/all	9	11	9	11
Total	100	100	100	100
(*N*, weighted)	(369)	(506)	(400)	(1275)

Source: CBS News-*New York Times* poll, April 14, 1986, Question 7.

Note: Registered voters in the survey were asked the following question: "Sometimes people decide to vote for somone for the House because of national issues. Sometimes, it's because of local or state issues. And sometimes, it's because of the candidate's personal qualities. This year, what will make the biggest difference in how you vote—a national issue, a local or state issue, or the candidate's personal qualities?"

[a] Includes "political party" as a volunteered response.

paramount—for example, gun control, abortion (pro or con), or crucial ethnic issues. Even if small, such groups can decide close contests. That is why legislators dislike taking positions on issues that evoke extreme responses— issues that prompt certain voters to oppose them despite their stewardship on other matters.

Regardless of how issues sway voters directly, they exert powerful indirect effects upon election outcomes. For one thing, issues motivate that segment of voters who are opinion leaders, who can lend or withhold support far beyond their single vote. Issues are carefully monitored by organized interests, including PACs, in a position to channel funds, publicity, or volunteer workers to the candidate's cause. It is more than superstition, then, that makes legislators devote so much time and attention to cultivating these "attentive publics."

Conclusion

What overall portrait do we gain of voters in congressional elections? It is a rather complicated picture in which three factors—party, candidates, and issues—play varying roles. Despite weakening partisan ties, a large segment of the electorate seems to have made a "standing decision" to vote for candidates by party affiliation. Individual candidate factors are, however, of substantial and growing importance. Congressional candidates, especially incumbents, strive to fashion unique appeals based not on party loyalty but on "home style"—a mixture of personal style, voter contacts, and constituent service.[51] Because of their superior resources for cultivating attractive home styles, incumbents have an edge at the polls. Through media exposure, Senate challengers can often overcome this advantage; lacking such outlets for their message, fewer House challengers can do so. Finally, issues and ideologies influence at least some voters in some elections.

Election Outcomes

The process by which representatives and senators reach Capitol Hill is a prime aspect of the two Congresses notion we have put forth. The most pervasive attribute of electoral processes is their local character. "All politics is local," as former Speaker Thomas P. "Tip" O'Neill, Jr., put it. Or as Thomas E. Mann and Raymond E. Wolfinger conclude, "In deciding how to cast their ballots, most voters are influenced primarily by the choice of local candidates." [52] Although national tides are the backdrop against which these local contests are fought, the candidates, the voters, and often the issues and styles are deeply rooted in states and districts. The aggregate of all these contests is a locally based legislative body charged with addressing national problems and issues. Selection processes, in short, are part of the *pluribus* from which the *unum* must emerge.

Party or Factional Balance

Despite the much-vaunted independence of candidates and voters, virtually all races are run with party labels. In 1988 no fewer than thirty-six different parties appeared on ballots somewhere in the United States. These included names such as Anti-Drug, New Union, Communist, Free Libertarian, Right to Life, Nuclear Freeze, and Socialist Workers.

In terms of governance only two parties really count: the Democrats or the Republicans have controlled Congress since 1855. The Appendix Table at the back of the book shows the partisan majorities in the House and Senate since 1901. Between 1896 and 1920 the two parties actually had approximately equal numbers of partisans in the electorate, but lower participation rates in Democratic areas tended to favor the Republicans. The GOP's relative position improved after 1920, when women received the vote. The 1932 realignment shifted the balance to the Democrats, and since then the Democrats have been virtually a permanent majority and the Republicans a permanent minority on Capitol Hill. In all that time, the Republicans controlled both chambers for only four years (1947-1949, 1953-1955) and the Senate alone for another six (1981-1987). Democratic sweeps in 1958, 1964, and 1974 padded their majorities. Republicans eventually recovered from the first two setbacks, but by the 1970s Democratic dominance, especially in the House, was harder to overcome because incumbents were successfully exploiting their reelection assets.

What has caused this longstanding partisan balance, or imbalance? A few of the answers to this question should already be apparent. Leaving the presidency aside, the Democratic party does appear to be the party of choice in this nation by a modest though surprisingly durable margin. Moreover, electoral majorities and minorities tend to be exaggerated by the winner-take-all system, especially when it comes to House seats. In addition, the Democrats claim more safe seats (and uncontested seats) than Republicans do. Turnout rates further cloud the picture: for demographic reasons, GOP areas tend to have higher vote totals than Democratic areas—making voting comparisons unreliable.[53] Some contend that Democratic control of the states has produced gerrymanders that unduly pad the Democrats' majorities. Despite some glaring examples of this, political scientists generally do not view gerrymandering as the major culprit in the GOP's misfortunes (see Chapter 3).

With its prolonged dominance below the presidential level, the Democratic party has developed long queues of qualified candidates extending into state, county, and city government. Conversely, "Republicans have suffered from certain self-fulfilling tendencies characteristic of a long-term minority party."[54] In the face of repeated defeats at the polls, the Republican party has found it more difficult to recruit strong candidates who are capable of raising war chests to challenge Democratic incumbents. Such candidates, remember, must normally emerge and be nurtured in the fields of local political affairs.

Despite the Democrats' preeminence on Capitol Hill over the past half century or so, this state of affairs need not last indefinitely. The GOP is traditionally well organized and generously funded. And it ought to be boosted by demographic changes. The party has enjoyed success in the South, where over the past quarter century its share of House seats has grown from 6 to 35 percent. Gone, too, is the "solid South" in the Senate. Population is shifting toward the South and West, where the GOP is thriving, and away from northern and eastern areas, traditional Democratic bastions.

Realignment or "Divided Government"?

Historically, political upheavals have shifted party control in the House or Senate with decisive results. Political scientists talk of "critical elections" or "critical periods" in which one party yields preeminence to another, or major voting groups alter the shape of the parties' coalitions. Three such watershed eras were the Civil War, the turbulent 1890s, and the New Deal 1930s. Each of these upheavals brought to Capitol Hill new lawmakers, new voting patterns, and new legislative priorities.[55]

For nearly fifty years political scientists have been on the lookout for a post-New Deal realignment; most have yet to spot one. Of course, meaningful changes can take place even without an underlying party realignment. The Wilson-era Democratic dominance (1912-1918), the Johnson-era "Great

Society" Congresses (1964-1966), the post-Watergate Democratic landslide (1974), and the Reagan juggernaut (1981-1982) involved changes in partisan strength on Capitol Hill that for one reason or another went far beyond any changes in attitudes or voting habits within the electorate as a whole. Elected officeholders, like most political activists, tend to be more committed to ideology or policy than are most voters, even those of the officeholder's own party. Thus, Congress turned leftward in the 1960s and 1970s and rightward in the 1980s without any dramatic shifts in voters' attitudes.

One-party Democratic dominance on Capitol Hill occurred alongside what increasingly seems to be a long-term Republican lease on the White House. While presidential contests are uniquely visible and highly competitive, Democratic contenders have captured only one presidential contest since 1964. Whether because of incumbents' strategies or voters' designs, the GOP's presidential successes have had surprisingly little effect upon the Democrats' control of Congress. (Republican control of the Senate from 1981 through 1986 was partly an exception to this rule, partly a product of unrelated factors.) The consequence of all this is that the voters have caused, and seem content with, the phenomenon of "divided government": split partisan control of the two policy-making branches.

Incumbents' tenacity means that there is less turnover of individual members, too. Can Congress remain vital and responsive with all this stability and changelessness? Of special concern is the House of Representatives, dubbed the "House of Lords" by the *Wall Street Journal* and described by journalist David S. Broder as "steadily, reliably, irresistibly or (some would say) irredeemably Democratic for 34 years."[56]

Of course, reelection rates should not be confused with turnover rates. While it is true that relatively few members these days are turned out of office by the voters, a goodly number leave Capitol Hill voluntarily—to retire, run for another office, or follow other pursuits. Indeed, voluntary retirements from Congress have remained relatively high. As the decade of the 1980s closed, 56 percent of representatives and 44 percent of senators had been elected to their current posts during that decade. The natural processes of membership renewal have not halted.

High turnover of members, whether by steady increments or by massive partisan realignments, does not seem to be required for Congress to be a responsive institution. Even if few lawmakers are turned out of office these days, all of them are keenly aware of the threat of defeat and take steps to prevent that eventuality by heightened attentiveness to constituents' needs through personal visits, speeches, newsletters, and polls. But are voters' views accurately reflected by the representatives they elect to Congress? This question is not easily answered. Popular control of policy makers is not the same thing as popular control of policies themselves. If this were the case, then constituents' views would be precisely mirrored by legislators' voting behavior and the laws passed by the legislature.

Registering Voters' Views

What sort of correlation exists between voters' attitudes and members' voting on issues? Miller and Stokes found that constituency attitudes correlated differently according to the type of policy.[57] In foreign affairs a slight negative correlation existed between constituents' attitudes and legislators' votes; in social and economic welfare issues the correlation was moderate; in civil rights issues the correlation was very high. In other words, in at least one and possibly two major policy areas the linkage was weak enough to cast some doubt on constituency control.

Political scientists explain the absence of strong linkages by noting how difficult it is to meet all the conditions needed for popular control of policies. Voters would have to identify the candidates' positions on issues, and they would have to vote by referring to those positions. Differences among candidates would have to be apparent, and winners would have to vote in accord with their preelection attitudes. These conditions aren't always met. Candidates' stands aren't always clear, nor do candidates invariably differentiate themselves on issues. As noted earlier, voters often ignore issues in voting; and once elected, legislators' views may diverge from their preelection attitudes.

Political scientists John L. Sullivan and Robert E. O'Connor tried to test these conditions by submitting a questionnaire to all House candidates covering three issue areas—foreign affairs, civil rights, and domestic policies—and then following the successful candidates' voting records in the House.[58] Their findings suggest that elements of popular control are present. First, according to their inquiries, voters had meaningful choices among candidates. Second, winning candidates generally voted according to their preelection stands. Third, candidates were ideologically distinct, with Democrats invariably more liberal than Republicans. To these pieces of evidence we can add another: according to recent surveys, most congressional voters can rank their representative on a liberal-conservative scale, and most of these claim an affinity with their representative's ranking.[59] In other words, voters' attitudes and legislators' views are roughly parallel—even though they may diverge on numerous specific points.

If ideological or attitudinal links between voters and their representatives are rough and variable, actual contacts between constituents and individual legislators are numerous and palpable. Individual legislators do not necessarily mirror their constituents, much less the nation as a whole in terms of demographic characteristics. Yet much of their time and effort while in office are devoted to dealing with "the folks back home." Constituency politics are ever-present in the daily lives of senators and representatives, and it is to this subject that we turn in the following chapter.

Notes

1. Keith Love, "Cranston's TV Campaign Narrated by Bridges," *Los Angeles Times,* April 29, 1986, I15.
2. David Shribman, "Cranston-Zschau Race May Offer a Glimpse of Future U.S. Politics," *Wall Street Journal,* October 8, 1986, 1.
3. Keith Love, "Cranston: A Man of Many Sides," *Los Angeles Times,* February 10, 1985, I28.
4. See Richard G. Niemi, Lynda W. Powell, and Patricia L. Bicknell, "The Effects of Congruity Between Community and District on Salience of U.S. House Candidates," *Legislative Studies Quarterly* 11 (May 1986): 187-201; and James E. Campbell, John R. Alford, and Keith Henry, "Television Markets and Congressional Elections," *Legislative Studies Quarterly* 9 (November 1984): 665-678.
5. U.S. Congress, Senate, *Congressional Record,* daily ed., 98th Cong., 2d sess., January 31, 1984, S575.
6. David S. Broder, "When Incumbency Is a Curse," *Washington Post,* October 7, 1986, A4; and Laura Parker, "Recasting Images in Washington Race," *Washington Post,* October 21, 1988, A8.
7. Peter Bragdon, "In 'Permanent Campaign' Era, Members' Funds Find Many Uses," *Congressional Quarterly Weekly Report,* September 12, 1987, 2185-2186.
8. Cited in David S. Cloud, "Big Bucks and Victory Often Go Hand in Hand," *Congressional Quarterly Weekly Report,* November 12, 1988, 3272.
9. Donald Philip Green and Jonathan S. Krasno, "Salvation for the Spendthrift Incumbent: Reestimating the Effects of Campaign Spending in House Elections," *American Journal of Political Science* 32 (November 1988): 900.
10. Gary C. Jacobson, "The Effects of Campaign Spending on Congressional Elections," *American Political Science Review* 72 (June 1978): 469-491.
11. Herbert E. Alexander and Brian A. Haggerty, "Misinformation on Media Money," *Public Opinion* 11 (May-June 1988): 7.
12. Ibid.
13. Quoted in Paul Houston, "TV and High Tech Send Campaign Costs Soaring," *Los Angeles Times,* October 2, 1986, I21.
14. Richard E. Cohen, "Costly Campaigns: Candidates Learn that Reaching the Voters is Expensive," *National Journal,* April 16, 1983, 782-788.
15. Edie N. Goldenberg and Michael W. Traugott, *Campaigning for Congress* (Washington, D.C.: CQ Press, 1984), 93.
16. Steve Farnsworth and Karen Tumulty, "These Races Not Always to the Thrift," *Los Angeles Times,* May 25, 1984, 1; and Cohen, "Costly Campaigns," 786.
17. Goldenberg and Traugott, *Campaigning for Congress,* 23.
18. Richard F. Fenno, Jr., *Home Style: House Members in Their Districts* (Boston: Little, Brown, 1978),46.
19. Merle Miller, *Lyndon: An Oral Biography* (New York: G. P. Putnam's Sons, 1980), 120.
20. Alan Ehrenhalt, "Technology, Strategy Bring New Campaign Era," *Con-*

gressional Quarterly Weekly Report, December 7, 1985, 2559-2565.
21. Lynda L. Kaid and Dorothy K. Davidson, "Elements of Videostyle: Candidate Presentation Through Television Advertising," in *New Perspectives on Political Advertising,* ed. L. L. Kaid, D. Nimmo, and K. R. Sanders (Carbondale, Ill.: Southern Illinois University Press, 1986), 184-209. See also Dorothy Davidson Nesbit, *Videostyle in Senate Campaigns* (Knoxville, Tenn.: University of Tennessee Press, 1988).
22. Peter Clarke and Susan H. Evans, *Covering Campaigns: Journalism in Congressional Elections* (Stanford, Calif.: Stanford University Press, 1983).
23. Raymond E. Wolfinger and Steven J. Rosenstone, *Who Votes?* (New Haven, Conn.: Yale University Press, 1980), 18ff.
24. M. Margaret Conway, "Political Participation in Mid-Term Congressional Elections," *American Politics Quarterly* 9 (April 1981): 221-244.
25. Milton C. Cummings, Jr., *Congressmen and the Electorate* (New York: Free Press, 1966).
26. Charles O. Jones, "The Role of the Campaign in Congressional Politics," in *The Electoral Process,* ed. M. Kent Jennings and L. Harmon Zeigler (Englewood Cliffs, N.J.: Prentice-Hall, 1966), 21-41.
27. Philip E. Converse, "The Concept of the Normal Vote," in *Elections and the Political Order,* ed. Angus Campbell, Philip E. Converse, Warren E. Miller, and Donald E. Stokes (New York: John Wiley & Sons, 1966), 9-39.
28. Norman J. Ornstein, Thomas E. Mann, and Michael J. Malbin, *Vital Statistics on Congress, 1987-1988* (Washington, D.C.: Congressional Quarterly, 1987), 65.
29. Martin P. Wattenberg, *The Decline of American Political Parties, 1952-1984* (Cambridge, Mass.: Harvard University Press, 1986), 20.
30. Larry J. Sabato, *The Party's Just Begun: Shaping Political Parties for America's Future* (Glenview, Ill.: Scott Foresman/Little, Brown, 1988), 129-130.
31. Gary C. Jacobson, "Meager Patrimony: Republican Representation in Congress After Reagan," in *The Reagan Legacy,* ed. Larry Berman (Baltimore: Johns Hopkins University Press, forthcoming).
32. Gary C. Jacobson, *The Politics of Congressional Elections,* 2d ed. (Boston: Little, Brown, 1987), 153.
33. Angus Campbell, "Surge and Decline: A Study of Electoral Change," in *Elections and the Political Order,* ed. Campbell et al. (New York: John Wiley & Sons, 1966), 40-62; and Raymond E. Wolfinger, Steven J. Rosenstone, and Richard A. McIntosh, "Presidential and Congressional Voters Compared," *American Politics Quarterly* 9 (April 1981): 245-255.
34. Eric M. Uslaner and Margaret Conway, "The Responsible Electorate: Watergate, the Economy, and Vote Choice in 1974," *American Political Science Review* 79 (September 1985): 788-803; and Samuel Kernell, "Presidential Popularity and Negative Voting: An Alternative Explanation of the Midterm Congressional Decline of the President's Party," *American Political Science Review* 71 (March 1977): 44-46.
35. Alan I. Abramowitz, "A Comparison of Voting for U.S. Senator and Representative in 1978," *American Political Science Review* 74 (September 1980): 633-650.

36. Edward R. Tufte, *Political Control of the Economy* (Princeton, N.J.: Princeton University Press, 1978), 112. See also Robert S. Erikson and Gerald C. Wright, "Voters, Candidates, and Issues in Congressional Elections," in *Congress Reconsidered*, 3d ed., ed. Lawrence C. Dodd and Bruce I. Oppenheimer (Washington, D.C.: CQ Press, 1985), 91-92.

37. Albert D. Cover, "Party Competence Evaluations and Voting for Congress," *Western Political Quarterly* 39 (June 1986): 304-312.

38. Michael Lewis-Beck, "A Model Performance," *Public Opinion* 9 (March-April 1987): 57-58; Francisco Arcelus and Allan H. Meltzer, "The Effect of Aggregate Economic Variables on Congressional Elections," *American Political Science Review* 69 (December 1975): 1232-1239; and John R. Owens, "Economic Influences on Elections to the U.S. Congress," *Legislative Studies Quarterly* 9 (February 1984): 123-150.

39. Robert S. Erikson, "The Advantage of Incumbency in Congressional Elections," *Polity* 3 (Spring 1971): 395-405; and Robert S. Erikson, "Malapportionment, Gerrymandering, and Party Fortunes in Congressional Elections," *American Political Science Review* 66 (December 1972): 1234-1245.

40. Warren Lee Kostroski, "Party and Incumbency in Postwar Senate Elections: Trends, Patterns, and Models," *American Political Science Review* 67 (December 1974): 1233.

41. Mark C. Westlye, "Competitiveness of Senate Seats and Voting Behavior in Senate Elections," *American Journal of Political Science* 27 (May 1983): 253-283.

42. Thomas E. Mann and Raymond E. Wolfinger, "Candidates and Parties in Congressional Elections," *American Political Science Review* 74 (September 1980): 62.

43. Alan I. Abramowitz, "Name Familiarity, Reputation and the Incumbency Effect in a Congressional Election," *Western Political Quarterly* 28 (December 1975): 668-684; Abramowitz, "A Comparison of Voting," 633-650; Thomas E. Mann, *Unsafe at Any Margin: Interpreting Congressional Elections* (Washington, D.C.: American Enterprise Institute, 1978); and Mann and Wolfinger, "Candidates and Parties," 623.

44. David R. Mayhew, *Congress: The Electoral Connection* (New Haven, Conn.: Yale University Press, 1974).

45. Michael J. Robinson, "Three Faces of Congressional Media," in *The New Congress*, ed. Thomas E. Mann and Norman J. Ornstein (Washington, D.C.: American Enterprise Institute, 1981), 91.

46. Gary C. Jacobson, "Incumbents' Advantages in the 1978 U.S. Congressional Elections," *Legislative Studies Quarterly* 6 (May 1981): 198.

47. Mann, *Unsafe at Any Margin*.

48. Donald E. Stokes and Warren E. Miller, "Party Government and the Saliency of Congress," *Public Opinion Quarterly* 26 (Winter 1962): 531-546.

49. Abramowitz, "A Comparison of Voting," 635.

50. Gerald C. Wright, Jr., and Michael B. Berkman, "Candidates and Policy in United States Senate Elections," *American Political Science Review* 80 (June 1986): 567-588.

51. Richard F. Fenno, Jr., *Home Style: House Members in Their Districts*

(Boston: Little, Brown, 1978).
52. Mann and Wolfinger, "Candidates and Parties," 630.
53. Edward R. Tufte, "The Relationship Between Seats and Votes in Two-Party Systems," *American Political Science Review* 67 (June 1973): 540-554.
54. Thomas E. Mann, "The Permanent Minority Party in American Politics," *The Brookings Review* 6 (Winter 1988): 33-38.
55. David W. Brady, "Electoral Realignments in the U.S. House of Representatives," in *Congress and Policy Change*, ed. Gerald C. Wright, Jr., Leroy N. Rieselbach, and Lawrence C. Dodd (New York: Agathon Press, 1986), 46-69.
56. David S. Broder, "An Unchanging House," *Washington Post*, May 8, 1988, B7; see also "The U.S. House of Lords," editorial, *Wall Street Journal*, April 18, 1988, 24.
57. Warren E. Miller and Donald E. Stokes, "Constituency Influence in Congress," *American Political Science Review* 57 (March 1963): 45-57.
58. John L. Sullivan and Robert E. O'Connor, "Electoral Choice and Popular Control of Public Policy: The Case of the 1966 House Elections," *American Political Science Review* 66 (December 1972): 1256-1268.
59. Mann and Wolfinger, "Candidates and Parties," 629.

House Majority Leader Richard A. Gephardt, a former presidential candidate, on the stump with farmers in his Missouri district.

CHAPTER FIVE

Being There:
Hill Styles and Home Styles

Since Theodore Roosevelt's presidency, Congress has created national parks and monuments to protect mountains, waterfalls, geysers, and historical sites. But a railroad yard in Scranton, Pennsylvania? Yes, in the 99th Congress Rep. Joseph M. McDade, R-Pa., managed to add $20 million to a supplemental spending bill to designate the old Lackawanna Railroad yards and a collection of steam locomotives as the "Steamtown National Historic Site." McDade's minor triumph flowed from his Capitol Hill position as second-ranking Republican on the House Appropriations Committee; his constituency made him an advocate for eastern Pennsylvania, where his activities did not escape notice:

> Articles in the *Scranton Tribune* recounted McDade's every move on the night of October 8, as he cut deals to pump millions into an economically distressed area. But now others are taking notice of one of those "little-noticed" amendments that suddenly placed a 40-acre collection of locomotives, railroad cars, tracks, and buildings into the same category as Abraham Lincoln's birthplace, Ford's Theatre, and the Rev. Martin Luther King's grave.[1]

Both a local advocate and a Washington insider, McDade personifies the "two Congresses." In this chapter we examine members of Congress and the two worlds in which they live and work. Who are these people? What are their jobs on Capitol Hill and back home in their states or districts? Do these two aspects of their work fit together? And how do the media shape the Hill styles and home styles that members adopt?

Hill Styles

Who Are the Legislators?

The Constitution names only three criteria for serving in Congress—age, citizenship, and residency. As we have seen, entrance requirements are really far more restrictive. It was Aristotle, after all, who first observed that elections are essentially oligarchic affairs that involve few active participants.

By almost any measure, senators and representatives constitute an economic and social elite. They are well educated. They come from a small number of prestigious occupations. Many of them possess or amass material wealth. An estimated one-third of all senators are millionaires (disclosure practices make it impossible to be precise). The House is more middle-class, economically speaking: the average freshman earned $61,600 a year, before entering the House in 1989, although at least thirty members are millionaires.[2]

The pay of senators and representatives ($89,500 in 1989) puts them in the top 1 percent of the nation's wage earners. Yet expenses are high, especially for members who maintain two residences; a federal pay commission reported in 1988 that "most members of Congress find it difficult to live on their current salaries."[3] Most have outside sources of income: a majority of them (70 senators and 250 representatives) reported 1987 earnings of at least $135,000 (the salary level proposed, and rejected, in early 1989).[4] Many income sources are legitimate, but among the problematic sources are honoraria—fees members accept from interest groups for speeches and appearances. These fees totaled $9.6 million in 1987. (Both chambers limit honoraria to $2,000 per event. The House limits outside earned income, including honoraria, to 30 percent of salary. The Senate limits honoraria to 40 percent of salary and places other restrictions on outside employment.)

Occupation. Some humorist proposed that our government "of laws and not men" is really "of lawyers and not men." When the 101st Congress convened, 247 members were lawyers. As Figure 5-1 indicates, lawyers typically outnumber other professions in the House of Representatives; the same is true for the Senate, where "no other occupational group even approaches the lawyers' record."[5]

In the United States, law and politics are closely linked. Many lawyers view forays into electoral politics as a form of professional advertising. The legal profession stresses personal skills, such as verbalization, advocacy, and negotiation, that are useful in gaining and holding public office. Important, too, is lawyers' monopoly over offices that serve as stepping-stones to Congress—especially elected law enforcement and judicial posts.[6] Lawyers also can move in and out of their jobs without jeopardizing their careers unlike doctors, engineers, or most other high-status professionals. In the 101st Congress there were only four physicians, four engineers, and three members of the clergy.

Business is the next most prevalent occupation of members. Many business people harbor antigovernment attitudes that make them reluctant to enter public life. Local proprietors (druggists or morticians, for example), while highly visible in their home towns, usually are hard pressed to leave their businesses in the hands of others. Corporate managers are neither very

Figure 5-1   Occupations of House Members in Eleven Selected Congresses

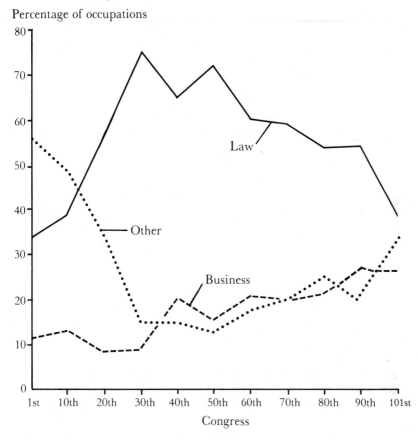

Percentage of occupations

Congress

Source: Roger H. Davidson, *The Role of the Congressman* (Indianapolis: Bobbs-Merrill, 1969), 238. Recent calculations by the authors.

visible nor mobile because temporary leaves of absence can bump them off the promotion ladder. However, executives in service industries—publishing, broadcasting, or real estate, for example—are visible and mobile enough to be ideal candidates and are found in growing numbers in Congress.

Other professions are represented in smaller numbers. Members of the "verbalizing professions"—teaching, journalism, public service, and even clergy—often win seats in Congress. Fifty members of the 101st Congress spent part or all of their early careers in education, and half that number were in communications.

Still other occupations are represented because they are uniquely visible. Historically, military heroes have been sought after, and following World

War II a surge of returning war veterans went to Congress. Two of those were representatives John F. Kennedy and Richard M. Nixon. Despite the influx of Vietnam veterans in the 1970s and early 1980s, the proportion of veterans, especially those with combat experience, is dwindling; military service seems no longer a special political asset.

Today's media-centered campaigns have spawned a few celebrity legislators. Several astronauts, including Sen. John Glenn, D-Ohio, have had political careers. Five one-time professional athletes served in the 101st Congress, including basketball players Bill Bradley, D-N.J., in the Senate and Tom McMillen, D-Md., in the House. And who could overlook the former stars of TV's "Loveboat" (Rep. Fred Grandy, R-Iowa) and "The Dukes of Hazzard" (Rep. Ben Jones, D-Ga.)?

Needless to say, many occupations are, and always have been, drastically underrepresented. Low-status occupations—including farm labor, service trades, manual and skilled labor, and domestic service—are virtually unknown on Capitol Hill. Only two representatives in the 101st Congress had blue-collar backgrounds; both of them were labor organizers. One blue-collar worker elected in recent years quit after one term because he was unhappy and self-conscious about his social status.

Education and Religion.   By every measure Congress is a highly educated body. Virtually every member has a college degree; a majority have advanced training. Many of the heavily represented occupations require postgraduate training. Earned doctorates are not unknown, and there are five Rhodes Scholars in the Senate.

While a few prestigious private universities are overrepresented, no schools hold the dominant position that Oxford and Cambridge do in British ruling circles. One reason is the lingering norm of localism in congressional recruitment, which means that local colleges and state universities have a large share of members. Of the senators sitting in 1989, sixty-one did their undergraduate work at in-state schools.

Most members of Congress are affiliated with organized religious bodies, at least in their public profession of membership. Virtually every member of the 101st Congress professed religious affiliation, compared with about six out of ten Americans. More than one-quarter of all House and Senate members are Roman Catholics, the largest single contingent. Twenty-three percent of the nation's population are Catholics. Most other legislators are Protestants, primarily the mainline denominations—Methodists, Episcopalians, Presbyterians, and Baptists. Jews, who comprise 2.6 percent of the total U.S. population, were at least 7 percent of the 101st Congress. In terms of trends, Catholics and Jews have enlarged their share of Congress's membership, while mainline Protestants have declined slightly.

On most issues religion probably has little impact on how members approach voting or other choices. However, intense social issues—among them abortion, school prayer, crime, pornography, and tuition tax credits for private schools—stir religious feelings. Members' religious ties probably tilt them toward the stands of highly motivated groups on these sensitive issues.

Race and Sex. Neither the Senate nor the House accurately mirrors the nation in terms of racial, ethnic, or sexual mixture. Throughout its history, Congress has been a bastion for white males.

Black Americans, who comprise 12 percent of the nation's population, account for under 5 percent of Congress's members. In 1989, twenty-four blacks (including one nonvoting delegate) served in the House, none in the Senate. Indeed, in all our history only about fifty blacks have served in Congress, three of them in the Senate and the rest in the House. Half of these served during the post-Civil War period of the nineteenth century. All were Republicans, loyal to the party of Lincoln. No blacks served in Congress from 1900 to 1928, when Oscar DePriest, a Republican, was elected from a heavily black district on Chicago's South Side. In the next twenty-five years only three more blacks entered Congress, but after the 1960s black representation rose steadily. And reflecting their longevity in Congress, more than half a dozen blacks have served as House committee chairmen. All but two of the twentieth-century black legislators were Democrats, reflecting blacks' modern-day partisan allegiance.

Black legislators typically see themselves representing members of their race wherever they may live. In 1971 they formed the Congressional Black Caucus, an alliance dedicated to working for policies of interest to blacks everywhere. They point out that, although very few constituencies are represented by blacks, no fewer than 172 districts have at least a 25 percent black population.[7] A few predominantly black districts are represented by whites.

Few blacks represent white areas; most come from minority-dominated districts. Of the blacks serving in the 1980s, only two came from areas of less than 50 percent minority population—Ron Dellums from Berkeley, California (39 percent minorities), and Alan Wheat of Kansas City, Missouri (25 percent). The average district represented by a black has a 67 percent minority population. Moreover, such districts tend to be in core cities dwindling in population. This suggests that black representation may have reached a plateau unless voters' attitudes change in predominantly white areas.

Other racial minorities are similarly underrepresented. Hispanics, who compose 5 percent of the nation's population, have no senators and only twelve representatives. Two senators and five representatives are Asian Americans. Other racial minorities are represented sporadically.

Unable to vote until 1920, women have always been underrepresented in Congress. Starting with Rep. Jeannette Rankin, R-Mont., elected in 1916, somewhat more than 125 women have been elected or appointed to Congress.

In 1989, two women served in the Senate (Nancy Landon Kassebaum, R-Kan., and Barbara A. Mikulski, D-Md.) and twenty-five in the House. At first, many women gained office on the death of husbands who were representatives or senators; some remained to have more notable careers than their husbands. As more women enter politics at all levels, the old tradition of the "widow's mandate" has faded, and women are being elected on their own merits.[8] Inevitably, the number of women lawmakers will rise.

Age and Tenure.   When the 101st Congress convened in January 1989, the average age in the two chambers was nearly fifty-three years. Representatives were in their early fifties, senators in their mid-fifties.[9] Early in our history, members of Congress usually were younger. House or Senate service was a part-time job, physically demanding but not especially exalted. Politicians stayed a few years and then moved on to other pursuits. After 1900, however, the seniority system and the political security of those from one-party areas—Democrats in the South, Republicans in the Midwest—led members to view congressional service as a long-term career. "Few die, and none retire," it was said. In the 1980s the average representative had served about 10.5 years, or 5.5 House terms. The average senator had served the same length of time, or 1.7 Senate terms. With each new election 10 percent or so of the two chambers' members are newcomers.

Trends in age and tenure reversed temporarily in the 1970s. Turnover was so high that by 1981 nearly half the representatives and fifty-five senators had served fewer than six years. Electoral defeats played some role, but most members left voluntarily. This "changing of the guard" involved both senior and junior members of Congress.[10] Veterans were disgruntled by new norms of scheduling, constituency attentiveness, and fund raising; newer members were dismayed by the job's low financial rewards and high costs—especially those borne by their families. In time, however, lawmakers seemed to adapt to contemporary working conditions; lower turnover in the 1980s reinforced membership stability.

A certain balance between new blood and stable membership is probably desirable for legislative bodies. "The youth is fine," observed Sen. Christopher Dodd, D-Conn., already in the top half of the House in seniority when he left in 1980 to enter the Senate, "but what we're missing to some degree is an institutional memory." [11] By the time the 101st Congress convened, fewer were newcomers: only 7 percent of the representatives and 10 percent of the senators.

Representation.   Must Congress demographically mirror the populace to be a representative institution? Probably not. At least an East Cambridge, Massachusetts, deli waitress didn't think so. When asked whether she was going to vote for another member of the Kennedy family, she retorted,

Are you kidding? I always vote for the Kennedys. They're like family. They're rich but they know all about us lower-class people.[12]

Legislators from farming districts can voice farmers' concerns even though they have never plowed a field; whites can champion equal opportunities for minorities. Few Hispanics serve in Congress, but the proportion of Hispanics in a district has been found to affect a member's support of issues supported by that group.[13] This is called *virtual representation*.

By and large, Congress is a body of local political pros for whom speaking for constituents comes naturally. Most of them keep in touch with the home folks without even thinking about it: a majority of representatives in one survey agreed with the statement that "I seldom have to sound out my constituents because I think so much like them that I know how to react to almost any proposal." [14]

Yet there is ultimately no real substitute for having a group's own member serve in Congress. When a member of an ethnic or racial minority goes to Congress, it is a badge of legitimacy for that group. Such legislators speak for members of their groups throughout the nation. Moreover, there are tangible gains in the quality of representation: the presence of those from underrepresented groups—women and minorities, for example—heightens Congress's sensitivity to issues such as parental leave, child care, and immigration.

Representation is not restrained by state or district boundaries. One member who suffers from epilepsy defends job rights for other sufferers from the disease; another whose grandson was born prematurely champions funds for medical research into birth defects; a third fled the Nazis as a child in the 1940s and has sworn to perpetuate awareness of the Holocaust. Such are causes close to members' hearts but virtually unnoticed by the press and public.

How Do Legislators Describe Their Jobs?

A few years ago the House Commission on Administrative Review asked 153 representatives to list "the major kinds of jobs, duties, or functions that you feel you are expected to perform as an individual member of Congress." This question elicited not so much the members' own priorities as their diverse perceptions of what colleagues, constituents, lobbyists, and others expect of them. The responses, summarized in Table 5-1, form a snapshot of members' jobs.[15]

Legislator. The rules, procedures, and traditions of the House and Senate place numerous constraints upon members' behavior. To be effective, new members must learn their way through the institutional maze. Legislators therefore stress the formal aspects of Capitol Hill duties and routines: legislative work, investigation, and committee specialization.

For many, being a legislator means gaining information and expertise on issues. One legislator declared:

Table 5-1   House Members' Views on the Jobs Expected of Them

Volunteered responses	Percentage[a]
Legislator	87
Constituency servant	79
Mentor/communicator	43
Representative	26
Politico	11
Overseer	9
Institutional broker	7
Office manager	6
Jack-of-all-trades	6
All other roles	4

Source: House Commission on Administrative Review, *Final Report,* 2 vols., H. Doc. 95-272, 95th Cong., 1st sess., December 31, 1977, 2: 874-875.
Note: $N = 146$.
[a] Many members mentioned two or more jobs.

> My first responsibility is to develop committee expertise. I'm expected to learn all there is to be known on an issue, to stay with it on a day-to-day basis. I want to be an expert, sought out by other members and able to help them.[16]

Expertise is pursued, not only because it is the way to shape public policy, but also because it sways others in the chamber.

The legislator's role dovetails with representing constituents. Most members seek committee assignments that will serve the needs of their states or districts. One House member related how his interest in flood control and water resource development impelled him to ask for a seat on the Public Works and Transportation Committee. "The interests of my district dictated my field of specialization," he explained, "but the decision to specialize in some legislative field is automatic for the member who wants to exercise any influence." [17]

Members soon learn the norms or folkways that expedite legislative bargaining and maximize productivity. Examining the post-World War II Senate, Donald Matthews identified six folkways governing behavior that were enforced in numerous informal ways. Senators should (1) serve an apprenticeship; (2) concentrate on Senate work rather than on gaining publicity; (3) specialize on issues within their committees or affecting their home states; (4) act courteously to colleagues; (5) extend reciprocity to colleagues—that is, provide willing assistance with the expectation that they will be repaid in kind one day; and (6) loyally defend the Senate, "the greatest legislative and deliberative body in the world." [18]

In recent years certain Senate folkways have faded in importance. New senators now participate immediately in most aspects of deliberation. Many senators, especially those with an eye on the White House, work tirelessly to attract national publicity and personal attention. Committee specialization, although still common, is less rigid than it once was: senators have numerous overlapping committee assignments and are expected to express views on a wide range of issues. Courtesy and reciprocity are still insisted upon, but institutional loyalty wears thin in an era of cynicism about government.[19]

The House relies more on formal channels of power than on informal norms. From interviews in the 1970s, however, Herbert Asher uncovered seven norms: (1) friendly relationships are desirable; (2) the important work of the House is done in committee; (3) procedural rules of the House are essential; (4) members should not personally criticize a colleague on the House floor; (5) members should be prepared to trade votes; (6) members should be specialists; and (7) freshmen members should serve apprenticeships.[20]

Even this loose network of norms has been diluted. Waves of new members, impatient with apprenticeship, plunge into the work of the House as soon as they learn their way around. Leadership comes earlier to members than it used to. Specialization is still attractive—more so in the House than in the Senate—but many members branch out into unrelated issues. No longer are committees the sole forums for influencing legislation. Looser norms of floor participation and voting have expanded members' chances for shaping bills outside their own committees' jurisdictions. Relaxation of norms such as apprenticeship and specialization is one aspect of the current diffusion of influence on Capitol Hill.[21]

Constituency Servant. Nearly eight out of ten respondents in the 1977 House survey mentioned the role of constituency servant. Constituency servants make sure their states or districts get their "fair share" of federal money and assistance. "It's a big pie down in Washington," former representative Michael "Ozzie" Myers, D-Pa., told FBI agents posing as aides of an Arab sheik.

> Each member's sent there to bring a piece of that pie back home. And if you go down there and you don't—you come back without milkin' it after a few terms . . . you don't go . . . back.[22]

The words are inelegant and the context sleazy, but the nub of truth is there. Members quickly develop a sharp eye for legislative provisions and how they affect particular areas. Often they join state and local officials in lobbying for federal funds or programs.

In addition to seeking a fat slice of the federal pie, a constituency servant attempts to solve citizens problems. This ombudsman role was cited by half the House members. Typically, this task is performed by legislators and their staffs as *casework*—individual cases triggered by constituent letters or visits. It is a chore that weighs heavily on members, even though many of them tire of it and most of them delegate it to staff aides. The philosophy of most legislators is expressed by one House member:

> Constituent work: that's something I feel very strongly about. The American people, with the growth of the bureaucracy, feel nobody cares. The only conduit a taxpayer has with the government is a congressional office.[23]

Sometimes members stress constituency service to gain breathing room for legislative stands that stray from district norms. This was a strategy successfully pursued by many Democrats of the 1974 "Watergate class"— thirty-six of whom captured seats formerly held by Republicans. Many combined a vigorous outreach program with some tailoring of positions for their districts.

Mentor/Communicator.   The mentor-communicator role is linked both to legislating and constituency errand running. Most members who stress this role view it in connection with issues that must be debated and voted on. As a respondent to the 1977 questionnaire phrased it:

> The role of the educator is first to learn, to assess the feelings of the district on particular issues, and to educate other members as to the aims of your constituency. To take the views of Washington back to the district. It's a two-way function.[24]

Another aspect of the mentor-communicator role is the act of keeping in touch with constituents by mail, by personal appearances, and by print and electronic media.

Closely allied is the role of the issue emissary (*representative*), articulated by a quarter of House members. Constituents expect their representatives to understand and express their views in Washington. This role is the essence of elective office, both in theory and in practice, and incumbents take it very seriously indeed.

Other Roles.   Some members act as Capitol Hill insiders and some as outsiders who adopt a maverick posture. Some members stress party leadership duties, others their social obligations, still others institutional brokerage—dealing with the executive branch, interest groups, and state and local governments. And a few members of Congress stress merely campaigning and gaining reelection. One former member placed this goal in perspective: "All members of Congress have a primary interest in being reelected. Some members have no other interest." [25]

How Do Legislators Spend Their Time?

Few things are more precious to senators and representatives than time; lack of it is their most frequent complaint about their jobs.[26] Allocating time requires exceedingly tough personal and political choices. Like the rest of us, legislators find that they lack the time to do all they want to do. So they, too, must reshape their expectations, and those of others, to conform to the real world of demands and resources.

Members' daily priorities are roughly as follows: (1) attend committee hearings, markups, and other committee meetings; (2) meet on legislative issues with constituents, government officials, lobbyists, and interest groups; (3) work back in the state or district; (4) study pending legislation or talk about legislation with other members or staff; (5) attend floor debate or watch the debate on television; (6) complete nonlegislative work (casework) for constituents in Washington; and (7) raise funds for the next campaign, for others' campaigns, or for the political party (see Table 5-2).[27] Staff members usually prepare daily schedules for members of Congress to refer to as they whirl through a busy day on Capitol Hill.

Scheduling is complicated by the large number of formal workgroups (committees, subcommittees)—more than 100 in the Senate, about 180 in the House—not counting joint, party, or ad hoc panels. These units offer senators more than 1,000 seats or positions, and representatives nearly 3,000 (see Chapter 7). The average senator sits on three to four committees and about seven subcommittees; representatives average two committees and five subcommittees. Leadership posts abound: nearly all majority party senators (now Democrats) and about half of all Democratic representatives chair a committee or subcommittee. The minority party's members are by no means left out: most of their senators and 80 percent of their representatives are ranking members of committees or subcommittees.

With so many assignments, lawmakers are hard pressed to control their crowded schedules. Scheduling problems are endemic. Committee quorums are difficult to achieve, and members' attentions are often focused elsewhere. During peak times—midweek (Tuesdays through Thursdays) and midsession (March through July)—members constantly face scheduling conflicts among two, three, or more of their committees.[28] Even within committees, scheduling can be haphazard. Quite often working sessions are composed of the chairman, perhaps one or two colleagues, and staff aides. Repeated floor votes, which lawmakers fear to miss, are another time-consuming duty. "We're like automatons," one senator said. "We spend our time walking in tunnels to go to the floor to vote." [29]

According to a study based on time logs kept by senators' appointment secretaries, lawmakers' daily schedules in Washington are "long, fragmented, and unpredictable"—adjectives that aptly describe representatives' days as well.[30] Members' schedules are splintered into so many tiny bits and pieces that effective pursuit of lawmaking, oversight, and constituent service is hampered. According to a management study of several senators' offices, an event occurs every five minutes, on the average, to which the senator or the chief aide must respond personally.[31] Often members have scant notice that

Table 5-2   Activities of Members of Congress: Actual and Ideal
(in percentages)

Activity	Time actually spent				Time would like to spend			
	Great deal	Some	A little	Almost none	Great deal	Some	A little	Almost none
Attend committee hearings, markups, other meetings	74	24	2	—	58	38	5	—
Meet on legislative issues with constituents, lobbyists, officials	61	34	5	—	23	57	16	4
Study pending legislation; talk about it with members, staff	24	61	13	2	63	35	1	1
Attend floor debate or follow it on television	13	46	35	7	25	49	20	6
Do nonlegislative work for constituents in Washington	13	35	35	17	9	24	40	27
Raise funds for the next campaign, for others, or for the party	10	22	38	30	2	13	27	59
Work back in the state	52	38	9	1	42	41	14	3

Source: Center for Responsive Politics, *Congressional Operations: Congress Speaks—A Survey of the 100th Congress* (Washington, D.C.: Center for Responsive Politics, 1988), 65-67.

Note: Senators and representatives were presented a list of activities and asked to indicate "how much time you spent on each activity in a typical week from last year." They were given the same list and asked how they would most *like* to spend their time. Of the 114 senators and representatives surveyed in the winter and spring of 1987, 111 and 112 responded to these questions.

their presence is required at a meeting or hearing. Carefully developed schedules can be disrupted by changes in meeting hours, by unexpected events, or by sessions that run longer than anticipated.

Political scientists may contend that Congress runs in harmony with members' needs, but the members think otherwise. In a 1987 survey of 114 House and Senate members, "inefficiency" was the thing that most surprised them about Congress (45 percent gave this response).[32] If given a free hand, members would like to spend more time studying and discussing legislation with colleagues and staff and following the floor debates. They would prefer to spend less time attending committee meetings, raising money for campaigns, and doing constituency casework (see Table 5-2).

In most cases senators felt more strongly about altering their work day than did representatives. Members, especially in the Senate, advocate schedule rearrangements that will facilitate planning and better use of their time. And they regret that their duties permit little time for personal and family affairs. Nearly half the respondents in the 1987 survey agreed that they had "no personal time after work"; a third said they had "no time for family." [33]

The dilemma legislators face in allocating their time is far more than a matter of scheduling. It is a case of conflicting role expectations. Look again at Table 5-2, where lawmakers' activities are arrayed to illustrate the tensions inherent in the two Congresses, from the legislative Congress (at the top of the list) to the representative Congress (at the bottom). By and large, members want to devote more time and effort to legislative duties and somewhat less time to constituency and political chores. The two Congresses pull members in different directions, and there is no pat formula for allocating time. As former House Budget Committee chairman Robert Giaimo, D-Conn., put it:

> One problem is that you're damned if you do and damned if you don't. If you do your work here, you're accused of neglecting your district. And if you spend too much time in your district, you're accused of neglecting your work here.[34]

Looking Homeward

Not all of a representative's or senator's duties lie in Washington, D.C. As we have stressed, legislators not only fashion policy for the nation's welfare; they also act as emissaries from their home states or districts. These dual spheres pervade legislators' consciousness and often create vexing day-to-day dilemmas. These choices are another reminder that members of Congress live in two distinct worlds, not just one.

What Is Representation?

Although found in virtually all political structures, representation most typifies democratic regimes dedicated to sharing power among citizens. In small communities, decisions can be reached by face-to-face discussion, but in populous societies this sort of personalized consultation is impossible. Thus, according to traditional democratic theory, citizens can exert control by choosing "fiduciary agents" to act on their behalf, deliberating on legislation just as their principals, the voters, would do if they could be on hand themselves.[35] Hanna Pitkin puts it this way:

> The representative must act in such a way that, although he is indepen-
> dent, and his constituents are capable of action and judgment, no conflict
> arises between them. He must act in their interest, and this means he must
> not normally come into conflict with their wishes.[36]

The arrangement does not always work out precisely as democratic theory
specifies. Unless it works fairly well most of the time, however, the system is
defective.

Incumbent legislators give high priority to representation. As we have
seen, four of five House members interviewed in 1977 saw themselves as
constituency servants. Many were mentor-communicators, others issue
spokespersons. In an earlier survey of eighty-seven members, the role most
often expressed was called the tribune: the discoverer, reflector, or advocate of
popular needs and wants.[37]

While legislators agree on the importance of representation, they
interpret it differently. One point of departure is Edmund Burke's dictum
that legislators should voice the "general reason of the whole," rather than
speak merely for "local purposes" and "local prejudices." [38] Burke's viewpoint has always had its admirers, and legislators who adhere to this notion in
the face of hostile public sentiment can at least hope for history's vindication.
Yet electoral realities mar the Burkean ideal. Burke himself was eventually
turned out of office for his candor. Modern electorates, motivated by self-
interest and schooled in democratic norms, prefer legislators who follow
instructions rather than exercise independent judgments.[39]

Two dimensions are embedded in the traditional distinction between the
Burkean Trustee and the Instructed Delegate. One turns on legislators' *styles
of representation:* whether they accept instructions (Delegate), act upon their
own initiatives (Trustee), or act upon some combination of the two (Politico).
The second is the *focus of representation:* whether legislators think primarily
in terms of the whole nation, in terms of their constituencies, or some
combination of these. Although conceptually distinct, style and focus of
representation are closely related. One study attempted to classify House
members according to their basic approaches to representation; the results are
shown in Table 5-3.

In practice, legislators assume different representational styles according
to the occasion; that is, they are Politicos. From his interviews with eighty-one
House members, David C. Kozak concluded that role orientations varied with
a "force field" of factors, including the amount of available information and
the level of controversy (whether the issue was "hot").[40] According to Thomas
Cavanagh, members ponder factors such as the nation's welfare, personal
convictions, and constituency opinions. "The weight assigned to each factor
varies according to the nature of the issue at hand, the availability of the
information necessary for a decision, and the intensity of preference of the
people concerned about the issue." [41]

Most lawmakers develop sophisticated ways of thinking about the

Table 5-3   Representational Roles of Eighty-Seven House Members

Representational styles		Representational focus	
Role	Percentage	Role	Percentage
Trustee	28	Nation dominant	28
Politico	46	Nation-district equal	23
Delegate	23	District dominant	42
Undetermined	3	Nongeographic	5
		Undetermined	3

Source: Roger H. Davidson, *The Role of the Congressman* (Indianapolis: Bobbs-Merrill, 1969), 117, 122.

choices they make, distinguishing those for which they can play the Trustee from those for which the Delegate mode is expected or appropriate. "Hot votes are associated with a delegate role and a local orientation," Kozak writes. "On low profile decisions, a perceived Trustee role and national orientation dominate." [42] Respondents in the 1977 House survey cited two categories of issues they reserved for personal conscience or discretion: issues of overwhelming national importance, such as foreign policy and national defense, and issues that entailed deep-seated convictions, such as abortion, gun control, or constitutional questions. In contrast, members said they deferred to districts on economic issues, such as public works, social needs, military projects, and farm programs. They give unqualified support to district needs because, as they see it, no other member is likely to do so.

If lawmakers fail to speak up for their constituents' interests, they will hear about it. "No effort will be spared," vowed Rep. Thomas J. Downey, D-N.Y., as he and his colleagues launched a campaign to save the Grumman Corporation's F-14 Tomcat fighter—a weapon that meant $2.4-billion savings to defense budget makers but 15,000 jobs to Long Island communities. "It's a no guts, no glory sort of issue," Downey explained. "If you win, you get to remind people of that. If you lose, you're going to have some explaining to do." [43]

When members of Congress act, take a position, or cast a vote, they weigh constituencies against their own knowledge and convictions. One element in the calculus is the knowledge that they may be called upon to *explain* their choices to constituents—no matter how many or how few people truly care about the matter.[44] The anticipated need to explain oneself shapes a member's choices and in fact is part of the dilemma of choice.

Consider the pay raises for members of Congress that are periodically debated on Capitol Hill and across the country, most recently in early 1989. Most members favor pay hikes but vote against them precisely because they fear explaining their support to skeptical constituents.

What Are Constituencies?

No senator or representative is elected by, interacts with, or responds to all the people in a given state or district. The constituencies fixed in lawmakers' minds as they campaign or vote may be quite different from the boundaries found on maps. Richard F. Fenno, Jr., describes a "nest" of constituencies, ranging from the widest (geographic constituency) to the narrowest (personal constituency), which is made up of supporters, loyalists, and intimates.[45]

Geographic and Demographic Constituencies. The average House district in the 1980s exceeded 550,000 people, the average state nearly 5 million. Because constituencies today are so much larger than in the early Congresses, face-to-face contacts have been replaced by a kind of building-block approach. Members view the electorate as an interlocking chain of locales, neighborhoods, factions, and groups. When they speak also of "the state" or "the district," it is usually such a network of blocks.

Politicians also are fond of talking about geographical subregions and their distinctive voting habits. Colorado, split by the Continental Divide, consists of an "eastern slope" and a "western slope." Western Connecticut's 5th Congressional District is split between the Naugatuck Valley's old mill towns with their blue-collar voters and the comfortable bedroom communities of conservative Fairfield County. Southern California's sprawling 37th district embraces smog-ridden suburbs around Riverside, irrigated farmland of the Coachella Valley, and wealthy desert oases of Palm Springs and Palm Desert where Gerald Ford, Bob Hope, and Frank Sinatra reside. Of course, such distinctions are grossly simplified. Most states and House districts contain diverse racial, ethnic, economic, and social groups.

Social and economic shifts can alter the face of electoral units. In 1960 Tucson was regarded a Democratic stronghold. But since then its population has soared as elderly people have retired to the Sun Belt. "Every time there's a blizzard in Buffalo or Detroit, we get 5,000 more conservative retirees in the district," said a campaign aide to Democratic representative Morris K. Udall.[46] Udall's initial constituency has steadily eroded, but he has hung on through bold campaigning, constituency service, and (in 1982) friendly redistricting.

As a rule, demographics are linked to partisan differences in voting. Because of this some areas are traditionally "Democratic" and others "Republican." In general, Democratic leanings are associated with the following demographic characteristics: dense population, blue-collar workers, ethnic groupings, nonwhite and noncollege educated residents, low-income families, and rental housing. Republican areas tend to display the opposite characteristics.[47]

In a sense, partisan differences are constituency differences translated into issues. Members whose voting records deviate from their party's norm may simply represent areas with attributes associated with the opposition party.[48] In the 1980s, for example, the "deviant" Republicans in the Senate included Arlen Specter of Pennsylvania and John Chafee of Rhode Island—both northeasterners. By the same token, the "maverick" Democrats—Richard C. Shelby of Alabama and David L. Boren of Oklahoma, for example—were from border or southern states.[49] Many of the House "Boll Weevils"—conservative Democrats who in 1981 backed President Reagan's budget and tax policies in defiance of their party leaders—hailed from areas where Reagan was popular. With the nationalization of our politics, these regional variations are fading: fewer southern boll weevil Democrats, or northeastern GOP liberals, are to be found these days. Some of these areas are now represented by parties new to them: Democrats in the North and West, Republicans in the South.[50] Other areas have simply lost much of their regional individuality.

Demographically, constituencies may be *homogeneous* or *heterogeneous*.[51] Some constituencies are uniform and one dimensional—mostly tobacco farmers or urban ghetto dwellers or small-town citizens. Others are diverse and embrace numerous, and not necessarily harmonious, interests. Compatibility is crucial: districts vary not only in numbers of interests but also in the level of conflict among them. "The less conflict a congressman perceives among his district interests," Fenno wrote, "the more likely he is to see his district as homogeneous, and the more conflict he perceives among district interests, the more likely he is to see his district as heterogeneous." [52]

Seasoned political observers instinctively recognize differences between homogeneous and heterogeneous constituencies, even though the concept lacks specificity and as a result has rarely been scrutinized by scholars. The following hypotheses seem plausible:

- States are more heterogeneous than House districts, in part because of their greater size.
- Because of increasing size, economic complexity, and educational levels, all constituencies, House as well as Senate, have become more heterogeneous.
- The more heterogeneous a constituency, the more challenging the representative's task.
- Increasingly heterogeneous districts may lead legislators to cultivate nonissue ties with voters (casework, local appearances, home style).[53]

Another attribute of constituencies is electoral balance, especially the incumbent's safeness or vulnerability. This is not the same thing as heterogeneity, although mixed districts tend to be more competitive than uniform ones. Needless to say, incumbents prefer "safe" districts—ones that contain a high proportion of groups sympathetic to their partisan or ideological stance. Not only do safe districts favor reelection; they also imply that voters will be easier to please.

Truly competitive districts, especially in the House, are comparatively rare (see Table 5-4). The number of competitive districts declined in the

Table 5-4 House and Senate Margins of Victory, 1970-1988

Election year	Percentage of vote				(N)
	Under 55	55-59.9	60 plus	Unopposed	
House					
1970	14	15	58	14	(435)
1972	15	14	59	12	(435)
1974	24	16	46	14	(435)
1976	17	14	56	12	(435)
1978	17	14	53	16	(435)
1980	18	14	60	8	(435)
1982	16	16	63	6	(435)
1984	12	13	61	14	(435)
1986	9	10	64	17	(435)
1988	6	9	67	18	(435)
Senate					
1970	40	23	33	3	(30)
1972	55	12	33	—	(33)
1974	41	18	35	6	(34)
1976	30	33	30	6	(33)
1978	24	33	36	6	(33)
1980	58	18	21	3	(34)
1982	30	27	43	—	(33)
1984	18	21	58	3	(33)
1986	38	15	47	—	(34)
1988	24	15	55	—	(33)

Source: *Congressional Quarterly Weekly Report* and authors' calculations.

1960s. Conversely, the proportion of elections captured by wide margins (60 percent or more of the two-party vote) has risen.[54] During the post-World War II years, about six out of every ten House elections were "safe" for the winner; after 1966 that figure rose to seven or eight out of ten. The Senate picture is more clouded, but in the 1980s about half the contests were won by comfortable margins.

Yet few incumbents regard themselves as truly "safe." The threat of losing is very real. A large majority of lawmakers have a close race at some time in their congressional careers, and a third of them eventually suffer defeat.[55] Incumbents worry not only about winning or losing but also about their margins of safety. Downturns in normal electoral support narrow the member's "breathing space" in the job and may invite challengers for future contests.[56]

Paradoxically, as members have become more successful at winning reelection, they seem less willing to make decisions that could stir controversy.

The heightened heterogeneity of constituencies is partly to blame as more and more issues arouse conflicting pressures. Another factor is members' heavy reliance on campaign funds and support from interest groups. If legislators resist the groups' priorities, they may face adverse publicity, unwanted controversy, and antagonistic voting blocs in the next election.

Political and Personal Constituencies. Inside the geographic and demographic constituencies are narrower "constituencies" that exist, often imprecisely, in candidates' or incumbents' minds as they analyze their electoral units: supporters (the reelection constituency); loyalists (the primary constituency); and intimates (the personal constituency).[57]

Supporters are people expected to vote favorably on election day. Of course, some of them do not. Candidates and their advisers repeatedly reassess these voters based on the area's political demography—registration figures, survey data, and recent electoral trends. The more elections a candidate has surmounted, the more precise ought to be the notions of where support comes from, reinforced by the most recent election results.

In waging campaigns, candidates and their managers pinpoint areas and groups with the biggest payoff—that is, sympathetic voters who can be persuaded to support and vote for the candidate. Such voters are not necessarily the candidate's most ardent supporters, but a little effort with them can pay off in a big way.

At the other end are groups rated as "hopeless" because they rarely vote for the candidate. Like most of us, legislators prefer to spend time with people whose outlook parallels their own. Contacts with hostile groups might seem futile, but candidates need to meet with such groups occasionally to "show the flag" and perhaps neutralize the opposition.

Loyalists are the politician's staunchest supporters and form the last line of electoral defense in a primary contest or other threat. They include early supporters and colleagues from preelectoral activities. For members once active in antiwar, civil rights, or environmental causes, they include people first drawn together in those movements. For other members, loyalists may be concentrated in religious or ethnic groups, political or civic clubs, or simply "friends and neighbors." From home-district travels with representatives, Fenno derived the notion of "at homeness" to denote the closeness between politicians and constituents.[58] Invariably, members felt most at home with loyalists, expressing their closeness with banter and familiar talk.

Loyalists are a bedrock campaign resource in terms of volunteer labor or financial contributions. For this reason candidates cannot ignore their loyalists. One of the favorite stories of Thomas P. "Tip" O'Neill, Jr., the former Speaker of the House, comes from his first, unsuccessful campaign for city council. A neighbor lady is supposed to have told him, "Tom, I'm going to vote for you even though you didn't ask me." "Mrs. O'Brien," replied a surprised O'Neill, "I've lived across the street from you for 18 years. I shovel your walk in the winter. I cut your grass in the summer. I didn't think I had to ask you for your vote." To this the lady replied: "Tom, I want you to know something: people like to be asked." [59]

Intimates are close friends who supply political advice and emotional support. Nearly every candidate or incumbent knows a few of them. They may be members of the candidate's family, trusted staff members, political mentors, or individuals who shared decisive experiences early in the candidate's career.

Fenno relates the following account of an informal gathering of intimates one Sunday afternoon in the home of a representative's chief district aide. Also present were the representative, a state assemblyman from the member's home county, and the district attorney of the same county.

> Between plays and at halftime, over beer and cheese, the four friends discussed every aspect of the congressman's campaign, listened to and commented on his taped radio spots, analyzed several newspaper reports, discussed local and national personalities, relived old political campaigns and hijinks, and discussed their respective political ambitions. Ostensibly they were watching the football game. Actually, the congressman was exchanging political advice, information, and perspectives with three of his oldest and closest political associates.[60]

The setting and the players differ from state to state and from district to district. Tip O'Neill's inner circle was the "boys" of Barry's Corner, a local club whose members and families he'd known intimately for over fifty years in political life. For Sen. J. Bennett Johnston, D-La., the inner circle is a "family" of long-time supporters and lobbyists who deal with his Energy and Natural Resources Committee and who raise funds for his political action committee, "Pelican PAC." [61] Such intimates play an indispensable role: they provide unvarnished advice on political matters and serve as sounding boards for ideas and strategies. The danger is that they may give faulty advice or inaccurately assess the larger constituencies. Long-term incumbents run a special risk if their intimates lose touch with constituency shifts. Politicians confront the constant dilemma of which advisers to trust; more than most of us, they pay a public price for those who fall short.

Home Styles

Legislators evolve distinctive ways of projecting themselves and their records to their constituents—what Fenno calls their home style. One aspect of this is the socio-psychological notion of presentation of self.[62] Legislators gain responses from others by expressing themselves in ways that leave distinct impressions or images. Such expressions may be verbal or nonverbal. Another facet of home style is how members explain what they have been doing while away from their home states or districts.

Legislators' home styles are communicated in various ways: personal appearances, mailings, newsletters, telephone conversations, radio or television spots, and press releases. We know little about how home styles arise, but they are linked to members' personalities, backgrounds, constituency features, and resources. The concept of home style shifts the focus of constituency linkage from *representation* to *presentation*. As Fenno states, "It is the style, not the issue content, that counts most in the reelection constituency." [63]

Presentation of Self. The core ingredient of a successful home style is trust—faith that legislators are what they claim to be and will do what they promise.[64] Winning voters' trust does not happen overnight; it takes time. Three major ingredients of trust are: *qualification,* the belief that legislators are capable of handling the job, a critical threshold that nonincumbents especially must cross; *identification,* the impression that legislators resemble their constituents, that they are part of the state or region; and *empathy,* the sense that legislators understand constituents' problems and care about them.

Given variations among legislators and constituencies, there are countless available home styles that effectively build the trust relationship. The legendary Speaker "Mr. Sam" Rayburn represented his East Texas district for nearly fifty years (1913-1961) as a plain dirt farmer. Once back in his home town of Bonham, his drawl thickened; his tailored suits were exchanged for khakis, old shirt, and slouch hat; and he traveled in a well-dented pickup truck, not the Speaker's limousine he used in the capital. A biographer relates:

> If Rayburn ever chewed tobacco in Washington, a long-time aide could not recall it, but in Bonham he always seemed to have a plug in his cheek. He made certain always to spit in the fireplace at his home when constituents were visiting, so that if nothing else, they would take away the idea that Mr. Sam was just a plain fellow.[65]

Today's legislators are no less inventive in fashioning home styles. Congressman A employs a direct style rooted in face-to-face contacts with people in his primary constituency. He rarely mentions issues because most people in his district agree on them. Congressman B, a popular local athlete, uses the national defense issue to symbolize his oneness with a district supportive of military preparedness. Congressman C displays himself as an issue-oriented, verbal activist who is not at home with conventional politicians. And so on; the repertoire of home styles is virtually limitless.

Voters are likely to remember style long after they forget issue pronouncements or votes. As one member told Fenno, "Most voters vote more on style than they do on issues." [66] Many legislators agree with and act upon this assumption.

Explaining Washington Activity. Even if the average voter is attracted less by issues than by style, incumbents are frequently challenged to explain what they have done while away from home. As we have noted, legislators make decisions in full awareness that they have to explain them to others.[67] Explaining is an integral part of decision making. In home-district forums, members expect to be able to describe, interpret, and justify their actions. If constituents do not agree with the member's conclusions, they may at least respect the decision-making style.

> They don't know much about my votes. Most of what they know is what I tell them. They know more of what kind of a guy I am. It comes through in my letters: "You care about the little guy."[68]

While few incumbents fear that a single vote can defeat them, all realize that voter disenchantment with their total record can be fatal. Thus, members stockpile reasons for virtually every position they take—often more than are needed. For thorny choices, an independent stance may be the best defense. Politicians tend to give the same account of themselves, no matter what group they are talking to. (Inconsistency, after all, is mentally costly—and can be politically costly as well.)

Legislators' accounts of Washington convey little of Congress's institutional life. Indeed, in explaining their behavior members often belittle this other Congress—portraying themselves as knight-errants battling against sinister forces and feckless colleagues.

Constituency Careers. Constituency ties evolve over the course of a senator's or representative's career. Constituency careers have at least two recognizable stages: *expansionism* and *protectionism*. In the first or expansionist stage the member constructs a reelection constituency by solidifying the help of hardcore supporters and reaching out to attract added blocs of support. This aggressive expansionism plus enterprising use of the perquisites of incumbency, such as the election year avalanche of mail to constituents, account for the "sophomore surge"—in which newcomers typically boost their margin in their first reelection bid.[69] In the second or protectionist stage the member ceases to expand the base of support, content with hoarding already-won support. Once established, a successful style is rarely altered.

Several developments might, however, lead to a change in constituency style. One would be a *contextual* change in the constituency: a population shift or redistricting that forces a member to cope with unfamiliar voters or territory. A second cause would be *strategic*, as a fresh challenger or a novel issue threatens established voting patterns. Because coalitions may shift over time, the results of the past election (or, if available, survey findings) are carefully scanned.

Finally, home styles may change with *personal* goals and ambitions. A member may seek higher office or may lose touch with voters and reject the reelection goal entirely. Growing responsibilities in Washington can divert attention from home business. Thirteen-term representative Charles Vanik, D-Ohio, retired with the following comments on these tensions:

When you become the most effective in this job, when you reach ... the epitome of your usefulness, you do so at the price of failing to keep up local communications. . . .

With me, it was a case of whether I wanted to refurbish my political base by being on the scene on an almost weekly, hourly basis back home and also of raising money, which I've lost the art of doing.[70]

Confronted with new aspirations and shifting constituency demands, not a few members decide to retire. Others struggle ineffectively and are defeated. Still others rejuvenate their constituency base and survive.

Office of the Member, Inc.

Home style is more than a philosophy for weighing constituents' claims. It affects how a member answers day-to-day questions: How much attention should I devote to state or district needs? How much time should I spend in the state or district? How should I maintain contact with my constituents? How should I deploy my staff aides to deal with constituents' concerns? One of the most vexing problems is how to balance demands for being in Washington with the need to be back home with constituents.

Road Tripping

During the nineteenth century legislators spent much of their time at home, traveling to Washington only when Congress was in session. After World War II, however, congressional sessions lengthened until they spanned virtually the entire year. Legislators began to set up permanent residence in the nation's capital—a practice that would have struck earlier voters as verging on arrogance. By the 1970s both houses adopted parallel schedules of sessions punctuated with brief "district work periods" (House) or "nonlegislative periods" (Senate).

At the same time the two houses authorized more paid trips to states or districts. In the early 1960s senators and representatives were allowed three government-paid trips home each year. Today they are allowed as many trips home as they want, subject to their official expense allowance limits. One researcher found a steady increase in the number of trips by House members during the 1970s.[71] In 1970 representatives spent close to fifteen weeks during the year in their congressional districts; by 1976 members were in their districts during twenty-two weeks of the year.

Travel increased for all members. However, the more time consuming it is to get home, the less often will members make the trip. When members' families are in Washington, they are less inclined to travel. Seniority is also a factor: senior members make fewer trips to their districts than junior members—perhaps reflecting junior members' greater district attentiveness. Members tend to avoid their districts during periods of congressional unpopularity but spend more time there during adverse economic conditions. As election day approaches, representatives stay closer to their districts.[72]

Constituency Casework

"All God's chillun got problems," exclaimed colorful former representative Billy Matthews, D-Fla., one day while brooding over constituent mail.[73] Helping citizens cope with the federal bureaucracy is a major task of every congressional office. While not all members are eager to handle casework personally, all of them concede that prompt and effective casework pays off at election time. This applies to senators no less than to representatives. "Many freshmen view their role differently than twenty-five years ago, when a senator was only a legislator," says Sen. Richard C. Shelby, D-Ala. "Now a senator is also a grantsman, an ombudsman, and a caseworker, and cannot ignore those other roles. When we are asked by our constituents to help, we can't say we don't have time because we are focusing on national and international issues." [74]

More numerous and more sophisticated electorates, not to mention the government's larger role in citizens' lives, have pushed legislators into the casework business in a big way. A few years ago, representatives estimated their average caseload at slightly more than 10,000 cases a year. Senators from small states averaged between 1,000 and 2,000; large-state senators had from 8,000 to 70,000 cases. Senators from New York and California received between 30,000 and 50,000 cases each year.[75]

As these figures suggest, casework loads vary from state to state and district to district. Some House offices studied by John R. Johannes handled no more than 5 or 10 cases a week, others nearly 500.[76] In both chambers senior legislators apparently receive proportionately more casework requests than do junior members.[77] Perhaps senior legislators are considered more powerful and better equipped to resolve constituents' problems; legislators themselves certainly cultivate this image in seeking reelection. Demographic variations among electorates can affect casework volume: some citizens are simply more apt to have contact with government agencies than others.

What are these "cases" all about? As reported by respondents in a nationwide survey, the most frequent reason for contacting a member's office (16 percent of all cases) is to express views or obtain information on legislative issues. Requests for help in finding government jobs form the next largest category, followed by cases dealing with government services such as Social Security, veterans' benefits, or unemployment compensation. Military cases (exemptions from service, discharges, transfers) are numerous, as are tax, legal, and immigration problems. Many are simply requests for information or government publications: copies of legislative bills and reports, executive branch regulations, agricultural yearbooks, infant care booklets, and tourist information about the nation's capital. And there are requests for flags that have flown over the U.S. Capitol (a special flagpole on the south side of the

Capitol is reserved for such flags, which are continually hoisted and lowered for that purpose).[78] Most cases come to legislators' offices by letter, although phone calls or walk-ins at district or mobile offices are not uncommon. Occasionally members themselves pick up cases from talking to constituents; many hold office hours in their districts for this purpose. When a request is received, it is usually acknowledged immediately by a letter that either fills the request or promises that an answer will be forthcoming.

If the request requires contacting a federal agency, caseworkers do this by phone, letter, or buckslip (a preprinted referral form).[79] Usually the contact in the executive agency is a liaison officer, although some caseworkers prefer to deal directly with line officers or regional officials. Once the problem has been conveyed, it is a matter of time before a decision is reached and a reply forwarded to the congressional office. The reply is then sent along to the constituent, perhaps with a covering letter signed by the member. If the agency's reply is deemed faulty, the caseworker may challenge it and ask for reconsideration, and in some cases the member may be brought in to lend weight to the appeal.

From all accounts, casework pays off in citizen support for individual legislators. In a 1977 national survey, 15 percent of all adults reported that they or members of their families had requested help from their representative.[80] Seven out of ten of them said that they were satisfied with the way their requests had been handled. As Morris P. Fiorina put it, "pork barreling and casework . . . are almost pure profit." [81]

Some criticize constituency casework as unfair or biased in practice. Citizens may not enjoy equal access to senators' or representatives' offices. Political supporters or cronies may get favored treatment at others' expense. Finally, administrative agencies may be pressured into giving special treatment to congressional requests, distorting the administration of laws.

A few critics advocate an independent, nonpartisan office of constituent relations, modeled after the Scandinavian *ombudsman*.[82] Although an arm of the legislature, such a facility would work independently of both members' offices and executive agencies. Proposals for an ombudsman's office have never taken hold at the national level, although they have been adopted by some states, municipalities, and administrative agencies. No doubt the leading reason is that senators and representatives don't want to forfeit the credit and advertising benefits of casework. When federal grants, contracts, or subsidies are allocated to a state or district, it is customary for the member to announce the award and thus claim some credit for it. Members of Congress enjoy another key advantage in performing the casework function: they have leverage over administrative agencies because their votes create those agencies and supply them with funds. This sort of clout would not be wielded by an independent office whose power was confined to recommending and publicizing.

Personal Staff

Representatives and senators head sizable office enterprises that reflect their "two Congresses" responsibilities. In 1989 each House member was entitled to an annual clerk-hire allowance of $379,480. With this money members may hire no more than eighteen full-time and four part-time employees. The average House member's staff numbers about fifteen. (Members' allowances are detailed on page 141.)

Representatives also are entitled to an annual official expenses allowance, which in 1989 amounted to more than $200,000. This money is used for travel, telecommunication, district office rental, office equipment, stationery, postage, computer services, and mass mailings.

Senators' personal staffs range in size from thirteen to seventy-one, with an average of about thirty-one. Unlike the House, there are no limits on the number of staff a senator may employ from clerk-hire money, which varies according to a state's population. In 1989 the allowance ranged from $716,012 for a senator representing fewer than 2 million people to $1,458,856 for a senator from a state with 21 million. There are sixteen population categories. Similarly, a senator's official expenses account varies from $36,000 to $156,000, depending upon factors such as the state's population and its distance from Washington, D.C.[83]

Staff Organization.   No two congressional offices are exactly alike. Each is shaped by the personality, interests, constituency, and position of the individual legislator. Members' role expectations are imprinted upon their staff organization. Those who specialize in legislation hire experts in the legislative process; those who stress constituency service closely supervise caseworkers. Political aspirants hire seasoned press aides and put great stock in producing press releases, targeted mailings, and radio and TV spots.

State and district needs weigh heavily in members' thinking about staff organization. Some districts require attention to government projects or programs; others have a large casework burden. A farm-state senator likely will employ at least one specialist in agricultural problems; an urban representative might hire a consumer affairs or housing expert. Traditions are important. If a legislator's predecessor had an enviable reputation for a certain kind of service, the new incumbent will dare not let it lapse.

The member's institutional position also affects staff organization. Committee and subcommittee chairmen have committee staff at their disposal. Members without such aides rely heavily on personal staff for committee work.

Staff Functions.   Most House and Senate personal aides are young and well educated, usually remaining in their positions about four years. The mix of personal staff functions is decided by each member. Most hire

Congressional Allowances, 1989

	House	Senate
Salary[a]	$ 89,500	$ 89,500
Washington office		
Clerk-hire	$379,480	$716,102-$1,458,856[b]
Committee legislative assistants	—[c]	$243,543
Interns	$ 2,000	—
General office expenses	$ 67,000	$ 36,000-$156,000[b]
Telephone/telegraph	15,000 long-distance minutes to district	—[d]
Stationery	—[d]	1.8-26.6 million pieces[b]
Office space	2,500 sq. ft.	4,800-8,000 sq. ft.
Furnishings	—[d]	—[d]
Equipment	Provided	Provided
District/state offices		
Rental	2,500 sq. ft.	4,800-8,000 sq. ft.
Furnishings/equipment	$ 35,000	$ 30,000-$41,744
Mobile office	—	one
Communications	—[d]	
Automated correspondence		Provided by Senate computer center
Audio/video recordings; photography	—[d]	—[d]
Travel	Formula (min. $6,200; max. approx. $67,200)	—[d]

Sources: Committee on House Administration; Senate Committee on Rules and Administration.

Note: In some cases no dollar value is given because of the difficulty in determining the range of reimbursed costs—for example, in travel or telephone reimbursements. Most of the 1989 allowances are transferable from one account to another.

[a] Established January 1, 1987; leaders' salaries are higher.
[b] A sliding scale linked to the state's population.
[c] Provided for members of Appropriations, Budget, and Rules committees.
[d] Covered within the "General office expenses" category. In most cases supplies and equipment are charged at rates well below retail levels.

administrative assistants (AAs), legislative assistants (LAs), caseworkers, and press aides as well as a few people from the home state or district. The administrative assistant supervises the office and imparts political and legislative advice. Often he or she functions as the legislator's alter ego, negotiating with colleagues, constituents, and lobbyists. Legislative assistants work with members in committees, draft bills, write speeches, suggest policy initiatives, analyze bills, and prepare position papers. They also monitor committee sessions that the member cannot attend.

Some members organize their personal staff differently. For example, Rep. William Natcher, D-Ky., "has no press secretary, administrative assistant or legislative assistant. Instead of the twenty-two aides to which he is entitled, he has eight, six in Washington and two in his district in West Central Kentucky. All are women." [84]

To emphasize the "personal touch," many members have moved casework staff to their home districts or states. In 1970, there were 1,035 district-based House staffers; in 1974, 1,519; and in 1987, 2,503.[85] At the same time there were 1,152 Senate staff based in state offices, compared with 303 in 1972. Virtually all House and Senate members have home offices in post offices or federal buildings; some members have as many as five or six. With the decline of party workers to assist local citizens, members' district staffs fill this need and, simultaneously, enhance members' reelection prospects.

Many other reasons are cited for decentralizing constituent functions. Congressional office buildings on Capitol Hill are crowded. Field offices have lower staff salaries and lower overhead. They are also more convenient for constituents, local and state officials, and regional federal officers. Computers and fax machines make it easy for Washington offices and district offices to communicate.[86] This decentralizing trend, which is likely to continue, implies a heightened division between legislative functions based on Capitol Hill and constituency functions based in field offices. "Office of the Member, Inc.," in other words, is increasingly split into headquarters and branch divisions— with the Capitol Hill branch dealing with legislative duties and the state or district office dealing with constituents.

Members and the Media

Both chambers' office allowances amply support lawmakers' unceasing struggle for media attention. Members' offices resemble the mail distribution division of a large business. Every day stacks of printed matter are released for wide distribution. In addition to press releases, newsletters, and individual and mass mailings, members communicate through telephone calls, interviews, radio and TV programs, and video tapes. Most of the time, these publicity offensives are aimed, not at the national media, but at individual media outlets back in the home state or district.

"Think Direct Mail"

The cornerstone of congressional publicity is the franking privilege—the right of members to send out mail under their signatures without cost to them. Rep. Bill Frenzel, R-Minn., notes that both parties teach newcomers three rules for getting reelected: "Use the frank. Use the frank. Use the frank." [87]

According to Postal Service estimates, members sent out 600 million pieces of franked mail in 1988—more than two items for every man, woman, and child in the country. The cost was $144 million, nearly twice that of 1978.[88] (Congress reimburses the U.S. Postal Service for the mailings on a bulk basis.)

When he was Senate Rules and Administration chairman, Charles McC. Mathias, Jr., R-Md., declared that mass mailings constituted 96 percent of the mail sent by senators; three-quarters of these mailings were constituent newsletters. Only 4 percent were individual letters responding to inquiries or requests.[89] Outgoing mail volume is much higher in election years than in nonelection years (see Figure 5-2).

With computerized address lists, mailings can be targeted at groupings—physicians, nurses, schoolteachers, teamsters, or home owners. By combining lists, groupings can be pinpointed even further. One congressional aide recounted his initiation into the wonders of direct-mail technology:

> I began with a personal letter to each of the special interest groups we have on file. The physicians received a letter from my congressman enclosed with a reprint from the *Congressional Record* of his recent remarks on the horrors of socialized medicine. The docs ate it up. The nurses got a letter pointing out the congressman's recent vote to increase funds in the federal budget for nurse training programs, along with a copy of his impassioned comments on the subject.
>
> Each of these letters began, "Knowing of your intense personal interest in any legislation affecting physicians/nurses, I thought you might be interested to see. . . ." On the average we received one response, invariably positive, for every two letters we sent—an absolutely phenomenal 50 percent rate of unsolicited response. Again, I was stunned. People cared about what we were saying! Amazing.[90]

One senator has four times as many names on his mailing list as there are mailboxes in his state. Another's administrative assistant instructed his staff to "think direct mail" and to send franked mailings to two new special-interest groups a week.[91]

A majority of mass mailings are general-purpose newsletters blanketing home states or districts. These are upbeat accounts of the legislator's activities, complete with photos of the legislator greeting constituents or conferring with top decision makers. The member's committee posts are highlighted, as are efforts to boost the home area. Recipients are urged to share their views or contact local offices for help. Perhaps once a year, the newsletter may feature an opinion poll asking for views on selected issues. Whatever the results, the

Figure 5-2   Incoming and Outgoing Congressional Mail, 1972-1988

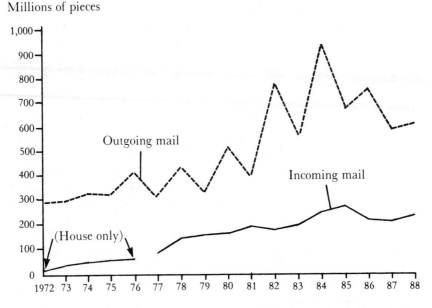

Millions of pieces

Source: John Pontius, "U.S. Congress Official Mail Costs: Fiscal Year 1972 to Present," Congressional Research Service Report, May 9, 1989, 27, 35, 45.

underlying message is that the legislator really cares what folks back home think.

The frank is as old as the nation—and so is criticism of it. A lawsuit filed in 1973 by Common Cause asked that franked mailings be halted on the grounds that they violated political challengers' right to compete for office free of government-imposed handicaps. Floods of publicly financed publicity, Common Cause argued, prevented opponents from effectively challenging the incumbents' records. Defenders of current franking practices were quick to respond. They emphasized members' need to inform constituents on issues and claimed that existing laws and rules were enough to prevent abuses. Ten years of litigation ended in 1983 when the Supreme Court affirmed a lower court's ruling upholding the validity of the franking law.

The existing franking law, passed in 1973 in response to the Common Cause suit, confers wide mailing privileges but forbids using the frank for mail "unrelated to the official business, activities, and duties of members." It also bars the frank for "mail matter which specifically solicits political support for the sender or any other person or any political party, or a vote or financial assistance for any candidate for any political office." In addition, House and Senate rules forbid mass mailings sixty days before a primary or general election. Just before the start of each sixty-day period, streams of Postal Service trucks are seen pulling away from loading docks of the congressional office buildings.

Franking usage continues to pose problems. The House has created a bipartisan Commission on Congressional Mailing Standards (the "Franking Commission") to advise members and investigate alleged violations of laws and regulations. The law requires the commission to advise House members on the content of all "postal patron" mailings (with no personal name). In 1988 the commission issued some 2,000 advisories. Commission chairman Morris K. Udall, D-Ariz., concedes that "the present law hasn't worked, and we have to go back and try again." However, the task is not simple, as he points out: "How do you write rules and regulations that distinguish between a thoughtful discussion of some important public issue and a self-promoting thing with the photograph of a member on every other page?" [92]

Feeding the Local Press

News outlets in this country are highly decentralized and dispersed. More than 11,000 newspapers are published in the United States, of which the 1,800 dailies are the most important in prestige and circulation. More than 12,000 periodicals are published. There are also more than 10,000 radio stations and 1,300 TV stations throughout the country.[93] These media outlets are locally based because of the vitality of local issues and local advertising.

Taken as a whole, local media outlets have inadequate resources for covering what their congressional delegations are doing in the nation's capital. Few of them have their own Washington reporters; most rely on syndicated or chain services that rarely follow individual members consistently. "If they report national news it is usually because it involves local personalities, affects local outcomes, or relates directly to local concerns." [94]

Relations with the press receive careful attention. Most legislators have at least one staffer who serves as a press aide; some have two or three. Their job is to generate coverage highlighting the member's work. Executive agencies often help by letting incumbents announce federal grants or contracts awarded in the state or district. Even if the member had nothing to do with procuring the funds, the press statement proclaims "Senator So-and-So announced today that a federal contract has been awarded to XYZ Company in Jonesville." Many offices also prepare weekly or biweekly columns that small-town newspapers can reprint under the lawmaker's byline.

The House, the Senate, and the four Capitol Hill parties have fully equipped studios and satellite links where audio or video programs or excerpts (called actualities) can be produced for a fraction of the commercial cost.[95] The TV studios feature a series of backdrops—including the familiar Capitol dome, an office interior, or a committee room setting. Some incumbents produce regular programs that are picked up by local radio or television outlets. More often, these outlets insert brief audio or TV clips on current issues into regular news broadcasts—to give the impression that their reporters have actually gone out and gotten the story. Increasingly, members create their own "news" reports and beam them directly to home-town stations—without ever talking to a reporter. With direct satellite feeds to local stations, many members regularly go "live at five" before local audiences.[96]

The Capitol Hill studios are heavily used. A survey found that nearly half of all congressional offices produced regular radio (usually weekly) and video (usually monthly) programs. Seventy-eight percent of the members sent brief radio spots by phone to district media outlets—an average of five times a month.[97] Michael Robinson's interviews with press secretaries indicate that members are using the studios more and more.[98] Recently elected representatives were more than three times as likely as senior members to use the recording studios at least once a week.

Like printed communications, radio and TV broadcasts pose ethical questions. House and Senate recording studios are not supposed to be used for "political" purposes, but the distinction between legitimate constituent outreach and political advertising remains blurred. (Party facilities have no such limits.) Some radio and television news editors have qualms about using such programs. "It's just this side of self-serving," said one television editor of the biweekly "Alaska Delegation Report." [99]

The Two Congresses and the Two Press Corps

In the eyes of home-district media outlets, incumbents fare splendidly. Robinson cites the case of "Congressman Press"—a midlevel House member untouched by scandal who has an average press operation. One year Congressman Press issued 144 press releases, about three a week. That year the major paper in his district ran 120 stories featuring or mentioning him; more than half the stories drew heavily on the press releases. "On average, every other week, Congressman Press was featured in a story virtually written in his own office." [100]

Even when not drawn from press releases, local stories tend to be respectful if not downright laudatory. During a reelection campaign in Wisconsin, the press aide of former Republican representative William Steiger observed that home-town stories were so lavish in their praise that no self-respecting press secretary would have dared put them out.[101] A detailed study of the local press corps in eighty-two contested races in 1982 highlighted the journalists' tendency toward "safety and timidity." Incumbents were rendered respectful coverage based on their experience; in contested open seats, journalists tended to keep their distance.[102]

Electronic media are even more benign than print media. Most local radio and TV reporters are on general assignment and do little preparation for interviews; their primary goal is to get the legislator on tape. As one legislator said, "TV people need thirty seconds of sound and video at the airport when I arrive—that's all they want." [103] National Public Radio correspondent Cokie Roberts concludes: "The emergence of local TV has made some members media stars in the home towns and, I would argue, done more to protect incumbency than any franking privilege or newsletter ever could, simply because television is a more pervasive medium than print." [104]

To influence legislation, members sometimes target the national media—TV networks and newspapers, such as the *New York Times* or *Washington Post,* that are read by elites. One of the most successful at promoting his work is Rep. Les Aspin, D-Wis., whose views on defense built his reputation. He explains the purpose of attracting national media:

> You're trying to influence the debate on the subject. You're trying to anticipate where the story is going, but you're also trying to push the story in a certain way. . . . You're trying to change the focus of the debate among the aficionados. [105]

Getting the attention of the national media is not easy for individual legislators, especially House members. Sometimes members resort to "leaking" information to gain press exposure.

The national press corps reports on Congress quite differently from local news organizations. Unlike most local reporters on general assignment, national reporters tend to specialize in the subjects they are covering. They also retain some distance from their news sources. With many sources to choose from, they do not depend on the goodwill of a single senator or representative. If they write an unflattering story about one of their sources, they are not likely to be boycotted; senators and representatives need reporters as much as or more than the reporters need them. If one source dries up, another can readily be found.

In general, national reporters maintain a cool, neutral stance toward their news sources on Capitol Hill. Following the canons of investigative journalism, many are on the lookout for scandals or evidence of wrongdoing. To the extent that they reveal bias in their work, it is the bias of the suspicious adversary. Thus, most close observers conclude that reporters are "tough" on Congress, especially in in-depth or interpretive analyses. Ethical problems, congressional pay and perquisites, and junkets abroad are frequent subjects for such stories.

In sum, the national press reports things differently from the local press. And individual members are not reported the same way as the institution of Congress. In all, the content and quality of press coverage underscore the two Congresses: Congress as collective policy maker, covered mainly by the national press, appears in a different light from the politicians who make up Congress, covered mainly by local news outlets. There are local variations, to be sure, and senators receive more searching coverage than House members. When scandals occur, all bets are off. But in general, press coverage widens the gap between the two Congresses.

Divergent press coverage also heightens the distinct images of the two

Congresses: positive for individual members, negative for the institution. "Americans love their congressmen much more than they love their Congress."[106] Individual lawmakers tend to be well known, favorably judged, respectfully covered by the local media, and—most important—reelected. Congress the institution, in contrast, is covered by the national press and judged by general impressions of the state of the nation—in recent years ranging from cautious to skeptical.

Here is another manifestation of the two Congresses: they are viewed through different lenses, reported by different channels of communication, and judged by different criteria.

Conclusion

Election is a prerequisite to congressional service. Incumbent legislators allocate much of their time and energy, and even more of their staff and office resources, to the care and cultivation of voters. Their Hill styles and home styles are adopted with this end in mind.

Yet senators and representatives do not live by reelection alone. Not a few turn their backs on reelection to pursue other careers or interests. For those who remain in office, reelection is not usually viewed as an end in itself, but as a lever for pursuing other goals—policy making or career advancement, for example. Fenno challenged one of the representatives whose constituency career he had followed, remarking that "sometimes it must be hard to connect what you do here with what you do in Washington." "Oh no," the lawmaker replied, "I do what I do here so I can do what I want to do there."[107]

Notes

1. Don Phillips, "The Little Museum That Could," *Washington Post,* November 25, 1986, A19.
2. John P. Gregg, "Average Freshman Earned Just $61,000 Before Entering House, Survey Shows," *Roll Call,* January 29, 1989, 3.
3. Commission on Executive, Legislative and Judicial Salaries, *Fairness for Our Public Servants* (Washington, D.C.: Government Printing Office, 1988), 23.
4. Walter Pincus, "Majority in Congress Already Make $135,000," *Washington Post,* January 24, 1989, A1.
5. Donald R. Matthews, *U.S. Senators and Their World* (Chapel Hill: University of North Carolina Press, 1960), 66.
6. Joseph Schlesinger, "Lawyers and American Politics: A Clarified View," *Midwest Journal of Political Science* 1 (May 1957): 26-39; and Allen G.

Bogue, Jerome M. Clubb, Carroll R. McKibbin, and Santa A. Traugott, "Members of the House of Representatives and the Processes of Modernization, 1789-1960," *Journal of American History* 63 (September 1976): 284.

7. *Congressional Quarterly's Guide to Congress,* 3d ed. (Washington, D.C.: Congressional Quarterly, 1982), 649.
8. Irwin N. Gertzog, *Congressional Women: Their Recruitment, Treatment, and Behavior* (New York: Praeger Publishers, 1984).
9. Julie Rovner, "Record Number of Women, Blacks in Congress," *Congressional Quarterly Weekly Report,* November 12, 1988, 3293-3295.
10. *New York Times,* June 14, 1981, E5.
11. Charles S. Bullock III and Burdett A. Loomis, "The Changing Congressional Career," in *Congress Reconsidered,* 3d ed., ed. Lawrence C. Dodd and Bruce I. Oppenheimer (Washington, D.C.: CQ Press, 1985), 66-69, 80-82.
12. Myra MacPherson, "Carrying the Camelot Torch," *Washington Post,* March 5, 1986, D1.
13. Susan Welch and John R. Hibbing, "Hispanic Representation in the U.S. Congress," *Social Science Quarterly* 64 (June 1984): 328-335.
14. Roger H. Davidson, *The Role of the Congressman* (Indianapolis: Bobbs-Merrill, 1969), 199.
15. House Commission on Administrative Review, *Final Report,* 2 vols., H. Doc. 95-272, 95th Cong., 1st sess., December 31, 1977, 2: 874-875.
16. Thomas E. Cavanagh, "The Two Arenas of Congress," in *The House at Work,* ed. Joseph Cooper and G. Calvin Mackenzie (Austin: University of Texas Press, 1981), 56-77.
17. Frank E. Smith, *Congressman from Mississippi* (New York: Pantheon Books, 1964), 129-130.
18. Matthews, *U.S. Senators.*
19. Norman J. Ornstein, Robert L. Peabody, and David W. Rohde, "The Senate through the 1980s: Cycles of Change," in *Congress Reconsidered,* ed. Dodd and Oppenheimer, 17-20.
20. Herbert B. Asher. "The Learning of Legislative Norms," *American Political Science Review* 67 (June 1973): 499-513.
21. Burdett A. Loomis and Jeff Fishel, "New Members in a Changing Congress: Norms, Actions, and Satisfaction," *Congressional Studies* 9 (Spring 1981): 81-94.
22. *New York Times,* August 14, 1980, B9.
23. Cavanagh, "The Two Arenas of Congress," 65.
24. Ibid., 66.
25. Smith, *Congressman from Mississippi,* 127. See also David Mayhew, *Congress: The Electoral Connection* (New Haven, Conn.: Yale University Press, 1974).
26. Davidson, *The Role of the Congressman,* 98; and Senate Commission on the Operation of the Senate, *Toward a Modern Senate,* S. Doc. 94-278, 94th Cong., 2d sess., 1977 committee print, 27.
27. Center for Responsive Politics, *Congressional Operations: Congress Speaks—A Survey of the 100th Congress* (Washington, D.C.: Center for

Responsive Politics, 1988), 65-67.

28. House Commission on Administrative Review, *Administrative Reorganization and Legislative Management*, 2 vols., H. Doc. 95-232, 95th Cong., 1st sess., September 28, 1977, 1: 27-31; and Senate Commission on the Operation of the Senate, *Toward a Modern Senate*, 35-38.

29. Ross A. Webber, "U.S. Senators: See How They Run," *The Wharton Magazine* (Winter 1980-1981): 38.

30. Senate Commission on the Operation of the Senate, *Toward a Modern Senate*.

31. Webber, "U.S. Senators," 37.

32. Center for Responsive Politics, *Congressional Operations*, 47-49.

33. Ibid., 62-64.

34. Vernon Louviere, "For Retiring Congressmen, Enough Is Enough," *Nation's Business*, May 1980, 32.

35. William H. Riker, *The Theory of Political Coalitions* (New Haven, Conn.: Yale University Press, 1962), 24-38.

36. Hanna Fenichel Pitkin, *The Concept of Representation* (Berkeley: University of California Press, 1967), 166.

37. Davidson, *The Role of the Congressman*, 80.

38. Ross J. S. Hoffman and Paul Levack eds., *Burke's Politics* (New York: Alfred A. Knopf, 1959), 114-116.

39. Carl D. McMurray and Malcolm B. Parsons, "Public Attitudes Toward the Representational Role of Legislators and Judges," *Midwest Journal of Political Science* 9 (May 1965): 167-185.

40. David C. Kozak, *Contexts of Congressional Decision Behavior* (Lanham, Md.: University Press of America, 1984).

41. Thomas E. Cavanagh, "The Calculus of Representation: A Congressional Perspective," *Western Political Quarterly* 35 (March 1982): 120-129.

42. Kozak, *Contexts of Congressional Decision Behavior*, 211.

43. Clifford D. May, "L.I. Starts a Dogfight in Congress to Save F-14," *New York Times*, May 9, 1989, B1.

44. John W. Kingdon, *Congressmen's Voting Decisions* (New York: Harper & Row, 1981).

45. Richard F. Fenno, Jr., *Home Style: House Members in Their Districts* (Boston: Little, Brown, 1978), 1.

46. Martin Tolchin, "Udall Re-election Imperiled by Newest Constituents," *New York Times*, October 30, 1980, B12.

47. See Lewis A. Froman, Jr., *Congressmen and Their Constituencies* (Chicago: Rand McNally, 1963), 91-93; Randall B. Ripley, *Congress: Process and Policy*, 4th ed. (New York: W. W. Norton, 1988), 295-297; and David M. Olson, *The Legislative Process: A Comparative Approach* (New York: Harper & Row, 1980), 425-428.

48. Lewis A. Froman, Jr., "Inter-Party Constituency Differences and Congressional Voting Behavior," *American Political Science Review* 57 (March 1963): 57-61.

49. *Congressional Quarterly Weekly Report*, January 10, 1981, 80.

50. Kenneth A. Shepsle, "The Changing Textbook Congress," in *Can the Government Govern?* ed. John E. Chubb and Paul E. Peterson (Washing-

ton, D.C.: The Brookings Institution, 1989), 249.
51. Fenno, *Home Style*, 4-8.
52. Ibid., 6.
53. Olson, *The Legislative Process*, 427; and Morris P. Fiorina, *Representatives, Roll Calls, and Constituencies* (Lexington, Mass.: Lexington Books, 1974), 90-101.
54. Albert D. Cover and David R. Mayhew, "Congressional Dynamics and the Decline of Competitive Congressional Elections," in *Congress Reconsidered,* ed. Dodd and Oppenheimer, 62-82.
55. James L. Payne, "The Personal Electoral Advantage of House Incumbents, 1936-1976," *American Politics Quarterly* 8 (October 1980): 465-482; Robert S. Erikson, "Is There Such a Thing as a Safe Seat?" *Polity* 8 (Summer 1976): 623-632.
56. Thomas E. Mann, *Unsafe at Any Margin: Interpreting Congressional Elections* (Washington, D.C.: American Enterprise Institute, 1978).
57. Fenno, *Home Style*, 8-27.
58. Ibid., 21
59. Thomas P. O'Neill, Jr., with William Novak, *Man of the House* (New York: St. Martin's Press, 1987), 25.
60. Fenno, *Home Style*, 24-25.
61. Joseph A. Davis, " 'Family' Raises Energy Funds for Pelican PAC," *Congressional Quarterly Weekly Report,* October 8, 1988, 2779-2781.
62. Erving Goffman, *The Presentation of Self in Everyday Life* (New York: Doubleday, 1959).
63. Fenno, *Home Style*, 153.
64. Ibid., 56.
65. Anthony Champagne, *Congressman Sam Rayburn* (New Brunswick, N.J.: Rutgers University Press, 1984), 28.
66. Ibid., 136.
67. Kingdon, *Congressmen's Voting Decisions.*
68. Fenno, *Home Style*, 153.
69. Rhodes Cook, "The Safe and the Vulnerable: A Look Behind the Numbers," *Congressional Quarterly Weekly Report,* January 9, 1982, 35-38.
70. Thomas J. Brazaitas, "Vanik Deplores Lack of Courage," *Cleveland Plain Dealer,* May 11, 1980, cited in *Congressional Record,* daily ed., 96th Cong., 2d sess., May 15, 1980, E2437.
71. Glenn R. Parker, "Sources of Change in Congressional District Attentiveness," *American Journal of Political Science* 24 (February 1980): 115-124.
72. Fenno, *Home Style*, 36, 209; and Parker, "Sources of Change."
73. Jim Wright, *You and Your Congressman* (New York: Coward-McCann, 1965), 35.
74. Richard E. Cohen, "Assertive Freshmen," *National Journal,* May 2, 1987, 1061.
75. House Commission on Administrative Review, *Final Report,* 1: 655; and Janet Breslin, "Constituent Service," in *Senators: Offices, Ethics, and Pressures,* in Senate Commission on the Operation of the Senate, 94th Cong., 2d sess., 1977 committee print, 21.

76. John R. Johannes, *To Serve the People: Congress and Constituency Service* (Lincoln: University of Nebraska Press, 1984), 34-36.
77. House Commission on Administrative Review, *Final Report*, 1: 655; and Breslin, "Constituent Service," 21.
78. House Commission on Administrative Review, *Final Report*, 2: 830.
79. Johannes, *To Serve the People*, chap. 5.
80. House Commission on Administrative Review, *Final Report*, 2: 830-831.
81. Morris P. Fiorina, *Congress: Keystone of the Washington Establishment* (New Haven, Conn.: Yale University Press, 1977), 45.
82. Walter Gellhorn, *When Americans Complain: Governmental Grievance Procedures* (Cambridge, Mass.: Harvard University Press, 1966).
83. Paul Dwyer, Congressional Research Service, provided information on congressional allowances.
84. *New York Times,* September 7, 1982, A18.
85. Norman J. Ornstein, Thomas E. Mann, and Michael J. Malbin, *Vital Statistics on Congress, 1987-1988* (Washington, D.C.: Congressional Quarterly, 1987), 144.
86. See Stephen E. Frantzich, *Computers in Congress* (Beverly Hills, Calif.: Sage Publications, 1982).
87. Charles R. Babcock, "Frankly, an Election-Year Avalanche," *Washington Post,* September 19, 1988, A19.
88. John Pontius, "U.S. Congress Official Mail Costs: Fiscal Year 1972 to Present," Congressional Research Service Report, May 9, 1989, 27, 35; and Walter Pincus, "Mail Funds Boosted in Hill Budget," *Washington Post,* January 11, 1989, A4.
89. *Congressional Record,* daily ed., 97th Cong., 2d sess., December 20, 1982, S15806-15808.
90. William Haydon, "How Congress's Computers Con the Public," *Washington Monthly,* May 1980, 45.
91. David Burnham, "Congress's Computer Subsidy," *New York Times Magazine,* November 2, 1980, 101; and Senator Charles McC. Mathias in *Congressional Record,* daily ed., December 29, 1982, S15806-15808.
92. Burnham, "Congress's Computer Subsidy," 98.
93. *Gale Directory of Publications,* vol. 2 (Detroit, Mich.: Gale Research, 1988), viii; and *Broadcasting Cablecasting Yearbook* (Washington, D.C.: Broadcasting Publishing, 1987), A-2, D-3.
94. Charles Bosley, "Senate Communications with the Public," in *Senate Communications with the Public,* 17.
95. For descriptions of congressional radio-TV studios, see Ben H. Bagdikian, "Congress and the Media: Partners in Propaganda," *Columbia Journalism Review* (January-February 1974): 5-6; Michael J. Robinson, "Three Faces of Congressional Media," in *The New Congress,* ed. Thomas E. Mann and Norman J. Ornstein (Washington, D.C.: American Enterprise Institute, 1981), 62-63; and Martin Tolchin, "TV Studio Serves Congress," *New York Times,* March 7, 1984, C22.
96. Carol Matlock, "Live from Capitol Hill," *National Journal,* February 18, 1989, 390.
97. Anne Haskell, "Live From Capitol Hill," *Washington Journalism Review*

4 (November 1982): 48-50.
98. Robinson, "Three Faces of Congressional Media," 62.
99. Tolchin, "TV Studio Serves Congress."
100. Robinson, "Three Faces of Congressional Media," 80-81.
101. John F. Bibby and Roger H. Davidson, *On Capitol Hill: Studies in the Legislative Process,* 2d ed. (Hinsdale, Ill.: Dryden Press, 1972), 72.
102. Peter Clarke and Susan H. Evans, *Covering Campaigns: Journalism in Congressional Elections* (Stanford, Calif.: Stanford University Press, 1983). See also Charles M. Tidmarch and Brad S. Karp, "The Missing Beat: Press Coverage of Congressional Elections in Eight Metropolitan Areas," *Congress and the Presidency* 10 (Spring 1983): 47-61.
103. Robinson, "Three Faces of Congressional Media," 84.
104. Cokie Roberts, "Leadership and the Media in the 100th Congress" (Paper prepared for the Dirksen Center-Congressional Research Service Congressional Leadership Project, October 27, 1989), 14.
105. "How to Get the News to Come Out Your Way," *Washington Post,* June 7, 1981, D1.
106. Glenn R. Parker and Roger H. Davidson, "Why Do Americans Love Their Congressmen So Much More Than Their Congress?" *Legislative Studies Quarterly* 4 (February 1979): 53-61.
107. Fenno, *Home Style,* 99.

PART THREE

A Deliberative Assembly of One Nation

In his first address to Congress, President George Bush promised to give the House and Senate "what friends deserve: frankness, respect, and my best judgment about ways to improve America's future." Bush backed up this positive rhetoric with many acts of personal consideration toward members of Congress. He invited members into the private residential quarters of the White House, snapped their pictures as they bounced on the Lincoln bed, and welcomed them to the White House for private meetings. As a consummate Washington "insider," President Bush recognized the need to make a good impression with the Democratic-run House (260 D, 175 R) and Senate (55 D, 45 R)—especially after conducting a bruising presidential campaign filled with partisan nastiness.

Some GOP professionals, however, viewed with concern Bush's efforts to promote a new spirit of bipartisanship with Congress. "The quicker we're rid of this bipartisanship the better," admitted a top Republican operative. "We have to run *against* the Congress." [1] Ed Rollins, executive director of the House Republican Campaign Committee, remarked that he wouldn't "steal, murder, lie, cheat, or pillage, but other than that I think just about anything goes" in GOP efforts to win control of the Congress.[2] Bush's legislative objectives conflicted with Republicans' electoral goals—a clash of the "two Congresses" in capsule form. As representatives of their districts or states, members of Congress struggle to win reelection; as lawmakers for the whole nation, they strive to make good national policy.

British statesman and philosopher Edmund Burke vividly described the dual character of the national legislature. The constituent-oriented Parliament, or Congress, he portrayed as "a Congress of ambassadors from different and hostile interests." The Parliament of substantive lawmaking was described as

> a deliberative assembly of one nation, with one interest, that of the whole—where not local purposes, not local prejudices, ought to guide, but the general good, resulting from the general reason of the whole.[3]

Part Three focuses on Congress as a legislative and deliberative body. Chapter 6 (party leaders) and Chapter 7 (committees) explain how the organization of the House and Senate shapes congressional lawmaking. Congress's relations with the president, bureaucracy, and interest groups are discussed in chapters 8, 9, and 10, respectively. As we shall see, the deliberative assembly of one nation is never very far from local purposes and local prejudices, especially given the overlay of partisan and institutional strategies crafted to win advantages in both the lawmaking and reelection processes.

Notes

1. *Newsweek,* March 20, 1989, 28.
2. Ibid.
3. Edmund Burke, "Speech to Electors at Bristol," in *Burke's Politics,* ed. J. S. Hoffman and Paul Levack (New York: Alfred A. Knopf, 1949), 116.

The Speaker's Lobby, with its stately chandeliers and portraits of former Speakers, is a symbol of the office and a gathering place for members.

CHAPTER SIX

Leaders and Parties in Congress

Being an elective party leader in the modern Congress is a challenging assignment. Today's rank-and-file members are simply more independent from party influence than many of their predecessors; they believe that their party leaders can do relatively little to them or for them. "We [members] all got here on our own," said Rep. Anthony Beilenson, D-Calif., "so we don't owe anything to the party." [1] In short, House and Senate leaders face a daunting prospect: the dearth of followers. As Rep. David Obey, D-Wis., lamented: "Once in a while we need more than good leadership, we also need good followership." [2]

The give and take between leaders and followers parallels the constant interaction between the "two Congresses," between the lawmaking institution and the representative assembly. In their "inside" role, party leaders guide institutional activities and influence policy. Good communications skills, parliamentary expertise, and sensitivity to the mood of the membership and of the electorate are important attributes of an effective leader. When Senate Republicans chose a new floor leader in 1984, they judged the five contenders primarily on their personal qualities. As Sen. Pete Wilson, R-Calif., explained, "That includes their intelligence, quickness, political shrewdness, tactical skill and knowledge of the rules and ability as a spokesman, strategist and builder of consensus within the party." [3] (Robert Dole of Kansas tested well, succeeding Howard Baker of Tennessee as GOP leader.) Four years later Senate Democrats elected a leader they believed would improve the "quality of life" inside the Senate (more predictability in scheduling and fewer late-night sessions, for example). [4] In a three-way contest George Mitchell of Maine succeeded West Virginian Robert C. Byrd, who had decided to retire as Senate majority leader.

In their "outside" role, party leaders not only help recruit candidates and assist them in their campaigns, but they must serve as the party's link to the president, the press, and the public. Not only was Senator Mitchell perceived, especially by younger senators, as well qualified to direct institutional reforms, but his widely acknowledged media skills would enable him to exert influence outside the Senate in presenting Democratic views to the entire nation. "The Democrats have realized the need, in the presence of the Republican administration," said Sen. Joseph Biden, D-Del., "to have a person who can not only make the Senate function well, but who can be a party spokesperson." [5]

Leaders also must find ways of persuading members who represent different constituencies, values, and interests to support legislation that addresses national concerns. "The only thing that counts is 218 votes, and nothing else is real," explained Richard Gephardt of Missouri, the majority leader of the House. "You have to be able [to attract a majority of the House] to pass a bill." [6]

As we look at the roles of leaders and parties, we must remember that Congress is a partisan body. The majority party in the House or Senate controls not only the top leadership posts, but also majorities on committees and subcommittees and all their chairmanships. This chapter identifies party leaders, describes their jobs, and assesses the sources of their influence; we also consider party structure—caucuses, committees, and groups. Finally, we look at continuity and change in the congressional party system.

Leaders of the House

Compared with the rules of the Senate, which emphasize minority rights, the rules of the House permit a determined majority to achieve its policy objectives. House leaders, especially the Speaker, are well positioned to advance institutional and party objectives if they can maintain winning coalitions in the face of dilatory tactics by the opposition. As House Minority Whip Newt Gingrich, R-Ga., once said, "The rules of the House are designed for a speaker with a strong personality and an agenda." [7] This description fit Speaker Jim Wright, D-Texas, whose forceful leadership and his knack of making Republican "minority status more painful," as one House GOP leader put it, embittered the minority party.[8] Gingrich brought ethical charges against the Speaker, and they were investigated by the Committee on Standards of Official Conduct. That panel eventually charged Wright with several violations of House rules, such as accepting gifts from a close business associate and circumventing limits on members' outside income through bulk sales of his book (*Reflections of a Public Man*) to lobbyists and interest groups. Speaker Wright did not survive these ethical and political challenges and left the House in June 1989.

The Speaker

No other member of Congress possesses the visibility and authority of the Speaker of the House. Part of the Speaker's prestige comes from the office's formal recognition in the Constitution, which states that the House "shall chuse their Speaker." Although the Constitution does not require the Speaker to be a House member, all of them have been. The Speaker is also second in line behind the vice president to succeed to the presidency. As the "elect of the elected," the Speaker stands near the president as a national figure.

The Speakership combines procedural prerogatives with policy and partisan leadership. As chief parliamentary officer and leader of the majority party (see Figure 6-1), the Speaker enjoys unique powers in scheduling floor business and in recognizing members during sessions. Occasionally, Speakers will relinquish the gavel to join in floor debate, but usually they vote only in case of a tie. The Speaker is also chief administrative officer for many House functions, and the distributor of a relatively small number of Capitol Hill patronage jobs. Speakers, like other members, must also represent their constituents' needs and interests.

Before 1899 it was not uncommon for Speakers to have only a few years' service as representatives. Whig Henry Clay of Kentucky still holds the record: election to the speakership on November 4, 1811—his first day in the House. Speakers elected since 1899 have served, on average, more than twenty years before their election to the post. Once in position, Speakers have traditionally been reelected as long as their party controlled the House. As a result of Speaker Wright's ethical dilemma, the bicentennial 101st Congress witnessed the only mid-course change in the Speakership in this century.

Cannon and Rayburn. During the Republic's first 120 years, Speakers gradually accrued power. By 1910 Speaker Joseph Cannon, R-Ill., dominated the House. He assigned members to committees, appointed and removed committee chairmen, regulated the flow of bills to the House floor as chairman of the Rules Committee, referred bills to committee, and controlled floor debate. Taken individually, Cannon's powers were little different from those of his immediate predecessors, but taken together and exercised to their limits they bordered on the dictatorial.

The House forced Cannon to step down from the Rules Committee in 1910. The next year, when Democrats took control of the House, the new Speaker (Champ Clark of Missouri) was stripped of his authority to make committee assignments, and his power of recognition was curtailed. The speakership then went into temporary eclipse. Power flowed to the majority leader, to the committee chairmen, and for a while to party caucuses.

Speakers since Cannon have exhibited differing leadership styles that reflected their personalities, the historical context in which they operated, and the partisan divisions and level of conflict within the chamber. Sam Rayburn, D-Texas (1940-1947, 1949-1953, 1955-1961), was a formidable leader because of his personal prestige as well as long political experience and immense parliamentary skills. As he himself explained, "The old day of pounding on the desk and giving people hell is gone. . . . A man's got to lead by persuasion and kindness and the best reason—that's the only way he can lead people." [9] Rayburn lent coherence to a House in which power was diffused among a relatively small number of powerful committee chairmen.

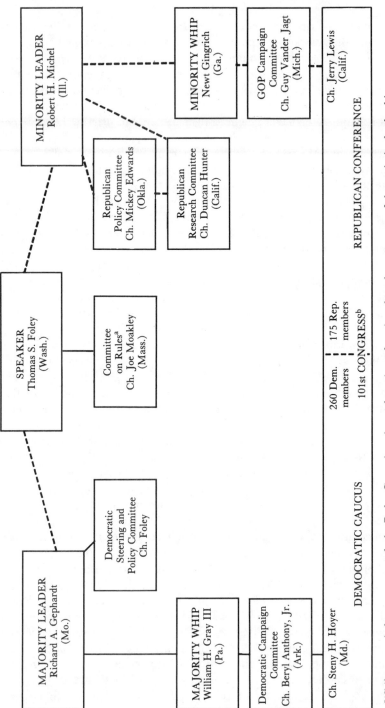

Figure 6-1 Organization of the House of Representatives, 101st Congress (1989-1991)

MINORITY LEADER
Robert H. Michel
(Ill.)

MINORITY WHIP
Newt Gingrich
(Ga.)

GOP Campaign
Committee
Ch. Guy Vander Jagt
(Mich.)

Ch. Jerry Lewis
(Calif.)

Republican
Policy Committee
Ch. Mickey Edwards
(Okla.)

Republican
Research Committee
Ch. Duncan Hunter
(Calif.)

SPEAKER
Thomas S. Foley
(Wash.)

Committee
on Rules[a]
Ch. Joe Moakley
(Mass.)

Democratic
Steering and
Policy Committee
Ch. Foley

MAJORITY LEADER
Richard A. Gephardt
(Mo.)

MAJORITY WHIP
William H. Gray III
(Pa.)

Democratic Campaign
Committee
Ch. Beryl Anthony, Jr.
(Ark.)

Ch. Steny H. Hoyer
(Md.)

260 Dem.
members

175 Rep.
members

101st CONGRESS[b]

DEMOCRATIC CAUCUS

REPUBLICAN CONFERENCE

[a] While not strictly a party panel, the Rules Committee in modern times functions largely as an arm of the majority leadership.
[b] As of January 3, 1989, when the 101st Congress convened.

Martin, McCormack, and Albert. Although the legacy of the historic 1910 revolt was weak central party leadership, modern Speakers have regained some of the former powers of the office. "In the few years that I served as Speaker," boasted Republican Joseph Martin of Massachusetts, "no Republican went on an important committee without my approval." [10]

Speaker John McCormack, D-Mass. (1962-1971), based his leadership on personal ties with his colleagues. But McCormack resisted congressional change and lost the support of many colleagues because he backed President Lyndon Johnson's controversial escalation of the Vietnam War. One of his critics, Morris Udall of Arizona, even tried to wrest the Speakership away from him.

The next Speaker, Carl Albert, D-Okla. (1971-1977), presided during a period of sweeping institutional changes. Under a 1975 reform, Democratic Speakers chair their party's Steering and Policy Committee, the group that assigns Democrats to committees. Another party change made that year permits the Speaker to nominate all Democratic members of the Rules Committee, including the chairman. The Speaker also acquired the authority to refer measures to more than one committee and to create ad hoc panels, subject to House approval. Albert supported other changes that dispersed power in the House to subcommittees and junior members, even though many of them limited his ability to exercise political and policy leadership.

O'Neill and Wright. O'Neill took the speakership in 1977 and was soon hailed as the most forceful Speaker since Rayburn. (Witness O'Neill's successful and expeditious maneuvering of President Jimmy Carter's omnibus energy program through the House.) With the election of Ronald Reagan, O'Neill encountered difficulties in leading a highly fragmented House and a fractured party. But it was O'Neill who found the administration's weakness— the "fairness" issue—and, as opposition to Reaganomics congealed, O'Neill as the ranking Democratic officeholder became his party's point man. In the process O'Neill transformed the Speakership into an office of high national visibility. As then Majority Leader Thomas S. Foley, D-Wash., pointed out:

> Sam Rayburn could have walked down the streets of Spokane, Wash., without anybody noticing him. Tip O'Neill couldn't do that. And it is very unlikely that any future Speaker will be anonymous to the country. The Speaker is going to join the vice president, the chief justice, and a few Cabinet members in the forefront of public recognition. [11]

When Wright became the forty-eighth Speaker in 1987, he aggressively expanded the post's public role in both national and international policy making. As a "superdiplomat" working for peace in Central America, he met with Nicaraguan leader Daniel Ortega, contra emissaries, and various ambassadors, and he endorsed peace proposals. This activism represented a unique foray into foreign policy making for modern Speakers. [12]

In the domestic arena Wright also risked boldly. He prodded committee chairmen to move on priority legislation by a certain date, recommended policies (such as raising taxes to cut deficits) over the opposition of the Reagan White House and many of his Democratic colleagues, and employed procedural tactics that aroused the ire of Republicans—and sometimes Democrats. O'Neill strived for consensus, but Wright laid out an agenda and then worked diligently, by himself if necessary, to mobilize support. "Tip would take all 435 of us in a big bear hug and try to gradually move us one way or another," remarked Rep. Pat Williams, D-Mont. "Jim Wright goes way out there, where you can barely see him, and waves, 'Come on!' " [13]

Conclusion.   The fall of Speaker Wright, like that of Cannon eighty years earlier, demonstrates that the broad prerogatives of the Speakership rest fundamentally on party, institutional, and public consensus. The Speaker's management of the House is based on the premise that the office is essential for realizing the objectives of members—leaders and followers, majority and minority. When a Speaker pushes his entire range of prerogatives to the limit, the members' stake in the office is placed in jeopardy. In the instances of both Cannon and Wright, objections were couched in the rhetoric of ethics: the progressive call for broader participation in 1910 and the demand for higher standards of personal conduct in 1989. But there the similarity of the cases probably ends. The Cannon revolt eclipsed the Speakership, which was rebuilt only after decades. The Wright case destroyed the individual's political career, but the office and its prerogatives presumably would remain intact as new Speaker Thomas S. Foley took charge.

Some scholars argue that leadership style in the House is largely contextual, dependent on the wider social and political environment. Factors such as the public's demand for legislation or the agenda of the president may restrict the Speaker or may present opportunities for activism. Other observers see leadership as primarily determined by institutional context (the diffusion of power among members, the autonomy of committees, party cohesiveness, and so on) rather than personal attributes. Still others contend that the "institutionalist thesis" is partially correct but inadequate. It discounts the capacity of talented individuals to lead by accommodating circumstances to their own objectives.[14] Wright's public agonies—triggered by charges of ethical improprieties but exacerbated by personal traits of impulsiveness and "hardball" partisanship—are but the most recent reminders of the Speakership's personal dimension. Clearly, personal capabilities and institutional context are both critical ingredients.

Floor Leaders

The Speaker's principal deputy—the *majority leader*—is the party's floor leader, elected every two years by secret ballot of the party caucus. Because the majority leader often succeeds the Speaker, some Speakers want to control that choice. The floor leader is not to be confused with a *floor manager*. The floor managers, usually two for each bill, are frequently the chairman and ranking minority member of the committee that reported the bill. They try to steer it to a final decision.

The House majority leader is usually an experienced legislator. Jim Wright, for example, had served twenty-two years on the Public Works and Transportation Committee and was slated to be its chairman in 1977 when he was elected floor leader with the strong backing of Speaker O'Neill.[15] O'Neill then advanced Majority Leader Wright's claim on the Speakership by giving him an extensive public role in managing the legislative affairs of the House. Before his election as majority leader in 1986, Representative Foley also had served for twenty-two years, including six as majority whip and six as Agriculture Committee chair.

By modern custom, neither the Speaker nor the Democratic or Republican floor leaders chair committees. Majority leaders, however, hold the leadership slot on the Budget Committee. The majority and minority floor leaders are also ex officio members of the Permanent Select Intelligence Committee.

House and party rules are silent concerning the majority leader's duties. The job is somewhat "open-ended," said Majority Leader Foley. "It is, to some extent, defined by relationship to the Speaker." [16] The key job defined by tradition is to be principal floor defender, negotiator, and spokesman for the party. "The reality," explained Foley, "is that in a modern, participatory Congress . . . the responsibility of leadership and the necessity of leadership is to constantly involve members in the process of decision and consensus." [17] The majority leader also helps to plan the daily, weekly, and annual legislative agendas; consults with members to gauge sentiment on legislation; confers with the president about administrative proposals, particularly when the president is of the same party; urges colleagues to support or defeat measures; and, in general, works hard to advance the purposes and programs of the majority party.

The *minority leader* is the floor leader of the "loyal opposition," the titular leader of his or her party. (Speakers assume that role for the majority.) Minority leaders promote unity among party colleagues, monitor the progress of bills through committees and subcommittees, and forge coalitions with like-minded members of the opposition party. Bertrand Snell, R-N.Y., minority leader from 1931 to 1939, thus described the duties:

> He is spokesman for his party and enunciates its policies. He is required to be alert and vigilant in defense of the minority's rights. It is his function and duty to criticize constructively the policies and program of the majority, and to this end employ parliamentary tactics and give close attention to all proposed legislation.[18]

Two main challenges face the minority, said GOP leader Robert H. Michel of Illinois: "To keep our people together, and to look for votes on the other side." [19] Michel took on a third challenge at the start of the 101st Congress: to return the House to GOP control. With Republicans the "permanent minority" since 1954, Michel devised a long-range strategy, called "Project Majority," to recapture the House for the GOP in November 1992 (in the wake of the reapportionment and redistricting that follows the decennial census). Part of Michel's strategy was to recruit able candidates to challenge Democratic incumbents and to use the House floor to draw contrasts between the two major parties.[20]

Like their majority counterparts, minority leaders are experienced legislators. Before Michel moved up from minority whip to Republican leader in 1981, he had spent twenty-four years in the House. His predecessor, John Rhodes of Arizona, was elected floor leader in 1973 after twenty years as a representative.

The Whips

An assistant majority or minority leader, the *whip,* is another elective post. Prior to a caucus rules change that took effect with the 100th Congress, the Democratic whip was appointed by the majority leader after consultation with the Speaker, whose voice usually prevailed. The switch from an appointive to an elective whip was advocated by junior Democrats who wanted a voice in determining which of their colleagues would step on the ladder that could lead to the Speakership.

In recent years both parties expanded their whip systems to include a variety of deputy, at-large, regional, and assistant whips who meet regularly to discuss issues and strategy. For instance, House Minority Whip Gingrich named two chief deputy whips—Steve Gunderson of Wisconsin to work on policy development and Robert Walker of Pennsylvania to concentrate on floor tactics.[21] Naming more members as whips involves them in leadership decision making and gives them additional incentives to back their top leaders. In the 101st Congress nearly one-third of all House Democrats belonged to the whip organization.

The whip system of each party aids the top leaders in various ways, including gathering intelligence, encouraging attendance, counting votes, and persuading colleagues. Whips frequently create party task forces to poll members and to involve junior members in building coalitions (the so-called "strategy of inclusion"—getting many legislators working on behalf of leadership initiatives). These task forces do more than count noses. "When the votes are not there, the task force and key committee players—under the aegis of the leadership—tinker with the substance of the bill [to marshal the votes]."[22] Whips in the House frequently stand by the chamber's doors and signal their arriving colleagues to vote yea (thumbs up) or nay (thumbs down). They also prepare weekly "whip notices" advising members of the upcoming floor agenda.

As the term implies, the whip's job is to encourage party discipline. In the modern Congress this is primarily accomplished by persuasion and hard work. As far as being able to "whip people into line," said the minority whip,

"I think we're more the 'whippees' than the 'whippers.' " [23] Yet some whips can be very persuasive. "What's it like when [Majority Whip] Tony Coelho asks for your vote?" inquired a House Democrat. "Let's see—ever been propositioned by a gorilla?" [24] To promote attendance at votes, whips must keep close track of their colleagues. Former GOP whip Leslie Arends of Illinois (1943-1975) once resorted to a unique stratagem to find an absent colleague. He notified the member's local radio station, which then announced at fifteen-minute intervals: "If anybody spies Congressman So-and-So, who should be representing us in Washington but isn't, tell him he's supposed to be in Washington tomorrow for an important vote." [25]

Leaders of the Senate

Today's Senate, even more than the House, is an institution rife with rampant individualism. Senators cherish their independence, which exacerbates the challenges faced by those elected to lead them. Unlike House leaders, Senate leaders lack the buttress of rules designed to expedite business and so must rely even more heavily on personal skills and negotiation with their colleagues.

Presiding Officers

The House majority's highest elected leader, the Speaker, presides over the House. By contrast, the Senate majority leader, the majority party's highest leader, almost never presides in the Senate chamber. In fact, the Senate has three categories of presiding officers.

First, the constitutional president of the Senate is the *vice president of the United States* (see Figure 6-2). Except for ceremonial occasions, he seldom presides over Senate sessions, and he can vote only to break a tie. Dan Quayle initially indicated that as president of the Senate he wanted to play a more activist role than some of his predecessors, but President Bush, who favored this expanded role, and Quayle were both counseled against such a course. Vice presidents experienced in the ways of Congress, such as former senators Quayle or Walter Mondale, can help bridge the gap between Capitol Hill and the White House. Vice President Quayle, for example, sits in on the weekly meetings of GOP committee chairmen and the luncheons that follow with all Republican senators. This participation enables him to learn the concerns of Republican senators and to inform them about White House intentions. The vice president can then share this Capitol Hill intelligence with President Bush. When votes on major issues are expected to be close, party leaders make sure that the vice president is presiding so he can break tie votes.

Second, the Constitution provides for a *president pro tempore* to preside in the vice president's absence. In modern practice this constitutional officer is the majority party senator with the longest continuous service. "Because of his

Figure 6-2 Organization of the Senate, 101st Congress (1989-1991)

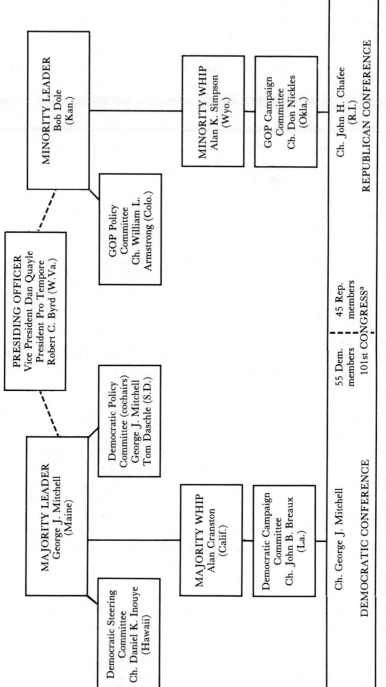

a As of January 3, 1989, when the 101st Congress convened.

position as a senior member of the party, and often the chairman of a key committee, the leadership regularly consults the president pro tempore as to his views on policies and actions of the party," said Senator Byrd when he was majority leader.[26] At the end of the 100th Congress, Byrd relinquished this post, but his longevity of service enabled him in the next Congress to serve as both president pro tempore and chairman of the Appropriations Committee. By passing a simple resolution, the Senate sometimes appoints a deputy president pro tempore. This majority party official presides over the Senate in the absence of the vice president and president pro tempore and is part of the leadership group that meets periodically at the White House with the president.

Third, a dozen or so majority senators, typically junior members, serve half-hour or so stints each day as the presiding officer. The opportunity to preside helps newcomers become familiar with Senate rules and procedures. None of these presiding officers have the influence or visibility of the House Speaker.

Floor Leaders

The *majority leader* is the head of the majority party in the Senate, its leader on the floor, and the leader of the Senate. Nowhere mentioned in the Constitution, the position evolved from the party post of conference (caucus) chairman during the late 1800s and early 1900s.[27] Similarly, the *minority leader* heads the Senate's minority party. Both officers are elected biennially by secret ballot of their party colleagues. Historically, the majority leadership has had its ups and downs, reflecting in part the differing leadership styles and political circumstances of each occupant. Democrat Scott Lucas of Illinois often was thwarted in trying to enact President Harry S Truman's program by a coalition of Republicans and southern Democrats. After two frustrating years Illinois voters ended his political career in 1951. Lucas's successor, Ernest McFarland of Arizona, also lost reelection after only two years as majority leader.

Strong Leadership, 1953-1960. The fortunes of the office changed, however, when Republican Robert A. Taft of Ohio became majority leader in 1953. Although Taft served less than a year before his death, he enhanced the stature of the office and underscored its potential as an independent source of authority. He "proved a master of parliamentary procedures" and contributed to his party's cohesiveness, which "showed more unity on key roll-call votes in 1953 than at any time in years." [28]

Unlike Taft, who served fourteen years before he became party leader, Lyndon B. Johnson was elected minority leader in 1953 after only four years in the Senate. In 1955 he became majority leader when the Democrats regained control of Congress. Johnson possessed singular attributes that helped him gain the top party office. "He doesn't have the best mind on the

Democratic side," declared Richard Russell of Georgia, the leader of southern Democrats. "He isn't the best orator; he isn't the best parliamentarian. But he's the best combination of all of these qualities." [29]

Known for his powerful persuasive abilities, Johnson transformed the Democratic leadership post into one of immense authority and prestige. His extensive network of trusted aides and colleagues made him better informed about more issues than any other senator. Opposition party control of the White House gave the aggressive Johnson the luxury of choosing which policies to support and which strategies to employ to get them enacted. And his pragmatic outlook, domineering style, and arm-twisting abilities made him the premier vote-gatherer in the Senate. The majority leader's awesome display of face-to-face persuasion has been called the "Johnson Treatment."

> The Treatment could last ten minutes or four hours. It came, enveloping its target, at the LBJ Ranch swimming pool, in one of LBJ's offices, in the Senate cloakroom, on the floor of the Senate itself.... Its tone could be supplication, accusation, cajolery, exuberance, scorn, tears, complaint, the hint of threat. It was all of these together. It ran the gamut of human emotions. Its velocity was breathtaking, and it was all in one direction. Interjections from the target were rare. Johnson anticipated them before they could be spoken. He moved in close, his face a scant millimeter from his target, his eyes widening and narrowing, and his eyebrows rising and falling. From his pockets poured clippings, memos, statistics. Mimicry, humor, and the genius of analogy made The Treatment an almost hypnotic experience and rendered the target stunned and helpless. [30]

Buttressing Johnson was an "inner club," a bipartisan group of senior senators, mainly southern Democrats such as Russell. The club, some people said, wielded the real power in the Senate through its control of chairman-ships and committee assignments. [31] There were even unwritten rules of behavior (for example, junior members should be seen and not heard) that encouraged new senators to defer to the "establishment."

Collegial Leadership, 1961-1989. Johnson's successor, Mike Mansfield, D-Mont., sharply curtailed the role of majority leader. He viewed himself as one among equals. "I can see a Senate with real egalitarianism, the decline of seniority as a major factor, and new senators being seen and heard and not being wallflowers," Mansfield said. [32] He permitted floor managers and individual senators to take public credit when measures were enacted. Significant organizational and procedural developments, such as increases in the number of subcommittees and staff aides, occurred in the Senate during his leadership.

When Byrd served as majority leader from 1977 to 1981 and 1987 to 1989, the Senate remained democratic, assertive, independent, and open to public view. Byrd's style was somewhere between that of the flamboyant Johnson and the relaxed Mansfield. "Circumstances don't permit the Lyndon

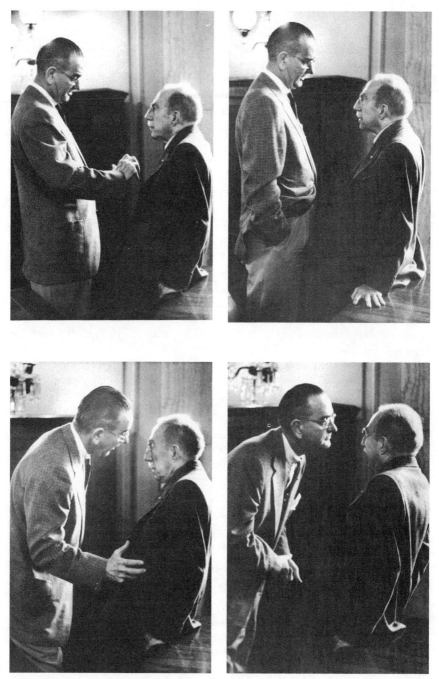

Senate Majority Leader Lyndon B. Johnson gives "The Treatment" to Sen. Theodore Francis Green, D-R.I.

Johnson style," he observed. "What I am saying is that times and things have changed. Younger Senators come into the Senate. They are more independent. The 'establishment' is a bad word. Each wants to do his 'own thing.' "[33]

Byrd recognized that he had to cater to individual members. On the other hand, the majority leader is charged with processing the Senate's workload. Caught between individual and institutional pressures, Byrd employed his formidable parliamentary skills and controls to accommodate colleagues and expedite the Senate's business.

Senator Howard Baker succeeded Byrd after the Republicans gained control of the Senate in 1981. As the first GOP majority leader in almost three decades, Baker wanted to make the Senate a truly deliberative body again. "I'd like to see us restore the nature of the Senate as a great debating institution," he said. "Our committees report too much legislation and we pass too many laws. We don't need more laws. We need less laws." [34]

When Baker retired from the Senate in 1984, he left a Congress less active in passing new laws, in part because of fiscal constraints and an antigovernment public mood. But Baker still complained that the "Senate floor is almost never the place where the great issues are thrashed out." More debate occurred, he lamented, "in the corridor near [my] office" than on the Senate floor itself.[35]

When Senator Dole, former chairman of the Finance Committee and 1976 vice-presidential nominee, became majority leader in 1985, he brought to the office experience, national visibility, quick wit, independence, and mastery of coalition building. As one White House official stated:

> He really knows how to count votes. He has a fine feeling for where his senators will be, when to press, when to back off, when to use persuasion on the facts and when to persuade on the politics of the situation.[36]

Dole faced two immediate challenges upon taking office: pushing President Reagan's second-term agenda through Congress, and retaining GOP control of the Senate. Although the Senate returned to Democratic control after the November 1986 elections, Senator Dole proved to be a hard-charging majority leader during his two-year stint in that post. "I didn't become majority leader to lose," he said. He established a "degree of tough control [of the Senate floor] unseen in a generation." On one occasion, angry at Dole's control of the floor amendment process through the majority leader's prerogative of being accorded priority of recognition by the presiding officer, Democratic leader Byrd exclaimed:

> I have had enough of this business of having the majority leader stand here and act as a traffic cop of this floor. . . . He determines who will call up an amendment, when they will call up an amendment and what will be in the amendment.[37]

When Senator Byrd returned as majority leader for the 100th Congress (1987-1989), he found a Senate significantly different from when he relinquished the post six years earlier. Republicans now controlled the White House and Byrd's senatorial majority was smaller than in years past. With both chambers of Congress in Democratic hands, Byrd and his House counterpart, Speaker Wright, had to develop a legislative agenda to counter President Reagan's. Democrats wanted to address national problems effectively and thus give their party a boost in the 1988 elections. Byrd's efforts at promoting party unity on issues were aided, ironically, by the Democrats' fresh memories of their minority status.

> But being in the minority for six years ... we learned that we don't have the luxury of each going his own way, and we do have to look at things together as a party. Because, while a given senator may be reelected on his own, quite independent of his party, at the same time he is a committee chairman or a subcommittee chairman because the party has control of the Senate. So, it's important that our party stay in control. Otherwise, we go back to being the ranking members and having far less influence and impact on national programs and the direction of our country. That's the penalty if we don't stick together.[38]

At the start of the 101st Congress, Majority Leader George Mitchell dispersed power to other Democrats that was previously consolidated in the majority leader's office. He named a senior Democrat, Daniel Inouye of Hawaii, to chair the Steering Committee, a panel heretofore always headed by the majority leader. Mitchell also appointed a first-term Democrat, Tom Daschle of South Dakota, to cochair with him the Democratic Policy Committee, an advisory and research unit of the majority leadership. Mitchell named another first-termer, Georgian Wyche Fowler, as assistant floor leader. Mitchell's initial goals, he said, were to establish a "good, fair and open relationship with the Republican leadership" and to "consult and involve Democrats in preparation and enactment" of a legislative program.[39]

Minority Leader. The Senate minority leader consults continually with the majority leader. If a member of the president's party, the minority leader has the traditional obligation of trying to carry out the administration's program. When Bush won the presidency—having beaten his arch-rival, Minority Leader Dole, for the GOP nomination—the two met to smooth their often stormy relationship. Each understood that the effectiveness of their dealings with one another was important in moving the GOP's agenda through the Democratically controlled Senate. "I want to be [Bush's] point man in the Senate," observed Dole, "as long as we're in on the takeoff and not just the landing." [40]

The minority leader also exercises a "watchdog" role over the majority party—offering criticism, frustrating majority actions, and formulating alternative proposals. Minority leaders' roles and operating styles are influenced by personality, colleagues' expectations, their party's size in the Senate, control of the White House, and the leader's view of the proper function of the office.[41]

Party Whips. The Senate's whip system is smaller than the House's but carries out a similar function of "counting noses" before a vote. In the 101st Congress the Democratic whip system consisted of Majority Whip Alan Cranston of California, elected by party colleagues to a record-setting fifth consecutive term; Chief Deputy Whip Alan Dixon of Illinois (elected by all Democrats); and eight regional deputy whips elected by the Democratic senators in their respective regions (East, South, Midwest, and West). And in an innovation advocated by the Democratic leaders of the 101st Congress, party members elected rather than appointed their chief deputy whip, the number four position in the party's hierarchy.

When the Republicans took control of the Senate in 1981, they dropped the practice of appointing assistant whips. Faced with numerous duties, such as chairing committees and subcommittees, GOP leaders lacked time for regular stints on the Senate floor as assistant whips. Moreover, there were plenty of other Republicans (floor managers, presiding officers, and elective leaders) to supervise and guard the floor. But after their return to minority status following the November 1986 elections, Republicans again appointed deputy minority whips to assist the minority whip (or assistant minority leader), Alan K. Simpson of Wyoming, in gathering votes and planning party strategy.

On occasion the two whip organizations cooperate as they did on the 1987 omnibus trade bill. Byrd, then the majority leader, offered this praise: "It was a remarkable piece of teamwork that we saw as Senator Cranston, Senator Simpson, and their respective whip organizations worked together" to expedite Senate consideration of members' amendments.[42]

Selection of Leaders

Senators and representatives elect their top leaders before the beginning of each new Congress by secret ballot in their party caucuses. Although the whole House votes for the Speaker, it is a pro forma election. With straight party voting the unspoken rule on this and other organizational matters, the majority party has always elected the Speaker. Since the 1980s, candidates for party leadership positions have often waged long and grueling campaigns to win support from their partisan colleagues. Members understand that a party leadership post can be a "career launching pad for members seeking advancement, either within the [Congress] or outside it." [43]

In the House the two parties treat their hierarchies differently—the Democrats as a ladder and the Republicans as a slippery slope. Democrats typically elevate their next-in-line officer—from whip to majority leader to Speaker—as vacancies occur. Although succession is not guaranteed, several recent Speakers attained office this way. Speaker Wright, who served as majority leader (but never as whip) for a decade, lauded the Democrats' "step up" pattern of succession because "it works" and produces leaders who understand the House. Representative Udall, however, questioned the leadership ladder tradition in the House: "You permit the past generation to pick the leaders of the future." [44]

Republicans, on the other hand, have a tendency to push people off the ladder, in part because of their frustrations at being the "permanent minority." In 1959 Charles Halleck ousted Joseph Martin as GOP leader; in 1965 Gerald Ford turned the tables on Halleck; and in 1980 colleagues persuaded John Rhodes to step down as party leader.

House Republicans' growing frustration with nearly four decades in the minority and with the conciliatory style of their leadership propelled Representative Gingrich into the minority whip post when President Bush named Richard Cheney, then GOP whip, as secretary of defense. Gingrich, who had never served in a leadership position or on any major House panel, eked out a narrow 87-85 victory over a consensus-practicing rival by stressing his video skills, determination to make Republicans the House majority in the 1990s, and aggressive style. "We had a choice of being attack dogs or lapdogs," said a House Republican about the election. "We decided attack dogs are more useful." [45]

Length of prior legislative service in Congress is not the only criterion that influences the election of party leaders. Other factors considered are ideological or geographical balance within the leadership, reputation for hard work and competency in procedural and organizational matters, and personal attributes such as intelligence, fairness, persuasive talent, political shrewdness, and media savvy. Not infrequently, partisans have to choose between internal skills (procedural expertise, for example) and external image.

Representative Michel, for example, waged a vigorous fight in 1980 to win election as House Republican leader. His opponent, Guy Vander Jagt of Michigan, stressed oratorical ability and talent as an effective party spokesman.

> House Republicans are a forgotten minority of a forgotten body.... That's why we need someone who can project to the American public.... Inevitably one winds up on "Face the Nation" or "Meet the Press." I think I would be a more forceful spokesman than Bob Michel.

Michel, on the other hand, emphasized parliamentary experience, service as minority whip, and bargaining skills.

> It takes more than a TV image to get things enacted into law. You can make beautiful speeches, but the bottom line is going to be enactment of the Reagan program.
>   Let's not forget we're still down 51 votes. Guy Vander Jagt has no experience on the floor and he'd be rebuffed on the other side of the aisle because he's been such a political partisan. A day-to-day diatribe would not serve the political process.[46]

By the late 1980s, however, members considered telegenic skills to be an important attribute of party leaders, as their election of Majority Leader

Mitchell and Minority Whip Gingrich suggest. "I'm the first leader of the C-Span [Cable Satellite Public Affairs Network] generation," declared Gingrich, who adhered to this formula: "conflict equals exposure equals power." [47]

For the most part, House and Senate leaders swim in the mainstream or center of their party. When he was majority leader, Byrd explained why: "As a member of the leadership it is my duty to bring north and south, liberals and conservatives together; to work out compromises. . . . I think it takes a centrist to do that." [48]

Byrd's successor, George Mitchell, was one of the Senate's most liberal members when he defeated the two less liberal contenders to be majority leader. "Clearly, Mitchell won not because of ideology," said fellow Democrat Lloyd Bentsen of Texas. "Mitchell won because he's Mitchell." [49] Sen. David Pryor, D-Ark., made this prediction: "I think you will see [Mitchell] become a centrist" because he will speak not just for Maine but for all Democrats and for the Senate. [50]

Once selected, party leaders enjoy a number of potent prerogatives and perquisites that augment their influence. For example, they are accorded priority in recognition on the floor, and they receive higher salaries, more office space, more staff, and more media attention than other members.

Serving as a party leader in the House is a full-time position. By contrast, every party leader in the Senate sits on several committees. The smaller size of the Senate allows leaders to participate in committee work while discharging their leadership duties. As majority leader, Johnson made a notable contribution on space policy, Mansfield and Baker on international affairs, Byrd on energy issues, Dole on tax questions, and Mitchell on environmental protection.

Jobs of Leaders

House and Senate leaders have basically the same job: to bring coherence and efficiency to a decentralized and individualistic legislative body. Leadership duties can be described in terms of "institutional maintenance" (ensuring that Congress and its members perform their lawmaking duties effectively) and "party maintenance" (crafting winning coalitions from among partisan colleagues). [51] Both kinds of functions point toward the parties' objective of influencing policy making in conformity with their political leanings.

Institutional Jobs

Organizing the Chamber. Party leaders influence congressional organization and procedure. They help select the chief administrative officers of the House or Senate, oversee committee jurisdictional revisions, and revise congressional rules.

In 1979 the Senate modernized its rules largely through the initiative of Democratic leader Byrd, who was instrumental in rules changes that curbed the filibuster in 1975 and realigned committee jurisdictions in 1977. Senate leaders Byrd and Dole were key actors in persuading the Senate in 1986 to permit gavel-to-gavel television coverage of its floor proceedings. Notable changes in House rules had occurred in 1890 when GOP Speaker Thomas B. Reed limited the minority party's ability to obstruct and conferred additional authority on the Speakership. Today's revisions sometimes have the same objectives. The majority convenes in caucus prior to the start of each Congress, drafts a rules package, and then approves it in the House on a party-line vote.

Scheduling Floor Business. "The power of the Speaker of the House is the power of scheduling," Speaker O'Neill once exclaimed.[52] After consulting with committee leaders, interested members, the president, and others, party leaders decide what, when, and in which order measures should come up for debate.

Once a bill is scheduled for action, the leaders' job is to see that members vote—a more difficult task than merely herding bodies into the chamber. Party leaders may seek out certain members to speak on an issue because their endorsement can persuade other legislators to support it. Or they may delay action until the bill's sponsors are present. "The leadership must have the right members at the right place at the right time," said Byrd when he was the Senate majority whip.[53] In short, leaders' scheduling prerogatives mold policy; arranging when bills reach the floor can seal their fate. A week's delay in scheduling a controversial White House initiative, for instance, gives the president, lobbying groups, and others additional time to mobilize votes for the proposal.

In 1988 the Senate began a new scheduling system. Every month the Senate is in session three weeks and off one week. This new schedule accommodates the two Congresses. It enables senators to meet with constituents in their states on a predictable basis; it also facilitates the Senate's business by enabling party leaders to plan a full five-day (Monday through Friday) work week. In the House, however, leaders typically plan little business for Mondays and Fridays, particularly in election years, to let campaigning members return home for long weekends.

Sometimes business is scheduled on the floor of the House and Senate with elections in mind. For example, Senate Democrats "put on the floor all the labor and social legislation they wanted to highlight in the closing weeks before the Nov. 8 elections." Their strategy was to embarrass GOP candidates who did not support these Democratic-formulated proposals on "family issues" and open them to charges of being antifamily. "This is solely a ploy to play games, to embarrass George Bush," retorted Senate Minority Whip Simpson.[54]

Influencing Colleagues.　Party leaders also have the the task of persuading members to support their legislation. In the modern Congress "twisting arms" means pleading and cajoling to coax votes. "If you have no sense of what other people's judgments, values or goals are," stated Speaker Foley about the negotiating process, "you're in a very poor position to evaluate how you might accommodate them." [55] While leaders generally seek to influence members of their own party and chamber, they also try to win cooperation from the other chamber and from the opposition party. Democratic and Republican leaders in the House and Senate regularly confer with each other to promote unity and understanding between the chambers.

Party leaders do not have to rely solely on their powers of persuasion, however. Informal political networks and access to strategic information give them an edge in influencing colleagues.

> Because of an improved whip system and because members will respond more candidly to leadership polls than to lobbyist or White House polls, [leaders] have perhaps the most important information in a legislative struggle—information on where the votes are and (sometimes) what it will take to win certain people over.[56]

Top leaders can bestow or withhold a variety of tangible and intangible rewards. They can name legislators to special or select committees, influence assignments to standing committees, aid reelection campaigns, smooth access to the White House or executive agencies, single out legislators for high praise, and furnish numerous other services. As Speaker O'Neill commented during an interview:

> You know, you ask me what are my powers and my authority around here? The power to recognize on the floor; little odds and ends—like men get pride out of the prestige of handling the Committee of the Whole, being named Speaker for the day. . . . [T]here is a certain aura and respect that goes with the Speaker's office. He does have the power to be able to pick up the telephone and call people. And Members oftentimes like to bring their local political leaders or a couple of mayors. And oftentimes they have problems from their area and they need aid and assistance. . . . We're happy to try to open the door for them, having been in the town for so many years and knowing so many people. We do know where a lot of bodies are and we do know how to advise people.[57]

Adroit leaders know how to wield these "little odds and ends" to advance their party's interests. They also weigh elements such as the public visibility of an issue, the extent of constituency interest in it, the size of their majority, and the likelihood of presidential intervention.

Consult the President.　A traditional duty of party leaders is to meet with the president about the administration's goals and to convey legislative sentiment about what the executive branch is doing or not doing. This consultative duty is performed mainly by leaders of the president's party. The

Informing the president by telephone of the new leadership in the 101st Congress are, from the left, Senate Minority Leader Robert Dole, Senate Majority Leader George J. Mitchell, House Majority Leader (now Speaker) Thomas S. Foley, and House Minority Leader Robert H. Michel.

origin of regular meetings between the president and congressional leaders has been attributed to Sam Rayburn:

> As majority leader, Rayburn was particularly embarrassed by the lack of adequate communication between the President [Franklin D. Roosevelt] and the House leadership. One day he told Tommy Corcoran, then a premier lobbyist for the White House: "The President ought to be having a meeting every week with his House and Senate leaders so we could tell him what we're planning, and he could tell us his plans. It could eliminate a lot of confusion. See what you can do—but don't you dare let him know I suggested it 'cause he thinks he 'borned' every idea that ever was."
>
> Corcoran handled the task skillfully. On Rayburn's next visit to the White House, Roosevelt said, "Sam, I've been thinking. Maybe it would be a good idea if I had a meeting with [Speaker] Bill [Bankhead] and you and [Vice President] Jack [Garner] and [Senate Majority Leader] Alben [Barkley] about once a week to talk over what all of us are planning."
>
> "Mr. President," replied Rayburn, "that's one of the smartest ideas I ever heard." So were born the periodic meetings with congressional leaders that all subsequent presidents have used to varying degrees.[58]

When leaders oppose programs sponsored by their party's president, usually they step aside so that other party leaders who support administration views can advocate and defend them on the floor. Alben W. Barkley, D-Ky., who served both as Senate majority leader (1937-1946) and minority leader (1947-1949), went so far as to say that usually "no matter what party is in power—no matter who is President—the majority leader of the Senate is expected to be the legislative spokesman of the administration." [59] The tug between institution and party is part and parcel of the job.

Party Jobs

Organizing the Party.   Top congressional leaders help organize their party by selecting partisan colleagues for standing committees, revising party rules, choosing other party leaders, and appointing party committees. Influencing policy formation is also very important. Speaker Wright, for example, responded to President Reagan's State of the Union address with his own remarks. "Consider the State of our Union with me," he said to the American public, "as we reflect upon five major steps the 100th Congress is taking to build America's future." One of these steps was aimed at improving the nation's competitive position in the world. "We can't build a vibrant economy by just delivering pizzas to each other," declared the Speaker.[60]

Promoting Party Unity.   Another leadership assignment is to encourage party unity in Congress on priority legislation. Senate GOP leader Everett Dirksen (1959-1969) used social gatherings to accomplish this goal.

> Dirksen brought the party members together in a series of social affairs. He held cocktail parties at the Congressional Country Club outside Washington, inviting all Republican senators and sometimes their wives too. These were calculated by Dirksen to improve party harmony and to build a friendly feeling for himself with the Republican senators.[61]

But party leaders' assistance to the rank and file goes far beyond extending them social invitations. Leaders schedule members' bills, provide them with timely political information, advise them on electoral issues, visit with their constituents, and help them obtain good committee assignments. For example, Senate Democratic and Republican leaders struggled for over two months before GOP senator David Karnes of Nebraska (appointed to fill the vacancy caused by the death of Democrat Ed Zorinsky) received the committee assignments of his choice: Agriculture and Banking. The partisan struggle involved the size and ratio—or balance of party power—of these two panels. In the end, with the aid of GOP leader Dole, Karnes got his assignments, although Democrats added another member to both panels.[62] This kind of assistance to members aids in the leaders' coalition-building activities on subsequent policy or political issues.

Publicizing Party Views.   Leaders are expected to publicize their party's policies and achievements. They give speeches in various forums, appear on radio and television talk shows, write newspaper and journal articles, and hold regular press conferences. House Speakers customarily meet with journalists before each day's House session. The Senate majority and minority leaders conduct what Senator Baker called "dugout chatter" sessions before the Senate convenes, when the press accredited to the Senate press gallery can question the two leaders.[63]

The spokesperson's role has increased in importance in recent years in part because of the political impact of the mass media. "We've created a situation," noted a scholar, "where the real way you drive the legislative process is by influencing public opinion, rather than by trading for votes." [64]

Providing Campaign Assistance. Leaders assist party members seeking reelection with campaign funds and endorsements. Many leaders sponsor fund-raising committees that dispense money to numerous colleagues. These so-called "leadership PACs" provide leaders with political IOUs that can be cashed in later. "I suppose that by making some contributions to colleagues, some colleagues might sense a little closer spirit of unity with the leadership program," Speaker Wright said.[65] However, as accusations about his ethics mounted, Wright provided less and less help to fellow Democrats. "How can he go to anybody's district?" asked a colleague. "He becomes the story." [66]

All three candidates for the job of Senate majority leader in the 101st Congress (Mitchell, Inouye, and Johnston) participated in fund-raising campaigns for their colleagues. As one account noted:

> It seems that the job of fundraiser is becoming more important to senators' expectations of what a majority leader should do. The candidates thus are not trying to buy votes so much as to demonstrate how well they can fulfill that role.[67]

It is worth noting that two recent party leaders—Mitchell and former House majority whip Coelho—previously chaired their chamber's congressional campaign committee. The ability to raise funds for colleagues, an increasingly important criterion for judging prospective party leaders, is yet another reminder that leaders stand at the conjunction of the two Congresses.

Congressional leaders maintain relations with national party organizations and with other groups. For example, House and Senate Democratic leaders are members of the Democratic National Committee and its executive committee; many serve as "superdelegates" (unpledged, ex officio delegates) to Democratic nominating conventions. Congressional leaders also are active in helping to draft their party's presidential platform. The 1988 GOP platform even contained a list of grievances against the Democratic-run House.

Party Caucuses, Committees, and Informal Groups

House and Senate leaders operate in different institutional contexts. In the larger, more impersonal House, majority party leaders sometimes ignore the wishes of the minority party. This seldom happens in the Senate, which emphasizes individualism, reciprocity, and mutual accommodation. Partisan conflict, as a result, tends to be somewhat more muted than in the House, where bitter party battles are commonplace.

Despite these differences between parties in the House and Senate, they are organized into the same three components: caucuses, committees, and informal party groups.

Party Caucuses

The organization of all partisans in a chamber is called the conference or (in the case of House Democrats) the caucus. Party conferences (caucuses) elect leaders, approve committee assignments, provide services to members, and debate party and legislative policies. A senior House Democrat explained how the caucus can serve to promote consensus on issues:

> The caucus is the place where a great deal of freewheeling debate over an issue takes place and where sometimes a consensus develops . . . with respect to how to handle reconciliation [legislation]. Most of the discussions, although they have taken place at leadership meetings and at chairmen's meetings and in whips' meetings, have ended up in the broader forum of the caucus where every member of the Democratic party participates. You don't take a vote, but you try to develop a consensus and make concessions where they're necessary and develop the strongest possible position that can be supported by the maximum number of Democrats.[68]

On rare occasions, party caucuses strip fellow members of their committee seniority.

Party caucuses, in brief, are useful forums where party members and leaders can assess and sway sentiment on substantive or procedural issues. During the 1970s House Democratic caucuses adopted procedural reforms that diluted committee chairmen's authority, strengthened subcommittees' autonomy, and emphasized "juniority" over seniority. The Senate GOP Conference has expanded its functions to provide media advice and services for its members. And some caucus chairmen in the House, such as Richard Gephardt, D-Mo., and Jack Kemp, R-N.Y., attracted sufficient national attention to be contenders for their party's presidential nomination.

Party Committees

The four congressional parties each establish committees to serve partisan needs and objectives (see Table 6-1). Of all the party committees, only the Senate majority and minority policy committees are created by law. This happened in 1947 after the House deleted a provision for policy committees from the Legislative Reorganization Act of 1946; the Senate then provided for

Table 6-1 Party Committees in the Senate and House

Committees	Number of members	Function
Senate Democratic		
Policy	9	Considers party positions on specific measures and assists the party leader in scheduling bills
Steering	22	Assigns Democrats to committees
Campaign	15	Provides campaign aid to Democratic senatorial candidates
Senate Republican		
Policy	23	Defines GOP positions on specific issues; researches procedural and substantive issues; drafts policy alternatives
Committee on Committees	17	Assigns Republicans to committees
Campaign	15	Provides campaign aid to Republican senatorial candidates
House Democratic		
Steering and Policy	31[a]	Assigns Democrats to committees; discusses and endorses party policy; serves as an executive arm of the Democratic caucus
Campaign	52	Aids in the election of Democrats to the House
Personnel	5	Oversees patronage appointments among Democratic members
House Republican		
Policy	32[b]	Considers policy alternatives to majority proposals and works for consensus among Republican members
Research	22	Appoints task forces to consider alternatives to majority legislation; conducts research
Committee on Committees	15[c]	Assigns Republicans to standing committees
Campaign	21	Seeks to elect Republicans to the House
Personnel	8	Aids in supervision of Republican employees

[a] Twelve members elected from regional zones, eleven ex officio members, and eight appointed by the Speaker.
[b] Eight members elected from regional zones, two members from the freshman class and two from the sophomore class, twelve ex officio members, and a maximum of seven members-at-large appointed by the GOP leader.
[c] In executive committee.

its policy units in a legislative branch appropriations act. The policy committees provide advice on scheduling, encourage party unity, study substantive and political issues, and discuss broad questions of party policy. They do not make policy, and their influence has varied over the years. They assume greater importance when the party does not control the White House and thus needs policy guidance.

Informal Party Groups

Informal party groups have long been part of the congressional scene. In the pre-1970 period conservative southern Democrats formed a loosely knit alliance (the "Boll Weevils") that held a powerful grip on legislation and congressional affairs through their disproportionate share of committee chairmanships and their coalition with conservative Republicans. Boll Weevils are becoming an endangered species in today's House in part because demographic and political changes in the South have brought the northern and southern wings of the Democratic party closer together on many substantive issues. But a modern variation of the Boll Weevils, called the Conservative Democratic Forum, played a pivotal role in the House during the 97th Congress (1981-1983). About fifty members of this group sided with Republicans to provide the margin of victory for Reagan's economic agenda.

On the liberal end of the spectrum, the House Democratic Study Group was the catalyst for changes during the 1960s and 1970s that shifted power from the "haves" (Democratic representatives with seniority) to the "have nots" (junior members seeking better committee assignments).

The GOP, too, has its informal party groups, such as the Conservative Opportunity Society (one of whose founders is Newt Gingrich) and the Republican Study Committee. Organized in 1973, the Republican Study Committee is the "self-proclaimed 'conservative conscience' of the Republican party in the House and has played a large role in countering Democratic legislative proposals and in initiating Republican legislative programs." [69] A group of about thirty moderate-to-liberal Republicans, called the House Wednesday Group, regularly meets to discuss and advance ideas for the House's agenda. "When you're in the minority," explained Rep. Bill Gradison of Ohio, "it's hard to influence by sheer numbers, so we have to try to impress with the force of ideas." [70] (For additional material on unofficial congressional groups, see Chapter 10.)

Party Continuity and Change

Several features of the contemporary party system stand out on Capitol Hill. Some of these features reflect elements of continuity; others highlight change. Among these features are the vigor of the congressional parties, the monopoly of the two-party system, the rise of divided party government, and the advent of new coalition-building practices.

Vigorous Congressional Parties

By any test one can use, congressional parties are flourishing: the organizational elements are healthy and active, leaders are increasingly prominent, and party voting is at relatively high levels (see Chapter 12). The Senate of the 1980s has even been called the "Leaders' Senate" because of the artful use of governing power. "Majority Leaders Howard Baker, Robert Dole . . . and Robert Byrd have set agendas for the body and pretty well determined how it will stand on issues. They have worked hard and used their particular and in each case rather different skills to hold almost all of their own parties together and to fashion positions which can command a few votes from the other side when necessary."[71] The same can be said of Majority Leader Mitchell.

That Democrats and Republicans are voting together on more issues is evident from recent analyses. One reason for this trend is a drop-off in the alliance between conservative southern Democrats and Republicans. Constituency changes in the South have led to the election of "new breed" Democrats who are more ideologically compatible with their party colleagues from the rest of the country. On the GOP side of the aisle, the ranks of "liberals" and moderates have thinned.

Another reason for voting cohesion is heightened partisanship in Congress, especially in the House. As one House GOP leader remarked: "Polarization often has very beneficial results. If everything is handled through compromise and conciliation, if there are no real issues dividing us from the Democrats, why should the country change and make us the majority?" [72] Congress is thus a partisan body—perhaps more so than at any time in modern history.

The Two-Party System

The Democratic and Republican parties have dominated American politics and the Congress since the mid-nineteenth century. Scholars have posited various theories for the dualistic *national* politics of a country as diverse as the United States. Some trace the origins of the national two-party system to early conflicts between Federalists (advocates of a strong national government) and Anti-Federalists (advocates of limited national government). Continuation of dualism occurred in subsequent splits, such as North versus South, East versus West, agricultural versus financial interests, and rural versus urban areas.[73] Constitutional, political, and legal arrangements are other bases of the two-party system. Plurality elections in single-member congressional districts encouraged creation and maintenance of two major parties. Under the winner-take-all principle, the person who wins the most votes in a state or district is elected to the Senate or House. This principle discourages the formation of third parties. In addition, many states have laws that make it difficult to create new parties.

Whatever mix of causes produced the two-party system, one thing is clear:

few third-party or independent legislators have been elected to Congress during the twentieth century. The 63d Congress (1913-1915) had the greatest minority party membership during this century: one Progressive senator and nineteen representatives elected as Progressives, Progressive-Republicans, or Independents. Since 1951 only three senators and three representatives have been elected from minor parties or as independents. Most of them convert to one of the major parties or vote with them in organizational matters, which hinge on party control. Third-party members have no institutional status. Their participation in Democratic or Republican affairs is "by invitation only."

Divided Government

There are two basic types of divided government: divided party control of Congress and split control of Congress and the White House. Both types occurred in the 1980s. Before the 1981-1987 period, control of Congress had been divided only twice: in the 62d Congress (1911-1913) and the 72d Congress (1931-1933).

The second type of divided government has become more common. For most of our history—that is, up to the end of World War II—one of the two major parties controlled all three power centers: the House, the Senate, and the White House. Yet in five of the presidential elections since 1968, Republicans won the White House while one or usually both legislative chambers remained in Democratic hands. It seems that the nation is in a period of more or less permanently divided government. Republicans are the "presidential party" and Democrats the "congressional party."

During President Reagan's first term, divided party control of Congress affected bicameral and legislative-executive relations in at least three noteworthy ways. First, President Reagan needed the support of some House Democrats to pass his proposals. His successes in the House, particularly in 1981, arose from disunity in Democratic ranks and unity among Republicans. Democrats held nominal control of the House, but real control on key issues rested with an ideological majority that consisted of "boll weevil" Democrats and Republicans. Second, the GOP-controlled Senate played a pivotal role either by accelerating action on the Reagan agenda (pressuring House Democrats in the process) or by seizing the initiative on issues when the White House failed to do so. Third, bicameral maneuverings took on greater complexity. Conference committees assumed more importance as each chamber sought to enact its version of disputed legislation. House Republicans even urged their majority Senate brethren to retaliate in kind against the Democrats if House Democrats shortchanged GOP representation on House committees. Or as a GOP House committee aide pointed out:

> Because we have a Republican Senate, [the Democratic committee majority] has come to recognize the value of getting the minority on board. . . . If they tick off the Republicans totally, what we will usually do . . . is get to the Senate people and say "we need to kill this bill." That

unspoken threat—the realization that the Republicans control the Senate and the White House—has been very important. . . . During the Carter administration, you found that [committee Democrats] were much less willing to accommodate Republican concerns.[74]

Some political commentators dislike divided government because it encourages policy deadlocks, diffuses public accountability, and promotes the "politics of blamesmanship." However, the ticket-splitting voters, with weakening ties to either party, seem to prefer this arrangement. Incumbency, especially for House members, is a huge electoral advantage, regardless of party. Differences in the parties' recruitment of candidates might help explain split control. Democrats seem to enlist more "quality" candidates for Congress; Republicans do the same for the presidency. Some analysts even argue that citizens prefer divided government because Democrats will "advance their interests as members of groups: whether the elderly, farmers, or home builders. But the Republicans take a national view on everything from the economy to foreign policy." [75] Whatever one thinks of it, divided government, in name or in spirit, is likely to be with us for some time. Some analysts foresee a split-level partisan alignment in which Republicans lock in the presidency while the Democrats control the House. "In terms of our recent political experience," noted former senator Thomas Eagleton, D-Mo., "we are left with the Senate as the only part of our governmental structure that may swing with change in voter attitude." [76]

Advances in Coalition Building

Party leaders today have many ways to build and mobilize winning coalitions on legislation. In an institution noted for diffusion of power and nonhierarchical character, party leaders increasingly use media strategies and omnibus bills to get the legislative results they desire. Procedural innovations also are important elements in the arsenal of the party leaders. These will be discussed in Chapter 7 (multiple referrals) and Chapter 11 (creative "rules" from the House Rules Committee and innovative unanimous consent agreements in the Senate).

Media Strategies.   Party leaders understand that media strategies (the use of the press, television, radio, polls, speeches, and so on) are essential to move or block legislation. No longer is the "inside" game—working behind the scenes to line up votes—sufficient to pass major, controversial measures. Also necessary is the "outside" game—influencing public opinion and creating grass-roots support for policy initiatives. "Being a good legislator means you have to do both," said House Majority Leader Gephardt. "If you are going to pass important legislation, you have to both deal with Members and put together coalitions in the country." [77] By getting constituents concerned about issues and policies, party leaders increase their chances of winning the support of congressional colleagues for their partisan priorities.

Omnibus Bills.   A phenomenon of modern lawmaking is the rise of mega-bills—legislation that is hundreds or thousands of pages in length. Much of Congress's most significant policy enactments are folded into four or five omnibus bills, such as continuing resolutions or reconciliation legislation (see Chapter 13). One reason for the rise of these "packages" is the politics of fiscal austerity. With the nation facing huge fiscal deficits, it is difficult for Congress to pass free-standing initiatives that involve money. As a result, some of these initiatives are incorporated into mega-bills to improve their chances of enactment. Presidents may sign a mega-bill even if it contains provisions offensive to them because a veto could cause the entire national government to shut down temporarily.

Omnibus bills have the indirect effect of recentralizing authority in party leaders because they possess the resources and authority to exercise coordinative and substantive influence over the packaging process. Mega-bills typically involve scores of committees. As a result, rank-and-file members look to party leaders for assistance in formulating a package acceptable to at least a majority of members. As one House member put it: "Our goal is to find something that's 60 percent acceptable to 52 percent of the members and I think we have a 75 percent chance of doing that." [78] No wonder House and Senate leaders often appoint ad hoc party task forces to mobilize support behind these priority matters.

Other factors, many of which are beyond the control of party leaders, affect successful coalition building. Some of these are the size of a party's majority in the House or Senate, the extent of presidential involvement in political mobilization, and the national mood. Still, at the heart of coalition building by party leaders are persuasion and the ability to serve members (speak at their fund raisers and schedule their bills, for instance).

Conclusion

Congressional parties have elaborate organizations, and their leaders a multiplicity of roles and duties. The Senate majority leader, explained Byrd when he held that post, "facilitates, he constructs, he programs, he schedules, he takes an active part in the development of legislation, he steps in at crucial moments on the floor, offers amendments, speaks on behalf of legislation and helps to shape the outcome of the legislation." [79] Party leaders can do many things, but they cannot command their colleagues. Party leaders "don't have punishments and rewards that we can hold in some cookie jar somewhere. That's not the way the system works," declared then Speaker Wright.[80] The art of leading, in sum, rests fundamentally on skill in persuading others to follow. "The most formidable tool I have is the power to persuade," noted Senate Majority Leader Mitchell.[81]

Congressional leaders' means of persuasion are numerous. They can schedule (or not schedule) bills for floor action, influence committee assignments, appoint special or select commitees, intervene with the White House, or arrange for campaign contributions to deserving members. When the leaders win key votes, it is sometimes because of personal prestige. Being liked makes a difference, as Rep. Barney Frank, D-Mass., explains:

> In some ways, being in Congress is more like being in high school than anything I've done since high school—I mean the way the structure is. Nobody in the House of Representatives can give any other member an order. The speaker is more influential than a new Republican from Texas, but he can't order anybody to do anything. Nobody can fire anybody. So what that means is that you become influential by persuading people, being likable, and having other people respect you but not resent you. That's why it's like high school.[82]

As we have seen, the "party principle" organizes Congress. The "committee principle," however, shapes the measures Congress acts upon. These two principles are often in conflict. The first emphasizes aggregation, the second fragmentation. Party leaders struggle to manage an institution that disperses policy-making authority to numerous work groups. In our next chapter we examine the important role of congressional committees.

Notes

1. Richard E. Cohen, "Congress' California Mavericks: By Conscience and Constituencies," *Los Angeles Times,* pt. V, April 26, 1987, 3.
2. *Congressional Record,* 100th Cong., 1st sess., December 3, 1987, H10975.
3. Richard E. Cohen, "The Race Is on to Replace Howard Baker as the Leader of Senate Republicans," *National Journal,* October 6, 1984, 1856.
4. Or as Sen. Charles Grassley, R-Iowa, put it, "Quality of life around here means making a plane reservation and being able to make the plane." Helen Dewar, "Mitchell's Orderly, Consultative Style Gets Early Plaudits in Senate," *Washington Post,* May 15, 1989, A11.
5. *Washington Times,* November 30, 1988, A8.
6. *Wall Street Journal,* January 30, 1985, 56.
7. John M. Barry, "The Man of the House: Jim Wright of Texas in Line to Succeed Tip O'Neill," *New York Times Magazine,* November 23, 1986, 109.
8. Tom Kenworthy, "House GOP Signals It's in a Fighting Mood," *Washington Post,* December 26, 1988, A8.
9. *U.S. News & World Report,* October 13, 1950, 30.
10. Joe Martin, *My First Fifty Years in Politics* (New York: McGraw-Hill, 1960), 181.
11. Alan Ehrenhalt, "Media, Power Shifts Dominate O'Neill's House," *Congressional Quarterly Weekly Report,* September 13, 1986, 2133.
12. Steven V. Roberts, "The Foreign Policy Tussle," *New York Times Maga-*

zine, January 24, 1988, 26.

13. *Washington Times,* December 28, 1987, A4.

14. See Joseph Cooper and David W. Brady, "Institutional Context and Leadership Style: The House from Cannon to Rayburn," in *Understanding Congressional Leadership,* ed. Frank H. Mackaman (Washington, D.C.: CQ Press, 1981); and Ronald M. Peters, Jr., "The Theoretical and Constitutional Foundations of the Speakership of the United States House of Representatives" (Paper delivered at the annual meeting of the American Political Science Association, Denver, Colo., September 2-6, 1982).

15. Bruce I. Oppenheimer and Robert L. Peabody, "How the Race for House Majority Leader Was Won—By One Vote," *Washington Monthly,* November 1977, 47-56.

16. Janet Hook, "Speaker Jim Wright Takes Charge in the House," *Congressional Quarterly Weekly Report,* July 11, 1987, 1484.

17. Christopher Madison, "The Heir Presumptive," *National Journal,* April 29, 1989, 1035.

18. Floyd M. Riddick, *Congressional Procedure* (Boston: Chapman & Grimes, 1941), 345-346.

19. Irwin B. Arieff, "Inside Congress," *Congressional Quarterly Weekly Report,* February 28, 1981, 379.

20. Richard E. Cohen, "Michel Has Designs on 1992," *National Journal,* December 17, 1988, 3194-3195.

21. Ronald D. Elving, "Gingrich Lieutenants Balance Political Style and Tactics," *Congressional Quarterly Weekly Report,* April 8, 1989, 733-734.

22. Ronald D. Elving, "Gingrich Lieutenants Keep Engines Running," *Congressional Quarterly Weekly Report,* March 18, 1989, 561.

23. *C-Span Update,* September 1, 1986, 4.

24. *Christian Science Monitor,* May 27, 1988, 4.

25. *Nation's Business,* January 1952, 52-53.

26. *Congressional Record,* 96th Cong., 2d sess., May 21, 1980, S5674.

27. Margaret Munk, "Origin and Development of the Party Floor Leadership in the United States Senate," *Capitol Studies* 2 (Winter 1974): 23-41.

28. James T. Patterson, *Mr. Republican: A Biography of Robert A. Taft* (Boston: Houghton Mifflin, 1972), 593.

29. Robert L. Peabody, *Leadership in Congress* (Boston: Little, Brown, 1976), 323.

30. Rowland Evans and Robert Novak, *Lyndon B. Johnson: The Exercise of Power* (New York: New American Library, 1966), 104.

31. See John G. Stewart, "Two Strategies of Leadership: Johnson and Mansfield," in *Congressional Behavior,* ed. Nelson W. Polsby (New York: Random House, 1971), 61-92; William S. White, *Citadel: The Story of the United States Senate* (New York: Harper & Bros., 1956); Joseph S. Clark, *The Senate Establishment* (New York: Hill & Wang, 1963); and Randall B. Ripley, *Power in the Senate* (New York: St. Martin's Press, 1969).

32. Richard E. Cohen, "Marking an End to the Senate's Mansfield Era," *National Journal,* December 25, 1976, 1803. See also *Congressional Record,* 88th Cong., 1st sess., November 27, 1963, 21754-21764.

33. *Congressional Record,* 96th Cong., 2d sess., April 18, 1980, S3294.

34. *New York Times,* December 3, 1980, A22.
35. *Wall Street Journal,* August 8, 1984, 58.
36. Hedrick Smith, "Bob Dole's Big Gamble," *New York Times Magazine,* June 30, 1985, 28.
37. *Washington Post,* March 9, 1987, A8.
38. Jacqueline Calmes, "Byrd Struggles to Lead Deeply Divided Senate," *Congressional Quarterly Weekly Report,* July 4, 1987, 1420.
39. Dewar, "Mitchell's Orderly, Consultative Style," A11.
40. *New York Times,* November 28, 1988, A20.
41. Charles O. Jones, *The Minority Party in Congress* (Boston: Little, Brown, 1970).
42. *Congressional Record,* 100th Cong., 1st sess., July 21, 1987, S10373.
43. *New York Times,* December 6, 1988, B13.
44. Jacqueline Calmes, "The Hill Leaders: Their Places on the Ladder," *Congressional Quarterly Weekly Report,* January 3, 1987, 6.
45. Jacob V. Lamar, "An Attack Dog, Not a Lapdog," *Time,* April 3, 1989, 22.
46. Vander Jagt and Michel quoted in the *Washington Post,* December 8, 1980, A2. See also Bill Keller, "New Minority Leader Michel: A Pragmatic Conservative," *Congressional Quarterly Weekly Report,* December 20, 1980, 3600-3601.
47. Howard Fineman, "For the Son of C-Span, Exposure Equals Power," *Newsweek,* April 3, 1989, 23.
48. *Congressional Record,* 94th Cong., 2d sess., February 16, 1976, 3137.
49. *Christian Science Monitor,* December 1, 1988, 3.
50. *Los Angeles Times,* November 30, 1988, 17.
51. Barbara Sinclair, *Majority Leadership in the U.S. House* (Baltimore, Md.: Johns Hopkins University Press, 1983).
52. *Congressional Record,* 98th Cong., 1st sess., November 15, 1983, H9856.
53. *Congressional Record,* 94th Cong., 1st sess., January 26, 1973, 2301.
54. Macon Morehouse, "Election-Year Politicking: Senate Fills Its Spare Time Feuding over 'Family Issues,'" *Congressional Quarterly Weekly Report,* October 1, 1988, 2708.
55. Madison, "The Heir Presumptive," 1036.
56. Sidney Waldman, "Majority Leadership in the House of Representatives," *Political Science Quarterly* 95 (Fall 1980): 377.
57. Michael J. Malbin, "House Democrats Are Playing with a Strong Leadership Lineup," *National Journal,* June 18, 1977, 942.
58. D. B. Hardeman and Donald C. Bacon, *Rayburn* (Austin: Texas Monthly Press, 1987), 227.
59. Simeon S. Willis et al., *The Process of Government* (University of Kentucky: Bureau of Government Research, 1949), 46.
60. *Congressional Record,* 100th Cong., 2d sess., January 27, 1988, H36-H37.
61. Neil MacNeil, *Dirksen,* 168-169.
62. *Roll Call,* May 18, 1987, 1.
63. *Congressional Record,* 98th Cong., 1st sess., November 15, 1983, S16130.
64. *New York Times,* June 7, 1984, B16.
65. *New York Times,* January 31, 1978, A13.
66. Gloria Borger, "A Cancer Grows on the Speakership," *U.S. News & World*

Report, May 22, 1989, 20.

67. Stephen Gettinger, "Potential Senate Leaders Flex Money Muscles," *Congressional Quarterly Weekly Report,* October 8, 1988, 2776.

68. Sinclair, *Majority Leadership in the U.S. House,* 96-97.

69. Edwin J. Feulner, Jr., *Conservatives Stalk the House: The Story of The Republican Study Committee, 1970-1982* (Ottawa, Ill.: Green Hill Publishers, 1983), 3.

70. *New York Times,* August 23, 1986, 5.

71. Michael Barone and Grant Ujifusa, *The Almanac of American Politics, 1988* (Washington, D.C.: National Journal, 1987), lxiv.

72. *The New Republic,* June 3, 1985, 9.

73. See V. O. Key, Jr., *Politics, Parties and Pressure Groups,* 5th ed. (New York: Thomas Y. Crowell, 1964); and Austin Ranney and Willmoore Kendall, *Democracy and the American Party System* (New York: Harcourt Brace Jovanovich, 1956).

74. Richard L. Hall, "Participation in Committees: An Exploration" (Paper presented at the 1984 annual meeting of the American Political Science Association, Washington, D.C., August 30-September 2, 1984), 21.

75. *Washington Post,* October 26, 1988, A23; and *Wall Street Journal,* November 14, 1988, A20.

76. *Congressional Record,* 101st Cong., 1st sess., April 6, 1989, S3402.

77. Richard Cohen, "Taking Advantage of Tax Reform Means Different Strokes for Different Folks," *National Journal,* June 22, 1985, 1459.

78. *Washington Post,* February 24, 1988, A22.

79. Richard E. Cohen, "Byrd of West Virginia: A New Job, A New Image," *National Journal,* August 20, 1977, 1294.

80. *New York Times,* April 27, 1982, A16.

81. Elaine S. Povich, "Majority Leader," *Chicago Tribune,* February 26, 1989, 9.

82. Hedrick Smith, *The Power Game* (New York: Random House, 1988), 54.

The Senate Labor and Human Resources Committee marks up a bill in the 100th Congress. From left, Republicans Quayle, Ind., and Hatch, Utah, argue with Democrats Kennedy, Mass., Pell, R.I., Dodd, Conn., and Simon, Ill.

CHAPTER SEVEN

Committees:
Workshops of Congress

Committees, like Congress as a whole, serve two broad purposes: individual and institutional. "As far as I can see, there is really only one basic reason to be on the Public Works Committee," admitted Rep. Douglas Bosco, D-Calif. "Intellectual stimulation" is not it. "Most of all, I want to be able to bring home projects to my district."[1] As Representative Bosco's remarks indicate, members of Congress understand the reelection connection between their committee assignments and their electoral opportunities two or six years down the road. Committees also enable legislators to develop expertise in areas that interest them. And some panels, such as the tax and appropriations "power committees," enable members to wield personal influence among their colleagues. "Members ask to be on" the House Appropriations Committee, explained Rep. Richard Armey, R-Texas, "because instanta-neously . . . they have a host of new friends, and we all know why": that panel controls the distribution of federal money.[2]

Institutionally, committees are the centers of policy making, oversight of federal agencies, and public education (largely through the hearings they hold). By dividing their membership into a number of "little legislatures," the House and Senate are able to consider dozens of proposed laws simulta-neously.[3] Without committees a legislative body of 100 senators and 440 House members could not handle 12,000 bills and nearly 100,000 nomina-tions biennially, a national budget of over a trillion dollars, and a limitless array of controversial issues. While floor actions often refine legislative products, committees are the means by which Congress sifts through an otherwise impossible jumble of bills, proposals, and issues.

Congressional committees serve another important institutional function in our political system: they act as "safety valves" or outlets for national frustrations and challenges. The United States' military and economic responsibilities, the social dislocations caused by technological advances, the trade deficit, global environmental concerns, the drug war, the rising cost of health care—these problems all place enormous strains on the political system. As forums for public debates, congressional committees help to vent, absorb, and resolve these strains. Moreover, the safety-valve function gives the citizenry a greater sense of participation in national decision making and helps educate members about public problems.

To be sure, the individual and institutional purposes of the committee system can conflict. Members often (though not always) gravitate to committees for constituency or career reasons, which means that they are not the most impartial judges of the policies they authorize. "It's one of the weaknesses of the system that those attracted to a committee like Agriculture are those whose constituents benefit from farm programs," acknowledged Rep. Charles Schumer, a Democrat from Brooklyn. "And so they're going to support those programs and they're not going to want to cut them, even the ones that are wasteful." [4]

Because good public policy may be impeded by the parochial orientations of individual members, Congress has a small number of centralizing or "control" committees that promote institutional and policy integration over committee and programmatic particularism. One of them is the Budget Committee of each house, which proposes limits on how much the various committees can authorize—limits that can be exceeded only through extraordinary means.[5] As House Budget chairman Leon Panetta, D-Calif., put it: "It's an enforcement committee. Once you set the budget goals, you have to enforce them. You have to say 'no' to a lot of people." [6]

However committees are characterized—power, housekeeping, constituency—it is plain that they are firmly rooted in the work of the House and Senate. In this chapter we will show how committees fit into the "two Congresses"—the lawmaking institution and the representative assembly. We also will address the following questions. How have committees changed since the first Congress? What are the different types of committees, and how are members assigned to them? How do committees make policy, and what duties do the staffs perform? In short, we will describe what happens in these busy workshops of Congress.

Evolution of the Committee System

In the early Congresses committees were mainly temporary panels created for a specific task. Proposals were considered first on the House or Senate floor and then referred to specially created panels that worked out the details—the reverse order of today's system. The Senate, for example, would "debate a subject at length on the floor and, after the majority's desires had been crystallized, might appoint a committee to put those desires into bill form." [7] About 350 ad hoc committees were formed during the Third Congress (1793-1795) alone.[8] The parent chamber closely controlled these temporary committees: it assigned them clear-cut tasks, required them to report back favorably or unfavorably, and dissolved them when they had completed their work.

By about 1816 for the Senate and a bit later for the House, they had developed a system of permanent or standing committees, some of which are still in existence. Standing committees, as historian DeAlva Alexander explained, were better suited than ad hoc groups to cope with the larger membership and wider scope of congressional business. Another scholar, George Haynes, pointed out that the "needless inconvenience of the frequent choice of select committees" taxed congressional patience. Perhaps, too, legislators came to value standing committees as counterweights to presidential influence in setting the legislative agenda.[9]

Permanent committees changed the way Congress made policy and allocated authority: the House and Senate now reviewed and voted upon recommendations made by specialized, experienced committees. And party leaders soon had to share authority with growing numbers of committee leaders. Standing committees also encouraged oversight of the executive branch. Members have called them "the eye, the ear, the hand, and very often the brain" of Congress.[10]

As committees acquired expertise and authority, they became increasingly self-reliant and resistant to chamber and party control. After the House revolted against Republican Speaker Joseph Cannon in 1910, power flowed to the committee chairmen, who took on substantial powers. Along with a few strong party leaders, they held sway over House and Senate policy making during most of the twentieth century. In rare instances committee members rebelled and diminished the chairman's authority.[11] But most members heeded the advice that Speaker John McCormack gave to freshmen: "Whenever you pass a committee chairman in the House, you bow from the waist. I do." [12]

The chairmen's authority was buttressed by a rigid seniority custom that flourished with the rise of congressional careerism. The majority party member with the most years of continuous service on a committee automatically became its chairman. There were no other qualifications, such as ability or party loyalty. As a result, committee chairmen owed little or nothing to party leaders, much less to presidents. This automatic selection process produced experienced, independent chairmen, but many members chafed under a system that concentrated authority in so few hands. The "have nots" wanted a piece of the action and objected that seniority promoted the competent and incompetent alike. They objected, too, that the system promoted members from "safe" one-party areas—especially conservative southern Democrats and midwestern Republicans—who could ignore party policies or national sentiments.

The late 1960s and 1970s saw a rapid influx of new members, many from the cities and suburbs, who opposed the conservative status quo. Allying themselves with more senior members seeking a stronger voice in Congress, they pushed through changes that diffused power among committee members and shattered seniority as an absolute criterion for leadership posts. Today House and Senate committee chairmen (and ranking minority members) must be elected by their party colleagues. No longer free to wield arbitrary authority, chairmen must abide by committee rules. And subcommittees have become more numerous, autonomous, and influential.

Types of Committees

Congress today has a shopper's bazaar of committees—standing, select, joint, and conference—and within each of these general types there are variations. For example, standing committees can be characterized as *authorizing* or *appropriating* panels. Authorizing committees (Agriculture, Armed Services, Banking, and so on) are the policy-making centers on Capitol Hill. As substantive committees, they propose solutions to public problems and advocate what they believe to be the necessary level of spending for the programs under their jurisdiction. The House and Senate Appropriations Committees actually recommend how much money agencies and programs will receive. Unsurprisingly, there is continuing conflict between the two types of panels, especially in areas of resource scarcity (see Chapter 13).

Standing Committees

For our purposes, the term *standing committee* means a permanent entity, created by public law or by amendment to House or Senate rules. Standing committees continue from Congress to Congress, except in those infrequent instances when they are eliminated or new ones are created. Table 7-1 compares the standing committees in the 101st Congress in terms of their size, party ratio, and number of subcommittees.

Standing committees process the bulk of Congress's daily and annual agenda of business. Seldom are measures considered on the House or Senate floor without first being referred to, and approved by, the appropriate committees. Put negatively, committees are the burial ground for most legislation. Stated positively, committees select from the thousands of measures introduced in each Congress those that merit floor debate. Of the hundreds of bills that clear committees, fewer still are enacted into law.

Sizes and Ratios.   The Legislative Reorganization Act of 1946 established the sizes of House and Senate standing committees and for the first time specified each panel's jurisdiction. Both chambers have since pushed those sizes upward, and in 1975 the House dropped from its rules any reference to committee size. Committee sizes and ratios (the number of majority and minority members on a panel) are set in the House by the majority leadership and are negotiated in the Senate by the majority and minority leaders. At the start of each new Congress, each chamber adopts two separate resolutions, one offered by the Democrats and the other by the Republicans, that elect members to the committees and thus set their size and ratio.

Table 7-1 Standing Committees of the House and Senate, 101st Congress

Committees	Size and party ratio		Number of subcommittees
House			
Agriculture	45	(D 27/R 18)	8
Appropriations	57	(D 35/R 22)	13
Armed Services	52	(D 31/R 21)	7
Banking	51	(D 31/R 20)	8
Budget	35	(D 21/R 14)	8
District of Columbia	11	(D 7/R 4)	3
Education and Labor	34	(D 21/R 13)	8
Energy and Commerce	43	(D 26/R 17)	6
Foreign Affairs	43	(D 26/R 17)	8
Government Operations	39	(D 24/R 15)	7
House Administration	21	(D 13/R 8)	6
Interior	37	(D 23/R 14)	6
Judiciary	35	(D 21/R 14)	7
Merchant Marine	43	(D 26/R 17)	6
Post Office	23	(D 14/R 9)	7
Public Works	50	(D 30/R 20)	6
Rules	13	(D 9/R 4)	2
Science, Space, and Technology	49	(D 30/R 19)	7
Small Business	44	(D 27/R 17)	6
Standards of Official Conduct	12	(D 6/R 6)	—
Veterans' Affairs	34	(D 21/R 13)	5
Ways and Means	36	(D 23/R 13)	6
Senate			
Agriculture	19	(D 10/R 9)	7
Appropriations	29	(D 16/R 13)	13
Armed Services	20	(D 11/R 9)	6
Banking	21	(D 12/R 9)	4
Budget	23	(D 13/R 10)	—
Commerce	20	(D 11/R 9)	8
Energy and Natural Resources	19	(D 10/R 9)	5
Environment and Public Works	16	(D 9/R 7)	5
Finance	20	(D 11/R 9)	8
Foreign Relations	19	(D 10/R 9)	7
Governmental Affairs	14	(D 8/R 6)	5
Judiciary	14	(D 8/R 6)	6
Labor and Human Resources	16	(D 9/R 7)	6
Rules and Administration	16	(D 9/R 7)	—
Small Business	19	(D 10/R 9)	6
Veterans' Affairs	11	(D 6/R 5)	—

Source: "Committees of the 101st Congress," *Congressional Quarterly Special Report,* May 6, 1989.

In the Senate, noted for its reciprocity and comity among members, panels may be enlarged to accommodate senators seeking membership on the same committees. Or senators may be granted waivers from Senate rules that limit them to service on no more than two major standing committees. Four Democrats up for reelection in 1990 (Max Baucus of Montana, Howell Heflin of Alabama, John Kerry of Massachusetts, and John Rockefeller of West Virginia) were granted waivers in the 101st Congress so they could sit on extra major committees that they deemed important to their reelection prospects—another example of the "two Congresses." [13]

House committee enlargements are engineered, scholars suggest, by majority party leaders who want to accommodate their colleagues' preferences. Pressured by individual legislators, minority leaders, state party delegations, and informal groups, and bound by the traditional right of returning members to reassignment to their committees, majority party leaders have expanded the number of committee slots. They recognize that party harmony can be maintained by boosting the number of committee seats.

Party ratios influence committee work as much as panel size does. Biennial election results frame the bargaining between majority and minority leaders. Ratios on most committees normally reflect party strength in the full House or Senate. They shape the committees' policy outlook, internal organization, and staffing arrangements. If the full committee is "stacked" against the minority, for example, that situation will repeat itself in subcommittee assignments and in the allocation of staff between the two sides.

Other practices and rules can affect ratios. House Democratic Caucus rules state that "committee ratios should be established to create firm working majorities on each committee. In determining the ratio on the respective standing committees, the Speaker should provide for a minimum of three Democrats for each two Republicans." Some House committees, like Appropriations, Budget, Rules, and Ways and Means, traditionally have disproportionate ratios to ensure majority party control.

Because it has the votes, the majority party can be the final arbiter if the minority protests its allotment of committee seats. Throughout the 1980s House Republicans complained bitterly that Democrats unfairly "packed" several major committees. Several GOP members even filed suit against Democratic leaders to gain more equitable committee ratios, but the case was dismissed by federal courts.

Subcommittees.   House rules require every standing committee with twenty or more members, except Budget, to have at least four subcommittees. (The Budget Committee has task forces, the functional equivalent of subcommittees.) Senators are prohibited from chairing more than one subcommittee on any one committee. This effectively limits the number of subcommittees to the number of majority party members on the parent committee.

Like standing committees, subcommittees vary widely in rules and procedures, staff arrangements, modes of operation, and relationships with other subcommittees and the full committee. Subcommittees perform most of the day-to-day lawmaking and oversight work of Congress. Their large number is attributed to several factors: complex problems requiring specialization, interest groups' demands for subcommittees to handle their subject area, and members' desires to chair subcommittees. As one scholar concluded:

> Subcommittee chairmanships are extremely valuable because most are now personal vehicles for the chair who can use them for agenda setting, for attempting to shape debate on an ongoing issue, for garnering personal publicity, for catering to specialized constituencies.[14]

A negative consequence of more independent subcommittees (a trend more evident in the House than in the Senate) is greater policy fragmentation.

Select or Special Committees

Select or special committees (the terms are interchangeable) are usually temporary panels that go out of business after the two-year life of the Congress in which they were created. But some select committees take on the attributes of permanent committees. The House, for example, has a Permanent Select Committee on Aging and a Permanent Select Intelligence Committee. Select committees usually do not have "legislative authority" (the right to receive and report out measures); they can only study, investigate, and make recommendations. Cases in point were the select Iran-contra panels that each chamber created in 1987 to explore the secret sale of U.S. arms to Iran in exchange for American-held hostages and the subsequent diversion of funds from those sales to the contras in Nicaragua.

Select panels are created for several reasons. First, they accommodate the concerns of individual members. The chairmen of these panels may attract publicity that enhances their political careers, as occurred during the 1970s for George McGovern (Select Committee on Nutrition and Human Needs), Walter Mondale (Select Committee on Equal Education Opportunity), and Claude Pepper (Select Committee on Aging). Harry S Truman came to public (and president Franklin Roosevelt's) attention as head of a special committee investigating World War II military procurement practices. Second, special panels are a point of access for interest groups such as owners of small businesses, the aged, and Native Americans. Third, select committees supplement the standing committee system by overseeing and investigating issues that the permanent panels lack time for or prefer to ignore. Finally, select committees can be set up to coordinate consideration of issues that overlap the jurisdictions of several standing committees. This approach is intended to reduce jurisdictional bickering.

Joint Committees

Joint committees, which include members from both chambers, have been used since the first Congress for study, investigation, oversight, and routine activities. Unless their composition is prescribed in statute, House members of joint committees are appointed by the Speaker, and senators by that chamber's presiding officer. The chairmanship of joint committees rotates each Congress or session between House and Senate members. In 1989 there were four joint committees: Economic, Library, Printing, and Taxation.

The Joint Library Commitee and the Joint Printing Committee oversee, respectively, the Library of Congress and the Government Printing Office. The Joint Taxation Committee is essentially a "holding company" for staff that works closely with the tax-writing committees of each house. The Joint Economic Committee conducts studies and hearings on a wide range of domestic and international economic issues.

Conference Committees

Before legislation can be sent to the president to be signed, it must pass both the House and Senate in identical form. Conference committees, sometimes called the "third house of Congress," reconcile differences between similar measures passed by both chambers. They are composed of members from each house. A representative highlighted their importance:

> When I came to Congress I had no comprehension of the importance of the conference committees which actually write legislation. We all knew that important laws are drafted there, but I don't think one person in a million has any appreciation of their importance and the process by which they work. Part of the explanation, of course, is that there never is a printed record of what goes on in conference.[15]

Conference bargaining can be roughly classified as traditional, offer-counteroffer, subconference, and pro forma. Traditional conferences are those in which the participants meet fact-to-face, haggle among themselves about the items in bicameral disagreement, and then reach an accord. The bulk of conferences are of this type. In offer-counteroffer conferences, often used by the tax-writing committees, one side suggests a compromise proposal; the other side recesses to discuss it in private and then returns to present a counteroffer. Conferences with numerous participants (on omnibus bills, for example) usually break into small units or subconferences to reconcile particular matters or to address special topics. Pro forma conferences are those in which issues are resolved informally—by preconference negotiations between conferee leaders or by staff—even before the conference formally meets. The conference itself then ratifies the earlier decisions.[16]

Some scholars argue that congressional committees are influential in large part because they possess unilateral authority at the conference stage to veto or negotiate alterations in legislation. Others dispute this contention and claim that the so-called "ex post veto is not a significant institutional foundation of congressional committee power." [17] (Selection of conferees, rules changes affecting conference committees, and conference reports are discussed in Chapter 11.)

The Assignment Process

Every congressional election sets off a scramble for committee seats. As noted earlier, legislators understand the linkage between winning desirable assignments and winning elections. Newly elected representatives and senators quickly make their preferences known to party leaders, to members of the panels that make committee assignments, and to others; at the same time, incumbents may be trying to move to more prestigious panels.

The Pecking Order

Among standing committees the most powerful and so most desirable are House Ways and Means and Senate Finance, which pass on tax measures, and the House and Senate Appropriations committees, which hold the federal purse strings. The Budget committees, established in 1974, also have become sought-after assignments because of their important role in economic and fiscal matters and their guardianship of the congressional budgeting process.

Among those that seldom have waiting lists are House District of Columbia, Senate Ethics, and House Standards of Official Conduct. The District of Columbia Committee is shunned by most members because it deals with local rather than national issues. The ethics committees in both chambers are unpopular because legislators are reluctant to sit in judgment of their colleagues. "It's dirty, dirty duty," acknowledged House GOP leader Robert H. Michel of Illinois. But there are rewards. Michel explained that

> once you've done that, boy, if you've got any other little special favors to ask [of party leaders], as distinguished from somebody else, I've got to tip the scales in favor of you, "Thanks, buddy, for putting up with all that. Now I'll give you the select committee on hunger or narcotics or something." [18]

The House and Senate ethics panels, it is worth noting, are required to have an equal number of Democrats and Republicans.

The attractiveness of committees can change. Once a coveted and choice assignment, particularly after its nationally televised impeachment inquiry of President Richard Nixon in 1974, the House Judiciary Committee subsequently lost much of its appeal. The panel not only deals with controversial social issues (abortion, school prayer, gun control, the death penalty), but it also authorizes very little money and attracts few campaign donations. The Senate Intelligence Committee, "once a congressional backwater that most members avoided because its mostly secret work had no home state impact," recently has attracted scores of applicants because of its expanding influence in international affairs.[19]

Preferences and Politicking

In an analysis of six House committees, political scientist Richard F. Fenno, Jr., found that three basic goals of lawmakers—reelection, influence within the House, and good public policy—influence the committee assignments that members seek. Fenno's study also revealed that the Interior and Post Office committees attract reelection-oriented members; Appropriations and Ways and Means, influence-oriented members; and Education and Labor and Foreign Affairs, policy-oriented members. Members with similar goals find themselves on the same committees, which may make harmonious but biased committees.[20]

Since Fenno's study, scholars have elaborated on the relationship between members' goals and committee assignments. They have divided House committees into reelection (or constituency), policy, and power panels and concur that "some mix of the three goals motivates" most activity on the committees. They agree, too, that members' goals "are less easily character-ized in the Senate than in the House." [21] Almost every senator has the opportunity to serve on one of the top four committees (Appropriations, Armed Services, Finance, and Foreign Relations). Hence, the power associ-ated with a particular committee assignment is less important for senators than for representatives.

Regardless of their committee assignments, senators are accorded wide latitude under their chamber's flexible rules to influence decision making on the floor. Asked why he ran for the Senate, Rep. Paul Simon, D-Ill., said, "In the House, you are restricted by your committee. But in the Senate, you're not tied down. You have a lot more room to exert influence." [22] (See House-Senate comparison of committees, Table 7-2.)

In the weeks after an election, members campaign vigorously for the committees they prefer. Sen. Daniel Patrick Moynihan, D-N.Y., successfully campaigned for a seat on the Finance Committee by pointing out that a New York Democrat had not served on the Finance Committee in 100 years. Moynihan gave each member of the assignment panel a card that outlined the history lesson, a "fact that he said impressed them." [23] With exceptions for some committees, members generally receive the assignments they request. In most cases, noted a scholar, "the assignment process has become an essentially routine, nondiscretionary procedure." [24] Both parties try and accommodate the assignment preferences of their partisans.

Only two days after her election to the Senate, Barbara Mikulski, D-Md., began to campaign for a coveted position on the Appropriations Committee. She pinpointed key senators and successfully lobbied for their support.[25] Veteran representative Robert Dornan, R-Calif., even enlisted President George Bush's support in his successful bid for a position on the

Table 7-2 House-Senate Committee Comparison

Category	House	Senate
Number of standing committees	22	16
Committee assignments per member	About 7	About 11
Power or prestige committees	Appropriations, Budget, Rules, Ways and Means	Appropriations, Armed Services, Finance, Foreign Relations; almost every Senator assigned to one of these four
Treaties and nominations submitted by the president	No authority	Committees review
Floor debate	Representatives' activity is somewhat confined to the bills reported from the panels on which they serve	Senators can choose to influence any policy area regardless of their committee assignments
Subcommittee government	The norm on many committees	Notable on some but not most committees
Committee consideration of legislation	More difficult to bypass	Easier to bypass (for example, by allowing "riders"—unrelated policy proposals—to measures pending on the floor)
Committee chairmen	Subject to party and House rules that limit their discretionary authority over committee operations	Freer reign to manage and organize their committees
Committee staff	Less assertive in advocating ideas and proposals	More aggressive in shaping the legislative agenda
Subcommittee chairmanships	Representatives of the majority party usually must wait at least one term	Majority senators, regardless of their seniority, usually chair subcommittees

Armed Services Committee. Dornan campaigned vigorously for Bush and asked him "to put in a good word" with GOP leader Michel.[26]

The assignments some members avoid are the same ones that others want. Or members may seek different benefits from different assignments. Sen. Alan Cranston, D-Calif., explained why he waited twelve years before seeking to join the Foreign Relations Committee:

> I had observed that that committee was not good as a political base. You can't do much for your constituents there, and you create vulnerabilities. . . . I selected three committees that I thought would help politically: the Labor Committee, which got me into basic social issues like education, health, and the troubles of working men and women, the more or less liberal concerns; the Banking Committee, to help me deal with the business constituency of California; and the Veterans' Committee, as an offset of my dove-like image.[27]

Inevitably, some members receive unwelcome assignments. Democratic representative Shirley Chisholm of Brooklyn was assigned in 1969 to the House Agriculture Committee. "I think it would be hard to imagine an assignment that is less relevant to my background or to the needs of the predominantly black and Puerto Rican people who elected me," she said. Her protests won her a seat on the Veterans' Affairs Committee. "There are a lot more veterans in my district than there are trees," she later observed.[28] By contrast, there are urban Democrats who welcome Agriculture Committee service; they fuse local with rural issues through food stamp, consumer, and other legislation.

How Assignments Are Made

Each party in each house has its own panel to review members' committee requests and hand out assignments: the Committee on Committees for House Republicans, the Steering and Policy Committee for House Democrats, the Republican Committee on Committees for Senate Republicans, and the Steering Committee for Senate Democrats (see boxes, pages 207, 209).

These panels' decisions are the first and most important acts in a three-step procedure. The second step involves approval of the assignment lists by each party's caucus. Finally, there is pro forma election by the full House or Senate.

Formal Criteria.   Both formal and informal criteria guide the assignment panels in choosing committee members. Formal criteria are designed to ensure that each member is treated equitably in committee assignments.

For example, the House Democratic Caucus divides committees into three classes: exclusive, major, and nonmajor. A member assigned to an exclusive panel (Appropriations, Rules, or Ways and Means) may not serve on any other standing committee (except House Administration) unless the

Party Assignment Committees

House Republicans. Two features characterize the GOP committee assignment group. First, each state with GOP representation elects a member to serve on the Committee on Committees. Because this can be an unwieldy group, the panel has an executive committee of about twenty members headed by the party's floor leader. The second feature is weighted voting. Each member casts as many votes as there are GOP members in his or her state delegation. The big-state members of the executive committee thus usually dominate assignments. To strengthen leadership influence in the assignment process, Republicans at the start of the 101st Congress authorized the minority leader and GOP whip to each cast twelve and six votes, respectively. Previously, each had but one vote. Decisions of the executive committee are subject to ratification by the full Committee on Committees.

House Democrats. Democrats on the House Ways and Means Committee functioned as their party's committee on committees from 1911 until 1974, when the Democratic Caucus voted to transfer this duty to the Steering and Policy Committee. This group (about thirty members) is headed by the Speaker and is balanced to reflect party views. The Speaker, subject to caucus approval, appoints all Democratic members of the Rules Committee.

Senate Republicans. The chairman of the Republican Conference appoints the assignment panel of about ten members. There are also ex officio members, including the floor leader.

Senate Democrats. The Steering Committee makes assignments for Democrats. Its size (about twenty-five members) is set by the party conference and may fluctuate from Congress to Congress. The party's floor leader appoints the members and chairman of this panel.

caucus waives the rules application. The intent of the caucus provision is to prevent members who receive the "plum" assignments from crowding members out of other spots.

Since 1953 when Senate Democratic leader Lyndon B. Johnson announced his "Johnson rule," all Senate Democrats are assigned one major committee before any party member receives a second major assignment. Senate Republicans followed suit.

Informal Criteria. Among the informal criteria used by parties in making assignments are the members' own wishes. "We like to give people committee assignments because they want them and because it broadens their political appeal," explained Gerald Ford when he was House minority leader.[29]

Scores of other informal factors affect committee assignments. Sen. Sam Nunn, D-Ga., sought assignment to the Armed Services Committee, in part because Georgia has a large military population. He was also following the tradition of distinguished Georgians who made their reputations in Congress on military matters. Nunn's great-uncle Carl Vinson was the longtime chairman of the House Armed Services Committee. Gender, too, may affect assignments. A Democrat on the House assignment panel explained why Colorado's Patricia Schroeder was placed on the Armed Services Committee as a freshman. "We thought we ought to have a woman on Armed Services because there are so many women in the service now," he said. "And Schroeder has a background in personnel. That was her field in law." [30]

Seniority.   The assignment panels normally observe seniority when preparing committee membership lists. The person with the longest service is always listed first. Senate Republicans, unlike House Republicans and House and Senate Democrats, apply seniority rigidly when two or more GOP senators compete for a committee position.

At the start of the 100th Congress, Republican senators Richard Lugar of Indiana and Jesse Helms of North Carolina both wanted to be the ranking minority member on the Foreign Relations committee. Senator Lugar had chaired the panel the previous Congress when Republicans controlled the Senate, but Senator Helms had more seniority on the committee. (When Republicans ran the 99th Congress and Lugar headed Foreign Relations, Helms, by choice, took the chair of the Agriculture Committee rather than Foreign Relations because in his tough 1984 reelection fight he promised North Carolinians that he would take the Agriculture post.)

The GOP members on Foreign Relations voted for Lugar, but Helms, arguing for the sanctity of the seniority system, pressed his case. Under the rules of the Senate Republican Conference, the committee's choice had to be agreed to by the majority of Senate Republicans. It was not: Helms defeated Lugar by a 24-to-17 secret vote. Interestingly, one of the most liberal Senate Republicans, Lowell Weicker of Connecticut, endorsed the conservative Helms:

> Senator Lugar's challenge is a precedent-setting change of the Senate's traditional seniority system. The system provides for an equality of senatorial representation which transcends policy, philosophy, geography and personality. Should this system be destroyed, the effectiveness of today's Republicans in the Senate and tomorrow's minorities in our party would be severely undermined.[31]

Biases.   The decisions made by the assignment panels inevitably determine the geographical and ideological composition of the standing committees. Committees can easily become biased toward one position or another. Farm areas are overrepresented on agriculture panels and seacoast interests on House Merchant Marine. No wonder committees are policy advocates; they propose laws that reflect the interests of their members and the outside groups and agencies that gravitate toward them.

The Senate GOP Assignment Process

Briefly, the procedure generally works like this: after the election the total number of Republicans and Democrats are compared to determine a ratio. That ratio is then applied to each of the various committees, and adjustments in the size of the committee and the Republican/Democrat ratio are made.

The vacancies caused by the election results, plus any changes in the number of seats each party controls, provide the actual number of vacancies for the next Congress. A list of all committees and vacancies is compiled. Each Republican Senator and Senator-elect is asked to notify the Committee on Committees as to their preferences for committee assignment. Incumbent Senators may indicate that they wish to retain their current committee assignments, or they may want to move from one committee to another. If they want to change, they indicate in writing the committee(s) they wish to relinquish and their preferences, in order of priority, for new assignment. Newly elected Senators indicate, in order of priority, their desired assignments.

These letters are all compiled, through the use of a computer, into a list indicating each Senator, beginning with the most senior member, and on down the line, with his or her committee preferences.

When the Committee on Committees meets, after the reorganization of the Republican leadership, the two lists are compared. The Committee looks at the letter from the most senior Senator. If he requests any changes they look to the list of committees and, if the assignments he requests are available, they are made. The positions he is giving up are then reflected as vacancies on whatever committees he has relinquished, and the Committee turns to the next Senator, and so on through all incumbent Senators.

After each incumbent Senator is given his committee assignments, the Committee turns to the most senior freshman Senator. Each freshman Senator is allowed to make one committee selection before the most senior freshman Senator is permitted to make two committee selections. . . .

Source: Letter to Sen. William Cohen, R-Maine, from GOP Senate leader Howard Baker. See William S. Cohen, *Roll Call, One Year in the United States Senate* (New York: Simon & Schuster, 1981), 30-31.

Who gets on a panel or who is left off affects committee policy making in a variety of ways. "There are enormous policy implications in the committee selection process," said Rep. Henry Waxman, D-Calif.[32] Committees that are carefully balanced between liberal and conservative interests can be tilted one way or the other by the recruitment process. A committee's political philosophy also influences its success on the House or Senate floor. Committees ideologically out of step with the House or Senate as a whole are more likely than others to have legislation defeated or significantly revised through floor amendments.

Approval by Party Caucuses and the Chamber

For most of the twentieth century each chamber's party caucuses either ratified the assignment decisions of their committees on committees or took no action on them at all. During the 1970s, however, party caucuses became major participants in the assignment process. Chairmen and ranking minority members were subjected to election by secret ballot of their partisan colleagues, establishing the principle and reality that the committee leadership is no longer an automatic right.

Seniority today still encourages continuity on committees, but it has become more flexible and is under caucus control. In 1975 House Democrats ousted three incumbent committee chairmen and replaced them with younger men. A decade later the caucus unseated eighty-year-old Melvin Price of Illinois as chairman of Armed Services and replaced him with Les Aspin, the panel's seventh-ranking Democrat. Price's fragile health and the Democrats' desire to challenge the administration's defense budget contributed to his ouster.[33] Aspin nearly lost his position two years later when the Democratic Caucus voted to deny him the Armed Services chairmanship because he had supported several Reagan initiatives. However, under Democratic Caucus rules another vote was required; Aspin then went head-to-head against his challengers and regained the chairmanship.[34]

Each chamber's rules require that all standing committees, including chairmen, be elected by the entire House or Senate. The practice, however, is for each party's leaders to offer the caucus-approved membership lists to the full chamber. Normally, these are then approved quickly by voice vote.

Committee Leadership

Committee leaders are usually the chairman and the ranking minority member. Committee chairmen call meetings and establish agendas, hire and fire committee staff, arrange hearings, recommend conferees, act as floor managers, allocate committee funds and rooms, develop legislative strategies, chair hearings and markups, and regulate the internal affairs and organization of the committee.

The top minority party member on a committee is also an influential figure. Among his or her powers are nominating minority conferees, hiring and firing minority staff, sitting ex officio on all subcommittees, appointing minority members to subcommittees, assisting in setting the committee's agenda, and managing legislation on the floor. The ranking member also serves as official committee spokesperson for the panel's other minority members.

Beyond these powers, the ranking minority member's influence varies with the committee's partisan ratio and ideological mix. On the House Armed Services Committee, a panel with a bipartisan tradition, senior Alabama

Republican Bill Dickinson is a pivotal figure who also serves as the committee's emissary to the defense secretary.[35]

On some committees ranking Republicans like Dickinson are in tune with the committee's basic policy outlook and work to gain compromises across the aisle, perhaps to the chagrin of more junior GOP firebrands. The ranking Republican on the Judiciary Committee, Hamilton Fish of New York, is "a very lonely man," remarked Rep. Mike Synar, Okla., a Democratic panel member.[36] Fish is sometimes the only Republican to vote with Judiciary Democrats. On other committees there may be intense rivalry between the chairman and ranking Republican.

The chairman has many procedural powers. Simply refusing to schedule a bill for a hearing may be sufficient to kill it. Or a chairman may convene meetings when proponents or opponents of the legislation are unavoidably absent. The chairman's authority derives from the support of a committee majority and a variety of formal and informal resources, such as substantive and parliamentary experience and control over the agenda, communications, and financial resources of the committee. When told by a committee colleague that he lacked the votes on an issue, House Energy and Commerce chairman John Dingell, D-Mich., replied: "Yeah, but I've got the gavel." [37] Dingell banged his gavel, adjourned the meeting, and the majority got no chance to work its will before the legislative session ended.

How a chairman uses these powers is partly a matter of personal style. Wilbur Mills's control of Ways and Means from 1959 to 1974 is legendary. "Wilbur, why do you want to run for the president and give up your grip on the country?" once asked Rep. Sam Gibbons, D-Fla.[38] And during his long tenure as chairman of the Senate Finance Committee, Russell Long, D-La., left no question who was boss.

Committee leaders can no longer run their committees as personal fiefdoms, however. Particularly in the House, procedural changes have limited the authority of the standing committee chairmen. By House and Democratic Caucus rules, for instance, chairmen have less control than before over their panel's internal structure. As two scholars explained:

> With their formal powers curtailed, House chairs became even more dependent on personal skills, expertise, and shrewdness to get things done. These factors still help to separate successful leaders from unsuccessful leaders. But remember that contextual factors severely constrain even the most talented House committee leaders. In this regard, House full committee chairs have become more like Senate full committee chairs, who long have operated in an environment characterized by a relatively equal distribution of resources among participants.[39]

Nevertheless, chairmen wield considerable power. "If you work hard, you can still win most of what you want," said House Interior chairman Morris K. Udall, D-Ariz. "But you can't do it the easy way, the way [some autocratic chairmen] did it." [40] As House Banking chairman Henry Gonzalez, D-

Texas, put it: the chairman's job is like "leading a fractious family across Pennsylvania Avenue in high traffic." [41]

Policy Making in Committee

Committees foster deliberate, collegial, fragmented decisions. They encourage bargaining and accommodation among members. In order to move bills through Congress's numerous decision points from subcommittee to committee, authors of bills and resolutions typically compromise differences with key committee members. These "gatekeepers" may exact alterations in a bill's substance. The proliferation of committees also multiplies the points of access for outside interests.

Overlapping Jurisdictions and Multiple Referrals

Each standing committee's formal responsibilities are defined by the rules of each house, various public laws, and precedents. Committees do not have watertight jurisdictional compartments. Any broad subject overlaps numerous committees. The Senate has an Environment Committee, but several other panels also consider environmental legislation; the same is true in the House. These House bodies, along with a brief sketch of their environmental responsibilities, are shown below:

Agriculture: pesticides; soil conservation; some water programs

Appropriations: funding environmental programs and agencies

Banking: open space acquisition in urban areas

Government Operations: federal executive organizations for the environment

Interior and Insular Affairs: water resources; power resources; land management; wildlife conservation; national parks; nuclear waste

Foreign Affairs: international environmental cooperation

Energy and Commerce: health effects of the environment; environmental regulations; solid waste disposal; clean air; safe drinking water

Merchant Marine and Fisheries: ocean dumping; fisheries; coastal zone management; environmental impact statements

Public Works and Transportation: water pollution; sludge management

Science, Space, and Technology: environmental research and development

Small Business: effects on business of environmental regulations

Ways and Means: environmental tax expenditures

Jurisdictional overlaps have both positive and negative results. On the plus side, they enable members to develop expertise in several policy fields, prevent any one group from dominating a topic, provide multiple access points for outside interests, and promote healthy competition among committees.

On the other hand, "healthy competition" can quickly turn to intercommittee warfare. During the 100th Congress, a "turf" battle developed over how much jurisdiction the House Energy and Commerce Committee should have over bank deregulation laws—part of the Banking Committee's territory. "The upshot was an impasse that could not be resolved." [42] As one representative said on another occasion:

> John Dingell feels about his committee [Energy and Commerce] much as Lyndon Johnson felt about his ranch. Johnson didn't want to own the whole world, he just wanted to own all the land surrounding his ranch. Dingell doesn't want his committee to have the whole world, just all the areas surrounding his jurisdiction. [43]

House and Senate rules acknowledge jurisdictional overlap. When a bill is introduced, it is usually sent to a single committee. But a bill that addresses many problems may be referred to multiple committees. There are three types of multiple referrals: joint referrals, when a bill is sent to two or more committees simultaneously; sequential referrals, when a bill is sent first to one committee and then to another; and split referrals, when different parts of a bill are sent to different committees. The Senate has long permitted multiple referrals by unanimous consent. The House has permitted them since 1975.

The use of multiple referrals, particularly in the House, has increased. Nearly a quarter of the bills and resolutions considered by House committees in the 98th Congress had been shared in some way with other panels. No longer is it simply "one bill, one committee"; instead it is often "one bill, many committees." [44] For example, fourteen House committees and nine Senate committees worked on an omnibus trade measure that passed the 100th Congress. As Senate Democratic leader Robert C. Byrd of West Virginia explained:

> I have worked closely with nine committee chairmen to develop a comprehensive bipartisan approach to international competition. In place of a series of individual bills, we adopted an omnibus approach in which different legislative initiatives were knitted together into a consistent whole. It is ... a procedural departure that has helped the existing Senate committee structure deal with a new and complex challenge. [45]

In addition to integrated policy making, multiple referrals promote public discussion of issues, access to the legislative process, and consideration of alternative approaches. They also enhance the Speaker's scheduling prerogatives. The Speaker can utilize the referral power to intervene more directly in committee activities, and even to set deadlines for committees to report multiply referred legislation. The reverse is also possible: delaying action on measures by referring them to other committees. House and Senate precedents require all committees that receive a bill to report it out before it can be scheduled for floor debate. In general, the more committees that review a measure, the longer it takes to process it. Thus, multiple referrals may slow down legislative decision making, and they may even result in the death of the bill.

Where Bills Go

Many bills referred to committee are sent by the chairman to a subcommittee. House Democratic Caucus rules require legislation to be referred to subcommittees within two weeks unless the full committee decides to consider those issues. Tax bills, for example, are considered by the full Ways and Means Committee rather than any subcommittee. The Senate has no formal or party rules that require chairmen to refer matters to their subcommittees. In the end committees and subcommittees normally select the measures they want to consider and ignore the rest. Committee consideration usually consists of three standard steps: public hearings, markups, and reports. Needless to say, there is plenty of staff research that precedes each of these "action" stages.

Hearings.   When committees conduct hearings on legislation, they listen to a wide variety of witnesses. These include the bills' sponsors, federal officials, pressure group representatives, public officials, and private citizens—sometimes even celebrities. Movie-star witnesses can help give a bill national visibility. When Elizabeth Taylor appeared before a Senate panel to testify on AIDS, the chairman said of the press coverage: "I haven't seen anything like this in the 30 days we have had hearings." [46]

Most hearings follow a traditional format. Witnesses read prepared statements. Then each committee member has a limited time to ask questions before the next witness is called. This procedure discourages lengthy exchanges, rebuttals, follow-up questions, or interaction among witnesses. To save time and promote give-and-take, committees occasionally use a panel format in which witnesses sit together and briefly summarize their statements.

The overlapping purposes served by hearings are many:

—to explore the need for legislation;
—to build a public record in support of legislation;
—to publicize the role of committee chairmen;
—to review executive implementation of public laws; and
—to provide a forum for citizen grievances and frustrations.

Sometimes committees conduct "field hearings" around the country to generate and assess public support for measures, or they hold joint hearings with other House or Senate panels.

Hearings are a necessary stage in the life of most measures. Witness lists are drawn up with an eye to "making a record" on an issue, generating maximum interest, and seeing that those vitally concerned have a chance to be heard. Hearings are shaped mainly by the chairman and staff, with varying degrees of input from other members, especially the ranking minority member. By revealing patterns of support or opposition and by airing substantive problems, hearings indicate to members whether a bill is worth taking to the full chamber. Chairmen who favor bills can expedite the hearings process; conversely, they can "kill with kindness" legislation they oppose by holding endless hearings. When a bill is not sent to the full chamber, the printed hearings are the end product of the committee's work.

Markups. After hearings the bill is "marked up." This is the stage where committee members decide the bill's actual language. Proponents try to craft a bill that will muster the backing of their colleagues, the other body, lobbyists, and the White House. This can be an arduous process because members often face the "two Congresses" dilemma: whether to support national initiatives or to oppose them because of constituency concerns (see box, page 216). Not uncommonly, the best bill that emerges from markup is the one that can attract majority support. As House Ways and Means Committee chairman Dan Rostenkowski, D-Ill., once said:

> We have not written perfect law. Perhaps a faculty of scholars could do a better job. A group of ideologues could have produced greater consistency. But politics is an imperfect process.[47]

Outside pressures are often intense during markup deliberations. Under House and Senate "sunshine" rules, markups must be conducted in public, except on national security or related issues. Compromises can be difficult to achieve in markup rooms filled with lobbyists watching how every member will vote. "Members ought to have the courage to look the lobbyists right in the eyes and go against them," said Rep. Don J. Pease, D-Ohio. "But as a practical matter, that's hard to do."[48] In recent years committees have increasingly voted to conduct their markups in secret. Sometimes they skirt "sunshine" rules in public by ploys such as the "football huddle" (members on the dais meet in small groups to conduct business in whispers) or the "squeeze play" (deliberately meeting in small rooms to exclude the public and lobbyists).

After conducting hearings and markups a subcommittee sends its recommendations to the full committee, which may conduct hearings and markups on its own, ratify the subcommittee's decision, take no action, or return the matter to the subcommittee for further study.

Reports. If the full committee votes to send the bill to the House or Senate, the staff prepares a report, subject to committee approval, describing the purposes and provisions of the legislation. Reports emphasize arguments favorable to the bill, summarizing selectively the results of staff research and hearings. Reports are noteworthy documents. The bill itself may be long, highly technical, and confusing to most readers. "A good report, therefore, does more than explain—it also persuades," commented a congressional staff

---

Markup Duel on Acid Rain

Opponents used stalling tactics May 13, 1986, to bring an acid rain control bill to a standstill, but House Energy subcommittee chairman Henry A. Waxman, D-Calif., one of the chamber's most skilled tacticians, insisted he could outlast the opposition.

The bill (HR 4567) was cosponsored by over 150 members, including a majority of Waxman's Subcommittee on Health and Environment, but it was opposed by full committee chairman John D. Dingell, D-Mich., and the subcommittee's ranking Republican, Edward R. Madigan of Illinois.

When Waxman began the markup, Madigan introduced a fifty-one-page substitute and insisted the entire text be read aloud. That kept the subcommittee busy most of the week. Under House rules, unanimous consent is needed to waive a public reading.

HR 4567 was aimed at reducing annual emissions of sulfur dioxide by 10 million tons and annual emissions of nitrogen oxide by 4 million tons by 1997. The substitute offered by Madigan, who was worried about Illinois's coal industry, would require only a 6 million-ton reduction in sulfur dioxide emissions by 2000. It would also have less stringent limits on nitrogen oxide levels, which would apply only to new power plants. HR 4567 would apply nitrogen oxide limits to existing power plants and automobiles as well.

Dingell, whose district is in the heart of the automobile industry, had argued that HR 4567 would pit one part of the country against another. Acid rain, a byproduct of coal-fired power plants prevalent in the Midwest, is blamed for environmental damage, particularly in the Northeast. At the May 13 markup, Dingell accused the bill's supporters of a "rush to judgment" and said more time is needed to fashion a bill acceptable to more people. "We cannot and should not force through the House a bill that entire congressional delegations . . . will have to oppose because of the adverse impacts on their states."

Waxman said the bill had broad geographical support, and he planned a marathon effort to break Madigan's stall. He scheduled a full day of markup on May 20, with additional sessions set for May 21-22. He wanted "to move the bill along as rapidly as possible," according to an aide.

Source: Adapted from Amy Stern, "Tactical Duel Marks Acid Rain Fight," *Congressional Quarterly Weekly Report*, May 17, 1986, 1129.

---

aide.[49] Reports also guide executive agencies and federal courts in interpreting ambiguous or complex legislative language.

The Policy Environment

Executive agencies, pressure groups, party leaders and caucuses, and the entire House or Senate form the backdrop against which a committee makes policy. These environments may be consensual or conflictual; some policy questions are settled fairly easily, while others are bitterly controversial. Environments also may be monolithic or pluralistic; some committees have a single dominant source of outside influence, while others face numerous competing groups or agencies.

Environmental factors influence committees in at least four ways. First, they shape the content of public policies and thus the likelihood that these policies will be accepted by the full House or Senate. The Judiciary committees, as noted earlier, are buffeted by diverse and competing pressure groups that feel passionately on volatile issues such as abortion and gun control. The committees' chances for achieving agreement among their members or on the floor depend to a large extent on their ability to deflect such issues altogether or to accommodate diverse groups through artful legislative drafting.

Second, policy environments foster mutual alliances among committees, federal departments, and pressure groups—the so-called "iron triangles" (see Chapter 10). The House Merchant Marine Committee, for example, regularly advocates legislation to benefit maritime industries and unions. This effort is backed by the Federal Maritime Commission. At the very least, "issue networks" emerge. These are rather fluid and amorphous groups of policy experts who try to influence any committee that deals with their subject area.[50]

Third, environments establish decision-making objectives and guidelines for committees. Clientele-oriented committees, such as the House Post Office and Civil Service Committee, try to promote the policy views of their satellite groups, such as mass-mailing firms and postal unions. Alliances between committees and federal departments also shape decisions.

Finally, environmental factors influence the level of partisanship on committees. Some committees, such as House and Senate Appropriations, are relatively free of party infighting. Perhaps "it is easier to reconcile numbers than philosophies." [51] But other committees—such as Labor and Human Resources in the Senate and Education and Labor in the House—consider contentious social issues like poverty and welfare that often divide the two parties.

Subcommittee Government

During most of Congress's history, the basic organizational unit was the standing committee. Today these committees are still crucial centers of decision making, but subcommittees, particularly in the House, have assumed greater importance. On many standing committees, subcommittees are now "where the action is."

House.   The movement toward subcommittee government began in the 1970s when liberals, frustrated by the tight control of committee business by conservative Southern Democrats, agitated for reform. The House Democratic Caucus in 1971 adopted a rule that no member could chair more than one legislative subcommittee. This change propelled young, liberal, nonsouthern members into subcommittee chairs. Then in 1973 Democrats adopted a subcommittee "bill of rights" that created on each standing committee a mini-Democratic caucus with authority to select subcommittee chairmen. Democrats also established a more equitable subcommittee assignment process; each Democrat can select one subcommittee before any colleague can select two.

Today subcommittee assignments in the House are limited to five per member. Each subcommittee chairman and each ranking minority subcommittee member can have one staff aide. Standing committees are limited to eight subcommittees (with some exceptions). "We've got so many committees and subcommittees now that if you can't remember somebody's name, you just say 'Hi, Mr. Chairman,'" said Representative Udall, the chairman of the House Interior Committee.[52]

Subcommittee government in the House, like any institutional change, has pluses and minuses. Among them are (1) slower decision making because majority consensus is harder to achieve, given the large number of participants; (2) wider opportunities for members to exercise initiative in lawmaking and oversight; (3) a heavier workload as members scurry to attend meetings called by activist subcommittee leaders; (4) heightened pressures on party leaders to schedule subcommittee-reported issues and amendments for floor consideration; and (5) difficulties in coordinating approaches to public problems.

Senate. Subcommittee government is less prevalent in the Senate. Several committees—Budget, Rules and Administration, and Veterans' Affairs—do not even have subcommittees. The majority of the other standing committees employ subcommittees for hearing purposes and little more. Policy making on these panels is concentrated at the full committee, which is the norm for Senate committee decision making. Nevertheless, there are standing committees that approach subcommittee government. These include Commerce, Judiciary, and Labor. Efforts to recentralize these committees have met with strong resistance.

Committee Staff

Throughout the three principal stages of committee policy making—hearings, markup, and report—staff aides play an active part. Representatives and senators (to a greater degree because there are fewer of them) cannot handle the heavy workload on their own and so must rely heavily on the "unelected lawmakers"—about 2,200 in the House and 1,200 in the Senate. Their influence can be direct or indirect, substantive or procedural, visible or invisible.

The discretionary agenda of Congress and its committees is largely shaped by the congressional staff. In the judgment of former senator Norris Cotton, R-N.H., "most of the work and most of the ideas come from the staffers. They are predominantly young men and women, fresh out of college and professional schools. They are ambitious, idealistic, and abounding with ideas." [53] Staff turnover on Capitol Hill is fairly high; many aides use their committee experience as a steppingstone to other jobs.

Policy proposals emanate from many sources—the White House, administrative agencies, interest groups, state and local officials, scholars, and citizens—but staff aides are strategically positioned to advance or hinder these proposals. As one Senate committee staff director recounted, "Usually, you draw up proposals for the year's agenda, lay out the alternatives. You can put in some stuff you like and leave out some you don't. I recommend ideas that the [chairman's] interested in and also that I'm interested in." [54]

Some members and scholars contend that unelected staffs are too active in shaping policy and thus undercut the lawmaking role of elected members. We are "elected Senators and we should try to do our business, occasionally, with ourselves and among ourselves and between ourselves," remarked GOP whip Alan K. Simpson in response to comments made by Senator Robert C. Byrd, when he was the Democratic leader. [55]

Staff aides negotiate with legislators, lobbyists, and executive officials, on issues, legislative language, and political strategy. Sometimes they even go to foreign countries to conduct investigations. In 1987 three staff aides of the Senate Foreign Relations Committee went to Iraq to assess firsthand the military prospects in the Iran-Iraq war. [56] Congress's investigative power undergirds its ability to make informed judgments on policy matters. And it is staff who do the essential spadework that can lead to changes in policy or new laws. Staff aides sometimes make policy decisions, however. Consider their crucial role on a 1983 defense appropriations bill:

> The dollar figures in the huge piece of legislation [were] so immense that House-Senate conferees, negotiating their differences . . . , relegated almost every item less than $100 million to staff aides on grounds that the members themselves did not have time to deal with such items, which Sen. Ted Stevens (R-Alaska) called "small potatoes." [57]

During hearings, aides recruit witnesses, on their own or at the specific direction of the chairman, and plan when and in what order they appear. In addition, staff aides commonly accompany committee members to the floor to give advice, draft amendments, and negotiate compromises. The number of aides who can be present is limited, however, by House and Senate regulations.

For information, analyses, policy options, and research projects, committee staff can turn to the four legislative support agencies: the Congressional Research Service, established in 1914; the General Accounting Office, established in 1921; the Office of Technology Assessment, established in

1972; and the Congressional Budget Office, established in 1974. Unlike committee or personal aides, these agencies operate under strict rules of nonpartisanship and objectivity. Staffed with experts, they provide Congress with analytical talent matching that in executive agencies, universities, or specialized groups.

Committee Reform

Since passage of the Legislative Reorganization Act of 1946, Congress has made numerous attempts to reform the committee system. Many legislators have questioned the effectiveness of committee operations and the propriety of congressional staff taking such an active role in policy. But this questioning has infrequently led to reform.

In 1973 and 1974 the Select Committee on Committees, headed by Rep. Richard Bolling, D-Mo., tried to eliminate several standing committees and make extensive changes in the jurisdiction of other committees. Instead, the House adopted a watered-down version of the committee proposal because of strong opposition from members who stood to surrender subcommittee chairmanships or favored jurisdictions.[58]

The Senate tried committee reform in 1977, with somewhat greater success. A select committee, chaired by Adlai E. Stevenson, D-Ill., recast jurisdictional responsibilities along more functional lines, limited senators' assignments, and reduced all types of committees (standing, select, and joint). The Senate adopted about 60 percent of what the Stevenson committee asked compared with only about 25 percent of the Bolling committee's plan.[59]

Since then Congress has moved gingerly on committee restructuring, given the decidedly mixed results of these earlier efforts. In 1979 another House select committee, chaired by Jerry Patterson, D-Calif., proposed a new standing committee on energy. The House turned down this proposal—a victim of turf politics, indecisive leadership, and the divisiveness of energy issues. In 1984 the Senate created a select panel, headed by Sen. Dan Quayle, R-Ind., to address committee reform and assignment limitations, but its recommendations were generally not acted upon by the Senate.

Committee reform will continue to be difficult to achieve because of a central paradox. On the one hand, lawmakers in both chambers profess impatience at the fragmentation and overlap in the committee system. On the other hand, members—and, perhaps more important, the staff and outside interests that support them—profit from these very attributes of the system. Committee reorganization thus would require skillful accommodation of members and pressure groups who stand to lose—or think they will lose— from any alteration in the status quo. The chances of success are slim without this accommodation and the hard bargaining necessary to produce a winning coalition. When asked to comment on congressional committee reform, House Speaker Thomas S. Foley of Washington said he wouldn't suggest touching it "with a 10-foot pole. . . . I went through the committee reform in 1974, and I have a general attitude toward reorganization. . . . [T]he first rule is probably, don't do it." [60]

Conclusion

In conclusion, at least seven generalizations can be made about committees today. First, they dominate the House and Senate agendas. The bills they report largely determine what each chamber will debate and in what form. House and Senate rules and practices favor committees in the lawmaking process by making it extraordinarily difficult to get around them.

Second, committees differ in their policy-making environments, mix of members, decision-making objectives, and ability to fulfill individual member's goals.

Third, committees typically operate independently of one another. This longtime custom fosters an attitude of "mutual noninterference" in the work of other committees. Paradoxically, such jurisdictional insulation results in numerous and longstanding "turf battles" on Capitol Hill. Needless to say, multiple referrals are spawning broader interrelationships among committees.

Fourth, committees often develop an esprit de corps that flows across party lines. Committee members usually will defend their panels against criticisms, jurisdictional trespassing, or any attempt to bypass them.

Fifth, recruitment methods and the custom of seniority reinforce the committees' autonomy. Committees frequently are imbalanced ideologically or geographically. They are likely to advocate policies espoused by agencies and outside groups interested in their work.

Sixth, the reforms of the 1970s promoted subcommittee government and further dispersed power in Congress. This has made the job of party leaders more difficult than ever. With more centers of power, it takes party leaders longer to forge compromises and develop winning coalitions.

Finally, the committee system contributes fundamentally to policy fragmentation although a few committees—Rules and Budget, for example— act as policy coordinators for Congress (see Chapters 11 and 13).

Notes

1. *Washington Post,* May 14, 1987, A23.
2. *Congressional Record,* 100th Cong., sess., June 25, 1987, H5564.
3. "Little legislatures" was a term coined by Woodrow Wilson in *Congressional Government* (Boston: Houghton Mifflin, 1885), 79.
4. *New York Times,* July 11, 1988, A14.

5. John W. Ellwood, "The Great Exception: The Congressional Budget Process in an Age of Decentralization," in *Congress Reconsidered*, 3d ed., ed. Lawrence C. Dodd and Bruce I. Oppenheimer (Washington, D.C.: CQ Press, 1985), 329. For the classic discussion of committee and member roles, see Richard F. Fenno, Jr., *Congressmen in Committees* (Boston: Little, Brown, 1973).

6. *New York Times*, December 19, 1988, B6.

7. Roy Swanstrom, *The United States Senate, 1787-1801*, Senate Doc. No. 64, 87th Cong., 1st sess., 1962, 224.

8. Lauros G. McConachie, *Congressional Committees* (New York: Thomas Y. Crowell, 1898), 124.

9. De Alva Stanwood Alexander, *History and Procedure of the House of Representatives* (Boston: Houghton Mifflin, 1916), 228; George H. Haynes, *The Senate of the United States: Its History and Practice*, Vol. 1 (Boston: Houghton Mifflin, 1938), 272; and Ralph V. Harlow, *The History of Legislative Methods in the Period Before 1825* (New Haven, Conn.: Yale University Press, 1917), 157-158.

10. *Cannon's Procedures in the House of Representatives*, House Doc. No. 122, 80th Cong., 1st sess., 1959, 83.

11. From 1953 to 1967, there were at least four "revolts" against House committee chairmen, including Clare Hoffman, R-Mich., of Government Operations; Wright Patman, D-Texas, of Banking; Adam Clayton Powell, D-N.Y., of Education and Labor; and Thomas Murray, D-Tenn., of Post Office and Civil Service.

12. *Wall Street Journal*, May 3, 1979, 1.

13. Mike Mills, "Senate Democrats Make Panel Assignments," *Congressional Quarterly Weekly Report*, December 3, 1988, 3438.

14. Barbara Sinclair, "The Distribution of Committee Positions in the U.S. Senate: Explaining Institutional Change," *American Journal of Political Science* 32 (May 1988): 298.

15. Charles L. Clapp, *The Congressman: His Job As He Sees It* (Washington, D.C.: Brookings Institution, 1963), 245.

16. Lawrence D. Longley and Walter J. Oleszek, *Bicameral Politics, Conference Committees in Congress* (New Haven, Conn.: Yale University Press, 1989), 196.

17. Keith Krehbiel, Kenneth A. Shepsle, and Barry R. Weingast, "Why Are Congressional Committees Powerful?" *American Political Science Review* 81 (September 1987): 935. See also Kenneth A. Shepsle and Barry R. Weingast, "The Institutional Foundations of Committee Power," *American Political Science Review* 81 (March 1987): 85-104.

18. Michael Oreskes, "Politics," *New York Times*, April 10, 1989, B7.

19. *Washington Times*, January 10, 1985, 1A.

20. Richard F. Fenno, Jr., *Congressmen in Committees* (Boston: Little Brown, 1973). See also Heinz Eulau, "Legislative Committee Assignments," *Legislative Studies Quarterly* (November 1984): 587-633.

21. Steven S. Smith and Christopher J. Deering, *Committees in Congress* (Washington, D.C.: CQ Press, 1984), 84, 111.

22. *Chicago Tribune*, July 21, 1983, 9.

23. *New York Times,* January 23, 1977, E5.
24. Irwin N. Gertzog, "The Routinization of Committee Assignments in the U.S. House of Representatives," *American Journal of Political Science* 20 (November 1976): 705.
25. Eric Pianin, "The Abrasive Lady from Baltimore Polishes Her Act," *Washington Post Magazine,* June 14, 1987, 22.
26. Josh Getlin and David Lauter, "Bush Rules Out Congressmen in His Cabinet," *Los Angeles Times,* pt. I, December 14, 1988, 30.
27. *Washington Post,* January 12, 1984, A12.
28. Shirley Chisholm, *Unbought and Unbossed* (Boston: Houghton Mifflin, 1970), 84, 86.
29. *Committee Organization in the House,* House Doc. 94-187, 94th Cong., 1st sess., 1975, 32.
30. *Washington Post,* March 4, 1973, E6.
31. *Washington Post,* January 1, 1987, A8. See also John Felton, "In Victory for Seniority System, Helms Wrests Post from Lugar," *Congressional Quarterly Weekly Report,* January 24, 1987, 143-144.
32. *New York Times,* January 5, 1983, B8.
33. Nadine Cohodas and Diane Granat, "House Seniority System Jolted; Price Dumped, Aspin Elected," *Congressional Quarterly Weekly Report,* January 5, 1985, 7-9.
34. *Los Angeles Times,* pt. I, January 23, 1987, 1.
35. Michael Glennon, "Special Report: The House Armed Services Committee," *Congressional Quarterly Weekly Report,* March 31, 1984, 735.
36. Nadine Cohodas, "Fish Plays Pivotal But Difficult Judiciary Role," *Congressional Quarterly Weekly Report,* April 30, 1988, 1160.
37. *Washington Post,* November 20, 1983, A9.
38. *Washington Post,* September 12, 1971, B1.
39. Smith and Deering, *Committees in Congress,* 168-169.
40. *Wall Street Journal,* May 3, 1979, 24.
41. Robert A. Rosenblatt, "New Stance for House Banking Panel," *Los Angeles Times,* pt. IV, December 10, 1988, 1.
42. John R. Cranford, "Caught in House Turf Battle, Banking Deregulation Bill Dies," *Congressional Quarterly Weekly Report,* October 15, 1988, 2977.
43. David Maraniss, "Powerful Energy Panel Turns on Big John's Axis," *Washington Post,* May 15, 1983, A14.
44. Roger H. Davidson, Walter J. Oleszek, and Thomas Kephart, "One Bill, Many Committees: Multiple Referrals in the U.S. House of Representatives," *Legislative Studies Quarterly* 13 (February 1988): 3-28. See also Melissa P. Collie and Joseph Cooper, "Multiple Referral and the 'New' Committee System in the House of Representatives," *Congress Reconsidered,* 4th ed., ed. Lawrence C. Dodd and Bruce I. Oppenheimer (Washington, D.C.: CQ Press, 1989), 245-272.
45. *Congressional Record,* 100th Cong., 2d sess., April 19, 1988, S4216.
46. Elizabeth Kastor, "The Capital Star System," *Washington Post,* May 9, 1986, D8.
47. *Washington Post,* November 25, 1985, A4.
48. Jacqueline Calmes, "Few Complaints Are Voiced as Doors Close on Capitol

Hill," *Congressional Quarterly Weekly Report,* May 23, 1987, 1059-1060.

49. Eric Redman, *The Dance of Legislation* (New York: Simon and Schuster, 1973), 140.

50. Hugh Heclo, "Issue Networks in the Executive Establishment," in *The New American Political System,* ed. Anthony King (Washington, D.C.: American Enterprise Institute, 1978), 87-124. See also David E. Price, "Policy Making in Congressional Committees: The Impact of 'Environmental Factors,'" *American Political Science Review* (Fall 1978): 548-574.

51. Diane Granat, "Special Report: House Appropriations Committee," *Congressional Quarterly Weekly Report,* June 18, 1983, 1213.

52. *Washington Times,* April 13, 1988, F4.

53. Norris Cotton, *In the Senate* (New York: Dodd, Mead, 1978), 65.

54. *Washington Post,* March 20, 1977, E9.

55. *Congressional Record,* 100th Cong., 2d sess., July 8, 1988, S9134.

56. *New York Times,* October 19, 1987, A16.

57. *Washington Post,* November 20, 1983, A13.

58. Roger H. Davidson and Walter J. Oleszek, *Congress against Itself* (Bloomington: Indiana University Press, 1977).

59. Judith H. Parris, "The Senate Reorganizes Its Committees: 1977," *Political Science Quarterly* 94 (Summer 1979): 319-337; and Roger H. Davidson, "Two Roads of Change: House and Senate Committee Reorganization," *Congress Reconsidered,* 2d ed. (Washington, D.C.: CQ Press, 1981), 107-133.

60. Christopher Madison, "The Heir Presumptive," *National Journal,* April 29, 1989, 1037.

At the White House briefing room, President Bush appears with Senators Mitchell (l.) and Dole to announce a foreign policy bargain between the two branches.

CHAPTER EIGHT

Congress and the President

On March 9, 1989, the Senate took an unprecedented action against a new president starting his first term: it rejected by a 53-47 vote George Bush's nominee for secretary of defense, former Texas GOP senator John Tower. Where President Bush wanted consent, the Senate provided contrary advice, in part because of Tower's personal behavior.

The Tower nomination battle was a classic face-off between the executive and legislative branches of government. Tensions between the two branches are inevitable. The branches are organized differently; they have divergent responsibilities; they have different constituencies and terms of office; and they are jealous of their prerogatives. Executive officials see Congress as inefficient and meddlesome. Legislators perceive the executive branch as arrogant and arbitrary. At times these differences lead to conflicts that the media dramatize as "battles on the Potomac."

Yet day in and day out Congress and the president work together. Even when their relationship is guarded or hostile, bills get passed and signed into law. Presidential appointments are approved by the Senate. Budgets are enacted and the government is kept afloat. This necessary cooperation goes on even when the White House and the Capitol are controlled by different parties. Conversely, partisan control of both branches is no guarantee of harmony, as Jimmy Carter sadly learned.

Conflict between Congress and the president inheres in our "separation of powers" and "checks and balances" system. The Founders expected their governmental arrangement also to promote accommodation between the branches. As Justice Joseph Story noted, the Framers sought to "prove that a rigid adherence to [the separation of powers] in all cases would be subversive of the efficiency of the government and result in the destruction of the public liberties." [1] Other interpreters have echoed these themes: "While the Constitution diffuses power the better to secure liberty,' wrote Justice Robert Jackson in 1952, "it also contemplates that practice will integrate the dispersed powers into a workable government." [2]

The two branches worked together in the New Deal's early days (1933-

1936), during World War II (1941-1945) and the brief Great Society years following John Kennedy's assassination (1964-1965), and for the even briefer Reaganomics juggernaut (1981). At other times they fought fiercely; for example, during Woodrow Wilson's second term (1919-1921), after 1937 for Franklin Roosevelt, after 1966 for Lyndon Johnson, and for most of Richard Nixon's and Ronald Reagan's tenure.[3]

The President as Legislator

Presidents are sometimes called the "chief legislators" because of their close involvement in the decisions Congress makes. Article II, Section 3, of the Constitution directs the president from time to time (today this means annually and during prime time) to "give to the Congress Information of the State of the Union and recommend to their Consideration such Measures as he shall judge necessary and expedient." Soon after delivering the annual State of the Union address, the president sends to Congress draft "administration bills" for introduction on his behalf. By enlarging the list of messages required from the president—annual budget and economic reports, for example—Congress has further involved the chief executive in designing legislation. Crises, partisan considerations, and public expectations all make the president an important participant in congressional decision making. And the president's constitutional veto power ensures that White House views will be listened to, if not always heeded, on Capitol Hill.

The concept of the legislative presidency did not become widespread until after World War II. Only then could it be said that the role was institutionalized, performed not because of some unique combination of personality and circumstance but because everyone—including Congress, the press, and the public—expected it.[4]

Setting the Agenda

Presidents have shaped Congress's agenda in varying degrees from the beginning. The first Congress of "its own volition immediately turned to the executive branch for guidance and discovered in [Treasury Secretary Alexander] Hamilton a personality to whom such leadership was congenial."[5] Two decades later (from 1811 to 1825) the "initiative in public affairs remained with [Speaker Henry] Clay and his associates in the House of Representatives" and not with the president.[6]

Preeminence in national policy making may pass from one branch to the other. Strong presidents sometimes provoke efforts by Congress to reassert its own authority and to restrict the executive's. Periods of presidential ascendancy often are followed by eras of congressional dominance.

Carter, Reagan, and Bush.   Agenda setting by Carter, Reagan, and Bush followed three very different patterns. Agenda control was the hallmark of Reagan's leadership during his first year in office. He shrewdly limited the number of his legislative priorities, most encapsulated as "Reaganomics" (tax and spending cuts). He introduced them soon after the 1980 elections, which was both a political honeymoon period and a time of widespread anticipation of a new era of GOP national political dominance. He dealt skillfully with Congress to mobilize support and galvanized public backing through dramatic television appeals. Later, when Reagan's control over the agenda loosened, Congress was still confined to a playing field largely demarcated by the president. It was forced to respond to, although not always accept, the positions he had staked out on taxes, spending, defense, and social issues.

By contrast, President Carter quickly overloaded Congress's agenda and never made clear what his priorities were. Three major consequences resulted:

> First ... there was little clarity in the communication of priorities to the American public. Instead of galvanizing support for two or three major national needs, the Carter administration proceeded on a number of fronts.... Second, and perhaps more important, the lack of priorities meant unnecessary waste of the President's own time and energy.... Third, the lack of priorities needlessly compounded Carter's congressional problems.... Carter's limited political capital was squandered on a variety of agenda requests when it might have been concentrated on the top of the list.[7]

If Carter overloaded the congressional agenda, George Bush underutilized it, at least initially. When Bush assumed office as the forty-first president, Congress and the White House seemed ready for more cooperation. After eight years of often sharp confrontation between President Reagan and Congress, President Bush skillfully courted Democrats and Republicans in Congress to establish a new mood and tone for legislative-executive relations. The ability to "acknowledge one another and speak on a one-to-one basis and stroke one another is extremely important to our process of government," stated Leon E. Panetta, D-Calif., chairman of the House Budget Committee. "And that's what [President Bush is] good at." [8]

Some Republicans, looking ahead to the 1990 elections and beyond, began to worry about President Bush's bipartisan approach and agenda. They urged him to draw sharper policy lines between Democrats and Republicans. "We've go to start pretty soon to differentiate where we are from where the Democrats are," stated Sen. Charles Grassley, R-Iowa.[9]

President Bush refrained from Congress bashing, and he did scores of little favors to demonstrate his understanding of how Congress works. But unlike President Reagan, who made the most of his honeymoon with Congress by winning enactment of his economic agenda, Bush did not push quickly for dramatic policy changes or even articulate two or three major goals that he wanted to accomplish. Needless to say, the policy-making context in which Bush operated differed from that of his predecessor, as Table 8-1 shows.

Table 8-1   The Policy-Making Context for Presidential Leadership,
1981, 1989

Reagan (1981)	Bush (1989)
Democratic control of House; Republican control of Senate.	Democratic control of both houses.
Specific agenda (cut taxes, increase defense spending, reduce the domestic role of the government).	Broad agenda with few specifics.
"Great Communicator" who often used media appeals to pressure Congress.	Negotiates behind-the-scenes with Congress on key issues (budget deficit and contra aid, for example).
Many legislators fearful of Reagan's political clout.	Legislators confident of their own electoral mandate and unafraid to challenge the White House.
The electorate is ready for changes.	The electorate is largely content with continuity.
Political "coattails" (the GOP takes control of the Senate for the first time in twenty-six years and picks up over thirty seats in the House).	No political "coattails." For the first time since 1960, the party that won the White House lost seats in both the House and Senate.
Double-digit budget deficits.	Triple-digit budget deficits.
Partisan battles over the direction of foreign policy.	Largely bipartisan foreign policy consensus.
Antigovernment critic who favors the private sector.	Washington "insider" who supports public service.
Many ideologues appointed to high office.	Pragmatic and seasoned Washington hands appointed to high office.
Adversarial relationship with key legislators, especially in the House.	Generally friendly relationship with scores of legislators of both parties in both chambers.

President Bush wanted to avoid early mistakes that could tarnish his political and public reputation. However, Tower's defeat, Bush's failure to fill administration positions quickly, and legislative-executive differences over raising the minimum wage and cutting the budget soon dissipated the honeymoon spirit. Setting the agenda would be difficult in light of Bush's campaign pledge not to raise taxes ("read my lips"). As Democratic representative Barney Frank of Massachusetts pointedly stated:

Bush has promised himself into a corner from which extrication will be difficult. To be a no-new-taxes-keep-defense-at-the-same-level-education-and-environmental President is hard to do. We're going to say to him, "Please tell us how you do that." [10]

Indeed, Bush's chief priority seemed to be achieving negotiated settlements on some of the most divisive issues held over from the Reagan years. First came a bipartisan agreement on aid to the rebel forces (known as the contras) seeking to overthrow the Nicaraguan government. In a dramatic break with the policies of the Reagan administration, Bush endorsed diplomatic rather than military means to bring peace to Central America. The bipartisan accord, which Secretary of State James Baker privately negotiated with House and Senate leaders, provided $45 million in nonmilitary aid to the contras through February 1990, when free elections in Nicaragua were scheduled. To ensure interim congressional review, no money could be spent to assist the contras after November 1989 unless four congressional committees (the appropriations and foreign affairs panels in both houses) sent letters to President Bush agreeing to continue the aid.

This type of informal arrangement, which the White House counsel challenged as an infringement on the president's power to conduct foreign policy, was the price of winning Congress's support for the aid package. "By removing the irritant of Nicaragua," the Bush administration expected "to build bridges to Congress on such issues as debt policy, U.S.-Mexican relations and southern Africa and to present a united front to the Soviet Union." [11] Soon there followed legislative-executive "treaties" on other issues, most notably the budget.

The divergent agendas of Carter, Reagan, and Bush remind us that presidential leadership is an amalgam of personal and political ingredients. Presidential priorities may arise from personal beliefs, campaign experiences, or pressures from influential backers. They are filtered through the president's personal style and hastened or hindered by public attitudes. An engineer by profession, Carter preferred to work with a large number of technically detailed issues. Reagan had no patience for details but believed he had an electoral mandate to achieve a small number of fundamental changes. Bush had few firm policy commitments and ran a campaign in 1988 that targeted his opponent more than it highlighted his own views. Once elected, Bush, a habitual negotiator, instinctively moved toward a conciliatory, open-ended approach to Congress.

Proposal and Disposal.   A wide gap often separates what a president wants from what he can get. Congress can influence what, when, how, or even whether executive recommendations are sent to Capitol Hill. White House agendas are frequently shaped by expectations of what will pass Congress. This indirect priority-setting power of the House and Senate can affect whether the president even transmits certain proposals to Congress. It also works in the other direction: recommendations may be forwarded or endorsed because the White House knows they have broad legislative support. "The president proposes, Congress disposes" is, in short, an oversimplified adage.

Central Clearance.   In fashioning a legislative program presidents do not lack advice (see Table 8-2). Coordinating and sifting through these recommendations (central clearance) is a responsibility primarily of the Office of Management and Budget. President Reagan gave this agency broad authority in overseeing the budgets and activities of other departments. Also during the Reagan administration, OMB expanded beyond its traditional role of "neutral advocate" in budget preparation to "political advocate" in selling the White House's fiscal priorities on Capitol Hill. Central clearance enables the president "to monitor department requests to ensure that they are not in conflict with his own." [12]

Outside Events.   National and international developments influence a president's agenda. For example, the Great Depression of the 1930s promoted President Franklin Roosevelt's agenda-setting role. When Roosevelt took office in 1933, Congress wanted him to tell it what to do. And he did. During his first 100 days, Roosevelt sent Congress fifteen messages and signed fifteen bills into law—an astonishing number for those days.

The Constitution gives the president the authority to convene one or both houses of Congress "on extraordinary occasions." A few days after taking office, FDR called a special session of Congress to consider his emergency banking legislation. "The House had no copies of the bill; the Speaker recited the text from the one available draft, which bore last minute corrections scribbled in pencil." After thirty-eight minutes of debate, "with a unanimous shout, the House passed the bill, sight unseen." [13] Passing President Reagan's revised budget package in 1981 took Congress a little longer but featured the same kind of swift support of the White House.

Contrast this with the careful scrutiny given President Carter's 1977 energy proposals—and indeed most other major initiatives submitted by presidents. Early in his term Carter described America's need for a new energy policy as the "moral equivalent of war" (dubbed MEOW by critics). Carter tried to focus congressional, media, and public attention on his program to reduce U.S. reliance on imported oil, encourage energy conservation, and promote energy production. Yet the public was slow to recognize the crisis, and there was little consensus about how to cope with it. In the end Congress enacted a 1978 energy package that included the phased deregulation of natural gas and tax incentives to produce and conserve energy. (More than a decade later analysts continue to discuss the need for a national energy policy and to worry about future energy crises.)

Table 8-2 Sources of Ideas for the President's Domestic Agenda

Source	Percentage of respondents mentioning source
External sources	
Congress	52
Events and crisis	51
Executive branch	46
Public opinion	27
Party	11
Interest groups	7
Media	4
Internal sources	
Campaign and platform	20
President	17
Staff	16
Task forces	6

Source: Paul C. Light, *The President's Agenda* (Baltimore: Johns Hopkins University Press, 1982), 86.

Note: Respondents were asked the following question: "Generally speaking, what would you say were the most important sources of ideas for the domestic agenda?" The number of respondents, all White House aides, was 118.

Legislative Delegations. Congress frequently delegates legislative responsibility to the president, departmental officials, or regulatory agencies. In 1946, for example, Congress asked the president to recommend ways to keep the nation's economy healthy.[14] Another example is Congress's creation of government corporations. For example, it delegated to the Federal Home Loan Bank Board supervisory authority over the savings and loan industry.

The decision to transfer such authority typically occurs because Congress cannot overcome its own shortcomings—its decentralized committee structure that inhibits swift and comprehensive policy formulation, its lack of technical expertise, and its members' vulnerability to reelection pressures. Congress also appreciates the strengths of single-purpose executive or independent agents—their capacity for fact-finding and coordination, for example.

The Veto Power

Article I, Section 7, of the Constitution requires the president to approve or disapprove bills passed by Congress. In the case of disapproval, the measure dies unless it "shall be repassed by two thirds of the Senate and House of Representatives." Because vetoes are so difficult to override, the veto power makes the president, in Woodrow Wilson's words, a "third branch of the legislature." [15] Presidents usually can attract one-third plus one of their supporters in Congress to sustain a veto, and so presidential vetoes are not very often overridden, as Table 8-3 indicates.

The veto is more than a negative power, however. Presidents also use it to advance their policy objectives. Veto threats, for example, often encourage committees and legislators to accommodate executive preferences and objec-. tions. Strong in his opposition to tax increases, President Reagan regularly warned Congress, "If a tax hike makes it to my desk, I'll veto it in less time than it takes Vanna White to turn the letters V-E-T-O." [16]

For its part, Congress can discourage vetoes by adding its items to "must" legislation or measures strongly favored by the president. "The President is probably going to veto a pork bill," said Rep. Robert S. Walker, R-Pa., "but if we put the crime package in there it has got a better chance of getting enacted into law." [17]

Once he receives a bill from Congress, the president has ten days (excluding Sundays) in which to exercise four options:

1. He can sign the bill. Most public and private bills presented to the president are signed into law. President Reagan began to issue "signing statements" that expressed his interpretation of a new law's provisions.[18]
2. He can return the bill with his veto message to the originating house of Congress.
3. He can take no action, and the bill will become law without his signature. This option, seldom employed, is reserved for bills the president dislikes but not enough to veto.
4. He can "pocket veto" the bill. Under the Constitution, if a congressional adjournment prevents the return of a bill, it cannot become law without the president's signature.

During the 1970s and 1980s, Congress and the president have sharply disagreed over the meaning of "prevents" in item 4. For example, a federal appeals court ruled that President Reagan acted unconstitutionally when he pocket vetoed a measure during the holiday season between the first and second sessions of the 98th Congress. Congressional attorneys argued that during legislative recesses both chambers designate officials to receive executive communications, including veto messages. Pending a decision by the Supreme Court, the appeals court ruling makes clear that pocket vetoes are constitutional only when Congress adjourns *sine die* (that is, adjourned finally) at the end of its second session (see box, page 236).

Regular and pocket vetoes are sometimes employed with the "two Congresses" in mind. For instance, President Reagan pocket vetoed a bill at the end of the 100th Congress that would protect from development 1.4 million acres of federal land in Montana. His decision was designed to aid Conrad Burns, the GOP senatorial candidate, in his bid (successful) to unseat

Table 8-3   Number of Presidential Vetoes, 1789-1989

Years	President	Regular vetoes	Pocket vetoes	Total vetoes	Vetoes over- ridden
1789-1797	George Washington	2	0	2	0
1797-1801	John Adams	0	0	0	0
1801-1809	Thomas Jefferson	0	0	0	0
1809-1817	James Madison	5	2	7	0
1817-1825	James Monroe	1	0	1	0
1825-1829	John Q. Adams	0	0	0	0
1829-1837	Andrew Jackson	5	7	12	0
1837-1841	Martin Van Buren	0	1	1	0
1841	W. H. Harrison[a]	0	0	0	0
1841-1845	John Tyler	6	4	10	1
1845-1849	James K. Polk	2	1	3	0
1849-1850	Zachary Taylor	0	0	0	0
1850-1853	Millard Fillmore	0	0	0	0
1853-1857	Franklin Pierce	9	0	9	5
1857-1861	James Buchanan	4	3	7	0
1861-1865	Abraham Lincoln	2	5	7	0
1865-1869	Andrew Johnson	21	8	29	15
1869-1877	Ulysses S. Grant	45	48	93	4
1877-1881	Rutherford B. Hayes	12	1	13	1
1881	James A. Garfield[b]	0	0	0	0
1881-1885	Chester A. Arthur	4	8	12	1
1885-1889	Grover Cleveland	304	110	414	2
1889-1893	Benjamin Harrison	19	25	44	1
1893-1897	Grover Cleveland	42	128	170	5
1897-1901	William McKinley	6	36	42	0
1901-1909	Theodore Roosevelt	42	40	82	1
1909-1913	William H. Taft	30	9	39	1
1913-1921	Woodrow Wilson	33	11	44	6
1921-1923	Warren G. Harding	5	1	6	0
1923-1929	Calvin Coolidge	20	30	50	4
1929-1933	Herbert Hoover	21	16	37	3
1933-1945	Franklin D. Roosevelt	372	263	635	9
1945-1953	Harry S Truman	180	70	250	12
1953-1961	Dwight D. Eisenhower	73	108	181	2
1961-1963	John F. Kennedy	12	9	21	0
1963-1969	Lyndon B. Johnson	16	14	30	0
1969-1974	Richard M. Nixon	26	17	43	7
1974-1977	Gerald R. Ford	48	18	66	12
1977-1981	Jimmy Carter	13	18	31	2
1981-1989	Ronald Reagan	39	39	78	9
Total		1,419	1,050	2,469	103

Sources: *Presidential Vetoes, 1789-1976,* compiled by the Senate Library (Washington, D.C.: Government Printing Office, 1978), ix; Gary L. Galemore, Congressional Research Service.

[a] W. H. Harrison served from March 4 to April 4, 1841.

[b] James A. Garfield served from March 4 to September 19, 1881.

Pocket-Veto Controversy

As the 100th Congress approached its midterm recess, lawmakers worked amid legal uncertainty about the extent of the president's power to kill legislation while they were gone.

Congress had long been at odds with Reagan administration officials over their view that the president could "pocket veto" bills any time the House and Senate recessed for more than three days, as was expected beginning sometime in mid-December. Congressional leaders contended that his pocket-veto power was more limited.

A pocket veto allows the president to kill a bill by not signing it when Congress is not in session. Unlike a regular veto, it cannot be overridden.

Open conflict may be avoided if contested bills are cleared early enough to ensure that Congress is still in session if and when the president vetoes them.

"If there are people who want to be sure [bills are] not pocket-vetoed, they're probably working very hard to get those measures up now," said Michael Davidson, Senate legal counsel.

Concern about the pocket veto had been raised about a housing bill (S 825) stalled by budget objections in the Senate.

While Congress is in session, the president has ten days (not counting Sundays) to sign a bill or veto it by returning it to Congress unsigned.

No one questions the validity of the pocket veto when a two-year Congress has adjourned and the next has not yet taken office. At issue is whether a pocket veto is valid in recesses during a session of Congress. A case that had been expected to clarify the issue, *Burke v. Barnes,* was declared moot by the Supreme Court in January 1987.

Sen. Edward M. Kennedy, D-Mass., who was involved in pre-Reagan lawsuits over the issue, wrote to House and Senate leaders in November to warn of the danger of pocket vetoes during the forthcoming recess. A White House spokesman said the administration regarded the pocket veto as one option available to it during the recess, but declined to comment further.

While the *Burke* case was pending, Reagan had avoided pocket vetoes in disputed recesses, sending such bills back to Congress with a disclaimer that he believed he had the pocket-veto authority. All of Reagan's vetoes in 1987 came while Congress was in session.

Based on correspondence with the Justice Department after the *Burke* decision, Kennedy said he believed the administration would continue to send vetoed bills back to Congress during a recess. But he warned that the administration seemed to be "reserving the right to assert that the bill has been pocket-vetoed and has not become law" if Congress overrode the veto. That likely would provoke a new battle.

Source: Adapted from Janet Hook, "End of Session Resurrects Pocket-Veto Issue," *Congressional Quarterly Weekly Report,* December 5, 1987, 3002.

Democratic incumbent John Melcher. The bill, which Melcher had sponsored, had become a campaign issue with Burns charging that it would cripple Montana's depressed economy. Burns even announced the pocket veto before Reagan formally disclosed it.[19]

An omnibus trade bill also became a political football when Reagan vetoed it in the 100th Congress because the legislation contained a provision requiring companies to provide sixty days' notice before closing plants. The president's veto worried congressional Republicans who were running for reelection; they feared that Democrats would charge them during the upcoming campaign with callousness toward American workers. For their part, Democrats were delighted with Reagan's veto because of its potential to hurt Republican candidates. Surrounded by TV cameras and a delegation of laid-off workers, Speaker Jim Wright of Texas even conducted a mock "signing" ceremony to dramatize Democratic support for workers and to pressure the White House.

When the president's veto was sustained by the Senate, many believed that spelled the end of the trade bill. But there was considerable political momentum for legislative action on this issue. As a result, Speaker Wright, Lloyd Bentsen of Texas, and other Democrats devised a two-bill strategy. The vetoed omnibus trade bill would be split into two separate bills: one on plant closings (to be taken up first) and the second on trade. The popular plant closings bill passed both chambers with wide bipartisan backing—enough to override the president's threatened veto.

GOP congressional leaders urged Reagan not to veto the bill again because it would hurt Republican candidates in the fall election. Senate GOP leader Robert Dole of Kansas argued that Reagan should let the bill become law without his signature. "In that way," said Dole, "the President could maintain his opposition to the bill without raising the political stakes." [20] Reagan followed Dole's advice. Later he signed the trade bill.

The decision to veto is a collective administrative judgment. Presidents seek advice from agency officials, the Office of Management and Budget, and White House aides. Five reasons commonly are given for vetoing a bill: (1) the bill is unconstitutional; (2) it encroaches on the president's independence; (3) it is unwise public policy; (4) it cannot be administered; and (5) it costs too much. Political considerations may permeate any or all of these reasons. The cost rationale is a favorite of recent presidents.

Just as there may be strong pressure on the White House to veto or sign a bill, there can be intense political heat on Congress after it receives a veto message. A week after President Nixon's 1970 televised veto of a labor-welfare funding bill, House members received more than 55,000 telegrams, most of which urged support for the veto. Congress upheld the veto, in part because of Nixon's televised appeal. On the other hand, despite a massive telephone campaign to congressional offices (as many as 80,000 calls an hour) urging support for President Reagan's veto of a 1988 civil rights bill, the House and Senate easily overrode the veto.[21]

Congress need not act at all upon a vetoed bill. The chamber that receives it may refer it to committee or table it, if party leaders feel they lack the votes to override. Even if one house musters the votes to override, the other body may do nothing. No amendments can be made to a vetoed bill—it is all or nothing at this stage—and votes on vetoed bills are required by the Constitution to be recorded.

Congress's habit of combining numerous items in a single measure puts the president in the position of having to accept or reject the entire package. Presidents and supporters of executive power have long touted the line-item veto as a way to reduce government spending. As a constitutional amendment (there are statutory variants), it would permit the president to veto items selectively in appropriation bills without rejecting the whole bill. The proposal has received renewed attention with the burgeoning of federal deficits.

Proponents argue that the item veto would give the president an effective way to eliminate wasteful spending and to reduce the federal deficit. Too often presidents cannot use their constitutional authority to veto objectionable bills to fund the government because of their massive size and scope. Because a veto would close down the government, the president is faced with a take-it-or-leave-it dilemma. Thus, proponents conclude, an item veto would actually *restore* a presidential prerogative that has been emasculated by omnibus funding bills.

Forty-three states, the proponents add, permit their governors to veto items in individual appropriation bills. The item veto's success in controlling expenditures at the state level is cited to justify its use by presidents.

Opponents counter that the item veto would probably not reduce spending. It is Congress that normally cuts the president's budget—not the other way around. The largest items—entitlements and interest on the federal debt—would not be subject to the veto; and at least in the current political atmosphere it is questionable whether these would be cut significantly. Moreover, the state analogy is not necessarily valid; most state constitutions forbid deficits and limit legislative sessions, leaving governors to work out adjustments in funding. These constraints do not operate at the federal level. States do not have anything like the national government's responsibility for national security or the nation's economy.

The item veto, in short, is largely an institutional and not a partisan issue. What concerns so many Democrats and Republicans on Capitol Hill is that it would expand any president's authority and undercut Congress's power of the purse. "It doesn't take much imagination to consider how much more persuasive [the president] would be if his words were buttressed with a veto stamp over individual projects and activities within our districts," said Sen. Mark Hatfield, R-Ore.[22]

Sources of Legislative-Executive Cooperation

Unlike national assemblies where executive authority is lodged in the leader of parliament, called the prime minister or premier, Congress is truly separate from the executive branch. Yet the executive and legislative branches are mutually dependent in policy making. One hundred and two volumes of the *United States Statutes at Large* underscore the cooperative impulses of the two branches. Each volume contains the joint product of Congresses and presidents over the years, from the 108 public laws enacted by the first Congress (1789-1791) to the 714 enacted by the 100th Congress (1987-1989). These accomplishments are the result of party loyalties, public expectations, bargaining, and compromise.

Party Links

Presidents and congressional leaders have met informally to discuss issues ever since the first Congress, when George Washington frequently sought the advice of Rep. James Madison. But meetings between the chief executive and House and Senate leaders did not become common until Theodore Roosevelt's administration. Today congressional party leaders are two-way conduits who communicate legislative views to the president and inform members of executive preferences and intentions.

Presidents and members of their party are linked both psychologically and ideologically. This means that "bargaining 'within the family' has a rather different quality than bargaining with members of the rival clan." [23] During Reagan's first term, for instance, the president and his chief aides relied heavily on Howard H. Baker, Jr., the Senate majority leader, to marshal support. "Before we move on anything up there, we pick up the phone and get Howard Baker's judgment on what will or won't fly," said James Baker, the White House chief of staff (no relation to the senator).[24]

However, presidents and their partisan colleagues on the Hill sometimes have divergent goals, especially when the president's party is in the minority (as has been the case since 1987). Presidents need legislative results, which impels them to deal with the majority party; the congressional minority seeks a sharper delineation of their positions to embarrass their opponents. President Bush can expect congressional Republicans to support his legislative agenda whenever possible, but House Republicans, in the minority for over three decades, want to confront House Democrats aggressively. To increase their chances of winning majority control of the House in the 1990s they want to make Democrats look bad and themselves look good.

The dilemma was expressed by Richard Cheney of Wyoming when he was House GOP whip. "By virtue of having won the White House it is important for us to help George Bush get his program through. That requires a certain degree of cooperation with the Democrats." [25] House Speaker

Thomas S. Foley of Washington used a parable to illustrate the partisan connection between his colleagues and President Bush:

> There is a good elephant who wraps his trunk around you and walks with you . . . to the high savannas of bipartisan achievement. But behind is the rumble of the elephant rogue herd . . . whose principal purpose is to find Democrats and to stomp them to death. Now, which elephant are we going to be dealing with? That's our concern.[26]

Foley's question was answered by Ed Rollins, executive director of the House GOP campaign committee. "It's a two-track system," Rollins said. A positive, popular Bush will help all Republicans, Rollins claimed, while he and others attack Democrats "district by district, state by state." [27] All presidents hope that their "coattails" are long enough to help their partisans win close congressional races.[28]

Bargaining Relationships

The interdependence of the two branches provides each with the incentive to bargain. Legislators and presidents have in common at least three interests: shaping public policy, winning elections, and attaining influence within the legislature. In achieving these goals, members may be helped or hindered by executive officials. Agency personnel, for example, can heed legislators' advice in formulating policies, help them gain favorable publicity back home, and give them advance notice of executive actions. Executive officials, on the other hand, rely on legislators for help in pushing administrative proposals through the legislative process.

An illustration of effective presidential bargaining with Congress occurred on May 7, 1981, when the Democratic-controlled House adopted Reagan's controversial budget package, intended to cut federal spending for social programs and raise military spending. The plan easily passed the House because of Reagan's popularity and adroitness in dealing with representatives. The "greatest selling job I've ever seen," said Speaker Thomas P. O'Neill, Jr. On the key House vote all 191 GOP members and 63 Democrats backed the president's budget scheme.

The president's victory was made possible by a multipronged strategy. He bolstered the support of wavering Republicans. He convinced several governors to meet with representatives from their states who were opposing the program. He met or phoned conservative Democrats whose support was needed. Top executive officials were sent into targeted Democratic districts to drum up public support. Finally, a few days before the House vote, and in his first public appearance since he had been shot in an assassination attempt, Reagan made a nationally televised address before a joint session of Congress and appealed for support of his economic program.

South Carolina Democrat Butler Derrick, who saw Reagan at the White House, experienced the "two Congresses" dilemma we have posed in this book. He described the "inside-outside" pressures he was under prior to the House vote.

> We've had all sorts of conservative proposals come before the Congress that were not here a year ago or six or eight months ago. They're here because Reagan was a catalyst. Most people I talk to, and I think they're right, back in the district, say, "You know, I don't know if he's right or he's wrong, but I'm not pleased with what we've done up to now, so I say let's give the guy a chance to see if it'll work."
>
> I've had a lot of pressure on me. I'm considered, I guess as a member of the Rules Committee, part of the Democratic leadership and I have had a good bit of pressure put on me from members of the leadership and what not. And I've just explained it to them. Quite frankly, to vote other than to vote for [the president], which I plan to do, would be like throwing gasoline in the face of my constituents.[29]

In short, Reagan shrewdly encouraged representatives to back his economic priorities because their constituents demanded it. He even suggested how legislators might reconcile their budget-cutting and program-spending instincts. Vote for my budget, he told House members, but fight in committee or on the House floor for favored programs.

Informal Ties

Some presidents deal with Congress more adeptly than others. Lyndon Johnson assiduously courted members. He summoned legislators to the White House for private meetings, danced with their wives at parties, telephoned greetings on their birthdays, and hosted them at his Texas ranch. He also knew how to "twist arms" to win support for his programs. Johnson's understanding of what moved members and energized Congress was awesome. "There is only one way for a President to deal with the Congress," he said, "and that is continuously, incessantly, and without interruption." [30]

In contrast, President Carter, elected as a Washington "outsider," never developed an affinity for Congress. Although by one measurement Congress sided with Carter on 75 percent of the votes on which he took a position during 1977, the margin was low for a first-year president whose party also controlled the Congress (see Figure 8-1). A House Democrat recalled:

> When I came here President Kennedy would have six or seven of us down to the White House every evening for drinks and conversation. Johnson did the same thing, and they created highly personal, highly involved relationships. With Carter, he has 140 people in for breakfast and a lecture.[31]

In this respect Carter was like Nixon, who despite his service in Congress dealt clumsily with lawmakers. Nixon shunned informal contacts with members, rarely telephoned them, and "could not bring himself to ask for votes." [32]

Figure 8-1 Presidential Success on Votes, 1953-1988

Percentage

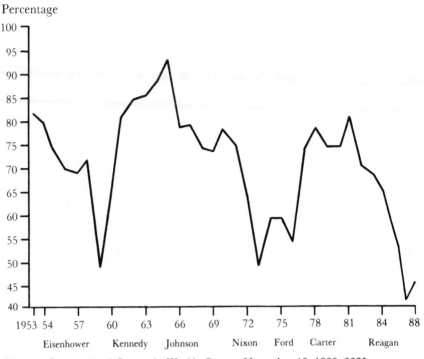

Source: *Congressional Quarterly Weekly Report,* November 19, 1988, 3325.
Note: Percentages are based on votes on which presidents took a position.

Other chief executives were more at ease with members. President Reagan, for example, enjoyed swapping stories with Democrats and Republicans alike. As former Senate majority leader Baker described him:

> In dealing with Congress, he's closer to Lyndon Johnson than anyone else.... Carter never understood the legislative process. Ford understood but he couldn't do anything about it. Nixon never paid enough attention to it to be successful. For give-and-take with Congress, Reagan is the best I've ever served with.[33]

Bush's personal style with Congress seems to fall somewhere between President Carter's (impersonal and detail-oriented) and President Reagan's (friendly and focused on the big picture). Bush is more involved in day-to-day policy making and personally consults with many members of Congress and friends around the country. "He makes and takes scores of phone calls each day," one report noted, "talking to an army of people in and out of government, from Congressmen to civil rights leaders to cronies from the Texas oil fields."[34]

Sources of Legislative-Executive Conflict

In 1987 Assistant Secretary of State Elliott Abrams testified before Congress about the secret scheme of President Reagan's national security aide, Col. Oliver North, and others to sell arms to Iran in exchange for American hostages. The profits were used to send weapons to the contras in Nicaragua. Sen. Howell Heflin, D-Ala., marveled at Abrams's ability to dodge tough questions about the affair through the artful use of words. "You are well-schooled in word-dancing," said Sen. Heflin. "I'm a lawyer," replied Abrams. "Maybe that's my problem."

Sen. Thomas Eagleton, D-Mo., however, took a tougher tack toward Abrams during hearings conducted by the Senate Intelligence Committee. This heated exchange occurred over Abrams's solicitation of $10 million from the Sultan of Brunei for the contras:

A: We made one solicitation to a foreign government.

E: Were you then in the fund-raising business?

A [with sarcasm]: I would say we were in the fund-raising business. I take your point.

E: Take my point: Under oath my friend, that's perjury. Had you been under oath, that's perjury.

A: You've heard my testimony.

E: I've heard it and I want to puke.[35]

This clash between a legislator and a member of the executive branch of government was extreme but not unprecedented. Legislative-executive conflicts were evident in 1789, they are present today, and they can be expected in the future for at least three reasons. First, the Constitution specifies neither the precise policy-making roles of Congress and the president, nor the manner in which they are to deal with one another. Second, presidents and Congresses serve different constituencies. Third, there are important variations in the timetables under which the two branches operate.

Constitutional Ambiguities

Article I invests Congress with "all legislative Powers," but it also authorizes the president to recommend and to veto legislation. In several specific areas the Constitution also splits authority between the president and Congress. The Senate, for example, is the president's partner in treaty making and nominations under "advice and consent" clauses. And before treaties can take effect, they require the concurrence of two-thirds of the Senate. The Constitution is silent, however, on how or when the Senate is to render its advice to the president.[36]

In 1919 and 1920 a classic confrontation occurred when the Senate vehemently opposed the Treaty of Versailles negotiated by President Wilson. The treaty contained an agreement binding the United States to the proposed

League of Nations. Many senators had warned the president against including the league provision in the treaty, and during floor deliberations the Senate added several "reservations" strongly opposed by the president. Spurning compromise, Wilson launched a nationwide speaking tour to mobilize popular support for the treaty. Not to be outdone, senators opposed to the pact organized a "truth squad" that trailed the president and rebutted his arguments. During his tour, Wilson suffered a stroke from which he never fully recovered. In the end the treaty was rejected. The Constitution, in short, intermingles presidential and congressional authority and also assigns each branch special duties.

Different Constituencies

Presidents and their vice presidents are the only public officials elected nationally. To win, they must create vastly broader electoral coalitions than do legislators, who represent either states or districts. Only presidents, then, can claim to speak for the nation at large. It is important to note, however, that

> there is no structural or institutional or theoretical reason why the representation of a "single" broader constituency by the President is necessarily better or worse than the representation of many "separate" constituencies by several hundred legislators. Some distortion is inevitable in either arrangement, and the question of the good or evil of either form of distortion simply leads one back to varying value judgments.[37]

Presidents and legislators tend to view policies and problems from different perspectives. Members often subscribe to the view that "what's good for Seattle is good for the nation." Presidents are apt to say that "what's good for the nation is good for Seattle." In other words, public officials may view common issues differently when they represent diverging interests.

For example, a president might wish to reduce international trade barriers. A representative from a district where the automobile industry is threatened by imported Japanese products is likely to oppose the president's policy. The importers and retailers of shoes from Italy, however, are likely to support the president. The challenge to national policy making is forging consensus within an electorate that simultaneously holds membership in two or more competing constituencies.

Disparities in constituencies are underscored by differences in the ways voters judge presidents and members of Congress. Studies of presidential popularity ratings suggest that presidents are judged on the basis of general factors—economic boom or bust, the presence or absence of wars or other types of crises, the impact of policies on given groups.[38] Legislators, by contrast, tend to be assessed on the basis of their personalities, their communication with constituents, and their service to the state or district in material ways. Not only do presidents and legislators serve differing constituencies; they labor under divergent incentives.

Different Time Perspectives

Finally, Congress and the president operate on different timetables. Presidents have four years, possibly eight, to win adoption of their programs. They are usually in a hurry to achieve all they can before they leave office. In practice, they have even less time—in view of the typical fall off of presidential support after the hundred-day honeymoon, roughly speaking. Thus, presidents and their advisers have a year, perhaps even less, to sell their basic program to Congress and the public.

Congress, on the other hand, moves slowly. Seldom does Congress pass presidential initiatives quickly. Moreover, many legislators are careerists. Once elected, House members are likely to be reelected, and senators serve six-year terms. Most members, then, will hold office a good deal longer than will presidents. Skeptical legislators, reluctant to follow the president, realize that if they resist long enough another person will occupy the White House. In addition, the lawmakers' attitude toward the president depends on whether the chief executive is up for reelection. Comparing Reagan's first and second terms, one congressional Republican said:

> The main political undercurrent is that Ronald Reagan will not run for re-election. His agenda is now a little bit different from Republicans in Congress. In the first term Ronald Reagan's agenda was the same as the Republicans—to get re-elected. Now it's a little different. While there's certainly times when both want the same thing, members of Congress ask, "Is this really in my best interest if I want to get re-elected?" Reagan doesn't have to ask that question anymore.[39]

Like his predecessor, George Bush confronted an election imperative. Electoral history shows that since the late 1800s, with one exception in 1934, the president's party has always lost mid-term seats. This political reality shadowed Bush's dealings with his partisan legislative allies.

Lobbying the Congress

"Merely placing a program before Congress is not enough," declared President Johnson. "Without constant attention from the administration, most legislation moves through the congressional process at the speed of a glacier."[40] Johnson regularly admonished his aides and departmental officers to work closely with Congress. "[Get off] your ass and see how fast you can respond to a congressional request," he told his staff. "Challenge yourself to see how quickly you can get back to him or her with an answer, any kind of an answer, but goddamn it, an answer."[41]

White House liaison activities with Congress, patronage services, and public appeals for support are several of the ways presidents enhance their bargaining power with the legislative branch. They help presidents exercise their constitutional and persuasive powers, and they also may minimize the delay and deadlock built into executive-legislative relationships.

White House Liaison

Presidents have always maintained informal contacts with Congress. George Washington dispatched Alexander Hamilton, his secretary of the Treasury, to consult with members; Thomas Jefferson socialized with his congressional allies. But not until the administration of Harry S Truman in 1949 did any president create an office to maintain ties with Congress. Truman's liaison unit consisted of two persons inexperienced in legislative politics.

In 1961 President John F. Kennedy upgraded the congressional relations unit. He realized that without aggressive liaison his New Frontier program faced tough sledding in a Congress controlled by conservatives. Kennedy named Lawrence F. O'Brien to head the Office of Congressional Relations and gave him high status on the White House staff. As a result, O'Brien said, "I could speak for the president with the Congress and deal directly with the Leadership of the House and Senate on behalf of the president." [42]

O'Brien worked diligently to establish cordial relations with members. He designated certain staff to be responsible for the House or Senate and for regional and partisan blocs. Liaison staff familiarized themselves with the members from each geographical area, learning their interests and calculating how their votes might be won for the president's program. O'Brien also coordinated departmental and agency liaison activities with Congress.

> We surveyed Congressional Relations in the Departments and Agencies and established a procedure whereby each Cabinet Member and Agency Head submitted to me by Monday noon of each week, a written report detailing his Department's activity on the Hill during the previous week and a projection of activity for the current week. We summarized these reports during Monday afternoon and sent the summary to the President for his night reading on Monday evenings along with a suggested agenda for his use when he met with the Democratic Leadership each Tuesday. In addition, we called the Congressional Liaison Heads of the Departments and Agencies, numbering about 40, to the White House periodically for in-depth discussions of our program and specific assignments.[43]

Every president since Kennedy has had his own system for lobbying Congress. Carter's liaison unit employed computers to analyze congressional votes and thus target members who were perhaps "gettable" for certain issues. In the Reagan White House overall legislative strategy on major issues was formulated by a Legislative Strategy Group. The group's objectives were to promote enactment of the president's agenda by building winning coalitions on Capitol Hill. And Reagan, like Carter before him and Bush after, appointed White House aides to contact groups and constituencies needed to win legislative battles. In effect, their job was to "lobby the lobbyists."

Bush's congressional relations office got off to a rocky start. The president's chief of staff, former New Hampshire governor John Sununu, was an outsider to Washington's norms and folkways, and the team assembled to deal with the House and Senate came under early criticism, especially for moving late to try and rescue the Tower nomination. "There has been a sense of miscalculating, a lack of accurate information, an inability to strategize on the mix of issues and an inability to get Bush to play offense on the issues," remarked a Bush GOP supporter. A Bush adviser noted that there "are not a lot of heavy hitters" at the White House because "that's the way Bush wants it." Bush wants a Cabinet stronger than the White House staff.[44]

No president has an easy task persuading Congress to act in a certain way. Numerous factors influence how members vote on issues important to the White House. While the personal legislative skills of presidents are significant, other considerations—members' constituency interests, policy preferences, and ideological dispositions, as well as public opinion and the number of partisan seats in each house—usually are more important in shaping congressional outcomes. As a result, the White House legislative liaison operation is concerned less with specific "arm twisting" and more with the "longer-term strategic task of creating an atmosphere of cooperation between the White House and Congress."[45]

Patronage Services

To win congressional support for their programs, presidents commonly grant or withhold their patronage resources. Broadly conceived, patronage involves not only federal and judicial positions, but also federal construction projects, location of government installations, offers of campaign support, availability of strategic information, plane rides on Air Force One, White House access for important constituents, and countless other favors both large and small. Their actual or potential award enables presidents to amass political IOUs they can cash in later for needed support in Congress. Some presidents, such as Lyndon Johnson, even keep records of the political favors they grant to members. A story illustrates the dynamics of trading:

> John Kennedy was trying to make a case to Senator Robert Kerr for an investment credit tax bill that was bottled up in the Senate Finance Committee, of which Kerr was an influential member. Kerr responded by asking why the administration opposed his Arkansas River project and by demanding a trade. Kennedy smiled and replied, "You know, Bob, I never really understood that Arkansas River bill before today." Kerr got his project as well as several other benefits. In return, he provided Kennedy with important support and managed the president's high-priority Trade Expansion Act in the Senate.[46]

Sen. Everett Dirksen, R-Ill., an influential minority leader from 1959 to 1969, insisted that patronage was a "tremendous weapon" of the president.

"It develops a certain fidelity on the part of the recipient," he said.[47] Yet there are limitations, including the shrinkage of patronage jobs in attractiveness if not in numbers. Presidents try to avoid the irritation of members whose requests are turned down, sometimes assigning to other officials the job of saying "no."

Public Appeals for Support

To generate grass-roots or indirect support for their programs, presidents may take their case to the people. The assumption is that citizens and pressure groups, energized by a president's "fireside chat" or nationally televised address, will lobby their representatives and senators to back the president. "With public sentiment, nothing can fail; without it nothing can succeed," Abraham Lincoln once observed.[48]

Presidents employ various means to win support and reduce opposition for their actions. The White House can sponsor regional conferences to drum up public support for the administration's program. Groups from members' states and districts can be invited to the White House to receive briefings from high-level officials. Or the president can undertake a nationwide speaking tour, woo press and media correspondents, conduct "town meetings," or dispatch key aides and executive officers to address groups around the country.

"Going public" on an issue is not without its risks. The president can raise expectations that cannot be met, make inept presentations, lose control over issues, infuriate legislators whose support he needs, or further stiffen the opposition. Also, many legislators are more popular than the president in their districts or states. The president goes public to gather support, for "if he had the votes he would pass the measure first and go to the public only for the bill-signing ceremonies." [49]

President Reagan was an acknowledged master at using electronic media to orchestrate public support. The Hollywood actor turned president not only was at home in front of cameras and microphones, but he also had a keen sense of public ritual and symbolism as means of rallying support. It is in the media arena where Reagan's legacy will loom large for future presidents and Congresses. He showed that "one man using the White House's immense powers of communication can lift the mood of the nation and alter the way it does business. It will be hard for future presidents to complain again about malaise in the country or the unbearable burdens of the presidency." [50]

Early analyses of President Bush's public relations techniques indicate that he has "abandoned the elaborate, tightly controlled machinery developed in recent years to project, manipulate and polish a presidential image" in the television age.[51] Instead, Bush is using traditional methods—meeting with small groups of reporters, inviting journalists to lunch, or traveling outside Washington, for instance—to build public support through communications.

The Balance of Power

"The relationship between the Congress and the presidency," wrote Arthur M. Schlesinger, Jr., "has been one of the abiding mysteries of the American system of government." [52] Part of the mystery inheres in the Constitution, which enumerates many powers for Congress as well as those "necessary and proper" to carry them out, while leaving the president's powers largely ambiguous. Where does the balance of power lie? There is no easy answer, but at certain times the scale has tipped toward Congress and at other times toward the president. Scholars have even identified periods of "congressional government" or "presidential government." [53]

Several points need to be remembered about the ups and downs of Congress and the presidency. First, the power balance is in constant flux. The stature of either branch can be influenced by issues, events, or personalities. Partisan circumstances also come into play. Today congressional Republicans generally support executive authority because their party regularly wins the White House (five of the six elections from 1968 to 1988). Consequently, Republicans seem to act as the "executive party" and Democrats as the "congressional party." Moreover, "party rivals have come increasingly to dominate the *institutional* rivalry of president and Congress." Each party, therefore, may seek ways to shift power from the president to Congress, or vice versa, depending upon their partisan, policy, and philosophical preferences. The battle over the Tower confirmation, then, can be perceived as "entrenched Democratic congressional power challenging entrenched Republican executive power." [54] Rejection of Tower was more than a judgment on his suitability to be defense secretary; it was also a "warning shot" across the administration's bow that was meant to convey caution in making future nominations.

Even during periods when one branch is called the "junior partner," actual relationships in specific policy areas may be exactly the reverse. The mid-1960s and early 1970s, for example, are cited as a time of "imperial presidents" and compliant Congresses.[55] But Congress during this period was hardly passive. While it enacted much of President Johnson's Great Society program, it also initiated scores of laws, including consumer, environmental, health, and civil rights legislation. Executive actions did not go unchallenged. Nationally televised hearings conducted in 1966 by the Senate Foreign Relations Committee helped mobilize congressional and public opposition to Johnson's Vietnam War policies.

Second, legislative-executive relationships are not zero-sum games. If one branch gains power, the other does not necessarily lose it. If one branch is up, the other need not be down. The expansion of the federal government since World War II has augmented the authority of both branches. Their growth rates differed, but each expanded its ability to address complex issues, initiate legislation, and frustrate proposals of the other.

Third, events contribute importantly to policy-making power. Conventional wisdom states that wars, crises, nuclear weapons, military expansion, and public demands fostered the imperial presidency. Such factors certainly enlarge the likelihood of executive dominance, but we should note that in the wars of 1812 and 1898, military action was encouraged in part by aggressive Congresses. Economic panics and depressions under Presidents James Monroe, James Buchanan, or Ulysses S. Grant did not lead to losses of congressional power.

Fourth, shifts of power occur within each branch. In Congress aggressive leaders may be followed by less assertive leaders. In the executive branch the forces for White House leadership regularly battle the forces for agency decentralization. These internal power fluctuations clearly affect policy making. As recently as the Eisenhower presidency, powerful committee and party leaders could normally deliver blocs of votes to pass legislation. More recent presidents can never be quite sure which of the 540 members will form a winning coalition.

Fifth, pendulum swings affect issue areas and how they are addressed by the two branches. In foreign relations, cycles of isolationism and internationalism, noninterventionism and interventionism, have succeeded each other at fairly regular intervals. Debates on health policy may shift from emphasizing government-run programs to approaches stressing private-sector competition. Or Congress may grab the initiative away from the president in policy making. The consensus seems to be "not that the President is less important than generally supposed but that Congress is more important" as policy formulator.[56]

Finally, public expectations that Congress ought to assert its authority, especially in domestic policy, encourage it to do so (see Table 8-4). These expectations further enable Congress to fashion national policies.

Congress and the president, in short, are institutions shaped by diverging imperatives. Executive officials want flexibility, discretion, and long-range commitments from Congress. They prefer few controls and consultations with a limited number of legislators. Where the executive tends to be hierarchical in decision making, Congress is collegial. One of the legislative branch's strengths, however, is to give voice and visibility to diverse viewpoints that the executive branch may have overlooked or ignored. The dispersion of power can slow down decision making, but it also can promote public acceptance of the nation's policies. Hence, what are often viewed as Congress's vices have some virtue.

Conclusion

Legislative-executive relations are characterized by accommodation, conflict, and flux. Of these, accommodation is the most important. Neither branch is monolithic. Presidents find supporters in Congress even when they are

Table 8-4 The Roles of Congress and the President in Policy Making (in percentages)

Who should have the major responsibility?	Energy policy	Economic policy	Foreign policy	General responsibility
Congress	40	40	27	36
Equal	19	20	18	22
President	35	34	49	37
Don't know	6	6	6	5

Sources: Gallup Poll; Thomas E. Cronin, "A Resurgent Congress and the Imperial Presidency," *Political Science Quarterly* (Summer 1980): 211.

Note: Respondents were asked the following question: "Now I would like to ask you some questions about the President and Congress. Some people think that the President ought to have the major responsibility for making policy, while other people think that Congress ought to have the major responsibility. In general, which do you think should have the major responsibility for setting policy?"

opposed by a majority of either house. Both branches seek support for their policy preferences from each other and from outside allies in an atmosphere usually free of acrimony.

However, it is also true that confrontation is a recurring theme in dealings between Capitol Hill and the White House. The Framers consciously distributed and mixed power among the branches. They left it unclear how Congress or the president was to assert control over the bureaucracy and over policy making. No wonder they tend to be adversaries even when they are controlled by the same party.

Finally, legislative-executive relations are constantly in flux. Either branch may be active on an issue at one time and passive on the same or different issues at another time. So many circumstances affect how, when, what, or why changes are brought about in their relationship that it is impossible to predict the outlook.

It is clear, however, that over the past generation Congress has equipped itself with a formidable arsenal of resources. As a result, it can play a more active role and even initiate policies of its own. This development need not be a formula for stalemate. "Our proper objective," counseled former senator J. William Fulbright, D-Ark., "is neither a dominant presidency nor an aggressive Congress but, within the strict limits of what the Constitution mandates, a shifting of the emphasis according to the needs of the time and the requirements of public policy." [57]

Notes

1. Joseph Story, *Commentaries on the Constitution of the United States,* 5th ed., vol. 1 (Boston: Little, Brown, 1905), 396.
2. *Youngstown Sheet and Tube Co. v. Sawyer,* 343 U.S. 579, 635 (1952).
3. See Wilfred E. Binkley, *President and Congress* (New York: Alfred A. Knopf, 1947); William S. Livingston et al., eds., *The Presidency and the Congress: A Shifting Balance of Power?* (Austin, Texas: Lyndon B. Johnson School of Public Affairs, 1979); and Richard E. Neustadt, *Presidential Power: The Politics of Leadership from FDR to Carter* (New York: John Wiley & Sons, 1980).
4. See Stephen Wayne, *The Legislative Presidency* (New York: Harper & Row, 1978).
5. Leonard D. White, *The Federalists* (New York: Macmillan, 1948), 55. See also Paul C. Light, "The President's Agenda: Notes on the Timing of Domestic Choice," *Presidential Studies Quarterly* (Winter 1981): 67-82.
6. Leonard D. White, *The Jeffersonians* (New York: Macmillan, 1951), 35.
7. Paul C. Light, *The President's Agenda* (Baltimore: Johns Hopkins University Press, 1982), 230-231.
8. Robin Toner, "Congress Still Purring as Bush Applies the Right Strokes," *New York Times,* January 31, 1989, A20.
9. Donald Lambro, "Bipartisan Blues Beset GOP's Ranks," *Washington Times,* May 19, 1989, F3.
10. *New York Times,* December 14, 1988, B12.
11. Robert S. Greenberger, "Bush, with Contra Aid Plan, Shows Willingness to Work with Congress in Setting Foreign Policy," *Wall Street Journal,* March 27, 1989, A12.
12. Richard M. Pious, *The American Presidency* (New York: Basic Books, 1979), 159. See also Larry Berman, *The Office of Management and Budget and the Presidency, 1921-1979* (Princeton, N.J.: Princeton University Press, 1979).
13. William Leuchtenburg, *Franklin D. Roosevelt and the New Deal, 1932-1940* (New York: Harper & Row, 1963), 43-44.
14. Stephen K. Bailey, *Congress Makes a Law* (New York: Columbia University Press, 1950). On legislative delegations, see Sotirios A. Barber, *The Constitution and the Delegation of Congressional Power* (Chicago: University of Chicago Press, 1975); and Louis Fisher, "Delegating Power to the President," *Journal of Public Law* 19 (1970): 251-282.
15. Woodrow Wilson, *Congressional Government* (Boston: Houghton Mifflin, 1885), 52.
16. *Wall Street Journal,* July 13, 1987, 1.
17. *Congressional Record,* 98th Cong., 2d sess., September 25, 1984, H10028.
18. Frank B. Cross, "The Constitutional Legitimacy and Significance of Presidential 'Signing Statements,'" *Administrative Law Review* 40 (Spring 1988): 209-238.
19. *Washington Post,* November 4, 1988, A11.

20. *New York Times,* July 27, 1988, A16.
21. *Los Angeles Times,* pt. I, March 18, 1988, 4.
22. Thomas E. Cronin, "The Item Veto: An Idea Whose Time Shouldn't Come," *Christian Science Monitor,* September 4, 1984, 22.
23. Richard Neustadt, *Presidential Power* (New York: John Wiley & Sons, 1960), 187.
24. *Wall Street Journal,* April 8, 1981, 1.
25. *Washington Post,* December 26, 1988, A9.
26. Robin Toner, "Democrats in House Warn Bush Against GOP Partisan Warfare," *New York Times,* March 24, 1989, A17.
27. Kim Mattingly, "Ed Rollins: Hardball in the House Will Jibe with Bush's 'Kinder, Gentler' Approach," *Roll Call,* March 30, 1989, 3.
28. John A. Ferejohn and Randall L. Calvert, "Presidential Coattails in Historical Perspective," *American Journal of Political Science* (February 1984): 127-146.
29. *Washington Post,* May 10, 1981, A3.
30. Lyndon Johnson, *The Vantage Point* (New York: Popular Library, 1971), 448.
31. *New York Times,* May 27, 1979, E4.
32. Wayne, *The Legislative Presidency,* 160.
33. Hedrick Smith, "Taking Charge of Congress," *The New York Times Magazine,* August 9, 1981, 14.
34. Dan Goodgame, "Rude Awakening," *Time,* March 20, 1989, 23.
35. Kim I. Eisler, "Elliott Abrams, Esq.: Defiant and Elusive," *Legal Times,* June 8, 1987, 2-3.
36. See Joseph P. Harris, *The Advice and Consent of the Senate* (Berkeley: University of California Press, 1953); and G. Calvin Mackenzie, *The Politics of Presidential Appointments* (New York: The Free Press, 1981).
37. James MacGregor Burns, *Presidential Government* (Boston: Houghton Mifflin, 1966), 284.
38. See, for example, Stephen J. Wayne, "Great Expectations: What People Want from Presidents," in *Rethinking the Presidency,* ed. Thomas E. Cronin (Boston: Little, Brown, 1982), 185-199.
39. *New York Times,* September 9, 1985, A11.
40. Lyndon B. Johnson, *The Vantage Point* (New York: Holt, Rinehart & Winston, 1971), 448.
41. Jack Valenti, "Some Advice on the Care and Feeding of Congressional Egos," *Los Angeles Times,* April 23, 1978, 3.
42. *Congressional Record,* 89th Cong., 2d sess., October 10, 1966, 25956.
43. Ibid. See also John F. Manley, "Presidential Power and White House Lobbying," *Political Science Quarterly* (Summer 1978): 255-275.
44. James Gerstenzang, "Early Fumbles by Bush's Staff May Trigger Quick Shake-up," *Los Angeles Times,* pt. I, March 25, 1989, 18.
45. James P. Pfiffner, "The President's Legislative Agenda," *The Annals* (September 1988): 29. See also George C. Edwards, *At the Margins* (New Haven, Conn.: Yale University Press, 1989).
46. George C. Edwards III, *Presidential Influence in Congress* (San Francisco: W. H. Freeman, 1980), 129.

47. Neil MacNeil, *Dirksen: Portrait of a Public Man* (New York: World Publishing, 1970), 343. See also Stanley Kelley, Jr., "Patronage and Presidential Legislative Leadership," in *The Presidency,* ed. Aaron Wildavsky (Boston: Little, Brown, 1969), 268-277.
48. Roy P. Basler, ed., *The Collected Works of Abraham Lincoln,* vol. 3 (New Brunswick, N.J.: Rutgers University Press, 1953), 27.
49. Pious, *The American Presidency,* 194. See George C. Edwards III, *The Public Presidency* (New York: St. Martin's Press, 1983).
50. *Wall Street Journal,* December 4, 1987, 8D.
51. Tom Rosenstiel and James Gerstenzang, "Bush Team Rejects Public Relations Techniques of Reagan White House," *Los Angeles Times,* pt. 1, April 30, 1989, 1.
52. Arthur M. Schlesinger, Jr., and Alfred D. Grazia, *Congress and the Presidency: Their Role in Modern Times* (Washington, D.C.: American Enterprise Institute, 1967), 1.
53. Wilson, *Congressional Government;* and Burns, *Presidential Government.*
54. Everett Carll Ladd, "The New Workings of Separation of Powers," *Christian Science Monitor,* March 3, 1989, 19.
55. See Joseph S. Clark, *Congress: The Sapless Branch* (New York: Harper & Row, 1964); and Arthur M. Schlesinger, Jr., *The Imperial Presidency* (Boston: Houghton Mifflin, 1973).
56. Lawrence H. Chamberlin, *The President, Congress and Legislation* (New York: Columbia University Press, 1946), 453-454. See also James L. Sundquist, *Politics and Policy* (Washington, D.C.: Brookings Institution, 1969); Ronald Moe and Steven Teel, "Congress as Policymaker," *Political Science Quarterly* (September 1970): 443-470; David E. Price, *Who Makes the Laws?* (Cambridge, Mass.: Schenkman Publishing Co., 1972); and John R. Johannes, "The President Proposes and the Congress Disposes But Not Always: Legislative Initiative on Capitol Hill," *The Review of Politics* (July 1974): 356-370.
57. J. William Fulbright, "The Legislator as Educator," *Foreign Affairs* (Spring 1979): 726.

Former White House aide Lt. Col. Oliver North is sworn in by Sen. Daniel Inouye, D-Hawaii, during congressional probe of the Iran-contra affair.

CHAPTER NINE

Congress and the Bureaucracy

During his presidential campaign, Jimmy Carter pledged to work against big government and to "streamline the bureaucracy." Yet once elected, Carter did little streamlining and, in fact, created two new departments: Energy in 1977 and Education in 1979.

Ronald Reagan also campaigned on an anti-big-government platform. In his first inaugural address Reagan stated that "government is not the solution to our problems; government is the problem. . . . It is my intention to curb the size and influence of the Federal establishment." When Reagan left office, however, the budget and work force of the federal government were bigger, not smaller. The number of civilians working for the federal government rose from 2.8 million in 1981 to more than 3 million in 1988.

To be sure, Reagan used a combination of budget and tax cuts to shrink expenditures for numerous social programs, but he embraced big, activist government in other areas, especially in the realm of military expenditures. In his last year in office he even created a new Cabinet position—Veterans' Affairs. While some agencies were "winners" during the Reagan years, most dealing with domestic programs were "losers" (see Table 9-1). In short, Reagan's record was noted less for downsizing the government than for shifting its priorities. Conservatives and liberals, it seems, both like to spend, but for different purposes.

Why is it so difficult for presidents to cut back the government? One reason is the ambivalence of the citizenry. While professing to want to get government off their backs, Americans of virtually all ideological persuasions turn to government to fulfill their goals. Beneficiaries resist curtailing or eliminating favorite agencies or programs. Liberals applaud government intervention to achieve economic welfare, promote social equality, and protect consumer rights. Conservatives bridle at these programs but welcome government subsidies to producers and intervention to promote national defense, order, and morality. "It is not surprising," noted one scholar, "that people who in the role of citizens deplore the unprincipled extension of federal activity also support, in their occupational roles, organizations that

Table 9-1   Federal Civilian Work Force, 1977-1987

Agency	Number of workers (in thousands)			Percentage change, 1977-1987
	1977	1981	1987	
Winners				
Justice	53.3	56.1	66.5	24.8
Postal Service	660.5	663.6	881.0	22.8
Treasury	127.1	128.9	146.0	14.9
Veterans	222.7	233.0	243.2	9.2
Defense	996.6	986.3	1,072.5	7.6
Labor	16.7	22.7	17.6	5.4
Losers				
General Services Administration	37.1	36.3	22.0	−40.7
Housing and Urban Development	17.1	16.5	12.3	−28.1
Transportation	75.2	69.7	61.5	−18.2
Agriculture	129.6	127.9	107.3	−17.2
Health and Human Services	157.3	157.8	130.9	−16.8
State	30.1	23.6	25.3	−15.9
Interior	81.9	81.7	70.5	−13.9
Commerce	38.6	45.1	34.2	−11.4
Energy	N/A	21.2	16.6	N/A
Education	N/A	7.1	4.5	N/A
All others	159.1	177.2	152.2	−4.3
Total executive branch	2,802.9	2,854.7	2,994.1	6.8

Source: *Government Executive* (March 1988): 8.
Note: Figures include full-time, part-time, and temporary workers.

press for measures that will be of special benefit to them." [1] True libertarians—who oppose government intervention on principle—are few and far between.

Congress Organizes the Executive Branch

Both the president *and* Congress are responsible for the "fourth branch of government," the bureaucracy. The Constitution requires presidents to implement the laws, and by implication it empowers them to give managerial direction to the executive branch. But just as the president is a key player in the lawmaking process, so Congress "has at least as much to do with executive administration as does an incumbent of the White House." [2] Congress is constitutionally authorized to organize the executive branch. But the Framers could not have foreseen that their sparse references to "executive departments" would nurture the huge modern bureaucracy. George Washington supervised only three departments (State, War, and Treasury); President George Bush heads fourteen, from the oldest (State and Treasury, 1789) to the newest (Veterans' Affairs, 1988). Besides the departments, Congress also has a hand in creating independent agencies, government corporations, and intergovernmental commissions (see Figure 9-1).

The complex federal structure periodically undergoes four basic forms of reorganization. First, executive agencies are created or abolished by law. Second, the president may order administrative changes. Third, Congress can authorize departments and agencies to reorganize themselves. Finally, Congress may authorize the president to propose reorganization plans subject to some form of congressional review.[3]

Reorganizations have political as well as administrative results. Congress is unlikely to approve such plans if they disrupt committee relations with favored agencies and programs. "If by this [executive] reorganization you affect in a major way the powers of the various committees in the Congress, you may as well forget it," a House committee chairman once told President Richard Nixon.[4]

Senate Confirmation of Presidential Appointees

High-level federal appointments are subject to the Senate's "advice and consent" under Article II, Section 2, of the Constitution. After the president determines whom to nominate, the Senate decides whether to confirm (see Figure 9-2). Senate committees usually elicit the following promise from nominees they have confirmed: "The nomination was approved subject to the nominee's commitment to respond to any requests to appear and testify before any duly constituted committee of the Senate." [5]

Presidents sometimes circumvent the Senate's role by making "recess appointments" during breaks in the Senate's session. Recess appointees serve until the end of the next Senate session; for example, a person named in 1988 might serve until late 1989. The Senate resents this process, and its opposition to some recess appointees has caused them to give up their posts.

The Senate's refusal to confirm John Tower as secretary of defense, discussed in Chapter 8, was partly because of his personal habits. Also of concern to numerous senators were Tower's ties to defense contractors. Nominations to high executive posts today are subject to standards of judgment and evaluation that go beyond questions of competence or conflict of interest. Nominees' personal lives and morality are scrutinized as well. As one commentator explained:

Figure 9-1 Organization of the Federal Executive Branch

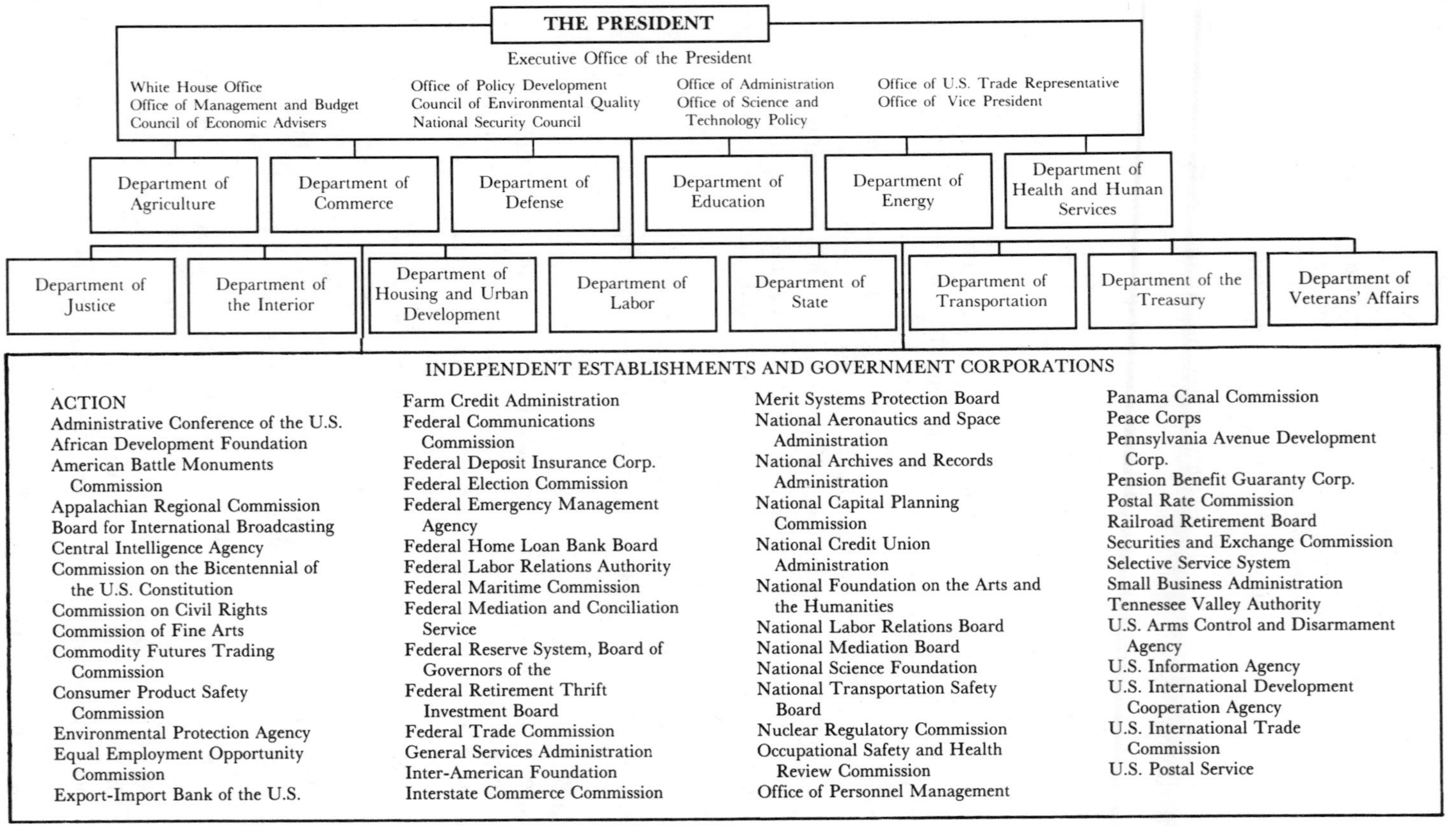

THE PRESIDENT

Executive Office of the President

White House Office
Office of Management and Budget
Council of Economic Advisers

Office of Policy Development
Council of Environmental Quality
National Security Council

Office of Administration
Office of Science and
Technology Policy

Office of U.S. Trade Representative
Office of Vice President

Department of Agriculture
Department of the Interior
Department of Commerce
Department of Housing and Urban Development
Department of Defense
Department of Labor
Department of Education
Department of State
Department of Energy
Department of Transportation
Department of Health and Human Services
Department of the Treasury
Department of Veterans' Affairs
Department of Justice

INDEPENDENT ESTABLISHMENTS AND GOVERNMENT CORPORATIONS

ACTION
Administrative Conference of the U.S.
African Development Foundation
American Battle Monuments
  Commission
Appalachian Regional Commission
Board for International Broadcasting
Central Intelligence Agency
Commission on the Bicentennial of
  the U.S. Constitution
Commission on Civil Rights
Commission of Fine Arts
Commodity Futures Trading
  Commission
Consumer Product Safety
  Commission
Environmental Protection Agency
Equal Employment Opportunity
  Commission
Export-Import Bank of the U.S.

Farm Credit Administration
Federal Communications
  Commission
Federal Deposit Insurance Corp.
Federal Election Commission
Federal Emergency Management
  Agency
Federal Home Loan Bank Board
Federal Labor Relations Authority
Federal Maritime Commission
Federal Mediation and Conciliation
  Service
Federal Reserve System, Board of
  Governors of the
Federal Retirement Thrift
  Investment Board
Federal Trade Commission
General Services Administration
Inter-American Foundation
Interstate Commerce Commission

Merit Systems Protection Board
National Aeronautics and Space
  Administration
National Archives and Records
  Administration
National Capital Planning
  Commission
National Credit Union
  Administration
National Foundation on the Arts and
  the Humanities
National Labor Relations Board
National Mediation Board
National Science Foundation
National Transportation Safety
  Board
Nuclear Regulatory Commission
Occupational Safety and Health
  Review Commission
Office of Personnel Management

Panama Canal Commission
Peace Corps
Pennsylvania Avenue Development
  Corp.
Pension Benefit Guaranty Corp.
Postal Rate Commission
Railroad Retirement Board
Securities and Exchange Commission
Selective Service System
Small Business Administration
Tennessee Valley Authority
U.S. Arms Control and Disarmament
  Agency
U.S. Information Agency
U.S. International Development
  Cooperation Agency
U.S. International Trade
  Commission
U.S. Postal Service

Source: *The United States Government Manual, 1988/89* (Washington, D.C.: Government Printing Office, 1988), 21.

Note: This chart shows only the most important agencies of the government.

Figure 9-2 The Appointments Process

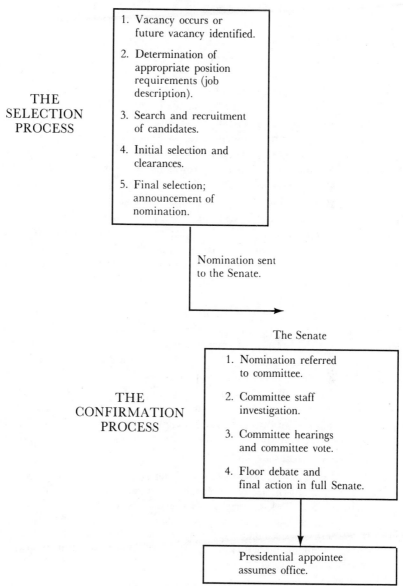

The White House

THE
SELECTION
PROCESS

1. Vacancy occurs or future vacancy identified.

2. Determination of appropriate position requirements (job description).

3. Search and recruitment of candidates.

4. Initial selection and clearances.

5. Final selection; announcement of nomination.

Nomination sent to the Senate.

The Senate

THE
CONFIRMATION
PROCESS

1. Nomination referred to committee.

2. Committee staff investigation.

3. Committee hearings and committee vote.

4. Floor debate and final action in full Senate.

Presidential appointee assumes office.

Source: G. Calvin Mackenzie, *The Politics of Presidential Appointments* (New York: The Free Press, 1981), xv. Reprinted with permission of Macmillan Publishing Company. Copyright © 1981.

These days, if you want to run for office or accept a position of public trust, everything is relevant. Your moral, medical, legal and financial background, even your college records, become the subject of public scrutiny. In the old days, the scrutiny was done in private, and certain transgressions could be considered irrelevant.[6]

This shift in standards stems in part from a shift in attitudes by the press and public. The press now reports more aggressively than in years past the private activities of public officials.[7] Mindful of the shift in standards, President Bush moved quickly after Tower's defeat to name House GOP whip Dick Cheney of Wyoming to be secretary of defense, a man with an impeccable personal and professional reputation. It took the Senate only a week to confirm him unanimously. Cheney "had very few allegations against him, and he had a financial report that was not complicated, and he had an FBI report that did not produce any impediments to his service," noted Sam Nunn, D-Ga., the chairman of the Senate Armed Services Committee.[8]

The confirmation process, however, is not always this smooth. Given the legal, ethical, and political scrutiny that most high-level appointees are subjected to, combined with what is likely to be a substantial reduction in salary for many, it is not surprising that the Bush administration had difficulty recruiting people for government service. Eighty percent of the top executive positions in the administration remained unfilled several months into Bush's presidency.[9]

Judicial appointments are subject to even closer Senate scrutiny than are high-level executive appointments. President Reagan's 1987 nomination of Robert Bork to the Supreme Court underscored the Senate's intensive role in the advice and consent process. During nationally televised hearings, members of the Senate Judiciary Committee probed Bork's constitutional and philosophical views in minute detail. Because Bork's nomination to a lifetime position came at a time of great public concern about the Supreme Court's ideological balance, and because Bork's views were perceived as controversial by many senators and outside groups, his nomination took on the appearance of a modern political campaign.

> Paid advertisements, grass-roots organizing and public opinion polls . . . played a highly visible role. Following very successful advertising campaigns by anti-Bork groups, pro-Bork advertisements and fund-raising appeals . . . assailed the integrity of those opposing the nomination. And Judge Bork himself found it necessary to give the first detailed, nationally televised testimony ever by a Supreme Court nominee about his positions on controversial issues.[10]

In the end the Senate rejected the Bork nomination.

Political, policy, and patronage considerations permeate the confirmation process. The Senate may refuse to consider a nominee if members invoke "senatorial courtesy." This tradition, dating from President George Washington's administration, generally means that the Senate will delay or not act upon nominations if a senator of the president's party opposes them.[11] Legislators, too, lobby the president to appoint their supporters to federal posts. Or senators, for personal and policy reasons, might threaten to block nominees they oppose. For example, Senators William Cohen, R-Maine, and Edward Kennedy, D-Mass., warned the Pentagon that they would seek to "block all future military appointments requiring congressional approval until the Defense Department puts into effect a law that reorganizes the military forces for anti-terrorism, commando missions and other special operations." [12]

The Personnel System

Congress wields wide authority—constitutionally, legally, informally—over the federal personnel system. The assassination of President James Garfield in 1881 by a disgruntled job seeker prompted Congress to curb the abuses of the "spoils system," the practice of handing out federal jobs to supporters of the party that had won the presidency. In 1883 Congress passed the first civil service law that substituted merit for patronage.

The modern legacy of the early patronage practices is the political appointee system. President Bush must appoint more than 4,000 persons to full-time government jobs; only 800 or so are subject to Senate confirmation.[13] Although the number of political appointees is small compared with the total number of federal employees, there is heightened concern about the "politicization" of high-level jobs in the civil service. In the State Department, for example, "roughly half the policy-making jobs . . . and more than 40 percent of ambassadorships are held by people from outside the career service." [14] In many agencies political appointees are replacing careerists—a development that does not alarm everyone. Some contend that more political appointees are needed "to monitor the permanent government" and "to develop aggressively new policies." [15]

The caliber of the federal work force sporadically concerns Congress. In the past decade observers identified a "quiet crisis"—namely, the need to attract able people to federal service. Some critics of the federal personnel system have argued that the national government "should be content to hire competent people, not the best and most talented people." [16] Most experts disagree. They believe the highest quality individuals must be recruited into the civil service if the federal government is to meet the myriad challenges it faces.

By law, Congress has wide control over federal employees. It can establish special requirements for holding office; terms of principal officers; employee performance standards; wages, benefits, and cost-of-living adjustments; personnel ceilings; and protections from reprisals for "whistleblowers" (employees who expose waste and corruption).

The "two Congresses" clash when pay raises are proposed for members and other federal employees. Few issues place senators and representatives in a more precarious position. Public criticism of pay hikes is real, as is the threat that potential opponents will seize upon the issue in the next election. "To vote for your own pay increase is an invitation to a 30-second-spot commercial against you in your next campaign," said Sen. John Glenn, D-Ohio.[17]

When the 101st Congress convened it considered a recommendation by the quadrennial Commission on Executive, Legislative, and Judicial Salaries to increase the salaries of members of Congress, federal judges, and senior civil servants from $89,500 to $135,000. "We're looking at a maharajah Congress," complained Ralph Nader, an opponent of the salary increase.[18] Others argued that congressional salaries had not kept pace with inflation for twenty years. To make the salary increase more palatable to the public, congressional leaders said they would pass rules banning honoraria. (Many legislators supplement their salaries by accepting fees from interest groups for making speeches.) But this strategy of a "pay raise for an honoraria ban" backfired completely because of vocal public dissent mobilized by outside groups. (For details of the legislative battle over the pay raise, see Chapter 15.)

Members, legislative staffers, and executive officers often take jobs with private-sector firms dealing with the government after they leave public office—the so-called "revolving door" phenomenon. In response to procurement abuses by the Pentagon, Congress in 1988 passed legislation designed to restrict federal officials who leave public service from immediately joining a private company to work on projects or contracts they had managed while in government service.

Independent Executive Units

Congress is largely responsible for the growth of executive units that are independent from direct presidential control. These include well-known regulatory agencies such as the Federal Trade Commission and Consumer Product Safety Commission. Established to protect the public interest, regulatory agencies sometimes develop friendly close ties to the industries they are supposed to regulate. President Reagan made deregulation a priority during his administration; however, by the Bush administration public and congressional sentiment had shifted somewhat toward reregulation, especially on matters involving the environment, public health and safety, and the savings and loan industry.[19]

Under the terms of the Administrative Procedure Act of 1946 and later changes to it, Congress established standards to guide rulemaking by regulatory agencies. Interested parties can participate in agency proceedings by testifying in public on the merits or demerits of proposed regulations. Regulations have the force and effect of law and are the means of implementing general legislation. All regulations, explained Sen. Charles Grassley, R-Iowa, are based ultimately on authority granted by this Congress. When an agency promulgates a rule, it is engaging in a legislative task—in effect, filling in the gaps on the implementation of policies that we in Congress have established through statute. Accordingly, all regulations must be accountable to this Congress.[20]

In addition to the regulatory agencies, Congress creates lesser known, quasi-governmental entities such as the Federal Home Loan Mortgage Corporation, the Legal Services Corporation, and the Corporation for Public Broadcasting. Organizations such as these give Congress fiscal and administrative flexibility in addressing public problems. Those units normally are exempt from requirements imposed on the other federal departments, such as civil service rules, salary limitations, presidential orders, or clearance of their legislative and regulatory proposals by OMB. These exemptions erode accountability to elected officials. "Profound constitutional questions are raised by the vesting of governmental duties and authorities in quasi-governmental institutions," warned one administrative expert.[21]

The federal civilian work force, contrary to many people's ideas, has remained relatively constant in size—only a 6.8 percent increase from 1977 to 1987, as Table 9-1 shows. How can the government do more, but keep its size relatively stable? The answer is that many subnational governments and private organizations perform federal functions indirectly. Weapons systems, for example, are built by private companies under contract to the government. The job of Defense Department personnel, like that of many federal workers, "consists of planning, coordinating, preparing and issuing regulations and contracts for, negotiating, paying for, overseeing, inspecting, auditing, and evaluating the work of others" [22] The "others" include state and local governments, universities, businesses, and hospitals.

"De-bureaucratizing" the federal government has advantages and disadvantages. So-called "third-party" government presents serious problems of accountability because companies under contract to the government are not directly responsible to Congress.[23] Yet third parties are sometimes faster, more flexible, and cheaper than the governmental machine.

The nation's largest single employment group consists of volunteers who work for nonprofit, nongovernmental, community groups such as churches, the Red Cross, and the Girl Scouts, to name a few. The total number of volunteers for all nonprofits probably exceeds 30 million.[24]

Both President Bush and congressional lawmakers have encouraged the private sector to shoulder more responsibility for national problems such as homelessness, drugs, crime, and illiteracy. During his acceptance speech to the Republican National Convention, Bush referred to volunteers across the country as "a thousand points of light." "What we need is 1,000 beds, not 1,000 points of light," rejoined the director of a shelter for homeless women.[25] Indeed, many wonder whether private volunteers can substitute adequately for public responsibility.

Sen. Barbara Mikulski, D-Md., sponsored legislation to create a citizens corps of civilian volunteers. In return for one or two years of public service and a subsistence wage, the volunteers would receive a $10,000 cash voucher that they could use to pay for college, finance a home, or use for other purposes. "Every one seems to have a sense of entitlement and no sense of obligation," noted Senator Mikulski.[26] Her bill was designed to encourage young citizens, as President Kennedy said in 1961, to "ask not what your country can do for you—ask what you can do for your country."

The Electoral Connection

Some observers suggest that Congress enlarged the executive establishment by passing vague laws that bureaucrats had to embellish with rules and regulations. Many regulatory laws, for example, call for a "reasonable rate," without defining "reasonable." Frustrated by government rules, people then turn to their senators and representatives for help. Lawmakers thus "take credit coming and going" by claiming credit both for getting programs enacted and for ironing out bureaucratic snarls they create.[27]

The electoral explanation of bureaucratic growth is disputable, however. There is little support for the argument that "congressmen's incessant quest for local benefits has somehow contributed to growth in government spending."[28] Federal expenditures have grown only slightly as a percentage of gross national product (18.1 percent in 1955 to 22.5 percent in 1988). Federal aid to localities even dropped off in the 1980s as states and communities looked less to Washington and established their own priorities. As the director of the U.S. Advisory Commission on Intergovernmental Relations explained:

> For 50 years—through the Great Depression, the New Deal, World War II, the Korean War, the Great Society, and Vietnam—the pendulum was swinging toward Washington because of its strengthened fiscal hand and national crises. Now the pendulum is swinging the other way—toward the state and local governments and a "do-it-yourself" federalism.[29]

Furthermore, programs such as Medicare and Medicaid "deliver benefits as a matter of right, not privilege, and congressmen have fewer opportunities to claim responsibility for them."[30]

Pork Barrel Politics.   For many federal programs Congress lets administrators decide how funds are to be spread among legislative districts. This is a resource that bureaucrats can employ to maintain and expand their influence in Congress.

> It is a mutually rewarding system. Congressmen can claim credit for whatever benefits flow into their districts, but at the same time they have insulated themselves from their constituents' anger when certain benefits cannot be secured. If Congress itself allocated benefits, constituents might well blame their congressmen for failing to acquire benefits, but as long as

bureaucrats have the final say, congressmen are partially protected from their wrath.[31]

Many considerations affect how federal projects are distributed. Crucial states may be awarded projects just before a presidential election. An agency may quickly process the requests of the president's congressional backers, while others' proposals are encased in red tape. Or key members of the committees with jurisdiction over certain agencies may receive the lion's share of federal benefits.

Of course, not all federal projects are worth attracting. Members compute the political risks of backing a missile base, hazardous waste dump, nuclear power plant, or other controversial projects strongly resisted by their constituents. Thus, Nevada and Utah senators led the counterattack against the Air Force's elaborate MX missile basing plan, opposed by many local influentials, including the Mormon Church.

Casework. As noted in Chapter 5, legislators frequently act as intermediaries between constituents and federal agencies. Constituent problems are handled by personal staff aides called caseworkers. In addition to the electoral payoff of effective casework, some members appreciate its value in oversight. "The very knowledge by executive officials that some Congressmen is sure to look into a matter affecting his constituents acts as a healthy check against bureaucratic indifference or arrogance," wrote a former senator.[32]

Informal Relations

Congressional-bureaucratic relations cover a wide spectrum of political understandings and information exchanges. Bureaucratic officials might "leak" information to members and committees, lobby members and staff, and negotiate policy agreements. Members and committees, for their part, rely on agency personnel for departmental analyses of legislation and for aid in drafting and interpreting bills and amendments. During Senate debate on a tariff measure, Robert Dole, R-Kan., informed his colleagues that the pending amendments had been assigned to one of three lists.

> One list will be those [amendments] that are under negotiations with Treasury, the Joint [Taxation] Committee, the majority and minority managers of the bill; the second will be those that are strongly opposed by Treasury; and, third, those where there has been agreement.[33]

Dole also stated that an assistant Treasury secretary was ensconced in an office near the Senate floor to discuss specific amendments with senators.

Congressional Control of the Bureaucracy

"Congressional power, like chastity," explained a scholar, "is never lost, rarely taken by force, and almost always given away." [34] Congress gives away to executive officials considerable discretion in interpreting and implementing the laws it passes. This is because legislators lack the knowledge and expertise to address numerous complexities in contemporary society (licensing interstate communications, for example), and no law can be sufficiently detailed to cover every conceivable or unforeseen circumstance.

In fact, Congress is sometimes criticized for drafting vague or sloppy legislation that gives executive officials and judges too much leeway in interpretation and administration (see later section in this chapter on Congress and the courts). "Administration of a statute is, properly speaking, an extension of the legislative process," and therefore Congress must watch over its programs lest they undergo unintended change.[35] Given the size and reach of the executive establishment, Congress's oversight role is more important today than when Woodrow Wilson wrote, "Quite as important as lawmaking is vigilant oversight of administration." [36]

The Constitution does not refer explicitly to the oversight role; it is implicit in Congress's right to, among other things, make laws, raise and appropriate money, give "advice and consent" to executive nominations, and impeach federal officials. Congress, however, has formalized its oversight duties. The Legislative Reorganization Act of 1946 directed all House and Senate committees to exercise "continuous watchfulness" over the programs and agencies under their jurisdiction. Subsequent statutes and House and Senate rules extended Congress's authority and resources for oversight.

Members understand their review responsibilities. "Congress' duty didn't end in passing this law," remarked Sen. Phil Gramm, R-Texas. "We have to make sure the law works." [37] To ensure that laws are working, Congress utilizes an impressive array of formal and informal processes and techniques. Much of it is indirect, ad hoc, and not subject to easy quantification or even recognition. "Oversight isn't necessarily a hearing," said John Dingell, D-Mich., the assertive chairman of the House Energy and Commerce Committee. "Sometimes it's a letter. We find our letters have a special effect on a lot of people." [38]

Hearings and Investigations

Many of Congress's most dramatic moments have occurred in legislative probes into administrative misconduct. Examples include the 1923 Teapot Dome inquiry, the 1973-1974 Senate Watergate hearings, and the 1987 Iran-contra investigation. But Congress's investigative authority is not without limits. As Chief Justice Earl Warren wrote in *Watkins v. United States* (1957):

> There is no general authority to expose private affairs of individuals without justification in terms of the functions of Congress. . . . Nor is the Congress a law enforcement or trial agency. These are functions of the executive and judicial departments of government. No inquiry is an end in itself; it must be related to, and in furtherance of, a legitimate task of the Congress.[39]

For two hundred years Congress has conducted investigations of varying types with varying results. There have been abuses and excesses, successes and accomplishments. Investigations aid in lawmaking by serving as Congress's eyes and ears. By collecting and analyzing information, House and Senate inquiries can clarify whether specific legislation is needed to address public problems. Investigations also strengthen Congress's ability to scrutinize executive branch activities, such as the expenditure of funds, the implementation of laws, and the discharge of duties by administrative officials. And investigations inform the public by disseminating and revealing information. "Congress provides a forum for disclosing the hidden aspects of governmental conduct," wrote two Senate members of the Iran-contra investigating committee. It allows a "free people to drag realities out into the sunlight and demand a full accounting from those who are permitted to hold and exercise power." [40] Hearings and investigations, in short, are valuable devices for making government accountable to the people.

Administrators are sensitive to the threat of hearings and inquiries and try to forestall them if possible. Occasionally, however, they encourage investigations, particularly if they are uneasy about their agency's policies. Michael Pertschuk, a liberal Democrat on the Federal Trade Commission during the early Reagan years, worked closely with the Democratic majority on a House Energy and Commerce subcommittee to publicize the new policy directions he opposed. "The subcommittee staff asks us what we think the problems are. We tell them what to look for," he said. "They investigate and come to some resolution." [41] Thus, hearings and investigations can strongly influence agency policies and priorities. They can spawn new laws or their functional equivalent: unwritten laws that change bureaucratic operations.

Congressional Vetoes

With unelected executive officials necessarily involved in the complexities of modern decision making, Congress has little choice but to delegate sweeping authority to administrative agencies—but with strings attached. One of the most popular strings is the *congressional veto,* a statutory enactment that permits presidents or agencies to take certain actions subject to later approval or disapproval by one or both houses of Congress (or in some cases committees of both or either). Legislative vetoes are arrangements of convenience for both branches: executives gain decision-making authority they might not have otherwise, and Congress retains a second chance to examine the decisions.

However, as mentioned in Chapter 2, the Supreme Court declared the legislative veto unconstitutional in 1983 in *Immigration and Naturalization Service v. Chadha.* The Court majority held that the device violated the separation of powers, the principle of bicameralism, and the "presentation" clause of the Constitution (legislation passed by both chambers must be presented to the president for his signature or veto). The decision, wrote Justice Byron White in a vigorous dissent, "strikes down in one fell swoop provisions in more laws enacted by Congress than the court has cumulatively invalidated in its entire history."

In the aftermath of the *Chadha* decision, Congress repealed some legislative vetoes, amended others, and employed its wide range of oversight techniques to monitor executive actions. The agreement to continue nonmilitary aid to the Nicaraguan contras forged by Secretary of State James Baker in the early months of the Bush administration with congressional leaders, permitted any of four congressional committees to suspend the aid program. This informal accommodation, which incorporated a committee veto on the exercise of presidential power, disregarded the *Chadha* ruling's spirit though not its letter (inasmuch as the agreement was nonstatutory). Even after the *Chadha* decision, legislative vetoes continue to be enacted into law. Public law scholar Louis Fisher sums up the status of legislative vetoes:

> Are they constitutional? Not by the Court's definition. Will that fact change the behavior between committees and agencies? Probably not. An agency might advise the committee: "As you know, the requirement in this statute for committee prior-approval is unconstitutional under the Court's test." Perhaps agency and committee staff will nod their heads in agreement. After which the agency will seek prior approval of the committee.[42]

In short, self-interest requires that agencies pay close attention to congressional wishes, especially those expressed by their authorizing or appropriating panels.

Mandatory Reports

Congress requires the president, agencies, and departments to assess programs and report their findings.[43] Although sometimes only marginally useful, reports can be important oversight tools for monitoring executive activities. For example, Congress directed the Reagan administration to submit a report on the security situation in the Persian Gulf and the ability of U.S. naval warships to protect "reflagged" Kuwaiti oil tankers (ships authorized to fly the American flag) from terrorist attacks or conventional military threats. Sen. Robert C. Byrd of West Virginia, then the Democratic leader, requested the chairman of three Senate committees—Armed Services, Foreign Relations, and Intelligence—to examine the report as to whether national security objectives had been adequately met.[44]

Nonstatutory Controls

Congressional committees also use informal means to review and influence administrative decisions. These range from telephone calls, letters, personal contacts, and informal understandings to statements in committee and conference reports, hearings, and floor debates.[45] Committee reports frequently contain phrases such as "the committee clearly intends that the matter be reconsidered," or "the committee clearly intends for the Secretary to promote," or "the committee clearly expects." One chairman, Jamie Whitten, D-Miss., of the House Appropriations Committee, "personally writes the multi-page essay on the state of agriculture that is printed at the beginning of each year's committee report on the agriculture appropriations bill." [46]

On occasion, OMB directors tell federal agencies to ignore appropriations report language because it is not legally binding. However, lawmakers of both parties and chambers (and even executive officials) mobilize to thwart such directives, sometimes by threatening to make all report language legally binding on agencies, thus limiting their flexibility and discretion in resolving issues.[47]

There is no measure of their usage, but nonstatutory controls may be the most common form of congressional oversight.

Inspectors General

In 1978 Congress created a dozen independent offices for inspectors general (IGs) in major federal departments and agencies. The act, said Rep. Frank Horton, R-N.Y., "was designed to improve the auditing and investigation of Federal programs so that taxpayers could be better assured that their money was being spent effectively and efficiently." Since then Congress has established inspector general offices in other departments and agencies. Reports of IGs on their efforts to root out waste, fraud, and abuse are submitted directly to Congress. The chairman of the Senate Committee on Governmental Affairs, John Glenn, D-Ohio, noted that "IGs have saved taxpayers more than $92 billion over the past five years." [48]

Saving taxpayers' money was a keen interest of former Sen. William Proxmire, D-Wis. For years he assumed a personal watchdog role over agency performance. Proxmire periodically gave "Golden Fleece" awards to agencies that wasted taxpayers' dollars. The awards not only encouraged program improvements, but also bestowed favorable publicity upon the senator.

The Appropriations Process

Congress probably exercises its most effective oversight of agencies and programs through the appropriations process. By cutting off or reducing funds (or threatening to do so), Congress can abolish agencies, curtail programs, or obtain requested information. By increasing funds, Congress can build up neglected program areas. The appropriations power is exercised mainly by the House and Senate Appropriations committees, particularly through their thirteen powerful subcommittees, whose budgetary recommendations are infrequently changed by the full committee or by the House and Senate.

These committees, or members from the House or Senate floor, may offer amendments that limit the purposes for which money may be spent or that impose other expenditure restrictions on federal agencies. For example, an antidrug amendment was added in 1988 to several appropriations bills that prohibited "federal agencies, including the Defense Department, from paying private contractors unless the companies have written policies . . . that bar drugs in the workplace." [49] Omnibus spending bills (or continuing resolutions) also may contain various policy directives to federal agencies, such as extending clean air deadlines or imposing airline smoking bans. (For a further discussion of the appropriations and authorization process, see Chapter 13.)

Impeachment

A rarely used oversight device is impeachment. Under the Constitution Congress can remove federal officials for "treason, bribery, or other high crimes and misdemeanors." (In 1986 Congress impeached Federal Judge Harry Claiborne for tax evasion.) The ultimate governmental "check" is the "power to remove all federal officials from office by impeachment," which is vested exclusively in Congress. [50] The House has the authority to impeach an official by majority vote; it then tries the case before the Senate. A two-thirds vote in the Senate is required for conviction. Only thirteen officials have been impeached: two executive officers and eleven federal judges. The House impeached President Andrew Johnson in 1868 because Radical Republicans in the House charged that he violated the Tenure of Office Act by dismissing the secretary of war. The Senate acquitted Johnson by a single vote. President Richard Nixon resigned in 1974 after the House Judiciary Committee voted articles of impeachment; he faced probable impeachment and conviction.

Oversight: An Evaluation

Each oversight technique has limitations. Hearings, for example, tend to be episodic with minimal follow-up; the appropriations process is hemmed in by programmatic needs for financial stability; and statutes are often blunt instruments of control.

Scholars have documented Congress's capacity and willingness in recent years to do more oversight. [51] This change stems from several factors. These include public dissatisfaction with big government, the growth of congressional staff, revelations of executive agency abuses, the influx of new legislators skeptical of government's ability to perform effectively, and recognition that in a time of fiscal and resource scarcity Congress must make every dollar count.

Despite the surge of interest, many legislators and scholars charge that Congress oversees ineffectively. "Members like to create and legislate," former Speaker Thomas P. O'Neill, Jr., said, "but we have shied from both the word and deed of oversight." [52] Others disagree. Two scholars contend that, contrary to conventional wisdom, Congress does not neglect its oversight role. Too many analysts, they argue, underestimate congressional surveillance because they are looking for "police patrol" oversight—active, direct, systematic, regular, and planned surveillance of executive activities. Instead, they claim, Congress usually waits until "fire alarms" go off from interest groups, the press, staff aides, and others about administrative violations before it begins to review in detail agencies' activities. Political scientist Joel Aberbach disputes this contention. He argues that the police patrol approach is more frequently employed on Capitol Hill than the fire alarm method.[53]

Plus, opinions differ on whether Congress is a sufficiently wary "watchdog." Some doubt there are enough institutional or political incentives to reward those who conduct oversight. There is a "high cost and low benefit . . . ratio in the oversight effort," remarked former representative John B. Anderson, R-Ill. The "high cost in terms of the time that must be expended, you might even call it drudgery, and the low benefit in any real public recognition."[54] In a period of divided government, however, there are more electoral and political incentives for members to oversee the bureaucracy. One of these is the opportunity to receive favorable publicity back home (the "two Congresses" connection); another is prodding by interest groups and the media; and still another is the contemporary climate of fiscal austerity. "Actual or threatened budget cuts and competition for scarce resources foster both adversarial and supportive oversight," noted Frederick Kaiser.[55] Committee and subcommittee chairmen, such as Representative Dingell and Rep. Jack Brooks, D-Texas, also "seek a high pay off—in attention from both the press and other agencies—when selecting federal programs to be their oversight targets."[56]

Cozy Relationships. "Sweetheart" alliances often develop between the committees that authorize programs, the agencies that administer them, and the interest groups that benefit from the services. Many committees are biased toward the programs or agencies they oversee; they want to protect and nurture their progeny and make program administration "look good." Without concrete allegations of fraud or mismanagement, committees may lack the incentive to scrutinize and reevaluate their programs. This type of "cooperative" oversight can dissuade committees from conducting hard-hitting inquiries.

Unclear Program Objectives. A standard rationale for oversight is ensuring that laws are carried out according to congressional intent. In practice, however, many laws are vague and imprecise, which thwarts assessment. Moreover, evidence that programs are actually working as intended can take years to emerge. Congressional patience may wane as critics charge that there are no demonstrable payoffs for the taxpayer. Alternatively, program flaws may be identified, but oversight may not reveal what will work or even whether there is any ready solution.

Committee Limits. Other obstacles to effective oversight include inadequate coordination among committees that share jurisdiction over a program, unsystematic committee review of departmental activities, and frequent turnover among committee staff aides, which limits their understanding of programs passed by Congress.

Proposed Improvements

Legislators and critics advocate various oversight reforms. "Sunset" legislation, for example, would direct committees to review all programs and agencies under their jurisdiction within a prescribed time period. Unless the programs and agencies were formally reauthorized, the "sun would set on them." [57] For example, Congress let the sun set on the Civil Aeronautics Board in December 1984 and transferred most of its functions to the Department of Transportation.

Another proposal, dubbed "sunrise," would require committees to identify the goals of bills and specify planned annual achievements. Polls and surveys could also be used to gather information about the effectiveness of the programs and services provided to beneficiaries. Some favor the creation of independent groups to investigate agency performance. All of these attempts to improve legislative oversight seek to buttress but not replace traditional review processes.

Micromanagement

Because oversight tends to be specific rather than general, committees are open to complaints about "micromanagement"—legislative intrusion in administrative details. Senator Nunn once noted that Congress required the Defense Department in 1970 to conduct thirty-six studies; by 1985 that figure had increased to 458 studies and reports.[58] Since then Congress has cut back on the number of required Pentagon reports. No clear lines distinguish excessive from effective micromanagement. In some areas—the ailing savings and loan industry, for example—Congress has managed too little.

Perhaps to the chagrin of executive officials, Congress's focus on administrative details is as old as Congress itself. The structural fragmentation of the House and Senate encourages examination of manageable chunks of executive actions. Members understand that power inheres in details, such as prescribing personnel ceilings for agencies. Presidents who oppose certain programs can "starve" them to death by shifting employees to favored activities. Thus, Congress may specify personnel ceilings for some agencies. "It is one of the anomalies of constitutional law and separated powers," wrote Louis Fisher, "that executive involvement in legislative affairs is considered acceptable (indeed highly desirable) while legislative involvement in executive affairs screams of encroachment and usurpation." [59] Legislative involvement in judicial affairs has been similarly problematic, as the next section will show.

Congress and the Courts

Federal courts are heavily involved in policy making and administrative affairs. Interest groups, for example, may sue federal agencies for misconstruing their statutory mandates or for issuing regulations contrary to Congress's intent. More often, contending groups turn to the courts to clarify issues left vague by Congress or sidestepped by agency regulations. No doubt everyone concerned—including legislators and staff aides—fully expects activist judges to intervene in complex questions of administrative law and policy making. In fact, the 1980s witnessed the "federal judiciary's growing role as referee between the political branches." [60] Issues involving the separation of powers—for instance, the legislative veto, the pocket veto, war powers, and budget matters—became regular items on federal court dockets.

Communications between Congress and the federal courts are less than perfect. Neither branch understands the workings of the other very well.[61] Judges are often unaware that ambiguity, imprecision, or inconsistency may be the price for winning enactment of measures. The more members try to define, the more they may divide or dissipate their support. Federal Judge Abner Mikva, who was a three-term House Democrat from the Chicago area, recounted an example from his Capitol Hill days. The issue involved a controversial strip-mining bill being managed by the chairman of the House Interior Committee, Morris Udall, D-Ariz.

> They'd put together a very delicate coalition of support. One problem was whether the states or the feds would run the program. One member got up and asked, "Isn't it a fact that under this bill the states will continue to exercise sovereignty over strip mining?" And Mo replied, "You're absolutely right." A little later someone else got up and asked, "Now is it clear that the Federal Government will have the final say on strip mining?" And Mo replied, "You're absolutely right." Later, in the cloakroom, I said, "Mo, they can't both be right." And Mo said, "You're absolutely right." [62]

Called upon to interpret such statutes, judges may not appreciate the efforts required to get legislation passed on Capitol Hill or understand how to divine "legislative history"—as manifested in hearings, floor debate, and reports.

A group of federal judges, led by Supreme Court Justice Antonin Scalia, argue that legislative history is open to "manipulation by individual members of Congress, [executive officials], Congressional staff members and lobbyists" and is therefore unreliable as an indicator of congressional intent. Other federal judges urge caution in downplaying the value of legislative history and assert that much of it is important to statutory interpretation. The debate about legislative history has special import on Capitol Hill because an increasing number of "conservative Republican judges are interpreting law passed by a Democratic Congress." [63]

For their part, legislators become exasperated when judges misinterpret their intent. For instance, the Supreme Court ruled in 1984 that parents of handicapped children who prevail in civil suits intended to protect their children's right to suitable school services are not entitled to attorneys' fees under the Handicapped Children's Protection Act. The Supreme Court said if Congress wanted those fees awarded it would have stated so explicitly. So Congress passed another law. Today we "correct this error," said the Senate floor manager of the bill, and reaffirm the "original intention of Congress." Congress and the courts, like Congress and the executive branch, are constantly engaged in constitutional and statutory interpretation and reinterpretation.[64]

Conclusion

The age-old issue of executive and judicial independence versus congressional scrutiny cannot be settled conclusively because of continual shifts in the balance of legislative, executive, and judicial prerogatives. The recent resurgence of oversight has had little discernible impact on the size and scale of the executive branch or on the main roles and responsibilities of the judicial and legislative branches. After all, committees are not disinterested overseers but guardians of the agencies and programs under their jurisdiction. Together with their satellite interest groups, committees and agencies form "subgovernments" or "issue networks" that dominate many policy-making areas. Our next chapter focuses on these complex relationships.

Notes

1. Edward C. Banfield, *The Democratic Muse* (New York: Basic Books, 1984), 197.
2. Richard E. Neustadt, "Politicians and Bureaucrats," in *The Congress and America's Future,* 2d ed., ed. David B. Truman (Englewood Cliffs, N.J.: Prentice-Hall, 1973), 199. See also Louis Fisher, *The Politics of Shared Power: Congress and the Executive* (Washington, D.C.: CQ Press, 1981).
3. See Herbert Emmerich, *Essays on Federal Reorganization* (University: University of Alabama Press, 1950); Peter Szanton, ed., *Federal Reorganization: What Have We Learned?* (Chatham, N.J.: Chatham House Publishers, 1981); and Harold Seidman, *Politics, Position, and Power,* 3d ed. (New York: Oxford University Press, 1980).
4. Harold Seidman, "Congressional Committees and Executive Organization," in *Committee Organization in the House,* House Doc. No. 94-187, 94th Cong., 1st sess., 823.
5. *Congressional Record,* 100th Cong., 1st sess., May 1, 1987, S5848.
6. William Schneider, "New Rules for the Game of Politics," *National Journal,*

April 1, 1989, 830.

7. Paul Houston, "Scrutiny of Public Officials Puts Standards to the Test," *Los Angeles Times,* pt. I, March 1989, 14.

8. Pat Towell, "The Cheny File: Relatively Simple," *Congressional Quarterly Weekly Report,* March 18, 1989, 594.

9. David E. Rosenbaum, "80% of Senior Positions Under Bush Still Empty," *New York Times,* May 13, 1989, 9.

10. *New York Times,* October 21, 1987, A23.

11. See Joseph P. Harris, *The Advice and Consent of the Senate* (Berkeley: University of California Press, 1953); Ronald C. Moe, "Senate Confirmation of Executive Appointments," in *Congress Against the President,* ed. Harvey C. Mansfield, Sr. (New York: Academy of Political Science, 1975), 141-152; and *America's Unelected Government,* ed. John W. Macy, Bruce Adams, and J. Jackson Walter (Cambridge, Mass.: Ballinger Publishing, 1983).

12. Stephen Engelberg, "Tug and Pull over a Vacant Chart," *New York Times,* May 22, 1987, A32.

13. *Los Angeles Times,* pt. I, December 15, 1988, 20.

14. *Washington Post,* January 6, 1989, A17.

15. *Federal Times,* December 12, 1988, 6; and *Washington Post,* August 6, 1987, A2.

16. *Wall Street Journal,* May 21, 1986, 32.

17. *Newsweek,* December 19, 1988, 37.

18. *Wall Street Journal,* December 14, 1988, A20.

19. *New York Times,* December 11, 1988, A1.

20. *Congressional Record,* 100th Cong., 1st sess., July 29, 1987, S10850.

21. Harold Seidman, "The Quasi World of the Federal Government," *The Brookings Review* (Summer 1988): 24.

22. Frederick C. Mosher, *The GAO: The Quest for Accountability in American Government* (Boulder, Colo.: Westview Press, 1979), 297.

23. *Congressional Record,* daily ed., 96th Cong., 2d sess., July 1, 1980, E3320.

24. *Wall Street Journal,* September 8, 1988, 30.

25. Gwen Ifill, " 'Thousand Points of Light' Dimly Understood," *Washington Post,* February 13, 1989, A3.

26. Robert Shogan, "Volunteer 'Citizen Corps' Proposed," *Los Angeles Times,* pt. I, January 26, 1989, 18.

27. Morris P. Fiorina, *Congress: Keystone of the Washington Establishment* (New Haven, Conn.: Yale University Press, 1977), 48.

28. R. Douglas Arnold, "The Local Roots of Domestic Policy," in *The New Congress,* ed. Thomas E. Mann and Norman J. Ornstein (Washington, D.C.: American Enterprise Institute, 1981), 284.

29. "The States Make a Comeback," *Christian Science Monitor,* February 12, 1987, 18.

30. Arnold, "The Local Roots," 284.

31. R. Douglas Arnold, *Congress and the Bureaucracy: A Theory of Influence* (New Haven, Conn.: Yale University Press, 1979), 209.

32. Joseph S. Clark, *Congress: The Sapless Branch* (New York: Harper & Row, 1964), 63-64.

33. *Congressional Record,* 98th Cong., 2d sess., April 12, 1984, S4423.

34. David B. Frohnmayer, "The Separation of Powers: An Essay on the Vitality of a Constitutional Idea," *Oregon Law Review* (Spring 1973): 330.
35. David B. Truman, *The Governmental Process,* rev. ed. (New York: Alfred A. Knopf, 1971), 439.
36. Woodrow Wilson, *Congressional Government* (Boston: Houghton Mifflin, 1885), 297.
37. *Washington Times,* December 29, 1986, A1.
38. Rochelle Stanfield, "Plotting Every Move," *National Journal,* March 26, 1988, 796.
39. *Watkins v. United States,* 354 U.S. 178 (1957). See also James Hamilton, *The Power to Probe* (New York: Vantage Books, 1976).
40. William S. Cohen and George J. Mitchell, *Men of Zeal: A Candid Inside Story of the Iran-Contra Hearings* (New York: Viking Penguin, 1988), 305.
41. *New York Times,* January 28, 1983, A18.
42. Louis Fisher, from *Extensions,* a newsletter for the Carl Albert Congressional Research and Studies Center (Spring 1984): 2.
43. John R. Johannes, "Study and Recommend: Statutory Reporting Requirements as a Technique of Legislative Initiative—A Research Note," *Western Political Quarterly* (December 1976); 589-596.
44. *Congressional Record,* 100th Cong., 1st sess., June 17, 1987, S8206.
45 Michael W. Kirst, *Government Without Passing Laws* (Chapel Hill: University of North Carolina Press, 1969).
46. Elizabeth Wehr, "Chairman Whitten Takes Long View in Agriculture," *Congressional Quarterly Weekly Report,* June 18, 1983, 1217.
47. Joseph A. Davis, "War Declared over Report-Language Issue," *Congressional Quarterly Weekly Report,* June 25, 1988, 1752-1753; and David Rapp, "OMB's Miller Backs Away from Report-Language Battle," *Congressional Quarterly Weekly Report,* July 9, 1988, 1928.
48. "Senate Votes to Add Four Inspectors General," *Congressional Quarterly Weekly Report,* February 6, 1988, 258.
49. *Los Angeles Times,* pt. I, September 22, 1988, 38.
50. *Congressional Record,* 95th Cong., 1st sess., April 30, 1975, E2080.
51. See Joel D. Aberbach, *Keeping a Watchful Eye: The Politics of Congressional Oversight* (Washington, D.C.: The Brookings Institution, 1990).
52. *Workshop on Congressional Oversight and Investigations,* H. Doc. 96-217, 96th Cong., 1st sess., 1979, 3.
53. Matthew McCubbins and Thomas Schwartz, "Congressional Oversight Overlooked: Police Patrol Versus Fire Alarm," *American Journal of Political Science* (February 1984): 165-177; and Joel D. Aberbach, "The Congressional Committee Intelligence System: Information, Oversight, and Change," *Congress and the Presidency* 14 (Spring 1987): 51-76.
54. *Workshop on Congressional Oversight and Investigations,* 78.
55. Frederick M. Kaiser, "Congressional Oversight of the Presidency," *The Annals* (September 1988): 89.
56. Richard Cohen, "The King of Oversight," *Government Executive* (September 1988): 17.
57. Ann Cooper, "The CAB Is Shutting Down, But Will It Set an Example for Other Agencies?" *National Journal,* September 29, 1984, 1820-1823.

58. *Congressional Record,* 99th Cong., 1st sess., October 1, 1985, S12341.
59. Louis Fisher, "Micromanagement by Congress: Reality and Mythology" (Paper presented at a conference sponsored by the American Enterprise Institute, Washington, D.C., April 8-9, 1988), 8.
60. Nadine Cohodas, "Courts Play Larger Role as Interbranch Referee," *Congressional Quarterly Weekly Report,* January 7, 1989, 13.
61. See Robert A. Katzmann, ed., *Judges and Legislators* (Washington, D.C.: The Brookings Institution, 1988).
62. *New York Times,* May 12, 1983, B8.
63. Charles Rothfeld, "Judging Law: Never Mind What Congress Meant? " *New York Times,* April 14, 1989, B8.
64. *Congressional Record,* 99th Cong., 2d sess., July 17, 1986, S9277. See also Louis Fisher, *Constitutional Dialogues* (Princeton, N.J.: Princeton University Press, 1988).

Lobbyist Sheila Bamberger makes a last-minute appeal to Senate Minority Leader Robert Dole, R-Kan., before a Senate floor vote.

CHAPTER TEN

Congress and Organized Interests

Capitol Hill lobbyists regularly fill committee hearings and markups, jam into conference committee rooms, and pack House and Senate galleries. These emissaries of organized interests do more than observe congressional events. They wield their vast resources—money, personnel, information, and organization—to win passage of legislation they favor, and to reward the politicians who help them. To become more effective, some even enroll in college courses that enable "both aspiring and already established lobbyists the chance to learn the nuts and bolts of the business." [1]

Practically every major corporation, trade association, and professional group has Washington lobbyists. They even have their own associations: the American Society of Association Executives and the American League of Lobbyists.[2] Like many other groups, both are based in Washington, where more national associations are located than in any other city. (In 1986, 3,200 associations were headquartered in Washington compared with 2,600 in New York City.)[3]

Looking in the Washington telephone directory under "associations" reveals as much about what moves Congress as the Constitution. More than 80,000 employees work for various associations. Scores of law firms have moved to the District of Columbia, and growing cadres of consultants and lawyers represent diverse clients, including foreign governments.[4]

A Nation of Joiners

The American penchant for joining groups was observed long ago by the French chronicler Alexis de Tocqueville. Americans of all "conditions, minds, and ages, daily acquire a general taste for association and grow accustomed to the use of it," he wrote in 1825.[5] In 1988, 70.5 percent of the population belonged to at least one organization, a 2.5 percent increase from four years earlier and a 5.5 percent increase from eight years before. Table 10-1 lists some of the more popular types of groups that people join, such as church, sports, or service organizations.

Table 10-1   Membership in Various Groups, 1980, 1984, 1988

Organization	Percentage of population who belong		
	1980	1984	1988
Church-affiliated groups	30.0	33.3	34.3
Sports groups	17.0	21.1	19.5
Labor unions	13.0	14.1	12.8
Professional or academic societies	12.8	15.3	13.5
Fraternal groups	10.4	9.1	8.4
School service groups	9.9	12.2	12.4
Service clubs	8.9	10.4	11.0
Hobby or garden clubs	8.4	8.8	10.3
Literary, art, discussion or study groups	8.4	8.7	8.5
Youth groups	8.0	9.4	10.7
Veterans groups	7.4	6.9	8.4
School fraternities or sororities	4.2	5.8	4.3
Farm organizations	4.0	4.2	3.4
Political clubs	3.1	3.9	4.4
Nationality organizations	2.5	3.3	2.2

Source: National Opinion Research Center, General Social Surveys, *1972-1988: Cumulative Codebook,* July 1988. Data compiled by Royce Crocker, Congressional Research Service.

Not all groups seek to influence congressional policy making, but each has the right to do so. The First Amendment protects the people's right to "petition the Government for a redress of grievances." Throughout American history, groups speaking for different subsets of "the people" have swayed public policies and politics. Such groups have included the abolitionists of the nineteenth century and their fight to end slavery, the Anti-Saloon League's crusade for prohibition in the 1900s, the antiwar and environmental movements of the 1960s and 1970s, and the equal rights, balanced budget, and nuclear freeze efforts of the 1980s.

A free society nurtures politically active groups. "Liberty is to faction what air is to fire," wrote James Madison in *The Federalist,* Number 10. Until recent years national policy making was dominated by a few well-organized, well-financed groups: farm, labor, business, and medical interests. The current era has seen an explosion of narrower based groups that focus their energies on single issues, such as abortion or gun control.[6]

Pressure Group Methods

Groups have influenced congressional decisions from the beginning. During the nation's early technological and industrial expansion, railroad interests lobbied for federal funds and land grants to build their routes. Some of the lobbyists' tactics—offering bribes, for example—helped foster the traditional public suspicion of pressure tactics. In 1874 Sen. Simon Cameron, R-Pa., described an honest politician as one who "when he is bought, stays bought" (or stays "rented" with a long lease).[7]

Lobbying methods during the twentieth century became more varied, urbane, and subtle. Significantly, the move from limited to big government reinforced the mutual dependence of legislators and lobbyists.

> Groups turn to Congress as an institution where they can be heard, establish their positions, and achieve their policy goals. Members of Congress in turn rely on groups to provide valuable constituency, technical, or political information, to give reelection support, and to assist strategically in passing or blocking legislation that the members support or oppose. Groups need Congress, and Congress needs groups.[8]

Groups' modern-day methods vary according to the nature and visibility of the issue and the groups' resources. As Table 10-2 reveals, there is no dearth of techniques by which groups can influence Congress. Among the most important practices are direct and social lobbying, group alliances, and grassroots support.

Direct Lobbying

In the traditional method, lobbyists present their client's case directly to members and congressional staff. If a group hires a prominent lawyer or lobbyist, such as Clark Clifford or Charles E. Walker, the direct approach will involve personal discussions with senators or representatives. The personal touch is very important, as an aide to former Speaker Thomas P. "Tip" O'Neill, Jr., explains:

> They know members of Congress are here three nights a week, alone, without their families. So they say, "Let's have dinner. Let's go see a ballgame." Shmooze with them. Make friends. And they don't lean on it all the time. Every once in a while, they call up—maybe once or twice a year—ask a few questions. Call you up and say, "Say, what's Danny [Rostenkowski, chairman of the House Ways and Means Committee] going to do on this tax-reform bill?" Anne Wexler [a former official in the Carter White House, now a lobbyist] will call up and spend half an hour talking about left-wing politics, and suddenly she'll pop a question, pick up something. They want that little bit of access. That's what does it. You can hear it. It clicks home. They'll call their chief executive officer, and they've delivered. That's how it works. It's not illegal. They work on a personal basis.[9]

Hollywood movie stars, the sons and daughters of powerful members, and some former members of Congress are particularly effective at direct lobbying. "Since I will continue to be active in the Congressional Prayer Breakfast Group, in the House gym, the members' Dining Room and on the

Table 10-2   Lobbying Techniques Used by 174 Sampled Interest Groups

Technique	Percentage of groups that use techniques
Testify at hearings	99
Contact government officials directly to present your point of view	98
Engage in informal contacts with officials—at conventions, over lunch, etc.	95
Present research results or technical information	92
Send letters to members of your organization to inform them about your activities	92
Enter into coalitions with other organizations	90
Attempt to shape the implementation of policies	89
Talk with people from the press and the media	86
Consult with government officials to plan legislative strategy	85
Help to draft legislation	85
Inspire letter-writing or telegram campaigns	84
Shape the government's agenda by raising new issues and calling attention to previously ignored problems	84
Mount grass-roots lobbying efforts	80
Have influential constituents contact their congressman's office	80
Help to draft regulations, rules, or guidelines	78
Serve on advisory commissions and boards	76
Alert congressmen to the effects of a bill on their districts	75
File suit or otherwise engage in litigation	72
Make financial contributions to electoral campaigns	58
Do favors for officials who need assistance	56
Attempt to influence appointments to public office	53
Publicize candidates' voting records	44
Engage in direct-mail fund raising for your organization	44
Run advertisements in the media about your position on issues	31
Contribute work or personnel to electoral campaigns	24
Make public endorsements of candidates for office	22
Engage in protests or demonstrations	20

Source: Kay Lehman Schlozman and John T. Tierney, *Organized Interests and American Democracy* (New York: Harper & Row, 1986), 150.

House Floor, I will maintain contact with my good friends who affect legislation," a just-retired representative of twenty years wrote in a letter to prospective clients. He promised to "unravel red tape, open doors, make appointments, work with the Administration or government agencies, influence legislation, and assist in any other service required." [10] But some members are offended by the special entrée that ex-legislators who are lobbyists have to the floor and to other Capitol Hill locations not generally open to the public.[11]

In the House there are more occasions for lobbyists to contact members directly than in the Senate, where lobbyists are more apt to target the staff who surround each member. The tasks of direct lobbyists are diverse. They monitor committees and testify at hearings; interpret Hill decisions to clients and clients' interests to legislators; perform services, such as writing speeches for members; and provide campaign assistance. "Essentially, we operate as an extension of congressmen's staff," explained one lobbyist. "Occasionally we come up with the legislation, or speeches—and questions [for lawmakers to ask at hearings] all the time. We look at it as providing staff work for allies." [12]

The direct approach has limitations, however. From the client's perspective, rapid turnover in Congress weakens a lobbyist's personal rapport with members. From the legislator's perspective, it is sometimes unclear whether a lobbyist actually "speaks" for an organization. For example, Sen. Bob Packwood, R-Ore., sharply criticized the lobbying tactics of the American Trucking Associations (ATA):

> I don't think truckers realize in what bad repute their lobbying organization is held. These fellows here [at ATA] do their industry no good service. They're devious. They'll go around you. They will mislead you deliberately. You cannot rely on the word of their lobbyists.[13]

A particularly effective direct technique is member-to-member lobbying (see box, page 286). No outsider has the same access to members (or to certain areas of the Capitol) as another colleague. Often party and committee leaders put together their own whip task forces to lobby for priority measures.

Social Lobbying

Although the Washington social circuit is vastly overrated, some lobbyists gain access to members at dinner parties or receptions. "When you want to make an end run, meet someone at a party," explained an experienced power dealer.[14] Some lobbyists are famous (or infamous) social hosts. Until his downfall in the 1977-1978 "Koreagate" scandal about buying influence on Capitol Hill, South Korean lobbyist Tongsun Park was a noted Washington host. "His flamboyant social style earned him enormous good will and access in the Washington political community," noted a commentator. "That could often be cashed in for reciprocal good will and generosity toward the country he represented." [15]

A variation of social lobbying is offering legislators gifts, trips, or speaking fees (honoraria). Congressional rules require annual disclosure of speaking fees, impose a $2,000 limit for each appearance, and prohibit senators and representatives from accepting anything worth more than $100 from a lobbyist or organization with a direct interest in legislation pending

Member-to-Member Lobbying

On March 7, 1988, Harris W. Fawell, R-Ill., distributed a letter to House members urging them to defeat what he called the "maximum job-loss bill."

On April 27, Thomas J. Downey, D-N.Y., asked his colleagues, "If you are in favor of people working, and you don't want people on welfare, how can you oppose raising the minimum wage?"

As members decided how they would vote on a measure (HR 1834) that would raise the minimum wage from $3.35 an hour to $5.05, they were lobbied nearly as hard by their colleagues as they were by labor and business groups. At least thirty "Dear Colleague" letters were circulated on the bill; those from opponents outnumbered those from supporters by nearly 2-to-1.

Uncertainty about the outcome contributed to the intra-House lobbying. Most members, like Fawell and Downey, directly asked for a vote for or against the bill. But some tried to drum up support for their own proposals. Thomas E. Petri, R-Wis., for example, wrote a number of letters promoting an enhanced earned-income tax credit as an alternative to a minimum-wage increase.

Members like to quote "expert" and "neutral" sources to bolster their own positions. For example, when Republicans discovered that the Congressional Budget Office had issued a report (later withdrawn) indicating that the minimum-wage legislation could lead to massive job losses and increased inflation, at least three GOP members fired off "Dear Colleague" letters to capitalize on the bad news.

Newspaper articles and editorials also serve as political fodder. Buddy MacKay, D-Fla., sent out a letter March 22 stating, "Attached is a volume of editorials gleaned from half the country, including your state. . . . Consider what our district newspapers are saying about the minimum wage."

Augustus F. Hawkins, D-Calif., chief sponsor of HR 1834, circulated a letter April 29 that included a letter from five former secretaries of labor endorsing the wage increase. "In view of their experience, their call for an increase in the minimum wage should be highly considered as we prepare to vote on the issue," Hawkins wrote.

Like a choreographed conversation, some letters rebut arguments made by previous letters. For example, on May 3, a group of two Republicans and two Democrats issued a letter stating that "every economic study ever done on the consequences of increasing the minimum wage concludes some job loss occurs." Accompanying the letter were several pages abstracting such studies. Two weeks later, a group of five Democrats responded with a chart showing that "with the exception of recession years, no increase in the minimum wage has resulted in a drop in employment!"

HR 1834 failed to become law in the 100th Congress, but the issue of raising the minimum wage was high on the 101st Congress's agenda. President Bush favored raising the minimum wage, but he and Congress differed over the approach.

Source: Adapted from Macon Morehouse, " 'Dear Colleague,' Please Stop Writing . . ." *Congressional Quarterly Weekly Report,* June 4, 1988, 1519.

before Congress. Speaking fees are often augmented by expenses-paid trips. For example,

> the Electronic Industries Association paid $200 each to 17 members of Congress to attend a four-day "legislative roundtable" at the South Seas Plantation at Captiva Island, Fla. Sessions lasted only four hours a day, leaving plenty of time for fishing trips, golf and tennis tournaments, and swimming. About half the members brought their wives, whose expenses also were paid.[16]

Events such as this one provide lobbyists with good opportunities to influence members. "We've got them for two or three days, so they can't get away from us," said one lobbyist. "And it's hard for them to tell us no," he added, "after we've spent that much time, money, and effort on them." [17]

There have been attempts to reform social lobbying practices. At the end of his presidency, Ronald Reagan recommended that Congress "abolish supplemental income such as honoraria from private special-interest groups." [18] Although the ban on honoraria was not passed, public pressure for reform increased. Adverse publicity about the honoraria members of Congress receive can even affect constituents' voting behavior. In November 1988 Sen. Joseph Lieberman, D-Conn., unseated three-term GOP incumbent Lowell Weicker in part because he hammered away at Weicker "for missing Senate votes while making speeches for fees." [19]

Coalition Lobbying

"We have no permanent friends or permanent enemies—only permanent interests." This oft-repeated truism helps to explain why "coalitions, like politics, make strange bed fellows." [20] Lobbying rivals (chemical companies and environmental groups, for example) sometimes forge temporary coalitions to promote or defend shared goals. For instance, civil rights groups and the National Association of Realtors, often at odds over the issue of housing discrimination, joined to support passage of fair housing legislation. The several parties to the compromise agreement supported the measure because it was in their interest to do so:

> The realtors were tired of charges that they condoned discrimination and wanted to refurbish their public image; Republicans, led by [then] Vice President Bush, wanted to demonstrate a commitment to civil rights before the November [1988] election; civil rights advocates, worried about the dwindling days of the legislative calendar, were willing to make concessions in order to capitalize on election-year pressures.[21]

Coalition building, in sum, is standard operating procedure. Some lobbyists even specialize in building coalitions and coordinating their activities.

Grass-Roots Lobbying

Instead of contacting members directly, many organizations mobilize citizens to pressure their senators and representatives. "They came in waves, first the

Washington lobbyists and then people from companies in my district," said Rep. Donald E. "Buz" Lukens, R-Ohio, about those opposed to a proposed ban against the Japanese company Toshiba from U.S. markets.[22] Masters of grass-roots lobbying know how to be very specific. Here is what one lobbyist said when he called a woodsman about a proposal to make hunting a nondeductible business expense: "Hello, Johnny Bob? This is J. D. in Washington. Got a pencil handy? Now, this is who your congressman is. This is how you write him." [23]

Interest groups often send mass mailings to targeted congressional districts with enclosed letters or postcards for constituents to sign and mail to their legislators. Legislators understand that lobby groups orchestrate this "spontaneous" outpouring of mail, but they don't wholly disregard it.

> Members have to care about this mail, even if it's mail that is almost identically worded. Labor unions do this sort of thing a lot. The congressman has to care that *somebody* out there in his district has enough power to get hundreds of people to sit down and write a postcard or a letter—because if the guy can get them to do *that,* he might be able to influence them in other ways. So, a member has no choice but to pay attention. It's suicide if he doesn't.[24]

Grass-roots lobbying is not new, but it has become more prevalent, effective, and sophisticated. Many groups use computers to identify supporters, target specific constituencies, or generate "personalized" mass mailings. Advanced technology, such as laser printing, is used to mass produce letters that appear to be personally written by constituents. Some of the correspondence even includes tape recorded messages or unusual visual aids: Realtors, protesting high interest rates, once sent bags of keys to members to symbolize the homes they couldn't sell.[25]

Proxy mailings are another sophisticated technique that produces a flood of mail to Capitol Hill. Organizations request their members to participate in mass mailings by authorizing headquarters staff to send messages on their behalf. The Medical Society of Virginia wrote its members with this advice:

> On highly critical issues, a heavy barrage of communications to Congress might be useful within a very narrow time frame. In such cases, the [American Medical Association] would prepare several variations of a basic message, furnishing these to the Western Union Service Center. Automatically and immediately, all stored names would be matched by zip code to the desired congressional districts (or by state, in the case of the Senate) and the variations of the message sent on a random basis, with a copy in each case going to the physician "sender." [26]

Other grass-roots techniques include petition drives, rallies, radio and television advertising blitzes, and national door-to-door campaigns. The U.S. Chamber of Commerce even has its own satellite television network, "Biznet," to reach corporate subscribers instantly. And large defense companies skillfully spread work and subcontracts throughout the nation to build ad hoc constituencies that will push Congress to support military weapons.

Today direct-mail specialists, survey researchers, and media consultants are often more critical to the election of legislators than are party organizations. As a result, parties are less able to protect members from grass-roots pressure campaigns. As Rep. Mike Synar, D-Okla., explained, "Through their computers these groups get to more of my voters, more often, and with more information than any elected official can do. I'm competing to represent my district against the lobbyists and the special interests." [27]

Groups and the Electoral Connection

Groups help reelect members to Congress in many ways, but at least three are worth noting. They raise funds, make financial contributions through political action committees (PACs), and rate the voting record of legislators.

Fund-Raising Assistance

Legislators who dislike raising money—seemingly a majority of them (see Table 5-2)—turn to lobbyists or professional fund raisers to sponsor parties, luncheons, dinners, or other social events where admission is charged. Lobbyists buy tickets or supply lists of people who should be invited.

Fund-raising events have consumed more and more of legislators' limited time and created new scheduling conflicts—further evidence of the imperatives of the "two Congresses," the representative assembly and the lawmaking institution. Members can't "chase money" and vote on bills at the same time. To minimize these conflicts between members' electoral and lawmaking responsibilities,

> the practice has grown up in the last several years of providing "windows" in the Senate schedule. A window is a period of time in which it is understood that there will be no roll-call votes. Senators are assured that they won't be embarrassed by being absent for a recorded vote. Windows usually occur between six and eight in the evening, which is the normal time for holding fundraising cocktail parties.[28]

When he was majority leader, Sen. Robert Byrd, D-W.Va., expressed concern that members were "being forced to spend more and more time raising money than in legislating." [29]

Congressional critics, and even legislators and lobbyists, question the propriety of fund-raising practices. Members are concerned about implied obligations when they accept help or money from groups. For their part, lobbyists may resent pressure from members to buy tickets to their fund raisers.

Despite such complaints, fund raisers are likely to persist. The situation could change if Congress provided stricter spending limits or public financing for congressional elections. These proposals, however, face stiff opposition from incumbents who fear it would aid or underwrite their challengers. As for public funding, it is questionable whether taxpayers favor this approach. In an era of fiscal scarcity, "I do not think it is time for us to enact an entitlement program for candidates for Congress," said Sen. Ted Stevens, R-Alaska.[30]

PACs and Policy Making

Political action committees have grown rapidly from 600 in 1974 to more than 4,000 in 1989 (see Chapter 3). Moreover, PAC contributions are growing as a percentage of total congressional campaign spending, and "nearly all PAC money goes to incumbents, regardless of party or beliefs" (see Table 10-3).[31] One effect of this has been to help the Democratic party because a majority of incumbents are Democrats. By the late 1980s, the partisan effects of PAC giving began to grate on Republicans, especially in the House, where the GOP has been the "permanent minority" since 1954. Many Republicans who previously opposed changes in campaign financing started to realize "that further opposition to campaign-finance reform will relegate them to minority status indefinitely." [32] Whether bipartisan consensus will emerge to produce changes is uncertain at this juncture, but so long as huge sums of money are required to get elected, the debate surrounding PACs will not be easily resolved.

More troublesome is the possible influence of PACs on voting behavior. Some see a "direct linear correlation" between a member's votes and the amount he or she received from a PAC. Others refute such a cause-and-effect relationship and argue that legislators are resistant to the importunings of PACs because they receive campaign funds from diverse and competing sources. It is a mistake, warned another analyst, to overstate the influence of money on policy making and ignore other considerations that influence how members vote. These include constituency pressures, party ties, friendship with other legislators or lobbyists, conscience, and personal idiosyncracies and prejudices.[33]

But on one issue nearly everyone agrees: money buys access. "Access is important precisely because there is no equal access," said a knowledgeable Washington activist. "It's unequal access because there's a limited amount of time for members to consider anything. Access is important because it's what comes up on a legislator's screen that influences him." [34] Or as one senator explained,

> If someone came in and said, "I contributed $1,000, or am about to contribute $1,000, to your campaign and I expect you to vote No," I think most Members would, if not kick 'em out of the office, at least make an outraged statement. But, a contributor calls you on a busy day when your inclination is not to take any calls, and if that person says, "I must speak to you urgently," the chances are you will take that call when you wouldn't have taken any other calls. So to that extent I think money does have impact.[35]

Table 10-3   PAC Donations to House Candidates, January 1, 1987–October 19, 1988 (in millions)

Type of candidate	Donation
Democratic incumbents	$44.9
GOP challengers	1.4
GOP incumbents	24.3
Democratic challengers	5.7
Open seats	
Democratic	3.3
GOP	1.8
Total Democrats	$53.9
Total GOP	$27.5

Source: *Wall Street Journal,* November 15, 1988, A24.

Rating Legislators

About 100 groups keep pressure on legislators by issuing "report cards" on their voting records. Groups select key issues and then publicize the members' scores (from 0 to 100) based on their "right" or "wrong" votes on those issues. The ratings of the liberal Americans for Democratic Action (ADA) and the conservative American Conservative Union (ACU) are well known and widely used. Many groups target members for electoral assistance or defeat and assign them attention-catching names: "heroes and zeroes" (consumer advocates) or the "dirty dozen" (environmental polluters).

One must beware of the "ratings game." It is always simplistic, oftentimes misleading and inaccurate. The selected issues are often biased, oversimplified, self-serving, and in any case inadequate to judge a member's record. Group strategists, however, defend ratings as "a shorthand way for voters to tell something about their congressman." [36] These legislative score cards are used by the groups themselves to determine which candidates will win endorsements and which will receive campaign contributions. Incumbents who hold closely contested seats are usually careful when casting their vote. As Rep. Philip Sharp, D-Ind., who represents a marginal district, said, "If I cast a vote, I might have to answer for it. It may be an issue in the next campaign. Over and over I have to have a response to the question: Why did you do that?" [37]

Groups and Legislative Politics

The lobbyist's job is time consuming because power in Congress is diffused. "Instead of selling his idea to a few senior members," observed one lobbyist, "he must work all members of a committee, on both sides of the aisle, and repeat that work when legislation reaches the floor." [38] Reflecting on the changing styles of modern lobbying, Washington lawyer-lobbyist Stuart Eizenstat (formerly President Jimmy Carter's domestic policy adviser) said:

> Because of the increasing sophistication of staff, you have to be armed with facts, precedents and legal points. Sure it's a political environment, but it's much more substantive. The old-style, pat-'em-on-the-back lobbyist is gone, or at least going.[39]

Congress is an open, decentralized institution that affords lobbyists multiple opportunities to shape the fate of legislation. Groups affect, directly or indirectly, virtually every feature of the congressional environment, such as committee activities, legislative agendas, and floor decision making.

Lobbyists and Committees

As we have seen, many congressional committees reflect the concerns of specific groups, such as farmers, teachers, or veterans. As long as the outside group wields political clout, Congress is unlikely to eliminate the committee it supports. For example, in 1977 the Senate considered abolishing its six-year-old Veterans' Affairs Committee and merging its functions with those of other standing committees, but veterans' groups adamantly objected and the committee remains. Congress's problem, observed Sen. Bob Packwood, R-Ore., is that "if everybody has an ear, a direct ear in the form of a committee, we are not going to have any kind of coherent [committee] structure." [40]

In their campaigns for choice committee assignments, legislators sometimes enlist the support of outside organizations. Lobbyists also encourage friendly legislators to bid for committees and subcommittees that handle issues important to their group's interests. Democratic representative Barbara Kennelly, whose hometown of Hartford, Connecticut, is a hub of the insurance industry, waged a successful campaign to join the tax-writing Ways and Means Committee. "The insurance industry must have a representative [on Ways and Means]," explained one House member, "and they pulled in all their due bills." [41]

Subgovernments

Committees often form alliances with the bureaucrats and lobbyists who regularly testify before them and with whom members and staff aides periodically meet. Scholars and journalists have called the three-way, policy-making alliances of committees, executive agencies, and interest groups *subgovernments*. Other names include "cozy little triangles," "triple alliances," "policy whirlpools," or "iron triangles." [42] By whatever name, these subgovernments directly affect program development.

> Committee members want campaign contributions, help in their election campaigns, and honoraria for speeches. They rely on the expertise of

lobbyists in writing laws. Interest groups expect members of committees to provide them with formal and informal access to the bureaus and with funds for programs that benefit them. They expect help in winning cabinet and subcabinet appointments for prominent group members.[43]

The influence of subgovernments varies with different policy areas depending upon the nature of the issue, its visibility, conflict among alliance members, and the existence of competing subgovernments. (One competing group, called the "dissident triangle," is made up of "the Pentagon's intellectual critics, their allies in Congress, and the press, which harvests news leaks from both." [44]) Subgovernments' efforts succeed or fail according to public tolerance. Are citizens agitated about an issue, or are they simply looking the other way? As one analyst pointed out,

> The iron triangle is really an iron quadrangle. The fourth side is the American public. The public is perfectly aware of the programs Congress is spending money on. The public likes most of those programs and wants to see more money allocated to them.[45]

The subgovernments' ability to dominate given policy arenas shifts with historical changes in institutions, processes, and the larger political environment. Scholar Hugh Heclo contends that "issue networks"—knowledgeable people and groups that flow in and out of several policy areas—have replaced the old triangles.[46] Issue network participants are united in their policy expertise but not in their domination over policies themselves. One can point to several factors that appear to be contributing to the decline of the iron triangle as an autonomous force in public policymaking: the rise of large numbers of new citizens' groups and advocacy organizations, new patterns of investigative reporting and the enlarged role of the media in national politics, the greater policymaking role of the federal courts, and the increasing aggressiveness of presidents intent on controlling the bureaucracy.[47]

Lobbyists and Legislation

Lobbyists are active during all phases of the legislative process. During the committee phase, lobbyists draft bills and amendments for members and testify at hearings. They often "help the policy-making process by pointing out how different industries and regions might be affected by various provisions, perhaps in ways unintended by those who drafted them." [48]

When major measures reach the House and Senate floor, groups focus on influencing votes. They plan strategy with their friends in Congress, prepare arguments for and against expected floor amendments, work to get their supporters on the floor for key votes, and draft floor statements and amendments. A newspaper report described one such scene:

> There is a flurry in the Senate gallery, where a group of wealthy western farmers and their lawyers is watching the debate. The Senate is trying to

decide if these landowners will be exempted from legislation putting sharp limits on the amount of federal irrigation water they can receive.

Their champion is Sen. Alan Cranston, D-Calif., arguing mightily [for the water exemption].

In the gallery, Sen. Rudy Boschwitz, R-Minn., is talking with the farmer-lobbyists. In the hallway, one of their lawyers is drafting language that Cranston will use to make his case. A Cranston aide runs relays between the gallery and the Senate floor.[49]

Groups help to frame Congress's policy and oversight agenda by pushing the House and Senate to address their concerns. Many legislative preoccupations of the past two decades—civil rights, environmental and consumer protection, and child care among them—stemmed at least in part from vigorous outside lobbying.

In 1984, for instance, Congress passed a bill to encourage states to raise their drinking age to twenty-one. States that passed such a law would receive increased federal funds for highway safety; states that did not would find their share of federal highway funds reduced. The impetus for this national program came from a lobbying organization started by mothers whose children were the victims of drunk drivers. Called Mothers Against Drunk Drivers (MADD), the group mobilized public and legislative backing for the anti-drunk-driving legislation.

For their part, members sponsor bills and amendments that win them group support—the "two Congresses" again. Sen. Jesse Helms, R-N.C., is a case in point. Regularly, Helms offers amendments on controversial social issues such as abortion and school prayer and forces votes on them. "His amendments," wrote Elizabeth Drew, "gave him a kind of publicity that was useful, firmed up his relationships with a cluster of 'New Right' groups, helped him raise money, and provided material with which he and his allies could try to defeat opponents." [50]

Informal Groups of Members

Legislators may complain about limited-issue lobbying groups, yet they have formed many such groups of their own. In response to the numerous informal caucuses created in the 1970s, former Speaker O'Neill once said, "the House has over-caucused itself." [51] By the late 1980s nearly every representative and senator belonged to at least one of the approximately 120 informal legislative groups (see Table 10-4).

Congress always has had informal groups, caucuses, coalitions, clubs, alliances, blocs, and cliques. What makes today's groups different from earlier ones is their number; diversity (there are partisan, bipartisan, and bicameral groups); institutionalized character (many have paid staff, office space, dues-paying members, bylaws, and elected officers); and capacity to monitor developments that affect their interests. Some state delegations meet regularly on either a partisan or bipartisan basis. Perhaps at a weekly breakfast or lunch they discuss state and national issues and internal congressional politics, mobilize support to capture their share of federal funds and projects, champion colleagues for coveted committee assignments, or back candidates for party leadership positions. California's House Democrats have assembled formidable power bases in most committees. "Committee assignments are sought with an eye to the collective good. And to maximize the benefits of seniority, committee-hopping is discouraged." [52]

Types of Groups

Most unofficial congressional groups, called by the House "legislative service organizations," have ties with outside interests. Not surprisingly, the Steel Caucus maintains links with the steel industry and the Textile Caucus with textile manufacturers. Some outside groups provide staff and financial support to the informal legislative associations.

Interest groups can be instrumental in forming these legislative counterparts. The idea for the Mushroom Caucus (to protect mushroom producers from foreign imports) originated at a May 1977 luncheon sponsored for House members by the American Mushroom Institute. [53] The Black, Women's, and Hispanic caucuses were established to give their national constituencies—and the members themselves—more recognition and clout in Congress. The Congressional Hispanic Caucus declared that its creation in 1976 was "a sign of the growing power of our community, and we are looking forward to strengthening the Federal commitment to Hispanic citizens." [54]

To expand their reach further, several informal groups have created or aligned themselves with private institutes. These institutes conduct research and provide analysis that can be used in congressional decision making. One stimulus for their creation was adoption in 1981 of House regulations that prohibit legislative groups who want to maintain offices in congressional buildings from receiving funds from outside sources, such as businesses or industries. (The groups that chose to observe the 1981 ruling are funded from members' official allowances.) The Congressional Environmental and Energy Study Conference created the Environmental and Energy Study Institute, a private, tax-exempt organization. To advocate their favorite causes, Senators Packwood and Robert Dole, R-Kan., among others, established their own private tax-exempt foundations—the Freedom of Expression Foundation and the Dole Foundation, respectively. The Dole Foundation's objective is to aid the disabled. (During World War II Dole suffered wounds that paralyzed his left arm.) "This is a way a prominent politician can see a need and then use his prominence to try to resolve it," said the director of the foundation. "In recent years it seems it has become increasingly hard for legislators who have a pet issue to find Federal dollars for it." [55]

Other groups have a regional purpose. Members of the Northeast-Midwest Economic Coalition want to retain their share of energy supplies, federal aid to cities, and manufacturing capacity for the Frost Belt states. The

Table 10-4   Informal Congressional Groups, 1988

House

Democratic

Budget Study Group (85)
Congressional Populist Caucus (25)
Conservative Democratic Forum
  ("Boll Weevils") (36)
Democratic Members of the 100th
  Congress (27)
Ninety-ninth New Members
  Democratic Caucus
Democratic Study Group (225)
House Democratic Research
  Organization (100)
Ninety-Seventh Democratic Caucus
Ninety-Eighth Democratic Caucus

Republican

Conservative Opportunity Society
House Republican Study Committee
  (140)
House Wednesday Group (33)
Ninety-Fifth Republican Club (14)
Northeast-Midwest Republican
  Coalition ("Gypsy Moths")
Republican Freshman Class of the
  98th, 99th, 100th Congresses
The '92 Group

Bipartisan

Budget Commandos (62)
Conference of Great Lakes
  Congressmen (100)
Congressional Agricultural Forum
  (75)
Congressional Arts Caucus (200)
Congressional Automotive Caucus (37)
Congressional Aviation Forum (75)
Congressional Bearing Caucus (20)
Congressional Border Caucus (17)
Congressional Coal Group (62)
Congressional Coalition on
  Population and Development (35)
Congressional Grace Caucus (165)
Congressional Human Rights Caucus
  (150)

Bipartisan (continued)

Congressional Maritime Caucus
  (105)
Congressional Metropolitan Area
  Caucus (8)
Congressional Mining Caucus (39)
Congressional Mushroom Caucus (6)
Congressional Port Caucus (100)
Congressional Social Security Caucus
  (56)
Congressional Space Caucus (150)
Congressional Steel Caucus (110)
Congressional Sunbelt Caucus
Congressional Task Force on Haiti
  (30)
Congressional Territorial Caucus (4)
Congressional Textile Caucus (87)
Congressional Travel and Tourism
  Caucus (150)
Congressional Truck Caucus (50)
Export Task Force (70)
Forestry 2000 Task Force (100)
House Beef Caucus (48)
House Fair Employment Practices
  Committee
House Footwear Caucus (54)
House Task Force on Coal Exports
  (40)
Hudson River Caucus (15)
Insurance Caucus
Liability Insurance and Tort Reform
  Task Force (69)
Local Government Caucus (20)
Long Island Sound Caucus (10)
Northeast Agricultural Caucus (45)
Northeast-Midwest Congressional
  Coalition (100)
Pennsylvania Congressional
  Delegation Steering Committee (5)
Pro-Life Caucus
Rural Health Care Coalition
Third World Debt Caucus
Trade Expansion Caucus (30)

Senate

Republican

Senate Steering Committee
Senate Wednesday Group

Bipartisan

Border Caucus
Concerned Senators for the Arts (67)
Northeast-Midwest Senate Coalition (36)
Pro-Life Action Task Force for Women,
Children, and the Unborn
Senate Air and Space Caucus
Senate Anti-Terrorist Caucus (14)
Senate Beef Caucus (33)
Senate Caucus on International Narcotics
Control (7)

Senate Caucus on the Family (25)
Senate Children's Caucus (30)
Senate China Trade Caucus (21)
Senate Coal Caucus (40)
Senate Drug Enforcement Caucus
Senate Footwear Caucus (35)
Senate Grace Caucus
Senate Human Rights Caucus (10)
Senate Rail Caucus
Senate Rural Health Caucus
Senate Steel Caucus
Senate Textile Steering Committee (12)
Senate Tourism Caucus (74)
Senate Trucking Caucus
Senate Western Coalition (30)
Senate Wine Caucus (11)

Bicameral

Ad Hoc Congressional Committee on the
Baltic States and the Ukraine (150)
Ad Hoc Congressional Committee on Irish
Affairs (111)
Arms Control and Foreign Policy Caucus
(129)
California Democratic Congressional
Delegation (27)
Coalition for Peace through Strength (250)
Congressional Ad Hoc Monitoring Group on
Southern Africa (50)
Congressional Alcohol Fuels Caucus
Congressional Black Caucus (23)
Congressional Caucus for Science and
Technology (35)
Congressional Caucus for Women's Issues
(100)
Congressional Clearinghouse on the Future
(100)
Congressional Coalition for Soviet Jews
Congressional Coalition on Adoption (80)
Congressional Competitiveness Caucus (198)
Congressional Copper Caucus (35)
Congressional Corn Caucus

Congressional Crime Caucus (80)
Congressional Friends of Human Rights (162)
Congressional Hispanic Caucus (13)
Congressional Leaders United for a Balanced
Budget (137)
Congressional Olympic Caucus
Congressional Rural Caucus (70)
Congressional Soybean Caucus (100)
Congressional Task Force on Afghanistan (26)
Environmental and Energy Study Conference
(325)
Federal Government Service Task Force (50)
Fire Services Caucus (225)
Friends of Ireland (160)
House-Senate International Education Study
Group (85)
Long Island Congressional Caucus (8)
Military Reform Caucus (135)
New York State Congressional Delegation (36)
Nuclear Non-Proliferation Task Force
Pacific Northwest Trade Task Force (20)
Pennsylvania Congressional Delegation (25)
Tennessee Valley Authority Caucus (38)
Vietnam Veterans in Congress (55)

Source: Sula P. Richardson, Congressional Research Service.
Note: Number of members, where available, is in parentheses.

Sun Belt Caucus, a southern representative explained, was established in 1979 "in large part to counter lobbying and information-disseminating activities of the Northeast-Midwest Coalition." [56] A founder of the Steel Caucus, Rep. Joseph Gaydos, D-Pa., likened his group's function to that of a cactus.

> A cactus is armed with sharp spines that cause pain to anything that steps on it or brushes up against it. The spines are a defense mechanism to keep the plant healthy and whole and to ensure survival. The Steel Caucus has the same function vis-à-vis the steelworkers and steelmakers. We jab lawmakers and government officials who do not realize that in recent years this nation has followed self-abusive, timid, favor-seeking, short-sighted trade and domestic policies that are hammering down the most basic of all our industries—steel—in all its forms. [57]

Each move to protect a region's interests is likely to prompt a countermove.

Caucuses also are formed to focus on issues that overlap several committees' jurisdictions or that fail to receive sufficient committee attention. The Senate Children's Caucus, created to highlight children's issues, conducted nationally reported hearings on the sexual abuse of the young. The Military Reform Caucus, a bipartisan, bicameral group, was formed in part to challenge the consensus opinion on defense prevalent in the Armed Services committees. "This lack of alternative opinion . . .," said Rep. Jim Courter, R-N.J., "creates a void which the Military Reform Caucus attempts to fill." These groups also act as clearinghouses for information in their fields. [58]

Finally, informal groups can buttress their members' strength back home. Some legislative groups, such as the House Democratic Study Group, provide campaign and fund-raising assistance for their members. The House Coal Caucus offered its initiator, Rep. Nick J. Rahall, D-W.Va., significant political benefits. A group of moderate House Republicans even formed "the '92 Group" to plan for recapturing control of the chamber the electoral year following the 1990 census. Occasionally, group nonmembership is used against candidates for reelection. For example, the challenger in Indiana's 3d Congressional District lambasted Republican incumbent John P. Hiler for dropping out of the eighteen-state "Frostbelt Coalition," which he termed a "slap in the face" to constituents. [59]

Legislative Impact of Ad Hoc Caucuses

The impact of informal groups on policy making is not clear. Some legislators minimize them. Former representative John Erlenborn, R-Ill., opposed the spread of caucuses because they "led to nothing but increased expenses, increased staff, decreased available working space, and a further growth of purely provincial points of view." [60] Others believe informal groups undermine party unity and lead to the "Balkanization" of Congress.

Although their overall achievements are hard to assess, caucuses shape Congress's policy agenda and influence policy making. For example, the

Conservative Opportunity Society, a group of House GOP members, employs aggressive floor tactics to challenge the Democratic leadership and to promote attention and consideration of Republican proposals. The Congressional Caucus for Women's Issues won enactment during the 1980s of legislation that addressed sex discrimination, such as reform of pensions for military spouses and enforcement of child support payments.

Informal groups serve as contact points for liaison officers in the executive branch. Informal groups provide executive and White House officials with information and can be instrumental in coordinating a legislative strategy and building coalitions. Finally, ad hoc caucuses permit members to discuss common issues and join with other groups to pass or defeat legislation. Paradoxically, informal groups foster both decentralizing and integrative tendencies in Congress.

Regulation of Lobbying

For more than 100 years Congress intermittently considered ways to regulate lobbying, a right, as noted earlier, protected by the First Amendment: "the right of the people . . . to petition the Government for a redress of grievances." Not until 1946, however, did Congress enact its first—and only—comprehensive lobbying law: the Federal Regulation of Lobbying Act, Title III of the Legislative Reorganization Act of that year. The act covered only direct contacts with members; it addressed neither lobbyists' contacts with staff nor grass-roots efforts.

The 1946 Lobbying Law

The main objective of the 1946 act was public disclosure of lobbying activities. It required persons trying to influence Congress to register with the Clerk of the House or Secretary of the Senate and to report quarterly on the amount of money received and spent for lobbying. The law's authors, although loathe to propose direct control of lobbying, believed that "professionally inspired efforts to put pressure upon Congress cannot be conducive to well-considered legislation." Hence, the law stressed registration and reporting:

> The availability of information regarding organized groups and full knowledge of their expenditures for influencing legislation, their membership and the source of contributions to them of large amounts of money, would prove helpful to Congress in evaluating their representations without impairing the rights of any individual or group freely to express its opinion to the Congress.[61]

The lobby law soon proved ineffective, however. In 1954 the Supreme Court upheld its constitutionality, but the decision (*United States v. Harriss*) significantly weakened the law. First, the Court said that only lobbyists paid to represent someone else must register, exempting lobbyists who spend their own money. Second, the Court held that registration applies only to persons whose "principal purpose" is to influence legislation. As a result, many trade associations, labor unions, professional organizations, consumer groups, and Washington lawyers avoid registering because lobbying is not their principal purpose. There are even lobbyists who say they are not covered by the law because their job is to inform—not influence—legislators. Finally, the Court held that the act applies only to lobbyists who contact members directly. This interpretation excludes lobbying activities that generate grass-roots pressure on Congress.

Critics say also that the act is weakly enforced. The Clerk of the House and Secretary of the Senate compile the lobbyists' quarterly reports and publish them in the *Congressional Record,* but they lack authority to investigate or enforce compliance as Sen. Robert C. Byrd has noted:

> Only two lobbyists have ever been convicted under the Lobby Act. In 1956, Republican Senator Francis Case of South Dakota charged that he had been given a $2,500 campaign contribution to influence his vote. A Senate investigation followed, leading to fines ... and one-year suspended sentences for two lobbyists for the Superior Oil Company, and a $10,000 fine for their employer.[62]

Efforts to Revise the 1946 Law

As a result of lobbying scandals, Congress has tried several times to plug the 1946 law's gaping loopholes. These attempts foundered largely because it is difficult to regulate lobbying without trespassing on citizens' rights to contact their elected representatives.

Other practical and political obstacles hamper revision of the law. There is no agreement about what constitutes lobbying. Nor is there consensus on a threshold to trigger stricter registration and reporting requirements, such as number of hours or days spent lobbying, or the amount of money expended during a quarter. Groups agree that a threshold covering almost every lobbying activity would cause certain organizations to "opt out of the political process for any of a number of reasons: the cost of compliance; the stigma of being labeled a lobbyist; the fear of government meddling in the organization's affairs; the assessment by the organization that the benefit of contacting Washington might be outweighed by the burdens of complying with the registration and reporting requirements."[63]

Lobbying by Foreign Governments

Lobbying for or by foreign governments, corporations, or groups, such as the contras in Nicaragua, has become more prevalent. Given the major role of the United States in the global economy and in military security, it is understandable why scores of foreign nationals, or Americans who work for foreign clients, spend so much time and money lobbying Capitol Hill. In 1988, 113 American firms were hired to represent 152 Japanese companies and government agencies.

For this representation and grass-roots activities they will pay more than $100 million—more than the combined budgets of the U.S. Chamber of Commerce, the National Association of Manufacturers, The Business Roundtable, the Committee for Economic Development and the American Business Conference—the five most influential business organizations in Washington.[64]

Under the Foreign Agents Registration Act, lobbyists who work for foreign clients must register with the Department of Justice. Periodically, Congress considers ways to strengthen foreign lobbying restrictions.

Conclusion

From the nation's beginning, lobbyists and lobbying have been an integral part of lawmaking. Lobbying "has been so deeply woven into the American political fabric that one could, with considerable justice, assert that the history of lobbying comes close to being the history of American legislation." [65]

Recent years have witnessed an explosion in the number and types of groups organized to pursue their ends on Capitol Hill. Compared with a decade ago, there are more industry associations, public affairs lobbies (such as Common Cause), single-issue groups, political action committees, and agents representing foreign governments. Some of these groups employ new grass-roots lobbying techniques. Today many issues are won in Washington because of sophisticated lobbying campaigns back in home states or districts.

No one questions that groups and lobbyists have a legitimate public role. But other aspects of lobbying warrant concern. Groups do push Congress to pass laws that benefit the few and not the many. They frequently misrepresent members' voting records in their rating schemes and pour money into campaigns of their allies (mainly incumbents). Lawmakers who defy single-issue groups find at election time that these organizations pull out all the stops to defeat them. "It's true what they say," said Rep. Jim Slattery, D-Kan.; Congress "responds to pressure, especially in an election year." [66]

Built-in checks constrain group pressures, however. First, there often are competing groups on any issue, and legislators can play one off against the other. As former Democratic representative (later New York City mayor) Edward Koch said:

> I learn a lot from lobbyists because after they have given me all the arguments on their side I invariably ask this question: "What are the three major arguments your opponents use and how do you respond to them?" This sometimes causes consternation. Then I will say, "If you don't tell me, they will." This usually provides me with additional information which would not otherwise come to my attention.[67]

Second, knowledgeable staff aides can forearm members to counter the lobbyists' arguments. Still another informal check on lobbyists is lawmakers' own expertise. Finally, there are self-imposed constraints. Lobbyists who misrepresent issues or mislead members soon find their access permanently closed off.

In addition to groups, many other forces shape a member's vote, including the processes and procedures that Congress employs to make laws. The next chapter examines the major procedural elements of decision making in Congress.

Notes

1. *Roll Call,* December 18, 1988, 19.
2. There is even a Washington-based organization, the Advocacy Institute, that helps to train lobbyists. See *New York Times,* January 2, 1986, A16.
3. *New York Times,* August 3, 1988, B4.
4. *New York Times,* September 7, 1984, A13.
5. Alexis de Tocqueville, *Democracy in America,* ed. Phillips Bradley (New York: Alfred A. Knopf, 1951), 119.
6. See Sylvia Tesh, "In Support of 'Single-Issue' Politics," *Political Science Quarterly* (Spring 1984): 27-44.
7. Elise D. Garcia, "Money in Politics," *Common Cause,* February 1981, 11.
8. Norman J. Ornstein and Shirley Elder, *Interest Groups, Lobbying and Policymaking* (Washington, D.C.: Congressional Quarterly, 1978), 224.
9. Hedrick Smith, *The Power Game* (New York: Random House, 1988), 232.
10. Ronald J. Hrebenar and Ruth K. Scott, *Interest Group Politics in America* (Englewood Cliffs, N.J.: Prentice-Hall, 1982), 63.
11. Janet Hook, "Ex-Members Have Access, But Not Always Clout," *Congressional Quarterly Weekly Report,* June 18, 1988, 1651-1653.
12. *Wall Street Journal,* October 5, 1987, 54.
13. *Wall Street Journal,* February 21, 1984, 1.
14. *New York Times,* January 20, 1981, B3.
15. Norman J. Ornstein, "Lobbying for Fun and Policy," *Foreign Policy* (Fall 1977): 160.
16. *Wall Street Journal,* July 28, 1983, 1.
17. *Los Angeles Times,* pt. I, June 20, 1988, 1. See also *Washington Post,* June 20, 1988, A1.
18. *Washington Post,* January 6, 1989, A6.
19. Chuck Alston and Janet Hook, "An Election Lesson: Money Can Be Dangerous," *Congressional Quarterly Weekly Report,* November 19, 1988, 3366-3367.
20. Ernest Wittenberg, "How Lobbying Helps Make Democracy Work," *Vital Speeches of the Day,* November 1, 1982, 47.
21. Steven V. Roberts, "Old Rivals Make Peace to Write a Housing Bill," *New York Times,* June 28, 1988, A22.
22. *Los Angeles Times,* pt. IV, May 1, 1988, 1.
23. *Washington Star,* December 31, 1980, C2.

24. John T. Tierney and Kay Lehman Schlozman, "Congress and Organized Interests," in *Congressional Politics*, ed. Christopher J. Deering (Chicago: Dorsey Press, 1989), 212.
25. *USA Today*, January 24, 1983, 8A. See Bill Keller, "Proxy Mail Replaces Cold Sweat Letters: Computers and Laser Printers Have Recast the Injunction: 'Write Your Congressman,'" *Congressional Quarterly Weekly Report*, September 11, 1982, 2245-2247.
26. *Oversight of the 1946 Federal Regulation of Lobbying Act*, Hearings Before the Senate Committee on Governmental Affairs, November 15 and 16, 1983, 98th Cong., 1st sess., 421.
27. *New York Times*, January 24, 1980, A16.
28. Philip M. Stern, "The Tin Cup Congress," *The Washington Monthly*, May 1988, 24.
29. *Congressional Record*, 100th Cong., 1st sess., August 5, 1987, S11292.
30. Jeremy Gaunt, "Filibuster Threat Hangs over Campaign Financing Debate," *Congressional Quarterly Weekly Report*, June 6, 1987, 1187.
31. *Wall Street Journal*, July 1, 1988, 16.
32. *Roll Call*, January 15, 1989, 5.
33. Kirk Victor, "Making a Leap in Logic," *National Journal*, July 16, 1988, 1904.
34. Smith, *The Power Game*, 256-257.
35. *Roll Call*, June 19, 1988, 12. See also Brooks Jackson, *Honest Graft: Big Money and the American Political Process* (New York: Alfred A. Knopf, 1988).
36. Bill Whalen, "Rating Lawmakers' Politics by Looking into Their Eyes," *Insight*, October 20, 1986, 21.
37. *New York Times*, May 13, 1986, A24.
38. *Oversight of the 1946 Federal Regulation of Lobbying Act*, 228.
39. Kirk Victor, "New Kids on the Block," *National Journal*, October 31, 1987, 2727.
40. *Committee System Reorganization Amendments of 1977*, Hearings Before the Senate Committee on Rules and Administration, 95th Cong., 1st sess., 21.
41. *New York Times*, January 5, 1983, B8.
42. There is an extensive literature on *subgovernments*, a term coined by Douglass Cater, *Power in Washington* (New York: Random House, 1964). See J. Leiper Freeman, *The Political Process: Executive Bureau-Legislative Committee Relations*, rev. ed. (New York: Random House, 1965); James R. Temples, "The Politics of Nuclear Power: A Subgovernment in Transition," *Political Science Quarterly* (Summer 1980): 239-260; and Gordon M. Adams, "Disarming the Military Subgovernment," *Harvard Journal on Legislation* (April 1977): 459-504.
43. Richard Pious, *The American Presidency* (New York: Basic Books, 1979), 222.
44. Smith, *The Power Game*, 163.
45. William Schneider, "Read Voters' Lips: Spending Is OK," *National Journal*, December 31, 1988, 3282. President Reagan reformulated the triangular alliance: he dropped the bureaucracy and added the media. Some commentators suggested that Reagan's reformulation was a way to avoid blame for

the huge deficits that accumulated during his eight years in office. See *Wall Street Journal,* January 5, 1989, A12.

46. Hugh Heclo, "Issue Networks and the Executive Establishments," in *The New American Political System,* ed. Anthony King (Washington, D.C.: American Enterprise Institute, 1978), 87-124.

47. Tierney and Schlozman, "Congress and Organized Interests," 214.

48. *New York Times,* May 31, 1985, D16.

49. *Washington Post,* September 23, 1979, A1.

50. Elizabeth Drew, "A Reporter at Large, Jesse Helms," *New Yorker,* July 20, 1981, 80.

51. *U.S. News & World Report,* February 4, 1980, 59.

52. *Washington Post,* June 12, 1987, A13. See also Tom Watson, "State Delegations: Power's Payoffs and Pitfalls," *Congressional Quarterly Weekly Report,* January 3, 1987, 24-28.

53. *Washington Star,* May 22, 1978, A1.

54. *New York Times,* December 8, 1976, 32.

55. *New York Times,* December 24, 1984, 8.

56. *Congressional Record,* 96th Cong., 1st sess., April 3, 1979, 7065.

57. From "The Steel Caucus," *Metal Producing,* June 1981, 89. The quotation was in a class report for Walter Oleszek by student David A. Domansky of American University.

58. Representative Courter is quoted in *Congressional Record,* 98th Cong., 2d sess., April 12, 1984, E1622. See also *New York Times,* April 27, 1984, A1.

59. *New York Times,* October 17, 1984, A22. See also Daniel P. Mulhollan and Arthur G. Stevens, "Special Interests and the Growth in Information Groups in Congress" (Paper presented at the Midwest Political Science Convention, Chicago, April 24-26, 1980), 15.

60. John Erlenborn, "Rep. Erlenborn on the Caucus Delecti," *Roll Call,* April 27, 1978, 4.

61. *Organization of the Congress,* House Rept. 1675, 79th Cong., 2d sess., 1946, 26.

62. *Congressional Record,* 100th Cong., 1st sess., September 28, 1987, S12944.

63. Hope Eastman, *Lobbying: A Constitutionally Protected Right* (Washington, D.C.: American Enterprise Institute, 1977), 19.

64. Pat Choate, "How Foreign Firms Buy U.S. Clout," *Washington Post,* June 19, 1988, C1. See also Deborah M. Levy, "Advice for Sale," *Foreign Policy* (Summer 1987): 64-85.

65. Edgar Lane, *Lobbying and the Law* (Berkeley: University of California Press, 1964), 18.

66. Julie Rovner, " 'Pepper Bill' Pits Politics Against Process," *Congressional Quarterly Weekly Report,* June 4, 1988, 1493.

67. *Washington Star,* December 16, 1975, A1.

PART FOUR

Policy Making and Change in the Two Congresses

"To get along, go along," Speaker Sam Rayburn's famous adage, character-ized Congress's policy making during the mid-twentieth century. A few powerful committee chairmen and party leaders exercised predominant influence in the House and Senate. This situation changed dramatically during the 1960s and 1970s. Today scores of legislators—junior and senior—can exercise initiative and creativity in lawmaking and oversight. Today's independence and deference to electoral considerations are embodied in Republican senator Phil Gramm's declaration: "I'm gonna dance with them that brung me"—meaning his Texas supporters.

Congress now disperses power to many members and opens itself to public observation. These characteristics sharpen the inherent tension be-tween the "two Congresses." On the one hand, greater decentralization and openness enhance Congress's representative role. Members can easily hear diverse and competing constituent views. On the other hand, with so much democracy it frequently takes Congress longer to formulate public policies. Policy stalemate and immobility can result.

The coexistence of electoral and policy-making imperatives helps to explain much of Congress's behavior. Electoral incentives may promote congressional deference to the White House on some issues. For other problems Congress decisively exercises its prerogatives. In our final five chapters we explore the characteristics of congressional procedures, decision making, voting, domestic and foreign policy making, and the adjustments Congress has made to changes in its internal and external environments.

House of Representatives chamber, showing the Speaker's dais and the "well" (two lecterns) where most speeches are made.

CHAPTER ELEVEN

Congressional Rules and Procedures

During a recent Congress, Arkansas senators David Pryor and Dale Bumpers took the roles of gourmands and extolled the virtues of Arkansas rice. Their purpose was to employ the rules of the Senate, which permit filibusters (unlimited debate), to influence legislative outcomes.

"I think it is time at this point, with regard to this particular agriculture bill that is before the Senate," said Pryor, "to talk about a very, very famous recipe for Arkansas rice casserole, six servings. First, one cup of rice, uncooked. Then, Mr. President, one cup of water." [1] Pryor went on at length to explain the preparation of the dish. Bumpers, too, highlighted the nutritional benefits of Arkansas rice.

The Pryor-Bumpers discussion was intended to remind senators that unless rice producers were accorded benefits under the farm legislation, as were growers of wheat, corn, and cotton, the spring planting season would be over before the bill passed. Their filibustering strategy worked. As Bumpers noted during a discourse on the merits of Arkansas versus Iranian rice:

> [The Iranian] said: "You think your rice is long grain. You go into a grocery store in Teheran and look at Iranian rice and you will see long grain rice." He said, "We can put your rice on the grocery shelf next to ours"—well, I understand we have a deal on an amendment, so I will stop here. [2]

This episode dramatically illustrates the weight of parliamentary rules in making policy. Pryor and Bumpers used the rules to stall the bill until they won their policy objective.

Congress needs written rules to do its work. Compiling the Senate's first parliamentary manual, Thomas Jefferson stressed the importance of a known system of rules.

> It is much more material that there should be a rule to go by, than what the rule is; that there may be uniformity of proceeding in business not subject to the caprice of the Speaker or captiousness of the members. It is very material that order, decency, and regularity be preserved in a dignified public body. [3]

Jefferson recognized that *how* Congress operates affects *what* it does. Thus Congress's rules protect majority and minority rights, divide the workload, help contain conflict, ensure fair play, and distribute power among members. Because formal rules cannot cover every contingency, *precedents*—accumulated decisions of House Speakers and Senate presiding officers—fill in the gaps. These precedents are codified by House and Senate parliamentarians, printed, and distributed. There are also informal, unwritten codes of conduct such as courtesy to other members. These *folkways* are transmitted from incumbent members to newcomers.[4]

For bills to become laws, they must pass successfully through numerous veto points in each house (see Figure 11-1). Bills that fail to attract majority support at any critical juncture may never be passed. Congress, in short, is a procedural obstacle course that favors opponents of legislation and hinders proponents. This so-called "defensive advantage" promotes bargaining and compromise at each decision point.

Congressional rules are not independent of the policy and power struggles that lie behind them. There is very little that the House and Senate cannot do under the rules so long as the action is backed up by votes and inclination. Yet votes and inclination are not easily obtained, and the rules persistently challenge the proponents of legislation to demonstrate that they have both resources at their command. There is little to prevent obstruction at every turn except the tacit premise that the business of the House and Senate must go on and recognition that the rules can be redefined and prerogatives taken away or modified.

Introduction of Bills

Only members of Congress can introduce legislation. The reasons why they introduce the bills they do are fascinating and numerous.

> Lawmakers are led to their choice of legislation by many factors: parochial interest, party preference and, often, crass calculation connected to campaign fund raising. But there is a motivator that is rarely discussed that can be just as potent: a personal brush with adversity. Congress is an intensely human place where personal experience sometimes has powerful repercussions.[5]

Rep. Ronnie Flippo, D-Ala., is a strong supporter of the federal workmen's compensation program in large part because he barely survived a fall from a construction platform. Workmen's compensation provided "him and his family with a living wage even though he was unable to work. He went to college, eventually entered politics and never forgot workers' comp."[6] Personal experience, however, is not the only source of legislative proposals. Often members get ideas for bills from the executive branch, interest groups, scholars, state and local officials, and even their own staff.

Figure 11-1 How a Bill Becomes a Law

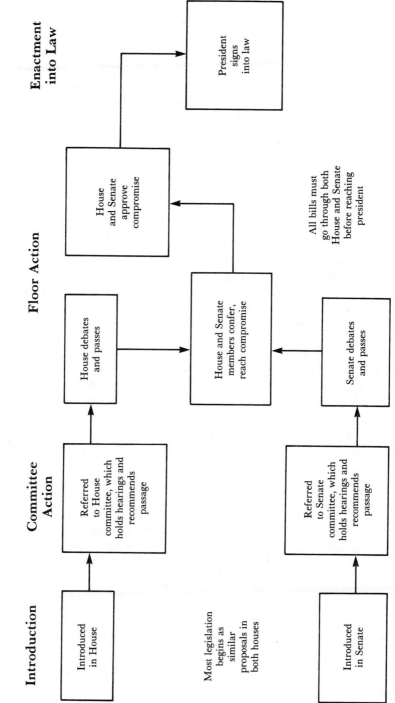

Introduction

Committee Action

Floor Action

Enactment into Law

Introduced in House

Referred to House committee, which holds hearings and recommends passage

House debates and passes

House and Senate members confer, reach compromise

House and Senate approve compromise

President signs into law

Most legislation begins as similar proposals in both houses

Introduced in Senate

Referred to Senate committee, which holds hearings and recommends passage

Senate debates and passes

All bills must go through both House and Senate before reaching president

A member who introduces a bill becomes its *sponsor*. This member may seek cosponsors to demonstrate wide support for the legislation. Outside groups, too, may urge members to cosponsor measures. "We were not assured of a hearing," said a lobbyist of a bill his group was pushing. "There was more hostility to the idea, so it was very important to line up a lot of cosponsors to show the over-all concern." [7] As important as the number of cosponsors is their leadership status and ideological stance. Cosponsors are not always like-minded politically. Massachusetts Sen. Edward Kennedy, a liberal Democrat, and Sen. Strom Thurmond of South Carolina, a conservative Republican, have, upon occasion, teamed up. Kennedy thus explained their alliance, "Whenever Strom and I introduce a bill together, it is either an idea whose time has come, or one of us has not read the bill." [8]

While it is easy to identify a bill's sponsors, it may be difficult to pinpoint its actual initiators. Legislation is "an aggregate, not a simple production," wrote Woodrow Wilson. "It is impossible to tell how many persons, opinions, and influences have entered into its composition." [9] President John F. Kennedy, for example, usually is given credit for initiating the Peace Corps. But Theodore Sorensen, Kennedy's special counsel, recalled that the Peace Corps was "based on the Mormon and other voluntary religious service efforts, on an editorial Kennedy had read years earlier, on a speech by General Gavin, on a luncheon I had with Philadelphia businessmen, on the suggestions of [Kennedy's] academic advisers, on legislation previously introduced and on the written response to a spontaneous late-night challenge he issued to Michigan students." [10] In short, the ideas behind many bills have tangled histories.

Required legislation, particularly budgetary measures, makes up much of Congress's annual agenda. Bills to authorize programs and specify how much money can be spent on them (authorization bills) and bills that actually provide the money (appropriation bills) appear on Congress's schedule at about the same time each year. Other matters recur at longer intervals, every five years perhaps. Emergency issues require Congress's immediate attention. Activist legislators also push proposals onto Congress's program. Bills not acted upon die automatically at the end of each two-year Congress. "Anybody can drop a bill into the hopper [a mahogany box near the Speaker's podium where members place their proposed bills]," said Rep. Dick Armey, R-Texas. "The question is, Can you make something happen with it?" [11]

Drafting

"As a sculptor works in stone or clay, the legislator works in words," declared one member.[12] Words are the building blocks of policy, and legislators frequently battle over adding, deleting, or modifying terms and phrases. For example, the "safe banking" bill was renamed the "Depository Institutions Deregulation and Monetary Control Act." There are no unsafe banks, the banking community protested.[13] Members sometimes give their bills catchy titles. Several legislators, for instance, sponsored the "Act for Better Child Care" so it could be easily publicized as the "ABC" bill.

Although bills are introduced only by members, anyone may draft them. Executive agencies and lobby groups often prepare measures for introduction by friendly legislators. Expert drafters in the House and Senate offices of legislative counsel assist members and committees. There are four basic types of legislation: bills, joint resolutions, concurrent resolutions, and simple resolutions (see box, page 312).

Congress nowadays acts frequently on comprehensive bills or resolutions (dubbed "packages" by the press). Packages contain an array of issues handled before as separate pieces of legislation. Their increasing use stems in part from members' reluctance to make hard political decisions without a package arrangement. As House Budget Committee chairman Leon Panetta, D-Calif., explained:

> You can use large bills as a way to hide legislation that otherwise might be more controversial, as a way to be able to slam-dunk issues that otherwise might be torn apart, as a way to avoid hard votes that Members would have to account for at election time, as a way to avoid angering special-interest groups that use votes [to decide] contributions to campaigns and as a way to guarantee that the President will have to accept it.[14]

Recent Congresses have seen fewer but bigger laws, as Table 11-1 shows.

The president, of course, plays a leading role in framing Congress's agenda. Presidential proposals reach Capitol Hill in a variety of ways, including bills, amendments, budgetary plans, or reports. While no president gets everything he wants from Congress, White House bills generally are treated as priority legislation. When President George Bush addressed Congress for the first time, he promoted several "kinder, gentler" issues—child care, education, environmental protection—that sharpened public and legislative attention to these topics.

Timing

"Everything in politics is timing," former Speaker Thomas P. O'Neill, Jr., used to say. A bill's success or failure often hinges on when it is introduced or brought to the floor. A bill that might succeed early in a session could fail as adjournment nears. On the other hand, it is sometimes possible to rush through controversial legislation during the last hectic days of a Congress.

Elections strongly influence the timing of legislation. Policy issues can be taken off or kept on Congress's agenda because of electoral circumstances—a good illustration of how the "two Congresses" are inextricably connected. "Everyone's afraid to leave without a drug bill," said Senator Bumpers about

Types of Legislation

Bill.   Most legislative proposals before Congress are in a bill form. They are designated H.R. (House of Representatives) or S. (Senate) according to where they originate, followed by a number assigned in the order in which they were introduced, from the beginning of each two-year congressional term. *Public bills* deal with general questions, and become public laws if approved by Congress and signed by the president. *Private bills* deal with individual matters, such as claims against the government, immigration and naturalization cases, and land titles. They become private laws if approved and signed.

Joint Resolution.   A joint resolution, designated H. J. Res. or S. J. Res., requires the approval of both houses and the president's signature, just as a bill does, and has the force of law. There is no significant difference between a bill and a joint resolution. The latter generally deals with limited matters, such as a single appropriation for a specific purpose. Joint resolutions also are used to propose constitutional amendments, which do not require presidential signatures, but become a part of the Constitution when three-fourths of the states have ratified them.

Concurrent Resolution.   A concurrent resolution, designated H. Con. Res. or S. Con. Res., must be passed by both houses but does not require the president's signature and does not have the force of law. Concurrent resolutions generally are used to make or amend rules applicable to both houses or to express their joint sentiment. A concurrent resolution, for example, is used to fix the time for adjournment of a Congress and to express Congress's annual budgeting plan. It might also be used to convey the congratulations of Congress to another country on the anniversary of its independence.

Resolution.   A simple resolution, designated H. Res. or S. Res., deals with matters entirely within the prerogatives of one house. It requires neither passage by the other chamber nor approval by the president and does not have the force of law. Most resolutions deal with the rules of one house. They also are used to express the sentiments of a single house, to extend condolences to the family of a deceased member, or to give "advice" on foreign policy or other executive business.

1988 election-year pressures to produce an omnibus antidrug measure.[15] With public opinion polls indicating strong voter sentiment for action on drugs, members wanted both to claim credit for addressing this issue and to avoid blame for not acting on a pressing national problem. Congress stayed in session beyond its scheduled adjournment date to pass the antidrug package. Conversely, this same 100th Congress abandoned clean air legislation in part because environmentalists "thought they could strike a better bargain" with Bush in the White House rather than Reagan.[16]

Table 11-1 Number and Length of Public Laws, 80th-99th Congresses (1947-1987)

Congress		Number of laws enacted	Total pages of statutes	Average pages per statute
80th	(1947-49)	906	2,236	2.5
81st	(1949-51)	921	2,314	2.5
82d	(1951-53)	594	1,585	2.7
83d	(1953-55)	781	1,899	2.4
84th	(1955-57)	1,028	1,848	1.8
85th	(1957-59)	936	2,435	2.6
86th	(1959-61)	800	1,774	2.2
87th	(1961-63)	885	2,078	2.3
88th	(1963-65)	666	1,975	3.0
89th	(1965-67)	810	2,912	3.6
90th	(1967-69)	640	2,304	3.6
91st	(1969-71)	695	2,927	4.2
92d	(1971-73)	607	2,330	3.8
93d	(1973-75)	649	3,443	5.3
94th	(1975-77)	588	4,121	7.0
95th	(1977-79)	633	5,403	8.5
96th	(1979-81)	613	4,947	8.1
97th	(1981-83)	473	4,343	9.2
98th	(1983-85)	623	4,893	7.8
99th	(1985-87)	664	7,198	10.8

Source: Norman J. Ornstein, Thomas E. Mann, and Michael J. Malbin, eds., *Vital Statistics on Congress, 1987-1988* (Washington, D.C.: Congressional Quarterly, 1987), 170.

Referral of Bills

After they are introduced, bills are referred to appropriate standing committees by the Senate presiding officer or the House Speaker. Committee jurisdictions and committee actions are discussed in Chapter 7, so here we will pass over this stage of legislation very quickly. A bill's phraseology can affect its referral and hence its chances of passage. This political fact of life means that members use words artfully when drafting legislation. The objective is to encourage the referral of their measures to sympathetic rather than hostile committees. If a bill mentions taxes, for example, it invariably is referred to the tax panels. To sidestep these committees, Sen. Pete Domenici, R-N.M., avoided the word *tax* in a bill proposing a charge on waterborne freight.

If the waterway fee were considered a tax—which it was, basically, because it would raise revenues for the federal treasury—the rules would place it under the dominion of the Senate's tax-writing arm, the Finance Committee. But Finance was chaired by Russell B. Long, of Louisiana, whose state included two of the world's biggest barge ports and who was, accordingly, an implacable foe of waterway charges in any form. Domenici knew that Long could find several years' worth of bills to consider before he would voluntarily schedule a hearing on S. 790 [the Domenici bill]. For this reason, [Domenici staff aides] had been careful to avoid the word *tax* in writing the bill, employing such terms as *charge* and *fee* instead.[17]

Domenici's drafting strategy worked; his bill was jointly referred to the Commerce and Environment committees.

Of the thousands of bills introduced annually, Congress takes up relatively few. A total of 10,588 public bills and joint resolutions were introduced during the 100th Congress; of these 1,391 were reported from committee, and only 713 became public laws. But there has been a veritable explosion of so-called "commemorative bills" that designate special days, weeks, or months and name federal buildings and sites after deceased former members of Congress and others. Figure 11-2 divides all public laws enacted between 1977 and 1985 into one of three broad categories based on their short titles: commemorative, administrative, and substantive. The proportion of commemorative enactments soared from about 4 percent in 1977 to nearly 60 percent in 1985; major substantive enactments declined from 83 percent to 30 percent. In sum, the 1980s witnessed fewer free-standing substantive enactments, more symbolic or commemorative enactments, and a tendency to embody numerous important programmatic changes in a small number of omnibus packages.

Members rely on committees to screen these various kinds of bills. House and Senate committees are governed by rules of procedure regarding the convening of hearings and meetings, proxy voting, and quorum requirements. House and Senate rules require, for example, that a majority of the full committee be physically present to report out any measure. If this rule is violated, a point of order can be made against the proposal on the floor.

Bills reported from committee have passed a critical stage in the lawmaking process. The next major step is reaching the House or Senate floor for debate and amendment. Our beginning point is the House because money matters (tax and appropriation bills) originate there—the first under the Constitution, the second by custom.

Scheduling in the House

All bills reported from committee are listed in chronological order on one of several *calendars,* lists that enable the House to put measures into convenient

Figure 11-2 Major Categories of Public Laws, 1977-1985

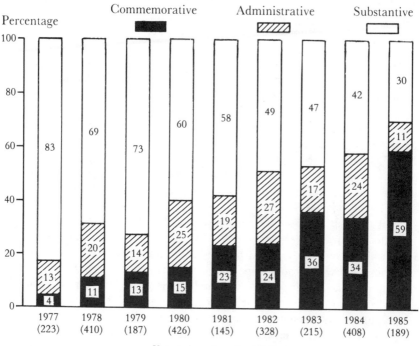

Year and number of public laws

Source: Roger H. Davidson, "The Legislative Work of Congress" (Paper presented at the annual meeting of the APSA, Washington, D.C., August 28, 1986), 54.

Note: *Substantive* public laws involve major or general policy decisions, including appropriations, authorizations, or substantive amendments to authorizations. *Administrative* laws are administrative decisions that do not involve major policy choices. Examples include Indian tribal claims settlements, land conveyances, interstate compacts, actions pertaining to the legislative process, and other administrative actions such as compensation adjustments and dispersion of income. The *commemorative* category includes designation of federal buildings or other facilities; authorization of commemorative days, weeks, or months; authorization of special medals; or granting of federal charters to organizations.

categories. Bills that raise or spend money are assigned to the so-called Union Calendar. The House Calendar contains all other major public measures. Private bills, such as immigration requests or claims against the government, are assigned to the Private Calendar, and noncontroversial bills are placed on the Consent Calendar. There is no guarantee that the House will debate legislation placed on the calendars. The Speaker and majority leader largely determine if, when, and in what order bills come up.

Shortcuts for Minor Bills

Whether a bill is major or minor, controversial or noncontroversial, will influence the procedure that is employed to bring it before the House. Most bills are relatively minor and are taken up and passed via the following shortcut procedures.

One shortcut is the designation of special days for considering minor bills. Measures on the Consent Calendar, for example, are in order for floor consideration on the first and third Mondays of the month. Bills brought up from the Consent Calendar, which cannot involve expenditures of over $1 million, are invariably passed with little debate by unanimous consent. (Members may speak briefly on the measure by "reserving the right to object," saying their piece, and then withdrawing the objection.) In fact, unanimous consent ranks first among the various procedural routes to the floor, which highlights the noncontroversial nature of much of the House's legislative agenda (see Table 11-2).

Another shortcut is the suspension-of-the-rules procedure, which is controlled by the Speaker through his power of recognition. Today roughly 30 percent of the measures passed by the House are considered under suspension, compared with around 8 percent a quarter century ago. Members may use this time-saving device every Monday and Tuesday to pass relatively noncontroversial measures. The procedure permits only forty minutes of debate, allows no amendments, and requires two-thirds vote for passage.

House members sometimes complain that weighty bills are rushed through under suspension, often late in the session. As journalist Elizabeth Drew observed:

> The theory is that this is an efficient way of clearing noncontroversial proposals, but the suspension procedure is used also for other purposes: to slip bills through or to deny members an opportunity to amend them, under the pretense that if a bill is on the suspension calendar it is by definition noncontroversial.[18]

In 1979 the use of suspension was limited. The Speaker cannot schedule for suspensions any bill exceeding $100 million in expenditures in any fiscal year unless authorized to do so by the Democratic Steering and Policy Committee.

Major measures reach the floor by different procedures. Budget, appropriation, and certain other measures are considered "privileged" and may be called up from the appropriate calendar for debate at almost any time. However, most major bills do not have an automatic "green light" to the floor. They get there by first obtaining a "rule" from the Rules Committee. Table 11-2 shows the proportion of measures that reach the floor under these various procedures.

The Strategic Role of the Rules Committee

Since the very first Congress there has been a House Rules Committee. During its early years, the committee prepared or ratified a biennial set of

Table 11-2   Procedural Route to the House Floor, 98th-100th
Congresses (1983-1989)

| | Percentage of measures | | |
Procedure	98th ($N = 1,461$)	99th ($N = 1,425$)	100th ($N = 1,543$)
Unanimous consent	34	38	30
Suspension of the rules	29	30	40
Privileged matter	20	19	14
Rules from Rules Committee	9	6	6
Private Calendar	4	3	5
Consent Calendar	3	2	2
Special procedures	1	2	1[a]

Source: Ilona B. Nickels, Congressional Research Service, April 1989.
[a] Less than 1 percent.

House rules and then went out of existence. As House procedures became more complex, the committee became more important. In 1858 the Speaker became a member of the committee and the next year its chairman. In 1880 Rules became a permanent standing committee. Three years later the committee launched a procedural "revolution": it began to issue *rules* (sometimes called *special orders*)—privileged resolutions that grant priority for floor consideration to virtually all major bills.

Because House rules require bills to be taken up in the chronological order listed on the calendars, many substantial bills would never reach the floor before Congress adjourned. The Rules Committee can put major bills first in line. Equally important, a rule from the committee sets the conditions for debate and amendment.

A request for a rule usually is made by the chairman of the committee reporting the bill. The Rules Committee conducts hearings on the request in the same way other committees consider legislation, except that only members testify. The House parliamentarian drafts the rule after consulting with committee leaders and staff. The rule is considered on the House floor and voted on in the same manner as regular bills (see box, page 318).

Types of Rules.   Traditionally, rules granted by the Rules Committee have been either open, closed, modified, or waived. Many bills receive an *open rule,* which means that any and all germane amendments can be proposed. Of the 138 rules granted during the 100th Congress, 79 were open, fewer than in the 95th to 98th Congresses (see Table 11-3). This general decline reflects efforts by the majority leadership to ensure greater predictabil-

---

Example of a Rule from the Rules Committee

Following are excerpts of a Rules Committee special order (rule), H. Res. 360, setting the terms of House debate on a 1988 bill, H. R. 3396, providing for the rehiring of certain air traffic controllers.

Resolved, That at any time after the adoption of this resolution the Speaker may, pursuant to clause 1(b) of rule XXIII, declare the House resolved into the Committee of the Whole House on the State of the Union for the consideration of the bill (H.R. 3396) to provide for the rehiring of certain former air traffic controllers, and the first reading of the bill shall be dispensed with. After general debate, which shall be confined to the bill and which shall not exceed one hour, to be equally divided and controlled by the chairman and ranking minority member of the Committee on Post Office and Civil Service, the bill shall be considered for amendment under the five-minute rule and each section shall be considered as having been read. At the conclusion of the consideration of the bill for amendment, the Committee shall rise and report the bill to the House with such amendments as may have been adopted, and the previous question shall be considered as ordered on the bill and amendments thereto to final passage without intervening motion except one motion to recommit.

Source: *Congressional Record,* 100th Cong., 2d sess., March 29, 1988, H1260.

---

ity in the amending process. A *closed rule* prohibits the offering of amendments. A *modified rule* permits amendments to some parts of the bill but not to others. *Waivers of points of order* set aside technical violations of House rules to allow bills to reach the floor.

During the 1980s, majority members of the Rules Committee displayed great procedural creativity and imagination. No longer is it sufficient to classify rules in the traditional manner (see box, page 320). "Instead of choosing from among a few patterns the Rules Committee has demonstrated a willingness to create unique designs by recombining an increasingly wide array of elements, or by creating new ones as the need arises, to help leaders, committees, and members manage the heightened uncertainties of decisionmaking on the House floor." [19]

The trend toward complex rules reflects several developments: the desire of majority leaders to exert greater control over floor procedures, members' restlessness with dilatory floor challenges to committee-reported bills, wider use of multiple referrals, and efforts by committee leaders to keep unfriendly amendments off the floor.

In summary, rules establish the conditions under which most major bills are debated and amended. They determine the length of introductory debate,

Table 11-3 Open and Restrictive Rules, 95th-100th Congresses
(1977-1989)

Congress	Total rules granted	Open rules Number	Open rules Percent	Restrictive rules Number	Restrictive rules Percent
95th (1977-79)	241	213	88	28	12
96th (1979-81)	198	161	81	37	19
97th (1981-83)	112	90	80	22	20
98th (1983-85)	145	105	72	40	28
99th (1985-87)	101	65	64	36	36
100th (1987-89)	138	79	57	59	43

Source: Survey of Activities, Committee on Rules, 95th-99th Congresses; Notices of Action Taken, Committee on Rules, 100th Congress (as of October 21, 1988). Published in *Congressional Record,* daily edition, October 21, 1988, E 3656-7.

permit or prohibit amendments, and may waive points of order. They are sometimes as important to a bill's fate as being favorably reported from committee.

Arm of the Majority Leadership.   Originally, the Rules Committee was an agent of the majority leadership. In 1910 the House rebelled against the arbitrary decisions of Speaker Joseph Cannon, R-Ill., and removed him from the committee. During subsequent decades, the committee became an independent power. It extracted substantive concessions in bills in exchange for rules. It blocked measures it opposed and advanced those it favored, often reflecting the wishes of the House's conservative coalition of Republicans and southern Democrats.

The chairman of the Rules Committee from 1955 to 1967, Howard W. "Judge" Smith, D-Va., was a master at devising delaying tactics. He might quickly adjourn meetings for lack of a quorum, allow requests for rules to languish, or refuse to schedule meetings. House consideration of the 1957 civil rights bill was temporarily delayed because Smith absented himself from the Capitol. His committee could not meet without him. Smith said he was seeing about a barn that had burned on his Virginia farm. Retorted Speaker Sam Rayburn, "I knew Howard Smith would do most anything to block a civil rights bill, but I never knew he would resort to arson." [20]

Liberal frustration with the coalition of conservatives who dominated the committee boiled over. After President Kennedy was elected in 1960, Speaker Rayburn realized he needed greater control over the Rules Committee if the House was to process the president's "New Frontier" program. This led to a titanic struggle between Smith and Rayburn over the latter's proposal to enlarge the committee from twelve to fifteen members.

Examples of Creative Rules

King-of-the-Mountain (or Hill) Rule.   To accommodate diverse factional preferences, the Rules Committee will outline a procedure that permits several major alternatives (or substitutes) to be offered to the legislation under consideration. However, no matter the outcome—yea or nay—on any of the substitutes, the king-of-the-hill procedure stipulates that the vote on the last substitute is the one that counts for purposes of accepting or rejecting national policy. As one Republican representative explained in discussing Democratic and GOP substitutes: "Debate your alternative; debate our alternative; vote on our alternative, and if it wins or fails, then you go to the majority proposal, and if it wins, you prevail because it is the king of the hill. The last to be voted on that passes, wins." [1]

Self-Executing Rule.   This special order provides that when the House adopts a rule it has also agreed simultaneously to pass another measure or matter. Adoption of a self-executing rule means that the House has passed one or more other proposals at the same time. Whether this rule is controversial or not usually depends on the nature of the policy being agreed to in the "two for one" vote.

Restrictive Rule.   The essential feature of this type of rule is that it limits the "freedom of Members to offer germane amendments to the bills made in order by those rules." [2] During the 1980s, there has been a steady increase in the number of restrictive rules. Rank-and-file members, especially Republicans, often rail against these rules because they restrict their opportunities to amend committee-reported measures or majority party initiatives.

Multiple-Step Rule.   This type of rule facilitates an orderly amendment process. One variation is for the Rules Committee to report a rule that regulates the debating and amending process for specific portions of a bill and then report another follow-on rule to govern the remainder of the measure and amendments to it. [3] Another variation is for the Rules Committee to state publicly that if a measure encounters difficulties on the floor, the panel "reserves its right to report a subsequent rule ... which might limit time for further debate or further amendments." [4]

Anticipatory Rule.   To expedite decision making on the floor, the Rules Committee may grant a rule even before the measure or matter to which it would apply has been reported by a House committee or conference committee. "In past years we used to call this buying a pig in a poke," said one Rules opponent of an anticipatory rule, "but now the language has been updated." [5]

1. *Congressional Record,* 100th Cong., 3d sess., March 3, 1988, H644.
2. *Congressional Record,* 100th Cong., 2d sess., July 7, 1988, H5352.
3. For an example, see *Congressional Record,* 100th Cong., 2d sess., April 26, 1988, H2496.
4. *Congressional Record,* 98th Cong., 1st sess., October 20, 1983, H8473.
5. *Congressional Record,* 100th Cong., 2d sess., May 26, 1988, H3689.

Superficially, the Representatives seemed to be quarreling about next to nothing: the membership of the committee. In reality, however, the question raised had grave import for the House and for the United States. The House's answer to it affected the tenuous balance of power between the great conservative and liberal blocs within the House. And, doing so, the House's answer seriously affected the response of Congress to the sweeping legislative proposals of the newly elected President, John Kennedy.[21]

In a dramatic vote the House agreed to expand the Rules Committee. Two new Democrats and one Republican were added, which loosened the conservative coalition's grip on the panel.

With the changes of the 1970s, the Rules Committee came under even greater majority party control. In 1973 the Democratic Caucus limited the committee's authority to grant closed rules. Two years later the caucus authorized the Speaker to appoint, subject to party ratification, all Democratic members of the Rules Committee. (Thirteen years later Republicans authorized their leader to name the GOP members of the Rules Committee.) The majority party maintains a disproportionate ratio on the panel (nine Democrats and four Republicans in the 101st Congress).

According to the former chairman of the Rules Committee, Claude Pepper, D-Fla., Speaker Jim Wright of Texas acted "more upon the assumption that the Rules Committee is a branch of the leadership than Speaker O'Neill did. Sometimes members chafe a little at that." [22] Republicans, in particular, protested the Rules Committee's formulation of rules that restricted their opportunities to offer amendments to major legislation and that provided tactical advantages to the Democratic party. When the House considered a defense authorization bill, the rule structured the amendment process so that Democratic members could balance antidefense with prodefense votes. The rule

> ensured that votes on important "anti-Reagan" amendments would be separated by roll calls on less crucial issues, so that moderates and conservatives could cast a "pro-defense" vote following particularly controversial amendments on which the leadership wanted a vote against the administration position.[23]

One GOP leader became so outraged at such rules that he dubbed them CRAP (Creative Rule Alteration Procedures) because they "restrict the rights of Members and distort normal legislative procedure beyond all recognition and rationality for narrow partisan purposes." In rebuttal, Rep. Thomas S. Foley, D-Wash., claimed that the real Republican complaint "is not to House procedures, but to the policies achieved with those procedures." [24] In June 1989 Foley was elected to succeed Wright as Speaker of the House.

Dislodging a Bill from Committee

Committees do not necessarily reflect the point of view of the full chamber. What happens when a standing committee refuses to report a bill, or when the Rules Committee does not grant a rule? To circumvent committees, members have three options but they are extraordinary actions and are seldom successful: the discharge petition, the Calendar Wednesday rule, and the device that enables the Rules Committee to extract a bill from committee.

The *discharge petition* permits the House to relieve a committee from jurisdiction over a stalled measure. If a committee does not report a bill within thirty days after the bill was referred to it, any member may file a discharge motion (petition) requiring the signature of 218 members, a majority of the House. Once the signatures are obtained, the discharge motion is placed on the Discharge Calendar for seven days and then can be called up on the second and fourth Mondays of the month by any member who signed it. If the discharge motion is passed, the bill is taken up right away. Since 1910, when the discharge rule was adopted, only two discharged measures have ever become law. Its threatened use, however, may stimulate a committee to act on a bill.

The discharge rule, with several variations, also applies to the Rules Committee. A motion to discharge the committee is in order seven days, rather than thirty days, after a bill has been before it. Any member may enter a motion to discharge the committee. This rarely happens. The last time the Rules Committee was discharged was in 1982 on a proposed constitutional amendment to balance the budget.

Adopted in 1909, the *Calendar Wednesday rule* provides that on Wednesdays committees may bring up from the House or Union calendars their measures that have not received a rule from the Rules Committee. Calendar Wednesday is cumbersome to employ, seldom used, and generally dispensed with by unanimous consent. Since 1943 fewer than fifteen measures have been enacted into law under this procedure.[25]

Finally, the Rules Committee has the power of extraction. It can introduce rules making bills in order for House debate even if the bills have not been reported by standing committees. Based on an 1895 precedent, this is akin to discharging committees without the 218-signature requirement. Again, this procedure is seldom used and stirs sharp controversy among members who think it usurps the rights of the other committees.

House Floor Procedures

The House normally meets Monday through Friday, usually convening at noon. At the beginning of each day's session, bells ring throughout the Capitol and the House office buildings, summoning representatives to the floor. The signal bells also ring to notify members of votes, quorum calls, recesses, and adjournments. Typically, the opening activities include a daily prayer; approval of the *Journal* (a constitutionally required record of the previous day's proceedings); receipt of messages from the president or the Senate; announcements, if any, by the Speaker; and one-minute speeches by members on any topic.

Preliminary House proceedings also include recitation of the Pledge of Allegiance. The practice, which began in the fall of 1988, grew out of partisan politics. House Republicans, who wanted to embarrass Democrats and aid their presidential nominee George Bush, introduced a surprise resolution on the floor to require daily recitation of the pledge. (On the campaign trail Bush repeatedly criticized Democratic nominee Michael Dukakis for vetoing a state law requiring teachers to lead their pupils in the pledge.) The Democrats voted to quash the resolution, but quickly they recognized their electoral predicament. They did not want to appear unpatriotic, especially those facing tough reelection contests, or in opposition to Dukakis's position. The end result: the majority leadership instituted the practice of having a Democrat and then a Republican alternate in leading the House in the Pledge of Allegiance.[26]

After these preliminaries, the House generally begins considering legislation. For a major bill a set pattern is observed: adoption of the rule, convening as a Committee of the Whole, general debate, amending, and final passage.

Adoption of the Rule

The Speaker, after consulting the majority leader and affected committee chairmen, generally decides when the House will debate a bill and under what kind of rule. When the scheduled day arrives, the Speaker recognizes a majority member of the Rules Committee for one hour to explain the rule's contents. By custom, the majority member yields half the time for debate to a minority member of the Rules Committee. At the end of the debate, which often takes less than the allotted hour, the House votes on the rule.

Opponents of a bill can try to defeat its rule and avert House action on the bill itself. But rules seldom are defeated because the Rules Committee is sensitive to the wishes of the House. Once the rule is adopted, the House is governed by its provisions. Most rules state that "at any time after the adoption of [the rule] the Speaker may declare the House resolved into the Committee of the Whole."

Committee of the Whole

The Committee of the Whole House on the State of the Union is a parliamentary artifice to expedite consideration of legislation. It is just the House in another form with different rules. For example, a quorum in the Committee of the Whole is only 100 members compared with 218 for the House. The Speaker appoints a majority party colleague to preside over the committee, which then begins general debate.

General Debate

A rule from the Rules Committee specifies the amount of time, usually one to two hours, for a general discussion of the bill. More controversial bills will require more time, perhaps four to ten hours. Control of the time is divided equally between the majority and minority floor managers—usually the chairman and ranking minority member of the committee or subcommittee that reported the legislation. The majority floor manager's job is to guide the bill to final passage; the minority floor manager may seek to amend or kill the bill.

After the floor managers make their opening statements, they parcel out several minutes to colleagues on their side of the aisle who wish to speak. General debate rarely lives up to its name. Most legislators read prepared speeches; give-and-take exchange occurs infrequently.

The Amending Phase

The amending process is the heart of decision making on the floor of the House. Amendments determine the final shape of bills and often dominate public discussion, as have Illinois Republican Henry J. Hyde's repeated amendments barring the use of federal funds for abortions.

An amendment in the Committee of the Whole is considered under the *five-minute rule,* which gives the sponsor five minutes to defend it and an opponent five minutes to talk against it. The amendment may then be brought to a vote. Amendments regularly are debated, however, for more than ten minutes. Legislators gain the floor by saying, "I move to strike the last word" or "I move to strike the requisite number of words." These pro forma amendments, which make no alteration in the pending matter, simply give members five minutes of debate time.

If there is an open rule, opponents may try to load down a bill with so many objectionable amendments that it will sink of its own weight. The reverse strategy is to propose "sweetener" amendments that attract members' support. Offering numerous amendments is an effective dilatory tactic because each amendment must be read in full, debated at least five to ten minutes, and then voted upon.

In this amending phase the interconnection of the "two Congresses" is evident: amendments can have electoral as well as legislative consequences. For example, Democratic representative Richard Stallings won a heavily Republican district in Idaho in 1984. Majority party leaders "called attention to his work on behalf of Idaho farmers by assigning him the visible job of offering perfecting amendments to the 1985 farm bill. Stallings, considered one of the vulnerable members in 1986, won reelection with 54 percent of the vote." [27] Two years later he won again.

The minority party's policy preferences often are expressed through amendments. "Since the liberal leadership more often than not refuses to schedule hearings on our bills," wrote a GOP member, "we counter by offering our legislation in the form of amendments to other bills scheduled for consideration by the House." [28] Again, the nature of the rule shapes amendment opportunities. Even some restrictive rules can be used to advantage by the minority party. As the GOP whip pointed out:

What happens when we have these restrictive rules, a rule that requires that we have a printing in the *Record* by a certain date in order for that amendment to be considered? Well, one thing that it does is cause the proliferation of amendments. . . . I am guilty of that myself. When you see you are fixin' to be cut off and not be able to have an opportunity to offer an amendment, then you start conjuring up all possible amendments, and you put them in the *Record*.[29]

The minority also guards the floor to demand explanations or votes on amendments brought up by the majority. Since 1981 the self-appointed GOP "watchdog" has been Rep. Robert S. Walker of Pennsylvania. He has portrayed the role as difficult and lonely. "You don't win much in the way of popularity contests when you're always trying to throw your body in front of other people's steamrollers," he said. "It's not a popular thing to constantly raise questions in areas where people don't want you to." [30]

Voting

Prior to passage of the 1970 Legislative Reorganization Act, the Committee of the Whole adopted or rejected amendments by voice votes or other votes with no public record of who voted and how. Today any legislator supported by twenty-five colleagues can obtain a *recorded* vote. How members decide which way to vote is principally discussed in Chapter 12; here we focus on the mechanics of voting.

With the installation of an electronic voting system in 1973, members insert their personalized cards (about the size of a credit card) into one of more than forty voting stations on the floor and press the Yea, Nay, or Present button. A large electronic display board behind the press gallery provides a running tally of the total votes for or against a motion (see photo, page 306). The voting tally, said a representative, is watched carefully by many members.

I find that a lot of times, people walk in, and the first thing they do is look at the board, and they have key people they check out, and if those people have voted "aye," they go to the machine and vote "aye" and walk off the floor.

But I will look at the board and see how [members of the state delegation] vote, because they are in districts right next to me, and they have constituencies just like mine. I will vote the way I am going to vote except that if they are both different, I will go up and say "Why did you vote that way? Let me know if there is something I am missing." [31]

After all pending amendments have been voted upon, the Committee of the Whole "rises." The chairman hands the gavel back to the Speaker and a quorum once again becomes 218 members.

Final Passage

As specified in the rule, the full House must review the actions of its "agent," the Committee of the Whole. The Speaker announces that under the rule the *previous question* has been ordered, which means that no further debate is permitted on the bill or its amendments. The Speaker then asks if any representative wants a separate vote on any amendment. If not, all the amendments agreed to in the committee will be approved. The next important step is the recommittal motion. It provides a way for the House to return (or recommit) the bill to the committee that reported it. By custom, the request is always made by a minority party member who opposes the legislation. Recommittal motions rarely succeed, but they do serve to protect the rights of the minority. Following the motion's defeat, the Speaker will say, "The question is on passage of the bill." Final passage is often by recorded vote.

Passage by the House marks the half-way point in the lawmaking process. The Senate must also approve the bill, and its procedures are strikingly different from those of the House.

Scheduling in the Senate

Compared with the larger and more clamorous House, which needs and adheres to well-defined rules and precedents, the Senate operates more informally. And unlike the House, whose rules permit a determined majority to make decisions, the Senate's rules emphasize individual prerogatives and minority rights (those of the minority party, a faction, or even one senator). "The Senate," said J. Bennett Johnston, D-La., "is run for the convenience of one Senator to the inconvenience of 99." [32] Moreover, what requires a simple majority to pass the House may require a supermajority in the Senate. Proponents of legislation may need to attract sixty votes to break a filibuster (extended debate) before they can get a final vote on the measure. No wonder some commentators say the Senate has only two rules: unanimous consent and exhaustion.

The scheduling system for the Senate is relatively simple: one calendar for all public and private bills (the Calendar of General Orders) and another for treaties and nominations (the Executive Calendar). It has nothing comparable to the scheduling duties of the House Rules Committee, and the majority and minority leadership actively cooperate in scheduling.

In 1988 the Senate leadership began a "three week-one week" experimental schedule to give senators more certainty and predictability in scheduling. This scheduling experiment continued in the 101st Congress. For every month, the Senate was in session for three weeks, Monday through Friday, and out of session for one week. As the majority leader stated:

> The 1 week out of session is not giving Senators anything. I am not doing it for the convenience of Senators, to give them a week off. That is not the point and they know that. They have work to do. They have work to do back in their States. They have work to do here. Committee work can go on and it would be unimpeded and uninterrupted by rollcalls and quorum calls. [33]

Legislation typically reaches the Senate floor in two ways: by unanimous consent or by motion. Unanimous consent is of utmost importance, and its use is regulated by the majority leader in consultation with the minority leader.

Unanimous Consent Agreements

The Senate frequently dispenses with its formal rules and instead follows privately negotiated agreements submitted to the Senate for its unanimous approval (see box, page 328). The objective is to expedite work in an institution known for extended debate. As Tom Daschle of South Dakota, cochairman of the Senate Democratic Policy Committee, pointed out:

> We aren't bringing [measures] to the floor unless we have [a unanimous consent] agreement. We could bring child-care legislation to the floor right now, but that would mean two months of fighting. We want to maximize productive time by trying to work out as much as we can in advance [of floor action].[34]

Unanimous consent agreements limit debate on the bill, any amendments, and various motions. Occasionally, they specify the time for the vote on final passage and impose constraints on the amendment process. For example, to facilitate enactment of an omnibus crime package that contained provisions with widespread Senate support, senators agreed to a unanimous consent request barring floor amendments on controversial issues such as gun control or the death penalty.[35]

The Senate's unanimous consent agreements are functional equivalents of special orders from the House Rules Committee. They waive the rules of their respective chambers, and each must be approved by the members, in one case by majority vote and in the other by unanimous consent. However, senators and aides draft unanimous consent agreements privately, whereas the Rules Committee hears requests for special orders in public session.

Ways to Extract Bills from Committee

If a bill is blocked in committee, the Senate can do one of several things to obtain floor action: add the bill as a nongermane floor amendment to another bill, bypass the committee stage by placing the bill directly on the calendar, suspend the rules, or discharge the bill from committee. Only the first procedure is effective; the other three are somewhat difficult to employ and seldom succeed.[36]

Because the Senate has no general germaneness or relevancy rule, senators can take an agriculture bill that is stuck in committee and add it as a nongermane floor amendment to a pending health bill. "Amendments may be made," Thomas Jefferson noted long ago, "so as to totally alter the nature of the proposition." Most unanimous consent agreements, however, prohibit nongermane amendments.[37]

Example of a Unanimous Consent Agreement

The unanimous consent agreement the Senate followed in debating S. 20, the Whistleblower Protection Act of 1989.

Ordered, That on Thursday, March 16, 1989 at 10:30 a.m., the Senate proceed to the consideration of S. 20, the Whistleblower Protection Act of 1989, and that no amendments be in order except an amendment to be offered by the Senator from Michigan (Mr. Levin), to remove the independent litigating authority of the special counsel and to strengthen the confidentiality protection of the whistleblower, on which there shall be 30 minutes, equally divided, and an amendment to be offered by the Senator from Kansas (Mr. Dole), regarding the desecration of the flag, on which there shall be 30 minutes, equally divided.

Ordered further, That time for a debate on the bill be limited to 30 minutes, to be equally divided and controlled, respectively, by the Senator from Michigan (Mr. Levin) and the Senator from Delaware (Mr. Roth), or their designees.

Ordered further, That no motion to recommit the bill, with or without instructions, be in order.

Ordered further, That the motion to reconsider the vote on passage of the bill be laid upon the table.

Ordered further, That the agreement be in the usual form.

Ordered further, That any roll call votes ordered with respect to S. 20 be stacked to occur, in sequence, beginning at 2:00 p.m. *(Mar. 15, 1989).*

Source: Senate of the United States, Calendar of Business, Thursday, March 16, 1989, 2.

Senate Floor Procedures

The Senate, like the House, regularly convenes at noon, sometimes earlier. Typically it opens with prayer; approval of the *Journal;* statements by the party leaders; routine business (the "morning hour"), such as the introduction of bills and receipt of messages; brief speeches by members; and then unfinished business or new business made in order by a unanimous consent agreement.

Normal Routine

For most bills the Senate follows these steps:

—The majority leader secures the unanimous consent of the Senate to an arrangement that specifies when a bill will be brought to the floor and the conditions for debating it.

—The presiding officer recognizes the majority and minority floor managers for brief opening statements.

—Amendments are then in order, with debate regulated by the terms of the unanimous consent agreement.
—There is a roll-call vote on final passage.

As in the House, amendments in the Senate serve different purposes. For example, floor managers might accept "as many amendments as they can without undermining the purposes of the bill, in order to build the broadest possible consensus behind it." [38] Some amendments bestow benefits to the electorate and can embarrass members who must vote against them. "My amendment can be characterized as a 'November amendment,' " remarked Sen. Jesse Helms, R-N.C., "because the vote . . . will provide an opportunity for Senators to go home and say, 'I voted to reduce Federal taxes' and 'I voted to cut Federal spending.' " [39]

Senators are nearly always eager to offer amendments to bills, especially to bills taken up just before Congress adjourns. For instance, scores of amendments were introduced to an electorally popular antidrug measure near the end of the 100th Congress. To expedite consideration of the drug bill, the bipartisan Senate leadership hammered out an unusual agreement to prevent the measure from bogging down with irrelevant amendments. An ad hoc bipartisan task force of four senior senators was created to decide which amendments would be offered. [40] This informal screening unit, which functioned somewhat like the House Rules Committee, highlights the informality that characterizes much of Senate procedure.

A bill is brought to a final vote whenever senators stop talking. This can be a long process, particularly in the absence of a unanimous consent agreement. On some bills unanimous consent agreements are foreclosed because of deliberate obstructive tactics, particularly the filibuster. In these instances bills cannot be voted upon until the filibuster has ended.

Filibusters

Generally, filibusters involve numerous blocking tactics besides extended debate—senators holding the floor for hours of endless speeches. Many contemporary filibusters are waged by those who skillfully utilize Senate rules. For example, they might offer numerous amendments, raise many points of order (parliamentary objections), or demand numerous and consecutive roll-call votes.

The right of extended debate is unique to the Senate. Any senator or group of senators can talk continuously in the hope of delaying, modifying, or defeating legislation. In 1957 Strom Thurmond, R-S.C., then a Democrat, set the record for the Senate's longest solo performance—twenty-four hours and eighteen minutes—trying to kill a civil rights bill.

The success of a filibuster depends not only on how long it takes, but also on when in the year it is waged. Late in a session a filibuster can be most effective because there is insufficient time to break it. [41] Needless to say, even the threat of a filibuster—the *silent filibuster*—can encourage accommodations or compromises between proponents and opponents of legislation. (Another form of silent filibuster is called the *hold,* which permits one or more senators to block floor action on measures or matters by asking their party leaders not to schedule them.)

Defenders say filibusters protect minority rights, permit thorough consideration of bills, and dramatize issues. Critics contend that they enable small minorities to extort unwanted concessions. During most of its history, the Senate had no way to terminate debate except by unanimous consent. In 1917 the Senate adopted Rule XXII, its first *cloture* (debate-ending) rule. After several revisions Rule XXII now permits three-fifths of the Senate (sixty of one hundred members) to shut off debate on substantive issues. Once cloture is invoked, there still remain thirty hours of debate time on the pending matter before the final vote. Thus, it is possible to stretch out the thirty hours for several days, producing what senators refer to as *postcloture filibusters.*

Senators complain about the frequent use of filibusters and cloture attempts. Once filibusters occurred on issues of great national importance; today they occur on a wide range of less momentous topics. "During the 25 years from 1940 to 1965," noted Senator Pryor, "there were only 18 filibusters in the Senate. During the 22 years since then, the number of filibusters skyrocketed to 88." [42] Attempts to invoke cloture also have increased, from twelve during the 90th and 91st Congresses to forty-three during the 98th and 99th Congresses. Moreover, the norm of one cloture vote per measure has changed. The modern Senate reached a record of eight cloture votes (all unsuccessful) on a controversial campaign financing measure during the 100th Congress.

The surge in filibusters and cloture attempts stems from a variety of factors. Among them is the influx of many senators who prefer to push their own agendas even if the Senate's institutional activities grind to a halt. The Senate amended Rule XXII in 1975 to make it easier to invoke cloture, and the filibuster is simply more potent in a Senate that today is workload packed and deadline driven. Some senators have recommended that cloture be made more difficult to invoke and more effective once invoked. Others have urged a return to greater comity among senators so the balance between institutional interests and individual prerogatives can be restored.

Resolving House-Senate Differences

The House and Senate must pass bills in identical form before they can be sent to the president. If neither chamber will accept the other's changes, a House-Senate conference committee must reconcile the differences. Conference committees meet to resolve the matters in dispute; they are not to reconsider provisions already agreed to. Neither are they to insert new matter.

But because congressional rules are not self-enforcing, members must object on .the floor to prevent new matter from appearing in conference reports.

Most public laws are approved without conferences. However, about 10 to 15 percent of the measures passed by Congress—usually the most important and controversial—are subject to bicameral reconciliation by conference committees. There are, of course, controversial measures that are not sent to conference. For example, sometimes conferences are deliberately avoided by the proponents of a measure to prevent an end-of-session Senate filibuster that might kill the legislation.

Selection of Conferees

Conferees usually are named from the committee or committees that reported the legislation. Congressional rules state that the Speaker and Senate presiding officer select conferees; actually, the decision is made by the respective chairmen and ranking minority members.

Each chamber may name as many conferees as it wants, and in recent years some conference delegations have grown quite large. The 1981 omnibus reconciliation conference set the record, with more than 250 conferees working in 58 subconferences.

In conference each chamber has a single vote determined by a majority of its conferees, who are expected to support generally the legislation as it passed their house. But as conference committees drag on, a senator confessed, the "individual attitudes of the various members begin to show." [43] House conferees on some occasions have a "knowledge advantage" over Senate conferees. Representatives serve on fewer committees than do senators and have greater opportunities to specialize in selected policy areas. This means that representatives on conference committees often find that they are "arguing with Senate staff," said Rep. Tom Tauke, R-Iowa. "For a House member, that's a frustrating experience." [44]

The ratio of Democrats to Republicans on a conference committee generally reflects their proportion in the House or Senate. Seniority frequently determines who the conferees will be, but it has become common for junior members to be conferees.

Openness

Secret conference meetings were the norm for most of Congress's history. In 1975, both houses adopted rules requiring open meetings unless the conferees from each chamber voted in public to close the sessions. Two years later the House went further, requiring open conference meetings unless the full House agreed to secret sessions. Some legislators hold that open conferences impair bargaining. Sen. Mark Hatfield, R-Ore., shares this opinion:

> When conferences were in executive [closed] session, members didn't have to pound the table and make speeches they hope will be reported back home. They could sit there and say, "You know where I sit and I know

where you sit so we've got to compromise." We do the same thing now but it takes much longer because we have to give all of our speeches first.[45]

This is yet another instance of individual-institutional cleavage. Under the watchful eye of lobbyists, conferees fight harder for provisions they might have dropped quietly in the interest of bicameral agreement. Needless to say, private bargaining sessions still permeate conference negotiations. As one senator pointed out:

> When we started the openness thing we found it more and more difficult to get something agreed to in the conferences; it seemed to take forever. So what did we do? We would break up into smaller groups and then we would ask our [conference] chairman . . . to see if he could find his opposite number on the House side and discuss this matter and come back and tell us what the chances would be of working out various and sundry possibilities.[46]

Senators and representatives anticipate that certain bills will go to conference and plan their strategy accordingly. For example, whether to have a recorded vote on amendments can influence conference bargaining. As Senate GOP leader Robert Dole of Kansas stated, "It seems to me we wanted a [floor] vote in case there is a conference. In case there is an effort [by House conferees] to strip out these amendments, they know they have a pretty solid vote on the Senate side." [47] Absent a recorded vote, amendments may be easier to drop in conference.

The Conference Report

A conference ends when its report (the compromise bill) is signed by a majority of the conferees from each chamber. The House and Senate then vote on this report without further amendment. At this stage the incentives are to approve it. "The threat of seeing two years of work wasted changed the mood of the conference," wrote a House committee staff aide.[48] This principle also applies to action by the full House and Senate on conference reports.

If either chamber rejects the conference report, an infrequent occurrence, a new conference may be called or another bill introduced. Once passed, the compromise bill is sent to the president for his approval or disapproval.

Conclusion

The philosophical bias of House and Senate rules reflects the character of each institution. Individual rights are stressed in the Senate, majority rule in the House. In both chambers, however, members who know the rules and precedents have an advantage over procedural novices in affecting policy outcomes.

Persistence, strategy, timing, compromise, and pure chance are also key elements in the lawmaking process. To make public policy requires building majority coalitions at successive stages where pressure groups and other parties can advance their claims. Political, procedural, personal, and policy considerations shape the final outcome. Passing laws, as one representative said, is like the "weaving of a web, bringing a lot of strands together in a pattern of support which won't have the kind of weak spots which could cause the whole fabric to fall apart." [49] The next chapter explores further the weaving of laws by analyzing factors that influence how Congress makes decisions.

Notes

1. *Congressional Record,* daily ed., 98th Cong., 2d sess., March 22, 1984, S3074.
2. Ibid., S3078. Also see Franklin L. Burdette, *Filibustering in the Senate* (Princeton, N.J.: Princeton University Press, 1940).
3. *Constitution, Jefferson's Manual, and Rules of the House of Representatives,* House Doc. 97-201, 97th Cong., 2d sess., 1983, 113-114. The rules of the Senate are contained in *Senate Manual,* Senate Doc. 98-10, 98th Cong., 1st sess., 1983.
4. Donald R. Matthews, *U.S. Senators and Their World* (Chapel Hill: University of North Carolina Press, 1960), chap. 5.
5. *Wall Street Journal,* October 2, 1987, 1.
6. Ibid.
7. *National Journal,* April 10, 1982, 632.
8. Julie Rovner, "Senate Committee Approves Health Warnings on Alcohol," *Congressional Quarterly Weekly Report,* May 24, 1986, 1175.
9. Woodrow Wilson, *Congressional Government* (Boston: Houghton Mifflin Co., 1885), 320.
10. Theodore Sorensen, *Kennedy* (New York: Harper & Row, 1965), 184.
11. *Wall Street Journal,* June 2, 1988, 56.
12. *Congressional Record,* daily ed., 95th Cong., 1st sess., May 17, 1977, E3076.
13. *Washington Post,* June 21, 1978, D7.
14. Lawrence J. Haas, "Unauthorized Action," *National Journal,* January 2, 1988, 20.
15. Janet Hook, "100th Congress Drags on but End Seems Near," *Congressional Quarterly Weekly Report,* October 15, 1988, 2971.
16. Joseph A. Davis, "All Sides Blamed for Death of Clean-Air Bill," *Congressional Quarterly Weekly Report,* October 8, 1988, 2812.
17. T. R. Reid, *Congressional Odyssey: The Saga of a Senate Bill* (San Francisco: W. H. Freeman, 1980), 17.
18. Elizabeth Drew, "A Tendency to 'Legislate,' " *New Yorker,* June 26, 1978, 80.
19. Stanley Bach and Steven Smith, *Managing Uncertainty in the House of Representatives: Adaptation and Innovation in Special Rules* (Washington, D.C.: Brookings Institution, 1988), 87.

20. Alfred Steinberg, *Sam Rayburn* (New York: Hawthorn Books, 1975), 313.
21. Neil MacNeil, *The Forge of Democracy* (New York: David McKay, 1963), 411.
22. Janet Hook, "GOP Chafes Under Restrictive House Rules," *Congressional Quarterly Weekly Report*, October 10, 1987, 2451.
23. Pat Towell, "House Rebuffs Reagan Views on Defense Spending, Policy," *Congressional Quarterly Weekly Report*, May 9, 1987, 901.
24. See *Roll Call*, June 12, 1988, 5; and *Roll Call*, June 19, 1988, 5. The GOP leader was Trent Lott of Mississippi, now in the Senate. Foley wrote the rebuttal when he was the majority leader.
25. Information supplied by Richard Beth of the Congressional Research Service.
26. Susan F. Rasky, "For House Democrats, a Pledge Lesson," *New York Times*, September 10, 1988, 1; and Tom Kenworthy, "Pledge Makes House Debut; A Long Run Appears Likely," *Washington Post*, September 14, 1988, A10.
27. Peter Bragdon, "Pork-Barreling to Win Votes Back Home May Not Always Be As Easy As It Seems," *Congressional Quarterly Weekly Report*, October 24, 1987, 2585.
28. *Mt. Vernon* [Ohio] *News*, September 20, 1980, 2.
29. *Congressional Record*, 100th Cong., 1st sess., June 17, 1987, H5085.
30. Irwin B. Arieff, "House Floor Watchdog Role Made Famous by H. R. Gross Has Fallen on Hard Times," *Congressional Quarterly Weekly Report*, July 24, 1982, 1776.
31. John F. Bibby, ed., *Congress off the Record* (Washington, D.C.: American Enterprise Institute, 1983), 23.
32. *New York Times*, November 22, 1985, B8.
33. *Congressional Record*, 100th Cong., 2d sess., January 26, 1988, S38.
34. Susan F. Rasky, "With Few Bills Passed or Ready for Action, Congress Seems Sluggish," *New York Times*, May 14, 1989, 24.
35. *Congressional Record*, 98th Cong., 2d sess., January 27, 1984, S328-S329.
36. Walter J. Oleszek, *Congressional Procedures and the Policy Process*, 3d ed. (Washington, D.C.: CQ Press, 1989), 193-196. See also Lewis A. Froman, Jr., *The Congressional Process* (Boston: Little, Brown, 1967); and Terry Sullivan, *Procedural Structure: Success and Influence in Congress* (New York: Praeger, 1984).
37. *Constitution, Jefferson's Manual, and Rules of the House of Representatives of the United States*, House Doc. 98-277, 98th Cong., 2d sess., 1985, 221.
38. Elizabeth Drew, *Senator* (New York: Simon & Schuster, 1979), 158.
39. *Congressional Record*, 97th Cong., 2d sess., May 20, 1982, 55648.
40. Hook, "100th Congress Drags On," 2971.
41. See comments by Senate Democratic whip Alan Cranston in *New York Times*, July 17, 1986, A3.
42. Senate Committee on Rules and Administration, *Report on Senate Operations*, 1988, Senate print, 100-141, 100th Cong., 2d sess., September 20, 1988, 55.
43. Randall B. Ripley, *Power in the Senate* (New York: St. Martin's Press, 1969), 128.

44. Janet Hook, "In Conference: New Hurdles, Hard Bargaining," *Congressional Quarterly Weekly Report,* September 6, 1986, 2081.
45. *Los Angeles Times,* December 22, 1979, 6.
46. *Congressional Record,* 99th Cong., 2d sess., February 20, 1986, S1463.
47. *Congressional Record,* 100th Cong., 2d sess., June 28, 1988, S8689.
48. Jennifer J. White, "Negotiating and the Congressional Conference Process: A Case Study of the Export Administration Act and the Omnibus Trade Bill," *The North Carolina Journal of International Law and Commercial Regulation* (Spring 1988): 338.
49. Barber B. Conable, "Weaving Webs: Lobbying by Charities," *Tax Notes,* November 10, 1975, 27-28.

Representatives vote at stations throughout the House chamber, inserting card and voting aye, no, or present. The lighted tally appears above the gallery.

CHAPTER TWELVE

Decision Making in Congress

The ordeal of Sen. Terry Sanford, D-N.C., began toward the end of the Senate's roll call vote on whether to override President Ronald Reagan's veto of a $87.5 billion highway and mass transit bill. The expected vote: sixty-six votes for the override, thirty-two against. Only Sanford and Republican whip Alan K. Simpson of Wyoming had not voted, Simpson holding back for tactical reasons. Sanford held the key. The sixty-seventh vote would defeat the president.

Before the roll call ended, Sanford was caught in a tug of war between the Senate's Democratic majority leadership and the White House. Democratic colleagues appealed to his loyalty; constituents and the White House thought he had pledged to stick with the president, supposedly because he was unhappy with the bill's funding for North Carolina roads. Swayed by the pressure, Sanford came down on three sides of the issue: first he voted "present," then he voted to sustain the veto, and finally he announced he would vote to override when the final vote was taken the following day—thus defeating the president.

Sanford, new to the Senate but a former governor and university president, was chastened by his experience. "Let's say I was slightly confused," he admitted. Later he contended that his position was "absolutely solid," though no one agreed with him.[1]

The Power to Choose

Sanford's awkward dilemma reflects the extraordinary power and freedom of individual House or Senate members. Although few votes command such public attention, every decision has the capacity to shape government. In both chambers every legislator has the right, indeed the obligation, to vote. (Delegates and resident commissioners in the House may vote in committee but not on the floor.) Legislators cast their own votes; no colleague or staff aide may do it for them. To exchange their votes for money or any other thing of value would be to accept a bribe, a federal crime.

Recorded votes on the House or Senate floor, while legislators' most visible decisions, are imperfect clues to their views. For a fuller measure of their performance, one must also consider how members participate in floor debate, take part in committee deliberations, gain expertise on issues, attend to party or caucus affairs, allocate time between legislative and constituent duties, hire and supervise staff, and gather and utilize information supplied by scores of agencies or interested parties. Countless such decisions—a few reached with the anguish of Senator Sanford's vote on the highway bill, others made hastily or inadvertently—define what it means to be a member of Congress.

In making choices members of Congress are relatively free and unfettered. There are no settled formulas for being a senator or a representative. Lawmakers are chosen from individual, discrete constituencies. Although virtually all wear party labels, they wear them loosely at best. Former Speaker Thomas P. O'Neill, Jr., once described House Democrats as "an organization of convenience." [2] Loyalty to the president, even when of the legislator's own political party, is not always expected or even rewarded. Although most members would prefer to support the president, especially on foreign policy questions, they are free to dissent when drawn by conscience or constituency pressures.

Capitol Hill norms strongly underscore lawmakers' independence. [3] Party leaders may plead, coax, or warn; using "roughhouse" tactics against members is frowned upon and if tried probably would backfire. Presidents also woo members, but their powers are limited. Neither are there constitutional grounds for attacking legislators for performing their duties, at least in legislative deliberations and votes. Anxious to prevent reprisals against legislators in the conduct of office, the Constitution's authors specified in Article I, Section 6, that "for any speech or debate in either House, they shall not be questioned in any other place."

Types of Decisions

One of the most basic decisions made by legislators is how much time to spend in the nation's capital. Members within 500 or 600 miles often remain at their home base, commuting to Washington for midweek sessions. Many of these "Tuesday-Thursday Club" members rarely if ever spend a weekend in Washington. For them, life in the Washington community is as alien as a foreign country. Others, with varying degrees of enthusiasm, plunge into the capital's social and political activities. Such individuals rarely "go back to Pocatello," as the saying goes. Between these two extremes are many degrees of "at homeness" in Washington, roughly measured by the amount of time spent in the home state or district.

A more subtle question is how to spend one's time and energies while in the nation's capital: whether to focus on legislative issues or on constituency relationships. Some members work hard to digest the mountains of reports and analyses that cross their desks; in the parlance of Capitol Hill, they "do their homework." By comparison, others seem to know or care little about legislative matters. They prefer to stress different aspects of the job (correspondence, outreach, and visits with constituents or lobby groups, for example). Such members rarely contribute to committee or floor deliberations; their votes are usually prompted by cues from colleagues, staff members, the White House, or interested groups.

Although either of these strategies can be successfully pursued, and distressingly few voters can tell the difference, most legislators claim to prefer legislative tasks, as we saw in Chapter 5. Whatever the distractions, they strive to make time for legislative work.

Specializing

Within the legislative realm, members may dig deeply in a particular area or range widely across issues and policies. Senators are more apt to be generalists, while representatives are inclined to cultivate a few specialties.

In both houses key policy-making roles are played by those whom David E. Price calls *policy entrepreneurs:* those recognized for "stimulating more than . . . responding" to outside political forces in a given field.[4] Often nearly invisible to the mass of citizens, these legislators are known to specialized publics for their contributions to specific policies—for example, Sen. Sam Nunn, D-Ga., on military policy; Rep. G. V. "Sonny" Montgomery, D-Miss., on veterans' affairs; Sen. Daniel Patrick Moynihan, D-N.Y., on welfare reform; and Rep. Bill Frenzel, R-Minn., on free trade questions.

Legislative specialties are often determined by constituency interests. On the Environment and Public Works Committee, Senator Simpson found a mission defending Wyoming's coal industry. A special target was a Clean Air Act provision in effect requiring power plants to install "scrubbers" to clean emissions from their burning of coal—thus reducing demand for clean-burning western coal and protecting "dirty" coal from other regions. Alaska lawmakers focus on the policies toward government-controlled Alaska lands, while the North Carolina delegation must show not only fealty but also success in promoting the state's tobacco industry.

Second, committee assignments may shape members' interests. While grappling with the Clean Air Act on the environment panel, Simpson was becoming embroiled in immigration reform because of his chairmanship of Senate Judiciary's Immigration and Refugee Policy subcommittee. Lee H. Hamilton, D-Ind., has used his seats on the House Foreign Affairs and Intelligence committees to stake out an independent and thoughtful course over more than twenty-five years. Neither specialty was calculated to appeal to home-state voters, but their assignments gave these lawmakers opportunities for serious legislative work.

Third, specializations may reflect personal interests nurtured by background or experience. Sidney Yates, D-Ill., whose parents took him to concerts as a child and who now collects modern art, easily cultivated the role of shepherding government funding for the arts through the House. Democrat Bob Graham, who as Florida governor was known for environmental initiatives like Save Our Rivers and Save Our Coasts, quickly adopted an environmental focus when he arrived in the Senate in 1987.

Prior to reforms of the 1960s and 1970s, lawmakers faced formidable obstacles if they wanted to affect policies not handled by their committees. Today, however, members have avenues of influence besides committee assignments—speeches, floor amendments, caucuses, and task forces, to name a few. As a freshman representative, Henry J. Hyde, R-Ill., began his fight against public funding for abortions by introducing floor amendments (the now famous "Hyde amendments") to various funding bills. Though only in his second term and not on the Armed Services Committee, Dick Armey, R-Texas, devised an ingenious scheme for closing unneeded military bases that avoided political sensitivities and won bipartisan support. Such spectacular feats are not everyday occurrences, but the fluidity of today's procedures makes even the most junior member a potential policy entrepreneur.

Whatever a member's specialty, the ability to influence the decision-making process is what really counts, as former senator Edmund S. Muskie, D-Maine, explains:

> People have all sorts of conspiratorial theories on what constitutes power in the Senate. It has little to do with the size of the state you come from. Or the source of your money. Or committee chairmanships, although that certainly gives you a kind of power. But real power up there comes from doing your work and knowing what you're talking about. Power is the ability to change someone's mind. . . . The most important thing in the Senate is credibility. *Credibility! That* is power.[5]

Staking Out a Position

Lawmakers, of course, do more than specialize in a given policy field. They must adopt positions or take stands sooner or later—what Richard F. Fenno, Jr., has called the "politics of timing."[6]

From his examination of the 1981 vote on selling AWACS (airborne warning and control system) reconnaissance planes to the Saudi Arabians, Fenno identified three types of decision makers. Some members are *early deciders*—that is, their positions are known from the outset, from declarations or prior voting records. Staunch supporters of Israel, for example, were certain to oppose arms sales to Arab countries. Such members still have important decisions to make—for example, the extent of their involvement in the issue—but they are shunned by most lobbyists because their position is fixed.

Active players are members who delay their commitment, thus inviting negotiation from various sides of the issue at hand. Somewhere along the line these members may become identified with a particular solution—for example, a compromise package. How they vote may be determined by the policy or by their desire to protect their professional reputation as independent-minded lawmakers. Whatever their motivation, they can maximize their influence over the final language of the legislation.

Finally, there are the *late deciders* like Senator Sanford on the highway bill. They delay their decision (or reconsider an earlier commitment) until the very last moment. While late deciders usually forfeit any influence over the basic framework of the measure, they are eagerly courted by all sides and may gain other concessions. Late deciders are concerned not only about political payoffs, but also about their professional reputation for independence.

Do legislators actually favor the bills and resolutions they introduce? Normally they do, but as Sportin' Life, the *Porgy and Bess* character, said, "It ain't necessarily so." Members may introduce a measure to stake out jurisdiction for a committee or to pave the way for hearings and deliberations that will air a public problem. Or they may introduce measures they do not personally favor to oblige an executive agency or to placate a given interest.

According to Senate and House rules, bills and resolutions may have an unlimited number of cosponsors. The author of a measure will often circulate a "Dear Colleague" letter detailing the virtues of the bill and soliciting cosponsors to demonstrate broad support and force committee action. Cosponsorship, no less than sponsorship, is politically motivated as freshman senator Dan Quayle, R-Ind., well understood when he asked arch-liberal Edward M. Kennedy, D-Mass., to sponsor his first major bill, the 1982 Job Training Partnership Act. Soliciting Kennedy's cooperation was a daring move for a young conservative embarking on his initial subcommittee assignment. "The decision to travel the bipartisan route . . . was his earliest strategic decision," wrote Fenno of Quayle's eventual legislative success. "It caused him a lot of trouble, but he never looked back." [7] Despite right-wing opposition and stonewalling from the Reagan administration, Quayle's decision won him passage of the job training act—his greatest Senate accomplishment.

Occasionally, however, cosponsors are shunned. Introducing his waterway users' fee bill, Sen. Pete V. Domenici, R-N.M., decided against seeking cosponsors for several reasons.[8] First, as ranking Republican on the subcommittee, he could arrange for hearings without cosponsors' support. Second, single sponsorship would be easier. ("If you've got cosponsors you have to clear every little change with them.") Third, if the bill became law, he would get full, undiluted credit. And finally, if by chance he found no cosponsors, his effort might suffer a devastating initial setback. Thus, for a time Domenici fought alone for his bill. In the end it was signed into law by President Jimmy Carter at a Democratic rally crowded with politicians who initially had opposed it; Domenici's role was barely mentioned. Such are the ironies of politics.

Casting Votes

Lawmakers' most visible choices are the votes they cast. Voting is a central ritual in any legislative body. Members place great stock in their voting records, under the assumption (sometimes borne out) that constituents will judge them at reelection time. Outside groups are keen-eyed followers of the votes on specific measures. Scholars, too, have a longstanding love affair with legislative voting, no doubt because votes provide concrete, quantifiable indicators that lend themselves to statistical analysis.

Most senators and representatives strive to be present for as many floor votes as they can. The average member participates in nine out of every ten recorded votes on the floor. A few members boast perfect voting records. The all-time champion is Rep. William Natcher, D-Ky., whose unbroken string of more than 16,000 floor votes and quorum calls began when he came to the House in 1954.[9] Not every vote merits the effort, but most members cultivate a record of diligence to buttress their home styles and to forestall charges of absenteeism by opponents. (For a discussion of the mechanics of how members vote, see Chapter 11.)

Offering Amendments

A chief strategy for shaping legislation during floor deliberations is to offer amendments. Sometimes amendments are intended to provide a test of strength. During debate on President Reagan's 1981 tax bill, for example, the floor manager, Republican senator Bob Dole of Kansas, moved to table his own amendment offsetting the windfall profits tax on oil companies. He thought his motion would be soundly defeated, but the narrow margin indicated that opponents of oil-tax loopholes were strong and could even sustain a filibuster.[10] Other amendments are intended to counteract the biases of the committees that drafted and reported the legislation.

In some cases amendments are designed to force members to declare themselves on symbolic issues that command public attention. Amendments on abortion funding or balanced budgets are prime examples. When the House debated creation of the Department of Education in 1979, the bill was laden with amendments having little to do with the new agency's charter or structure—on matters such as abortion, busing, school prayers, and racial quotas. Although the amendments were widely publicized and passed by wide margins, they were unceremoniously dropped by conferees before the measure could gain final approval.

In the Senate, which cherishes individual senators' prerogatives, amendments have always been a central part of floor debate, even though some amendments are designed to delay action. Even after the cloture rule was tightened in the 1970s, some senators found they could evade it by introducing delaying amendments after cloture had been invoked. Though a few of these loopholes were closed in the 1980s, floor participation in the Senate is open to everyone on a nearly equal basis.

If members can't vote in person, they can still be recorded on an issue. They may announce their views in floor statements or press releases. Or they may *pair* themselves with someone on the opposite side of an issue—a voluntary arrangement that allows members to go on record without actually voting or affecting the final tabulation. A *general pair* means that two members are listed without any indication of how either might have voted. A *specific pair* indicates how the two absent legislators would have voted, one for and the other against. A *live pair* matches two members, one present and one absent. In a live pair the member who is there casts a vote but then withdraws it, announcing that he or she has a live pair with a colleague and identifying how each would have voted on the issue. A live pair subtracts one vote, yea or nay, from the final tally and on rare occasions may influence the outcome of closely contested issues.

During committee deliberations, absent members often vote by *proxy,* entrusting their votes to an ally who is present at the session. Proxy rules vary by committee. A few prohibit proxies altogether. Some require written proxies, others do not; some require separate proxies for each vote, while others allow general proxies in which the member in attendance casts the votes on procedural matters that come up. Given scheduling difficulties and erratic attendance patterns, legislators leading the fight for or against a particular measure take care to gather proxies beforehand and use them according to the applicable rules.

What Do Votes Mean?

Like other elements in the legislative process, voting is open to manifold interpretations. A given vote may or may not be what it seems to be. Therefore, students of politics must be very cautious in analyzing legislative votes.

Votes are frequently taken on procedural matters that evoke responses independent of the issue at hand. Certain senators, for example, refuse to vote in favor of cloture, regardless of the issue under consideration. They cherish individual senators' right to speak at length on matters of intense concern—to filibuster, if necessary, to put their case before the final court of public opinion. Once thought the exclusive property of southern segregationists intent on blocking civil rights legislation, the filibuster is now employed by senators of every ideological stripe to block legislation they vehemently oppose.

House and Senate floor votes are imperfect channels for registering members' views. Members may favor a measure but feel constrained to vote against it in the form presented on the floor. Conversely, members unhappy with portions of a measure may go along because "on balance" it is a step forward. Or they may vote for a proposal they disagree with to prevent enactment of something worse. Or they may support an amendment they oppose with the expectation that the other body or the conference committee will kill it. Or they may accede to party leaders' wishes on measures they disagree with as long as their actions don't adversely affect their constituencies. And so on.

The dilemmas of voting were brought home to Rep. Steny H. Hoyer, D-Md., when he struggled late in the 1983 session to push a civil service health care bill desired by federal workers (65,000 of whom reside in his district). To facilitate action, he offered an amendment limiting abortions under federal health plans. His tactic was aimed at forestalling even stronger antiabortion provisions, and in any event he expected the amendment to be scuttled in a House-Senate conference. But the Senate fooled him, voting 44-43 to accept his amendment and adopting the House bill without a conference. So the "Hoyer amendment" became law, to the chagrin of its author and the anger of his prochoice allies.[11]

In some cases recorded votes are totally misleading. A favorable vote may really be negative or vice versa. A 1979 Senate vote to attach a school prayer amendment sponsored by Jesse Helms, R-N.C., to a measure dealing with Supreme Court jurisdiction was really a vote to kill the amendment because it was expected that the House would scuttle the Court bill. A vote later that year against automobile air bags was only a token vote because it was tied to an authorizing bill that would expire before the National Highway Traffic Safety Administration's air-bag regulations were to take effect. In such cases the meaning of a legislator's vote is, to say the least, very much in doubt.

Not infrequently, voting obscures a legislator's true position. Given the multiplicity of votes—procedural as well as substantive—on many measures, it is entirely possible for lawmakers to come out on both sides of an issue or at least appear to do so. For instance, members may vote to authorize a program but against funding it. Or they may vote against final passage of a bill but for a substitute version. This tactic assures the bill's backers that the lawmaker favors the concept, while pleasing voters who oppose the bill. Such voting patterns may reflect a deliberate attempt to obscure one's position or careful thought about complex questions. As in so many aspects of human behavior, lawmakers' motivations can be fully judged only in light of specific cases.

Where congressional votes are concerned, then, things are not always what they seem. "What I've lost in the Congress is not my ideals, but my illusions," observed Rep. Stephen J. Solarz, D-N.Y. "The good and the bad are frequently totally intertwined, and often the only way to get something good is to accept something bad." Or as Rep. Bill Gradison, R-Ohio, puts it, "The public has the view that the shortest distance between two points is a straight line, but that's not true in government. If you see 'compromise' as a dirty word, you're in the wrong place." [12]

Lawmakers' voting rationales are sometimes hard to explain to outsiders. In such cases members face a dilemma: either swallow their reservations and vote for appearance's sake, or vote their convictions and face the consequences. Regarding the highly attractive constitutional amendment requiring a balanced budget, Sen. Ernest F. Hollings, D-S.C., admitted he planned to vote for it because he got "tired of explaining" its deficiencies. It was easier "just to say put it in." [13]

This point is important for students because scholars often treat votes as if they were unambiguous indicators of legislators' views. It is important for citizens because lobbyists and reporters frequently assess incumbents on the basis of floor votes. As noted in Chapter 10, many groups construct voting indices for labeling "friendly" or "unfriendly" legislators. Citizens are well advised to examine such indices closely. A small business lobby, the National Federation of Independent Business (NFIB), based its 1981 House voting survey on only four votes—all Reagan-backed budget or tax bills. Loyal Democrats scored zero even though many had received NFIB's "guardian" awards the year before. Even more misleading was a right-wing group's "moral/family" voting record, under which "Christian" votes included those favoring military spending and the balanced-budget amendment, and against the Equal Rights Amendment, the National Science Foundation, and affirmative action. Not one member from the clergy ever passed, but a member who pleaded guilty to having sex with a House page got a perfect score.[14]

Determinants of Voting

The lesson of these examples is skepticism. Votes, particularly on single issues, should be examined, interpreted, and labeled with caution. With these caveats in mind, we turn to several factors that shape congressional voting: party affiliation, constituents' views, ideological leanings, and presidential leadership.

Party and Voting

One way for members to reach voting decisions is to consult the views of their political party colleagues. Party affiliation remains the strongest single correlate of members' voting decisions, and in recent years it has reached relatively high levels.[15]

Unlike parliamentary systems, the U.S. Congress rarely votes along straight party lines and never brings down the government in power (unless one counts impeachment of the president). In a typical year from one-third to one-half of all floor votes could be called *party unity votes,* defined by Congressional Quarterly as votes in which a majority of voting Republicans oppose a majority of voting Democrats. In a typical year the minority party wins about a third of all party unity votes, which indicates the looseness of party ranks. Figure 12-1 depicts House and Senate party votes from 1970 through 1988. The sawtooth pattern of recent years suggests that party votes are most frequent early in the two-year Congresses, falling off as the next election approaches and members pick their own way through controversial

Figure 12-1 Party Unity Votes in Congress, 1970-1988

Percentage

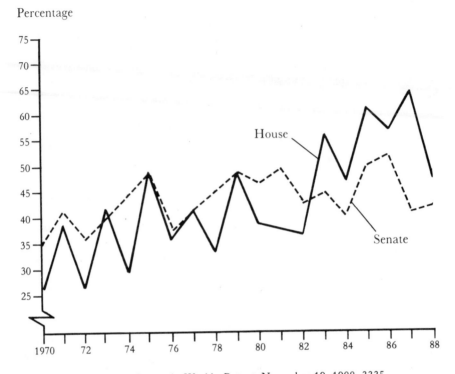

Source: *Congressional Quarterly Weekly Report,* November 19, 1988, 3335.
Note: Percentage of all House and Senate votes in which a majority of Democrats opposed a majority of Republicans.

end-of-session votes. Despite a recent revival of party voting, today's levels still fall short of the militant parties era of a century ago. Around 1900 about two-thirds of all roll calls were party unity votes. In several sessions a majority of the votes saw 90 percent of one party marshaled against 90 percent of the other; today such sharp partisan divisions appear in fewer than one roll call vote in ten.[16]

Individual members' *party unity scores* can be calculated—the percentage of party unity votes in which they vote in agreement with the majority of their party colleagues. According to these scores, the average legislator votes with his or her party two-thirds to four-fifths of the time. Aggregate Democratic and Republican party unity scores from 1970 through 1988 are displayed in Figure 12-2. Partisan voting blocs are prominent also in many committees. From their painstaking study of voting in eight House committees during the mid-1970s, Glenn and Suzanne Parker concluded that partisanship was a key explanatory variable in all of the panels except for Foreign Affairs, which has a bipartisan tradition.[17]

Partisan voting patterns have been extensively studied by scholars, although their conclusions by no means agree. Party voting levels in both houses were relatively high in the 1950s, fell in the 1960s, and rose again perceptibly in the 1970s. Sharp partisanship was evident throughout the 1980s. This condition reflected factors such as divided party control of Congress, the controversial and ideologically charged agenda of the Reagan presidency, and the use of ethics as a political weapon.

Republicans historically have displayed more cohesion than have Democrats, although the 1980s found Democrats uncommonly united. Democrats have often been badly divided—first by the historic North-South split, later by the Vietnam War. High points of Democratic cohesion occurred in 1965, at the zenith of President Lyndon B. Johnson's "Great Society"; during the struggles with President Richard Nixon in the early 1970s; and when opposition to President Ronald Reagan galvanized after 1981.

Partisan strength in voting is rooted in several factors. Some students argue that party loyalty is mainly a shorthand term for constituency differences; that is, partisans vote together because they reflect the same kinds of political and demographic areas. According to this reasoning, legislators stray from party ranks when they feel their constituents will not benefit from the party's policies. Today's Democratic mavericks tend to be from the South, whose voters are to the right of the party's mainstream. GOP mavericks are mostly from New England and the Northeast Corridor, where voters fall to the left of the party's center. To survive electorally in these areas, these elected officials must lean away from their parties' main thrust.

The constituency basis of party differences also accounts for the recent upsurge in lawmakers' party loyalty. Southern Democrats, for example, are more in step with their party's left-of-center thrust than they used to be. Race has subsided as a dividing line. Indeed, many southern lawmakers actively court black voters. Some of the most conservative areas in the South are now represented by Republicans, not Democrats. By the same token, the Republican congressional party is now more uniformly conservative than it used to be: Democrats have captured many areas once represented by GOP liberals, who are today a rare breed. As a result, today's Capitol Hill parties are more cohesive ideologically than they have been in many decades.

Party cohesion also flows from shared policy goals shaped early in a congressional candidate's career. Those who entered politics through the civil rights, environmental, or antiwar movements tend to cluster within the Democratic party and to reflect their shared values in voting. By contrast, individuals who became active to slash taxes or combat domestic welfare programs tend to gather under the GOP banner, underscoring that party's historic approach to such issues. More than three-quarters of the party-line

Figure 12-2 Levels of Party Voting in Congress, 1970-1988

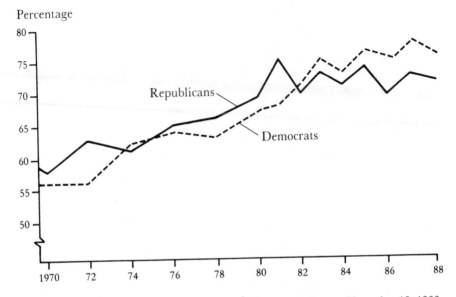

Source: Voting studies in *Congressional Quarterly Weekly Report*, November 19, 1988, 3338.

Note: The graph shows the percentage of time the average Democrat or Republican in Congress voted with his party majority in partisan votes for the years listed. These *composite party unity scores* are based on votes that split the parties in the House and Senate, a majority of voting Democrats opposing a majority of voting Republicans.

votes in the House in 1988 (90 percent of each party voting in opposition to the other) dealt with national security and foreign affairs—evoking such ideologically divisive questions as U.S. relations with Central America, South Africa, and the Soviet Union. In the Senate party-line votes dealt overwhelmingly with campaign finance, an intensely partisan issue. In party votes displaying less unity (a majority of one party opposing a majority of the other), domestic issues loomed large.[18]

Factors such as constituency or recruitment are reinforced by partisan activities on Capitol Hill. New members rely upon party bodies for committee assignments and usually organize into partisan "class clubs." When seeking out cues for voting, moreover, legislators tend to choose party colleagues as guides for their own behavior.[19]

Finally, as we saw in Chapter 6, partisan voting is encouraged by party leaders who contact members to solicit views and urge them to support the party. The more visible an issue, the harder party leaders must compete against other pressures for members' votes.[20] Leaders are more likely to muster votes if the issue is defined in procedural terms than if the issue is presented substantively. Whatever the legislator's personal leanings, the institutional push toward partisan voting cannot be ignored.

Constituency and Voting

Constituency traits often take partisan form. Certain types of areas are more likely to elect Democrats, while other areas tend to elect Republicans. Issue cleavages flow from these basic differences between "Democratic districts" and "Republican districts." [21] Representatives who deviate from their party's norms are apt to represent constituencies atypical for that party. According to one study, representatives' roll call voting records differ because their constituencies diverge demographically and electorally. [22]

Constituencies can control lawmakers' choices in two ways. First, people can elect representatives whose views so mirror their own that floor votes automatically reflect the will of the constituents. In other words, representatives vote their constituency because they are simply transplanted locals. Representatives' actions are constrained also by the threat of defeat. Occasionally, members voice policies or views at odds with those of their district's voters; often (but not always) incumbents subsequently shift their stands to retain their seats.

Apart from such vivid examples of constituency pressure, the precise impact of constituencies on congressional voting is hard to measure. Most constituents, after all, are unaware of most issues coming up for votes in the House or Senate chamber. Or constituency opinions may conflict so sharply that a clear mandate is lacking. Finally, legislators adopt varying strategies to interpret constituency interests and then explain their positions back home.

Ideology and Voting

The spirit of compromise supplies oil for the gears of the legislative process. Because grass-roots voters tend to cluster in the middle of the ideological spectrum, moderation appears to be prudent politics. Reporter-turned-novelist Ward Just voiced this view of the House in one of his short stories:

> It was not a place for lost causes. There were too many conflicting interests, too much confusion, too many turns to the labyrinth. . . . This was one reason why it was so difficult to build an ideological record in the House. A man with ideology was wise to leave it before reaching a position of influence, because by then he'd mastered the art of compromise, which had nothing to do with dogma or public acts of conscience. It had to do with simple effectiveness. [23]

Research studies, however, reveal striking ideological divisions in Congress. On the basis of roll call votes and interviews, Jerrold Schneider concluded that much congressional voting is ideological, that voting coalitions form because members carry with them well-developed ideological positions. Another study found that ideology affected voting more than state benefits or party commitments did. [24]

In the late 1930s a conservative coalition of Republicans and southern Democrats emerged in a reaction against the New Deal.[25] Historically, this coalition was stronger in the Senate than in the House, but its success rate in both chambers was impressive, with the conspicuous exception of the 89th Congress (1965-1967), when the anti-Goldwater landslide brought a horde of Democratic liberals to boost President Johnson's Great Society programs. In 1981 the coalition reappeared as President Reagan captured votes of conservative Democrats on budget, tax, and social issues, while pulling mainstream Democrats toward conservative positions on the other issues.[26] Today the coalition appears in roughly one vote out of every ten. A *conservative coalition vote* is defined as one in which a majority of voting Republicans and a majority of voting southern Democrats oppose a majority of voting northern Democrats. Figure 12-3 shows the percentage of recorded votes in each chamber in which the coalition appeared and the proportion of votes it won between 1970 and 1988.

A somewhat different picture emerges from a recent study of ideological voting by Jacob Stampen and John Davis. They ran every vote on the Senate floor from 1959 to 1981 through a supercomputer and tried to identify who voted together. What emerged were four recurring "mixed-motive coalitions" that combined party and ideology: the "Honey Bees" (liberal Democrats), the "Boll Weevils" (moderate to conservative Democrats, mainly southern), the "Yellow Jackets" (ideologically conservative Republicans), and the "Gypsy Moths" (GOP moderates, mostly from the Northeast). One Democrat was so independent he could not be categorized: William Proxmire of Wisconsin, the incurable maverick. The four groups showed impressive consistency, even over the years of the so-called "Reagan revolution" when the Senate fell into Republican hands.[27]

The Presidency and Voting

Although Congress often pursues an independent course and few members feel a deep loyalty to the occupant of the White House, presidents do influence voting.[28] Not only do presidents shape the legislative agenda, but they can pressure members to lend support. Figure 8-1 on page 242 depicts the percentage of times Congress voted with every president from Dwight D. Eisenhower to Reagan on issues on which the president announced a position. Many routine and uncontroversial matters are included in this index, but it still roughly gauges the president's standing on Capitol Hill and suggests several patterns.

First, modern presidents attain at least half of their legislative objectives. This success probably springs not so much from popularity or skill as from the routine nature of many of their initiatives. Yet some presidents—like Eisenhower and Johnson during their first two years, Kennedy during his three years in office, and Reagan in 1981—enjoy extraordinary success in steering their proposals through Congress.

Figure 12-3   Conservative Coalition Votes and Victories, 1970-1988

Percentage

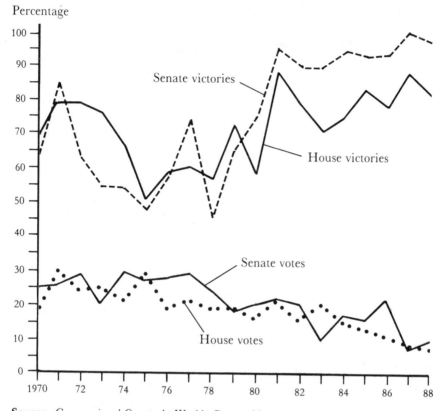

Source: *Congressional Quarterly Weekly Report,* November 19, 1988, 3345, 3349.

Note: *Votes* is the percentage of all roll call votes on which a majority of voting southern Democrats and a majority of voting Republicans—the conservative coalition—opposed the stand taken by a majority of voting northern Democrats. *Victories* is the percentage of conservative coalition votes won by the coalition.

Second, partisan swings affect presidential success rates. As long as their party controls Congress, presidents win at least three of four votes on which they have taken positions; with divided government, presidents fall well below that level. Success smiled even upon Jimmy Carter, whose reputation on Capitol Hill was battered by his stance as an outsider and the ineptness of his legislative liaison office at the beginning of his presidency. With heavy partisan majorities in both chambers, Carter's legislative record was actually quite strong.[29]

When partisan control of the White House and Congress is divided, presidents' success levels are far less reliable. A partial exception to this rule was 1981, Reagan's first year in office. (Republicans held the Senate but not the House). That year Reagan won more than eight votes out of every ten on which he took a position. Thereafter, however, his support levels fell dramatically—even by comparison with Eisenhower, Nixon, and Ford, all of whom faced a hostile Congress.[30]

Shifts in partisan strength in Congress sometimes have dramatic effects. President Eisenhower's success rate fell 24 percent following the Democrats' victories in the 1958 congressional elections. Building on the 1964 Democratic landslide, President Johnson achieved a modern high of 93 percent success. (Johnson's success rate was boosted also by his habit of sending up messages supporting measures he already knew would pass.)

Third, presidents tend to lose congressional support as their administrations age. Reagan's experience dramatically confirmed this finding: his support score fell thirteen points after his first year and dropped still further after the 1982 midterm elections boosted the Democrats' majority in the House. After the Democrats recaptured the Senate in 1986 and his administration was damaged by the Iran-contra revelations, Reagan's success rate hit a modern-day low point: 43.5 percent of his initiatives were approved by Congress.

Although presidents have taken clear-cut stands on an increasing *number* of issues over time, these represent a declining *percentage* of congressional votes because the workload of members is much heavier than it used to be.[31] In 1979 President Carter took a position on roughly one House and Senate vote out of every five; at a comparable stage in his administration Eisenhower was taking positions on about three out of five congressional votes.

Giving and Taking Cues

Various legislative voting models have been devised by scholars to explain how members of Congress make up their minds. As the following models show, party, constituency, ideology, and presidential support are not the only cues that influence members' voting decisions.

Cleo Cherryholmes and Michael Shapiro divided legislative decision making into two phases: *predisposition* and *conversation*. In the initial phase, party, region, committee, and other variables predispose each legislator for or against each measure. If the predisposition is indecisive, the lawmaker seeks cues from colleagues—the conversation stage. Cherryholmes and Shapiro assigned weights to various predispositions as well as to the probability that members will accept cues from colleagues. When applied to the 1960s votes on federal activism and foreign aid, this model predicted 84 percent of the results in both areas.[32]

In their study of selected votes from 1958 to 1969, Donald Matthews and James Stimson estimated the significance of nine sources of cues: state party delegations, party leaders, party majority, president, House majority, committee chairmen, ranking minority members, the conservative coalition, and the liberal Democratic Study Group. State party delegations proved to have the highest correlations with voting in both parties. Party and committee leaders were also effective cue givers, as were party and House majorities. Democratic presidents were potent cue-givers for the Democrats, and Republican presidents were moderately powerful in influencing their Hill partisans. In short, partisan cues were most potent when the White House and Congress were controlled by the same party. Taken as a whole, the Matthews-Stimson model was able to predict 88 percent of the votes actually cast.[33]

Policy dimensions form the basis of Aage Clausen's model, drawn from analyzing of roll call votes in the 1950s and 1960s. Clausen examined voting on government management, social welfare, international involvement, civil liberties, and agricultural aid. Scoring legislators on each policy dimension, he discovered great stability in members' positions over time and in the impact of various cue sources. Political party was an effective predictor for some issues (especially government management). Constituency controlled others (civil liberties, in particular). In still other cases a combination of factors was at work: party and constituency dominated social welfare and agricultural aid votes, while international decisions were affected by a combination of constituency and presidential influence. Clausen's work demonstrated that stable forces such as party, constituency, and presidential support induce members to assume long-term positions on legislative policy.[34]

These three models are based upon, or tested with, aggregate voting statistics. To compile these figures, individual members' votes are compared with factors such as the party majority or the president's position; high correlations are described as influence. Thus, the models are based on inferences gleaned from the conjunction of members' votes and other factors. A few researchers have tackled the arduous job of trying to tap the actual processes by which voting cues are given or received.

David Kovenock's communications audit supported the notion of cue giving and cue taking within Congress. "Most of the messages congressmen received, and most of those which influence them," he found, "originate at least in the first instance from sources within the Congress."[35] Nearly two-thirds of all incoming communications originated on Capitol Hill—from fellow representatives, staff aides, or senators. Of those communications dealing with subcommittee business and regarded as influential, 99 percent came from members and staff, governmental agencies, or organized interest groups. The kinds of communications lawmakers received depended on their positions. For example, the more vulnerable their electoral position, the less they focused on lawmaking messages and the more they communicated with folks back home.

John Kingdon's model of representatives' decisions is based on interviews with members immediately after their votes on specific issues.[36] Legislators have little difficulty making up their minds when they have strong personal convictions or when party leaders and interest groups agree and point them in the same direction. If all the actors in their field of vision concur, members operate in a "consensus mode" of decision making. Fellow members emerge as the most influential cue givers, with constituencies ranking second. As one lawmaker put it:

> I think that the other members are very influential, and we recognize it. And why are they influential? I think because they have exercised good judgment, have expertise in the area, and know what they are talking about.[37]

When members deviate from the consensus stance indicated by their cue givers, it is usually to follow their own consciences. Adding up these short-term forces, Kingdon in his model successfully predicted about 90 percent of the decisions.

Legislative voting models, no matter how elegant, cannot capture the full range of factors shaping decisions. "The two biggest political lies," former senator Thomas Eagleton, D-Mo., once declared, are "one, to say a senator never takes into account the political ramifications of a vote and secondly, almost an equal lie, is to say the only thing a senator considers is politics." [38] To unravel the chain of causality involved in congressional decision making would require a comprehensive model embracing demographic, sociological, psychological, and political motivations. Simplified models, without a doubt, pinpoint important components of legislators' decisions. As with all complex human behavior, however, such decisions elude wholly satisfactory description.

Legislative Bargaining

Legislators make choices on a staggering variety of matters, in relatively short periods of time, often with inadequate information. First, each legislator has separate and sometimes conflicting goals and information. Second, whatever their goals or information levels, every legislator wields one vote with which to affect the outcome.[39]

Such a state of affairs—disparate goals and widely scattered influence—is hazardous. Conflict may flare out of control if the contending policy objectives are not adequately met. On the other hand, stalemate is a constant threat, as when irresistible forces clash with immovable objects. In such a predicament members have to resort to politicking: that is, they must trade off goals and resources to get results. No wonder, then, that Congress is "an influence system in which bargain and exchange predominate." [40]

Bargaining is a generic term referring to several related types of behavior. In each case an exchange takes place: goals or resources pass from a bargainer's hands in return for other goals or resources that he or she values. Bargains may be implicit or explicit (see Table 12-1). Implicit bargaining occurs when legislators engage in actions designed to elicit certain reactions from others, even though no negotiation may have taken place. For example, legislators may introduce a bill or sponsor hearings not because they think the bill will pass, but because they hope the action will prod someone else—an executive branch official, perhaps, or a committee chairman with broader jurisdiction on the question—into taking action on the problem. Or a bill's managers may accept a controversial amendment knowing full well that the objectionable provision will be dropped in the other chamber or in conference. These are examples of the so-called "law of anticipated reactions." [41]

Another type of implicit bargaining occurs when legislators seek out or accept the judgments of colleagues with expertise on a given matter, expecting that the situation will be reversed in the future. What is being traded is information. As Sen. Carl Levin, D-Mich., said of Armed Services Committee Chairman Sam Nunn: "He knows more about the subject he talks about than anybody else by the time he starts talking about it." [42] The exchange not only saves the recipient the time and trouble of mastering the subject matter; it may also provide a credible "cover" in defending the vote. During the 1986 tax reform debates, Sen. Bill Bradley, D-N.J., was a trailblazer who gave members across the ideological spectrum guidance on tax issues. When conservative Republican Charles E. Grassley of Iowa made decisions on tax policy, he said there was always "another factor to consider: How does Bradley look at this?" [43] As we have seen already, exchanges of voting cues are endemic in both chambers.

Explicit bargains also take several forms. In *compromises*, legislators agree to split their differences. The most visible instances of compromises occur in House-Senate conferences, where differences in the two chambers' versions of a bill are ironed out. As former representative Edward J. Derwinski, R-Ill., described it, "members sit down and split the differences. If the House stipulates $100 million for an item and the Senate $200 million, the general tendency is to say, 'Okay, let's take $150 million.' " [44] Compromises are easiest in measures containing quantitative elements—for example, funding levels or eligibility criteria—that can easily be adjusted upward or downward. Compromise also occurs between factions. For example, members who favor a major new program and members who oppose any program at all may agree to a two-year pilot project to test the idea.

Logrolling is a bargaining strategy in which the parties trade off support so that each may gain its goal. The term originated in the nineteenth century when neighbors helped each other roll logs into a pile for burning. In its most visible form, trading is embodied in a something-for-everyone enactment—known as "pork barrel"—on subjects such as public works, omnibus taxation, or tariffs and trade. Derwinski explained how farmers, representing 4 percent

Table 12-1 Typology of Bargaining

Implicit	Explicit
Anticipated reaction	Compromise
Exchanges of cues	Simple logrolling, time logrolling, logrolling with side payments

Source: Adapted from Robert L. Peabody, "Organization Theory and Legislative Behavior: Bargaining, Hierarchy and Change in the U.S. House of Representatives" (Paper presented at the annual meeting of the American Political Science Association, New York, N.Y., September, 4-7, 1963).

of the nation's workers, put together a majority coalition to pass price supports, acreage allowances, and marketing agreements:

> What [the farmers] do is very interesting. The agriculture people from North Carolina, where agriculture means tobacco, discuss their problems with the man representing the rice growers in Arkansas or California. The sugar beet growers in Minnesota and sugar cane interests in Louisiana and Hawaii and the wheat and corn and soybean and other producers just gather together in one great big happy family to be sure there is a subsidy for every commodity. They put those numbers together again so that they have at least 218 supporters in the House and 51 in the Senate. A supporter of the tobacco subsidy automatically becomes a supporter of the wheat subsidy, or the sugar quota, or the soybean subsidy, or whatever else follows.[45]

Nonfarm interests were drawn into one of the most successful logrolling achievements of recent years: the food stamp program. It brought together farm lobbies, who wanted to boost the market, and urban welfare interests, who wanted to feed low-income people.[46]

At the personal level logrolling means bringing individual lawmakers into the finished legislative product by including (or anticipating) their special interests, proposals, or amendments. When a junior staffer once asked the late senator Henry "Scoop" Jackson, D-Wash., how he had assembled a majority for a new proposal, he responded something like this: "Maggie said he talked to Russell, and Tom promised this if I would back him on Ed's amendment, and Mike owes me one for last year's help on Pete's bill." [47] This attitude of reciprocity is especially prevalent in the Senate, dominated as it is by individuals. The sponsor of a Senate bill often must placate most or all of the interested legislators in order to gain clearance to bring the bill to the floor.

Lawmakers who enter into, and stand to profit from, a logroll are expected to support the final package, regardless of what that package looks like. A broad-based logroll is hard to stop. "It's not a system of punishment.

It's a system of rewards," explained Rep. Bill Frenzel, R-Minn., about the House tax-writing process.[48] President Reagan's veto of the 1987 highway bill was overridden by the House and Senate because it contained so many projects benefiting members' districts—including one in the Peoria, Illinois, district of House Republican leader Robert H. Michel, who voted to override.

Deficits and cutbacks of the 1980s, however, shifted the goal of logrolling. In a hostile fiscal environment logrolling is often aimed at equalizing sacrifices rather than distributing rewards. Broad-spectrum bills—authorizations, omnibus tax measures, continuing resolutions, and budget resolutions—may include numerous less-than-optimal provisions, many of which would fail if voted on separately. Such a *negative logroll* enables lawmakers to support the measure as "the best deal we can get." In other words, members find it easier to accept damage to their favorite programs as long as they are sure that everyone else is "taking their lumps" through cutbacks or across-the-board formulas that limit other programs or benefits. The former chairman of the Senate Appropriations Committee, Mark O. Hatfield, R-Ore., explained he would "hold my nose and do certain things here for the purpose of getting the job done, but certainly not with enthusiasm or anything other than recognizing that we are doing things under emergency conditions." [49] In a time of fiscal stringency legislators have fewer opportunities to claim credit for sponsoring new programs or obtaining added funding. Avoiding blame replaces claiming credit as a legislative objective, and these omnibus reverse logrolls are a result.[50]

Aside from its political value, logrolling can have policy virtues. As R. Douglas Arnold notes,

> It can draw under a single umbrella coalition a whole series of programs, each of which targets funds according to need. Districts then receive substantial benefits where their needs are greatest and nothing where they are marginal.[51]

Logrolling, however, can transform narrowly targeted programs into broad-scale ones. The late senator Paul H. Douglas, D-Ill., sponsored a depressed-areas bill that underwent this kind of transformation. Originally drafted to provide aid to older industrialized regions, the bill met sharp resistance from rural and southern legislators who called it "special legislation for a few spots in Illinois, Pennsylvania, and a few other places." [52] To gain their support, Douglas reluctantly agreed to expand his bill to provide an equal amount for rural areas. He ruefully called the new provisions "pass the biscuits, Pappy." The senator's fears that broadened language would water down the bill to the point of ineffectiveness were not unfounded: once the measure was enacted, two-thirds of all U.S. counties eventually qualified for aid.

In a *time logroll* members agree to support one measure in exchange for later support for another measure. Sometimes the logroll embodies a specified exchange; at other times it is open ended until the donor decides to call in the chips. One explicit exchange occurred in 1983 when the Reagan administration was fighting to fund the controversial MX missile. Playing a broker's role, liberal representative Les Aspin struck a bargain whereby MX funding was traded for the administration's promise to seek future arms control agreements with the Soviet Union. Aspin described the deal as "something that has to continue over several Congresses and several administrations . . . a deal that you're trying to hold together over . . . a period of time." [53]

In a logroll with *side-payments,* support is exchanged for nonissue benefits—for example, a federal project for the state or district, a better committee assignment, inclusion in an important conference, or access to the White House. During the Reagan administration, it was revealed that several GOP senators had bargained votes for judicial appointments they desired. Of course, White House officials are equally adept at such maneuvering. The Reagan administration's $1 billion program to open up new navy "home ports" was a classic pork barrel scheme designed to scatter economic benefits to communities of friendly lawmakers. San Francisco, a Democratic stronghold that already had naval installations, was not included despite concerted lobbying by Sen. Pete Wilson, R-Calif. In May 1985 Wilson left his hospital sickbed to cast a crucial Reagan-backed budget vote. Two San Francisco Bay locations were quickly named as home ports for several decommissioned ships. "The day Wilson was wheeled into the Senate chamber in his pajamas, he won the battleship," a navy official joked.[54] Sometimes the side benefits of bargains may seem trivial or parochial, yet in many cases such payoffs help the member achieve other valued goals.

Are there limits to negotiation? According to bargaining theory, a measure's sponsors will yield only what they absolutely must to gain a majority of supporters. Under this so-called "size principle," a *minimum winning coalition* will occur in legislative bargaining situations under ideal conditions—that is, when the bargainers act rationally and with perfect information.[55] Recounting Senate Majority Leader Lyndon Johnson's meticulous vote counting before a floor fight, political scientist John G. Stewart concluded, "And once a sufficient majority had been counted, Johnson would seldom attempt to enlarge it: Why expend limited bargaining resources which might be needed to win future battles?" [56]

For legislative strategists lacking Johnson's extraordinary skills, however, this advice assumes conditions rarely met in actual situations. Uncertainty about outcomes leads strategists to line up more than a simple majority of supporters. Moreover, at many points in the legislative process extraordinary majorities are required—for example, in constitutional amendments, veto overrides, or in ending Senate filibusters. Not surprisingly, therefore, minimum winning coalitions are not typical of Congress, even in the majoritarian House of Representatives.[57] Yet coalition size is the crux of legislative strategy. Bargainers repeatedly face the dilemma of how broadly or how narrowly to frame their issues or how many concessions to yield in an effort to secure passage.

Bargaining is reflected not only in the substance of legislation but also in many attributes of the legislative process—delay, obfuscation, compromise, and norms such as specialization and reciprocity. It is no exaggeration to say that bargaining is endemic to the legislative way of life. Legislative bargaining shapes the character of bills, resolutions, and other forms of congressional policy making. It is yet another point of contact and conflict between the two Congresses—the Congress of individual wills and the Congress of collective decisions.

Notes

1. Edward Walsh, "Freshman on the Spot," *Washington Post,* April 2, 1987, A1.
2. *Congressional Record,* daily ed., 96th Cong, 2d sess., 1980, H9699.
3. Randall B. Ripley, *Congress: Process and Policy,* 4th ed. (New York: W. W. Norton, 1988), 110-111.
4. David Price, *Who Makes The Laws?* (Cambridge, Mass.: Schenkman Publishing, 1972), 297.
5. Bernard Asbell, *The Senate Nobody Knows* (Garden City, N.Y.: Doubleday, 1978), 210.
6. Richard F. Fenno, Jr., "Observation, Context, and Sequence in the Study of Politics," *American Political Science Review* 80 (March 1976): 3-15.
7. Richard F. Fenno, Jr., *The Making of a Senator: Dan Quayle* (Washington, D.C.: CQ Press, 1989), 43-45.
8. T. R. Reid, *Congressional Odyssey: The Saga of a Senate Bill* (San Francisco: W. H. Freeman, 1980), 15.
9. Sen. William Proxmire, D-Wis., whose voting record extended twenty-two years, described a recurrent nightmare that made him wake up in a sweat: he was locked in a bathroom or trapped inside a stalled elevator, while outside the bells were ringing to summon senators for a floor vote. Proxmire pounded and pounded on the door, to no avail. The roll call was taken—and he was not there. Marlene Cimons, "On Being Perfect: It's Not Easy," *Los Angeles Times,* March 22, 1982, 1.
10. Edward Cowan, "House Panel Completes Tax Action," *New York Times,* July 23, 1981, D7.
11. Margaret Shapiro, "Hoyer Unwittingly Led Antiabortion Cause in Bill Snafu," *Washington Post,* November 15, 1983, E1.
12. Martin Tolchin, "What Becomes of Those Ideals, or Those Idealists," *New York Times,* August 7, 1984, B6.
13. Albert R. Hunt, "Balanced-Budget Measure Is Likely to Pass Senate Next Week, Faces Battle in House," *Wall Street Journal,* July 30, 1982, 2.
14. Mary McGrory, "The Logic of Hellfire," *Washington Post,* February 12,

1984, B1; and Myra McPherson, "Falwell: Big Time Politics from the Pulpit of Old-Time Religion," *Washington Post*, September 27, 1984, D14.

15. William R. Shaffer, *Party and Ideology in the United States Congress* (Lanham, Md.: University Press of America, 1980).

16. John R. Cranford, "Party Unity Scores Slip in 1988, But Overall Pattern Is Upward," *Congressional Quarterly Weekly Report*, November 19, 1988, 3335-3337.

17. Glenn R. Parker and Suzanne L. Parker, "Factions in Committees: The U.S. House of Representatives," *American Political Science Review* 73 (March 1979): 85-102.

18. Cranford, "Party Unity Scores," 3337.

19. Helmut Norpoth, "Explaining Party Cohesion in Congress: The Case of Shared Policy Attitudes," *American Political Science Review* 70 (December 1976): 1171.

20. Lewis A. Froman, Jr., and Randall B. Ripley, "Conditions for Party Leadership: The Case of the House Democrats," *American Political Science Review* 59 (March 1965): 52-63.

21. Lewis A. Froman, Jr., *Congressmen and their Constituencies* (Chicago: Rand McNally, 1963).

22. Thomas A. Flinn and Harold L. Wolman, "Constituency and Roll Call Voting: The Case of Southern Democratic Congressmen," *Midwest Journal of Political Science* 10 (May 1966): 193-199.

23. Ward S. Just, *The Congressman Who Loved Flaubert and Other Washington Stories* (Boston: Little, Brown, 1973), 13-14.

24. Jerrold E. Schneider, *Ideological Coalitions in Congress* (Westport, Conn.: Greenwood Press, 1979); Robert A. Bernstein and William W. Anthony, "The ABM Issue in the Senate, 1968-1970: The Importance of Ideology," *American Political Science Review* 68 (September 1974): 1203; and James B. Kau and Paul H. Rubin, *Congressmen, Constituents, and Contributors* (Boston: Martinus Nijhoff Publishing, 1982), 121-122.

25. John F. Manley, "The Conservative Coalition in Congress," *American Behavioral Scientist* 17 (December 1973): 223-247; Barbara Sinclair, *Congressional Realignment: 1925-1978* (Austin: University of Texas Press, 1982); and Mack C. Shelley, *The Permanent Majority: The Conservative Coalition in the United States Congress* (University, Ala.: University of Alabama Press, 1983).

26. Robert J. Donovan, "For America, A New Coalition?" *Los Angeles Times*, July 6, 1981, 4.

27. Jacob O. Stampen and John R. Davis, "Multi-Issue Coalitions in the Congress: The Appropriate Units of Analysis in Voting Studies" (Paper presented at the Supercomputing Conference '88, Orlando, Florida, November 14-18, 1988).

28. Ronald C. Moe and Steven C. Teel, "Congress as Policy Maker: A Necessary Reappraisal," *Political Science Quarterly* 85 (September 1970): 443-470; and Steven A. Shull, *Domestic Policy Formation: Presidential-Congressional Partnership?* (Westport, Conn.: Greenwood Press, 1983).

29. See Charles O. Jones, *The Trusteeship Presidency: Jimmy Carter and the*

United States Congress (Baton Rouge, La.: Louisiana State University Press, 1988).

30. For a discussion of divided government, see James L. Sundquist, "Needed: A Political Theory for the New Era of Coalition Government in the United States," *Political Science Quarterly* (Winter 1988-89): 613-635.

31. Norman J. Ornstein, Thomas E. Mann, and Michael J. Malbin, *Vital Statistics on Congress, 1987-1988* (Washington, D.C.: Congressional Quarterly, 1987), 198, 203-204.

32. Cleo H. Cherryholmes and Michael J. Shapiro, *Representatives and Roll Calls* (Indianapolis: Bobbs-Merrill, 1969).

33. Donald R. Matthews and James A. Stimson, *Yeas and Nays* (New York: John Wiley & Sons, 1975).

34. Aage R. Clausen, *How Congressmen Decide* (New York: St. Martin's Press, 1973).

35. David M. Kovenock, "Influence in the U.S. House of Representatives: A Statistical Analysis of Communications," *American Politics Quarterly* 1 (October 1973): 456; see also 455, 457.

36. John W. Kingdon, *Congressmen's Voting Decisions*, 2d ed. (New York: Harper & Row, 1981).

37. John F. Bibby, ed., *Congress Off the Record* (Washington, D.C.: American Enterprise Institute, 1983), 22.

38. Albert R. Hunt, "Politicians Don't Play Politics All the Time," *Wall Street Journal*, May 14, 1981, 26.

39. Roger H. Davidson, *The Role of the Congressman* (Indianapolis: Bobbs-Merrill, 1969), 22-23.

40. Robert L. Peabody, "Organization Theory and Legislative Behavior: Bargaining, Hierarchy and Change in the U.S. House of Representatives" (Paper delivered at the annual meeting of the American Political Science Association, New York, New York, September 4-7, 1963).

41. Carl J. Friedrich, *Constitutional Government and Democracy*, 4th ed. (Waltham, Mass.: Blaisdell Publishing, 1967), 269-270.

42. Pat Towell, "Sam Nunn: The Careful Exercise of Power," *Congressional Quarterly Weekly Report*, June 14, 1986, 1330.

43. Jeffrey H. Birnbaum, "Progress of the Tax Bill Enhances Reputation of Sen. Bill Bradley," *Wall Street Journal*, June 4, 1986, 24.

44. Edward J. Derwinski, "The Art of Negotiation within the Congress," in *International Negotiation: Art and Science*, ed. Diane B. Bendahmane and John W. McDonald, Jr. (Washington, D.C.: Foreign Service Institute, U.S. Department of State, 1984), 9.

45. Derwinski, "The Art of Negotiation," 11.

46. John Ferejohn, "Logrolling in an Institutional Context: A Case Study of Food Stamp Legislation," in *Congress and Policy Change*, ed. Gerald C. Wright, Jr., Leroy N. Rieselbach, and Lawrence C. Dodd (New York: Agathon Press, 1986), 223-253.

47. Elliott Abrams, "Unforgettable Scoop Jackson," *Reader's Digest*, February 1985. Quotation cited in *Congressional Record*, 99th Cong., 1st sess., February 20, 1985, E478.

48. David E. Rosenbaum, "The Favors of Rostenkowski: Tax Revision's Quid

Pro Quo," *New York Times*, November 27, 1985, B6.

49. Dale Tate, "Use of Omnibus Bills Burgeons Despite Members' Misgivings," *Congressional Quarterly Weekly Report*, September 25, 1982, 2379.

50. The politics of "blame avoidance" is outlined in R. Kent Weaver, "The Politics of Blame," *The Brookings Review* 5 (Spring 1987): 43-47. The term *credit claiming* originated with David R. Mayhew, *Congress: The Electoral Connection* (New Haven, Conn.: Yale University Press, 1974), 52-61.

51. R. Douglas Arnold, "The Local Roots of Domestic Policy," in *The New Congress*, ed. Thomas E. Mann and Norman J. Ornstein (Washington, D.C.: American Enterprise Institute, 1981), 286.

52. Sar A. Levitan, *Federal Aid to Depressed Areas* (Baltimore: Johns Hopkins University Press, 1964).

53. Michael Getler, "Ex-Maverick Aspin Helped President Get the MX," *Washington Post*, May 27, 1983, A14.

54. Michael Weisskopf, "Navy Port Proliferation Criticized as Politics, Not Strategy," *Washington Post*, August 12, 1985, A7.

55. See William H. Riker, *The Theory of Political Coalitions* (New Haven, Conn.: Yale University Press, 1962), 32. Theorists define legislative bargaining situations formally as n-person, zero-sum games where side payments are permitted. That is, a sizable number of participants are involved; when some participants win, others must lose; and participants can trade items outside the substantive issues under consideration.

56. John G. Stewart, "Two Strategies of Leadership: Johnson and Mansfield," in *Congressional Behavior*, ed. Nelson W. Polsby (New York: Random House, 1971), 67.

57. Russell Hardin, "Hollow Victory: The Minimum Winning Coalition," *American Political Science Review* 79 (December 1976): 1202-1214.

The annual Federal Budget, here starting its press run at the Government Printing Office, is the central instrument for domestic policy making.

CHAPTER THIRTEEN

Congress, Budgets, and Domestic Policy Making

Early in his administration President George Bush called upon "all elements of our society to participate in the fight against drugs because we are dealing with scarce resources in terms of Federal money." [1] Indeed, trying to wage a drug "war" with limited resources is part of the fiscal legacy handed to President Bush by the Reagan administration. With a near tripling of the national debt (from $1 trillion at the start of Reagan's first term to $2.6 trillion and counting eight years later) and budgetary deficits during this period ranging from $150 to $200 billion annually, it is no wonder that the politics of fiscal scarcity dominated policy making by the new president. "The budget deficit has become a deficit issue, a foreign policy issue, a health-care issue, and an education issue," said economic analyst Alice Rivlin. "Getting the budget deficit behind us has become a test of our ability to govern." [2]

Before discussing how Congress is meeting this test, we will first define our terms. What are public policies and how does Congress make them? What are the stages and pitfalls of the policy-making process? After addressing these questions, the chapter then focuses on Congress's budgetary process, including the perennial legislative-executive struggle to influence the size and composition of the federal budget. It is the annual budget, after all, that establishes the nation's policy priorities.

Definitions of Policy

Because policies ultimately are what government is about, it is not surprising that definitions of policy and policy making are diverse and influenced by the beholder's eye. David Easton's celebrated definition of public policy as society's "authoritative allocations" of values or resources is one approach to the question. To put it another way, policies can be regarded as reflecting "who gets what, when, and how" in a society. A more serviceable definition of policy is offered by Randall Ripley and Grace Franklin: policy is what the government says and does about perceived problems. [3]

How do we recognize policies when we see them? The answer is not as simple as it may seem. Many policies, of course, are explicitly labeled and recognized as authoritative statements of what the government is doing, or intends to do, about a given matter. The measures may be far-reaching, like financing the Social Security system; they may be trivial, like proclaiming a "Smokey Bear Week," "National Goat Awareness Week," or "National Ice Cream Month." Nonetheless, they are obvious statements of policy. They are written down, often in painfully precise legal language. They boast documented life histories in committee hearings, reports, or floor deliberations that indicate what legislators had in mind as they hammered out the policy's final provisions.

Not all policies, however, are formal enough to be considered "the law of the land." Some are articulated by officials but, for one reason or another, never set down in laws or rules. The "Monroe Doctrine," which declared U.S. resistance to European intervention in the Western Hemisphere, was developed by Secretary of State John Quincy Adams in the second decade of the nineteenth century and has been adhered to ever since by successive generations of policy makers. Other policies, especially of a symbolic or exhorting nature, gain currency in the eyes of elites or the public without formal or legal elaboration.

Some policies stress substance—programs designed to build the nation's defense, for example. Others stress procedure, such as those requiring contractor insurance for military weapons, imposing personnel ceilings on federal agencies, or mandating program management standards. Still other policies are amalgams of rules or practices meeting specific demands but not perceived as comprising a whole.

It was not until the 1970s that people began to talk about "energy policy," but in truth the nation had such a policy for several generations—a something-for-everyone mixture of producers' tax advantages, artificially low consumer costs, and gasoline-powered transportation (highways, for example). This hodge-podge of programs, which encouraged inefficient use of energy and guaranteed dependence upon foreign oil, haunts the nation's energy policy even today.

Finally, there are policies that are made by negation. Doing nothing about a problem often has results that are as profound as passing a law about it. The nation had no general immigration law prior to 1924 and no medical care program before 1965, but its policies on those matters—favoring unregulated private activity—were unmistakable.

The process of arriving at these policies is *policy making*. The process may be simple or complex, highly publicized or nearly invisible, concentrated or diffuse. It may happen virtually overnight, as when President Ronald Reagan decided in 1983 to dispatch U.S. troops to the Caribbean island of Grenada. Or it may require years or even decades to formulate, as in the case of Medicare or civil rights.[4]

Stages of Policy Making

Whatever the time frame, policy making normally has several distinct stages or phases: setting the agenda, formulating policy, adopting policy, and implementing policy.

Setting the Agenda

At the initial stage public problems are spotted and moved onto the *national agenda,* which can be defined as "the list of subjects to which government officials and those around them are paying serious attention." [5] In a large, complex country like the United States, this agenda at any given moment is extensive and strenuously debated.

How do problems get placed on the agenda? Some are heralded by a crisis or some other prominent event—the hijacking of a plane by terrorists, the demise of savings and loan associations, or a campaign funding scandal. Others are occasioned by the gradual accumulation of knowledge—for example, growing awareness of an environmental hazard like acid rain or new technologies that make telecommunications laws dating from the 1930s obsolete. Still other agenda items represent the accumulation of past problems that can no longer be avoided or ignored. Finally, agendas may be triggered by political processes—election results, turnover in Congress, or shifts in public opinion. [6]

Agenda items are pushed by *policy entrepreneurs,* people willing to invest time and energy to promote a particular issue. Numerous Washington "think tanks" and interest groups, especially at the start of a new president's term, issue reports that seek to influence the economic, social, or foreign policy agenda of the nation. Usually, however, elected officials and their staffs or appointees are more apt to shape agendas than career bureaucrats or nongovernmental actors. [7] Notable policy entrepreneurs on Capitol Hill are congressional leaders who push their party's policy initiatives. "We'll develop our proposals, [Bush] will submit his and then we'll try to mesh them," said Senate Majority Leader George Mitchell, D-Maine. "I don't think we have any obligation . . . just simply to sit and wait for him to make a proposal. There may be some areas in which he makes no proposal at all." [8]

Lawmakers are frequent policy entrepreneurs because they are expected to voice the concerns of constituents and organized groups and to promote legislative solutions. Generally speaking, politicians gravitate toward issues that are visible, salient, and solvable. Tough, arcane, or conflictual problems may be shunned because they offer few payoffs and little hope of success. Sometimes only a crisis—like the 1973 and 1979 oil price increases that triggered long gasoline lines and shortages—can force lawmakers to address such questions. Yet despite enactment of legislation designed to ameliorate future energy problems, Americans today are as dependent on imported oil as they were before. Forecasters predict another energy crisis unless steps are taken to reduce the demand for oil, especially from the volatile Middle East, and to develop alternative fuels. This type of "creeping crisis" is often difficult for members of Congress to grapple with in part because of the "two Congresses." As conscientious lawmakers, they may want to forge long-term solutions. But as representatives of their constituents, they are deterred from acting when most citizens don't see any problems with the immediate situation.

Formulating Policy

In the second stage of policy making, items on the political agenda are discussed and potential solutions explored. At this stage members of Congress and their staffs play crucial roles by conducting hearings and writing committee reports. They are aided by policy experts in executive agencies, interest groups, and the private sector.

Another term for this stage is *policy incubation,* which entails "keeping a proposal alive while it picks up support, or waits for a better climate, or while a consensus begins to form that the problem to which it is addressed exists." [9] Sometimes this process takes only a few months; more often it requires years. During the Eisenhower administration (1953-1961), for example, congressional Democrats explored and refined policy options that, while not immediately accepted, were ripe for adoption by the time their party's nominee, John F. Kennedy, was elected president.[10]

Although policy incubation occurs in both chambers, it is especially promoted in the Senate because of that body's flexible rules, more varied constituent pressures, and greater media coverage. The policy-generating role is particularly characteristic of senators with presidential ambitions who need to capture the attention of both the press and the public.

The incubation process not only brings policies to maturity but also refines solutions to the problems. The process may break down if workable solutions are not available. The seeming intractability of many modern issues complicates problem solving. Speaker Thomas S. Foley, D-Wash., finds issues today far more complicated than when he came to Congress in 1965. At that time

> the civil rights issue facing the legislators was whether the right to vote should be federally guaranteed for blacks and Hispanics. Now members are called on to deal with more ambiguous policies like affirmative action and racial quotas.[11]

Solutions to problems normally involve "some fairly simple routines emphasizing the tried and true (or at least not discredited)." [12] There exists a repertoire of responses—for example, blue-ribbon commissions, trust funds, or pilot projects—that can be applied to a variety of unsolved problems.

Adopting Policy

Laws are ideas whose time has come. The right time for a policy is what scholar John Kingdon calls the *policy window:* the opportunity presented by circumstances and attitudes to enact a policy into law. Policy entrepreneurs must seize the opportunity for the policy window may close and the idea's time pass.

Once policies are ripe for adoption, they must gain popular acceptance. This is the function of *legitimation,* the process through which policies come to be viewed by the public as right or proper. Inasmuch as citizens are expected to comply with laws or regulations—pay taxes, observe rules, or make sacrifices of one sort or another—the policies themselves must appear to have been properly considered and enacted. A nation whose policies lack legitimacy is in deep trouble.

Symbolic acts, such as voting on the House or Senate floor or bill signing by the president, signal to everyone that policies have been duly adopted according to traditional forms. Hearings and debates, moreover, serve not only to fine-tune polices but also to cultivate support among affected interests. Answering critics of Congress's slowness in adopting energy legislation, Sen. Ted Stevens, R-Alaska, asked:

> Would you want an energy bill to flow through the Senate and not have anyone consider the impacts on housing or on the automotive industry or on the energy industries that provide our light and power? Should we ignore the problems of the miner or the producer or the distributor? Our legislative process must reflect all of the those problems if the public is to have confidence in the government.[13]

Legitimating, in other words, often demands a measured pace and attention to procedural details.

Implementing Policy

In the final stage policies shaped by the legislature and the highest executive levels are put into effect, usually by a federal agency. Policies are not self-executing: they must be promulgated and enforced. A law or executive order rarely tells exactly how a particular policy will be implemented. Congress and the president usually delegate most decisions about implementation to the responsible agencies under broad but stated guidelines. Implementation then determines the ultimate impact of policies. Officials of the executive branch can thwart a policy by foot dragging or sheer inefficiency. By the same token, overzealous administrators can push a policy far beyond its creators' intent.

Therefore, Congress then must exercise its oversight role (see also Chapter 9). It may require executive agencies to report or consult with congressional committees or to follow certain formal procedures. Members of Congress get feedback on the operation of federal programs through a variety of channels: media coverage, group protests, and even constituent casework.

With such information Congress can and often does pass judgment by adjusting funding, introducing amendments, or recasting the basic legislation governing the policy.

Types of Domestic Policies

One way to understand public policies is to analyze the nature of the policies themselves. Scholars have classified policies in many different ways.[14] The typology we will use identifies three types of domestic policies: distributive, regulatory, and redistributive.

Distributive Policies

Distributive policies or programs are government actions that convey tangible benefits to private individuals, groups, or firms. Invariably there are subsidies to favored individuals or groups. The benefits are often dubbed *pork* (special-interest spending for projects in members' states or districts), although that appellation is sometimes difficult to define. After all, "one person's pork is another person's steak." The projects also come in several different varieties.

> Dams, roads and bridges, known as "green pork," are old hat. These days, there is also "academic pork" in the form of research grants to colleges, "defense pork" in the form of geographically specific military expenditures and lately "high-tech pork," for example the intense fight to authorize research into super computers and high-definition television (HDTV).[15]

Distributive politics—which make many interests better off and few, if any, visibly worse off—are natural in Congress, which as a nonhierarchical institution must build coalitions in order to function. A textbook example was the $1-billion-plus National Parks and Recreation Act of 1978. Dubbed the "park barrel" bill, it created so many parks, historical sites, seashores, wilderness areas, wild and scenic rivers, and national trails that it sailed through the Interior Committee and passed the House by a 341-to-61 vote. "Notice how quiet we are. We all got something in there," said one House member, after the Rules Committee cleared the bill in five minutes flat. Another member explained: "If it had a blade of grass and a squirrel, it got in the bill." [16] Distributive politics of this kind throws into sharp relief the "two Congresses" notion: national policy as a mosaic of local interests.

The politics of distribution works best when tax revenues are expanding, fueled by high productivity and economic growth—characteristics of the U.S. economy from the end of World War II through the mid-1970s. When productivity declines or zealous tax cutting squeezes revenues, it becomes difficult to add new benefits or expand old ones. Such was the plight of lawmakers in the 1980s. Yet distributive impulses remained strong, adding pressure to wring distributive elements out of tight budgets and to hand out more noneconomic, symbolic benefits (commemorative legislation, for example).

Regulatory Policies

Regulatory policies are designed to protect the public against harm or abuse that might result from unbridled private activity. Thus, the Food and Drug Administration (FDA) monitors standards for foodstuffs and tests drugs for purity, safety, and effectiveness. The Federal Trade Commission (FTC) guards against illegal business practices such as deceptive advertising. The National Labor Relations Board (NLRB) combats unfair labor practices by business firms.

Federal regulation against certain abuses dates from the late nineteenth century when the Interstate Commerce Act and the Sherman Antitrust Act were enacted to protect against transport and monopoly abuses. As the present century dawned, scandalous practices in slaughterhouses and food processing plants, colorfully reported by reform-minded muckraking reporters, led to meatpacking, food, and drug regulations. The 1929 stock market collapse and the Great Depression paved the way for the New Deal legislation regulating the banking and securities industries and labor-management relations. Consumer rights and environmental protection came of age in the 1960s and 1970s. Dramatic attacks on unsafe automobiles by Ralph Nader and others led to new laws mandating tougher safety standards. Concern about smog produced by auto exhausts led to the Clean Air Act of 1970. And concern about airline delay, congestion, and safety during the 1980s prompted Congress to consider new regulatory controls for the nation's air traffic system.

In these cases and many similar ones Congress responded to reformist pressure and passed laws to protect the public. Theorists refer to such policies as *protective regulation* because their purpose is to protect the public and prevent anticipated abuses. In most cases industries stoutly oppose protective regulation, arguing that the public would be better off with self-regulation or mild guidelines than with tough, detailed standards and cumbersone reporting and enforcement procedures. Faced with stiff competition from efficient foreign cars, for example, the auto industry blamed its plight on the plethora of government regulations—safety, low pollution, and fuel economy—and sought relief in quotas.

Competitive regulation is regulatory policy that grants firms or organizations a favored place in the market and helps protect that place by limiting the entry of newcomers to the field. Only occasionally are protective and competitive regulatory policies clearly differentiated. Most regulations serve the dual purpose of protecting the public while at the same time guarding the competitive position of firms within the regulated industry. The policy thus serves distributive as well as regulatory functions, and for this reason the line between distribution and regulation is hard to draw. Many policies, at least in their inception, contain regulatory elements. Potential confusion on the airwaves demands licensing for the public's convenience as well as broadcasters'. Certifying aircraft protects competitors but also guards against unsafe equipment. Many regulations serve the industry's convenience, which underscores the pervasiveness of distributive policies and the tendency of policies to slip into the distributive mode even though they originated for other purposes.

Conflicts about deregulation began in the late 1970s. The trucking, airline, banking, and broadcasting industries were deregulated because economists and consumer groups concluded that federal regulations wasted resources and ultimately hurt consumers. Initially, the industries and their allies, including the regulators and the relevant congressional committees, resisted deregulation. The predictable world of governmental protection seemed more comfortable than the unpredictable world of competition. In these cases the mounting costs of compliance, not to mention the consumers' benefits from competition, overcame the fears of the more conservative sectors of the industry, and Congress authorized relaxation of earlier regulation. By the late 1980s, however, there was growing public and congressional interest in reregulating areas such as public health and safety and industries such as savings and loans and the airlines (see Table 13-1). "I don't think you can ask the free market to make sure that airplanes are working or that the cockpit crew is rested," said Rep. Dan Glickman, D-Kan.[17]

Redistributive Policies

Redistribution is the most difficult of all political feats insofar as it shifts resources visibly from one group to another. Because it is controversial, redistributive policy engages a broad spectrum of political actors—not only in the House and Senate chambers, but in the executive branch, interest groups, and even the public at large. Redistributive issues tend to be ideological. They often separate liberals and conservatives because they upset relationships between social and economic classes. Theodore R. Marmor described the thirty-year fight over medical care for the aged as "cast in terms of class conflict."

> The leading adversaries ... brought into the opposing camps a large number of groups whose interests were not directly affected by the Medicare outcome. ... [I]deological charges and countercharges dominated public discussion, and each side seemed to regard compromise as unacceptable.[18]

Of all public issues, redistribution is the most visible because it involves the most conspicuous allocations of values and resources. Most of the diverse socioeconomic issues of the past generation—civil rights, affirmative action, school busing, aid to education, homelessness, abortion, tax reform—were redistributive problems. Fiscal policy making has taken on a redistributive character as federal expenditures run ahead of revenues and lawmakers are forced to find ways to close the gap. Cutting federal benefits and opening up

Table 13-1 The Regulatory Future

Anticipated action	Anticipated effect
Increased regulation for:	
Savings and loans	Tighter controls over loan making and deposit interest rates.
Airlines	Possible increase in mandatory aircraft inspections and greater regulation of flight times to reduce airport congestion.
Workplace (safety)	Stepped up inspections and tougher enforcement by the Occupational Safety and Health Administration.
Decreased regulation for:	
Electric utilities	Additional competition in power production.
Drug manufacturers	Fewer delays in approval of new drugs by the Food and Drug Administration.
Biotechnology	Streamlined approval of research, testing, and production of genetically engineered organisms.
Natural gas producers	Relaxation of price controls.
New regulatory approaches for:	
Environment	Market-based incentives not to pollute may replace traditional reliance on direct regulation.

Source: Adapted from the *Los Angeles Times,* pt. I, February 5, 1989, 16.

new revenue sources both involve redistribution because they turn "haves" into "have nots." That is why politicians today find budget and revenue issues so burdensome. "I wasn't here in the glory days, when a guy with a bright idea of a scholarship program or whatever could get a few hundred million dollars to pursue it," lamented Rep. Richard Durbin, D-Ill. "Now you've got to take from one to give to the other." [19]

Federal budgeting is marked not only by extreme conflict, but also by techniques to disguise the redistributions or make them more palatable. For example, omnibus packages permit legislators to approve cuts *en bloc* rather than one by one, and across-the-board formulas (like "freezes") give the appearance of spreading the misery equally to affected clienteles. In all such vehicles distributive elements are added to placate the more vocal opponents of change. Such is the unhappy lot of politicians consigned to a redistributive mode.

Characteristics of Congressional Policy Making

As a policy-making machine, Congress displays the traits and biases of its membership and structure. Congress is bicameral with divergent electoral and procedural traditions. It is representative, especially where geographic interests are concerned. It is decentralized, having few mechanisms for integrating or coordinating its policy decisions. And it is reactive, mirroring conventional public or elite perceptions of problems.

Bicameralism

Several differences between the House and Senate—terms of office, size and character of their constituencies, and size of their legislative bodies—powerfully influence the policies they make. Six-year terms, it is argued, allow senators to play the "statesman" for at least part of each term before they are forced by oncoming elections to concentrate on fence mending. This distinction may be more apparent than real, but empirical studies of senators' voting habits lend some support to it.

The different constituencies unquestionably pull in divergent directions, as already noted. The more homogeneous House districts often promote clear and unambiguous positions on a narrower range of questions than those considered by senators who must weigh the claims of many competing interests on a broad range of matters. The size of the chambers, moreover, dictates procedural characteristics. House rules are designed to allow majorities to have their way, as restless Republicans have found to their dismay. In contrast, Senate rules give individual senators great latitude to influence action. "One person can tie this place into a knot," said Senate GOP whip Alan K. Simpson. "And two can do it even more beautifully." [20]

Are the biases of the two bodies consistent? Probably not. For years the Senate appeared more "liberal" than the House because of the presence of urban configurations in most of the states and the lingering effects of malapportionment favoring rural areas in drawing House districts. [21] Today that generalization would be hard to sustain. During the 1980s, Republicans controlled the Senate for six years, while Democrats retained majorities in the House. The two chambers thus differed in outlook, constituency, and strategy. Viewing the mixed long-term policy results, Benjamin Page concludes that bicameralism is less important in promoting or discouraging particular kinds of policies than in "the furtherance of deliberation, the production of evidence, and the revealing of error." [22] In recent years commentators have been struck by the convergence of the two chambers. Senators, like House members, are constantly engaged in reelection activities.

Localism

Congressional policies respond to constituents' needs, particularly those that can be mapped geographically. Sometimes these needs are pinpointed with startling directness. For example, an aviation noise control bill required construction of a control tower "at latitude 40 degrees, 43 minutes, 45 seconds north and at longitude 73 degrees, 24 minutes, 50 seconds west"—the exact location of a Farmingdale, New York, airport in the district of the Democratic representative who requested the provision.[23]

Usually, however, programs are directed toward states, municipalities, counties, or geographic regions. Funds are often transferred directly to local government agencies, which in turn deliver the aid or services to citizens. Or local agencies may act, individually or in consortiums, as "prime sponsors" for a bundle of closely related services—in community development or worker training, for example—that can be tailored to local needs.

Although national and local policies are necessarily interwined, the level of government making a policy is important for several reasons. First, interest groups wield different degrees of influence at various governmental levels. Racial, ethnic, and labor groups, for example, traditionally prefer national legislation; business and industry groups tend to prefer local action, which they feel more confident of bending to their purposes. Second, policy makers are sensitive to local traditions, some of which may be far ahead of the "nationwide consensus" and others of which may lag behind. Members of Congress represent localities and often share local policy makers' views.

Finally, national policies can be advanced by state and local governments, or states and localities can develop innovations that can spur national action. "I can't think of a time when they [state governments] have been so involved in helping to shape federal legislation," stated Rep. Thomas Downey, D-N.Y.[24] With shrinking fiscal assistance from the federal government, states and localities are fashioning creative solutions to many problems that the national government has been unable or unwilling to address. Some states have been so active in passing laws and issuing regulations that original advocates of local controls, such as business executives, "have found themselves running back to the arms of the federal government, asking Washington to preempt [legal and regulatory] action taken by the states." [25]

Many policy debates therefore revolve around the governmental level at which they should be resolved. Ideology makes little difference: liberals seek to enforce national standards in civil rights or environmental protection, but conservatives are equally eager to override local preferences in drunk driving or drug trafficking standards, "equal access" of religious groups to school facilities, and other policies. Preference for a given level of government is invariably overridden by one's zeal for the policy itself.

Piecemeal Policy Making

Policies all too often mirror Congress's scattered and decentralized structure. Policies are typically considered piecemeal, reflecting the patchwork of committee and subcommittee jurisdictions. Sometimes policies are duplicative or even contradictory; committees may sponsor price supports and agricultural research promoting tobacco production at the same time they fund research on lung cancer. Congress's segmented decision making is typified by authorizing and appropriating processes in which separate committees consider the same programs often without consulting each other.

The structure of a given policy often depends on which committees have reported it. Working from varying jurisdictions, committees can take different approaches to the same problem. A program from the taxing committees will feature tax provisions, from the Appropriations committees a fiscal approach, from the commerce panels a regulatory approach, and so forth. The approach may be well or ill suited to the policy objective—it all depends on which committee was the best positioned to promote the bill.

Symbolic Policy Making

Despite its reputation for uncontrolled spending binges, Congress is actually addicted to solutions to problems that are inexpensive and often symbolic. Not infrequently a bold national policy is coupled with funds limited to a few pilot projects or scattered too widely for maximum effect. Underfunding of programs is at least as common as overfunding. Sometimes this happens because of unforeseen consequences (for example, the number of eligible citizens rises); just as often it flows from political wishful thinking.

A wide repertoire of low-cost options exist for any given policy goal. Rather than finance a new standard, Congress can mandate the standard and pass on the cost of compliance to manufacturers or consumers. In selecting policy targets, Congress can choose low-ticket items over really tough, expensive ones. Rather than finance a program completely, Congress can offer a pilot program or loan guarantees, with repayment expected. Finally, lawmakers can hold out the prospect of recovering funds by eliminating "fraud, waste, and abuse." [26]

At heart, congressional policy making deals with appearances as much or more than with substantive results. Symbolic actions are important to all politicians. This is not the same thing as saying that politicians are merely cynical manipulators of symbols. Words and concepts—*equal opportunity, affirmative action, cost of living, parity*—are contested earnestly in committee rooms and on the House and Senate floor. The result, however, is that federal goals frequently are stated in vague, optimistic language, not spelled out in terms of specific measures of success or failure.

Often measures are passed to give the impression that action is being taken when the impact or efficacy of the measure is wholly unknown. Groups outside of Congress continually demand: "Don't just stand there, do something." Doing "something" is often the only politically feasible alternative, even when no one really knows what to do or when inaction might be just as effective.

Reactive Policy Making

At any given moment elected officials are seldom far ahead or far behind the collective views of the citizenry. Hence, it would be misguided to expect the national legislature to express "radical" solutions to problems. Members know that radical views are unlikely to attract widespread public support.

Congress is essentially a reactive institution, as one House member explained:

> When decision rests on the consent of the governed, it comes slowly, only after consensus has built or crisis has focused public opinion in some unusual way, the representatives in the meantime hanging back until the signs are unmistakable. Government decision, then, is not generally the cutting edge of change but a belated reaction to change.[27]

The reactive character of Congress's policy making is evident in its budget process. Under pressures to reform, Congress reacted in 1974, 1985, and again in 1987 with changes in how it makes budget decisions. As noted at the beginning of this chapter, the annual budget passed by Congress reflects the policy priorities of the nation. Today's budget process, dating from the mid-1970s, was designed to bring coherence to the way standing committees handle the president's budget. Since then it has decisively shaped both Congress's internal decision making and legislative-executive relations.

Authorizations and Appropriations

Every committee wants a hand in the budget. Hence, Congress has a two-step financial procedure: *authorizations* and *appropriations*. Congress first passes authorization laws that establish federal agencies and programs and recommend funding them at certain levels. Then it enacts appropriation laws that allow agencies to spend money. An authorization, then, is like an "IOU" that needs to be validated by an appropriation.

There are different kinds of authorizations and appropriations: annual, multiyear, and permanent. Through the end of World War II, most federal agencies and programs were permanently authorized; they were reviewed annually by the appropriating committees but not the authorizing panels. Since the 1970s, there has been a trend toward short-term authorizations, giving the authorizing committees more chances to control agency operations.[28]

The authorization-appropriation sequence is an invention of Congress. It is required by House and Senate rules, not by the Constitution. Historically, the dual procedure stemmed from inordinate delays caused by adding *riders*—extraneous policy amendments—to appropriation bills. "By 1835," wrote a legislator, "delays caused by injecting legislation [policy] into these [appropriation] bills had become serious and John Quincy Adams suggested that they be stripped of everything save appropriations." [29] Two years later the House required authorizations to precede appropriations. The Senate followed suit.

Here is what happens after an authorizing committee—such as Agriculture, Banking, or Commerce—approves a new program or policy. Our hypothetical example recommends $20 million for an Energy Department solar research and development program. Under the authorization-appropriation procedure the bill must pass both houses and be signed by the president before the Energy Department has the "authorization" to establish the program.

Then the House Appropriations Committee (actually, one of its thirteen virtually autonomous subcommittees) must propose how much money ("budget authority") the solar program should receive. The Appropriations Committee can provide the whole $20 million (but not more), propose cuts, or refuse to fund the program at all. Let's assume that the House goes along with Appropriations in approving $15 million. Then the Senate Appropriations Committee, acting somewhat like a "court of appeals," hears agency officials asking the Senate to approve the full $20 million. If the Senate accedes, a House-Senate compromise is worked out under the procedure described in Chapter 11.

In practice it is hard to keep the two stages distinct. There are authorizations that carry appropriations and appropriation bills that contain legislation (or policy provisions). In the House *limitation riders* make policy under the guise of restricting agency use of funds. Always phrased negatively ("None of the funds...."), limitations bolster congressional control of bureaucracy. Members employed limitations so frequently (from 47 floor amendments in 1963 to more than 165 by 1980) that the House changed its rules in 1983 to make it more difficult to offer them.[30]

Among the authorizing committees, House Ways and Means and Senate Finance have especially strong roles in the budget process. Both tax panels have access to the staff experts of the Joint Taxation Committee. Because the House initiates revenue measures, it typically controls whether Congress will act on measures to raise, lower, or redistribute taxes. Occasionally, however, the Senate takes the lead. The Senate can technically comply with the Constitution by taking a minor House-passed revenue bill and adding to it a major Senate tax measure. In 1981 the Republican-controlled Senate acted first on President Reagan's sweeping tax-cut plan by employing this tactic.[31] To be sure, the House jealously guards its constitutional authority to originate tax measures and may return to the Senate any bills that violate the origination clause.

"Backdoor" Spending Techniques

To sidestep the appropriations axe, authorizing committees evolved "backdoor" spending techniques—that is, funding provisions that are outside the appropriations process. There are three types of backdoors. *Contract author-*

ity permits agencies to enter into contracts that subsequently must be liquidated by appropriations. *Borrowing authority* allows agencies to spend money they have borrowed from the public or the Treasury. And *mandatory entitlements* grant eligible individuals and governments the right to receive payments from the national government. The fastest growing of these three techniques, entitlements establish judicially enforceable rights without reference to dollar amounts; that is, spending for entitlement programs (Medicare and Social Security, for example) is determined by the number of citizens who qualify and the benefit levels established by law.

These backdoor devices weakened Congress's capacity to control federal spending. By 1973 only 44 percent of the federal budget was handled by the appropriating committees, and interest on the federal debt—another uncontrollable expenditure—was soaring. Today about 60 percent of the budget is relatively uncontrollable because of laws that mandate spending. If Congress adjourned on its very first day in session, the government would be legally empowered to spend huge sums. Moreover, spending rises automatically because many federal programs (Social Security and veterans' pensions, for example) are indexed to the cost of living.

Pressures for Reform

The loosening of Congress's purse strings opened it to charges of being spendthrift and financially irresponsible. President Richard Nixon blamed it for annual deficits, consumer price hikes, high joblessness, and inflation. He also impounded (refused to spend) monies duly appropriated by Congress. Although his administration lost every court challenge to the impoundments, Nixon won the political high ground. He made Congress's haphazard budget process a major issue of the 1972 presidential campaign. In October he told a nationwide radio audience:

> But, let's face it, Congress suffers from institutional faults when it comes to Federal spending. In our economy, the President is required by law to operate within the discipline of his budget, just as most American families must operate within the discipline of their budget.
>
> In the Congress, however, it is vastly different. Congress does not consider the total financial picture when it votes on a particular spending bill; it does not even contain a mechanism to do so if it wished.[32]

These diverse pressures prompted Congress to restructure its budget procedures.

The 1974 Budget Act

The Budget and Impoundment Control Act of 1974 created the House Budget Committee, the Senate Budget Committee, and the Congressional Budget Office (CBO), which prepares economic forecasts for Congress and issues fiscal, monetary, and policy reports. The 1974 act also established a rigorous timetable for action on authorization, appropriation, and tax measures.

Every year Congress was required to adopt at least two concurrent budget resolutions, but the resolutions had no legal effect and required no action by the president. The first budget resolution, which was supposed to be adopted by May 15, recommended targets for overall federal spending during the fiscal year. By September 15 the budget committees reported a second resolution that was shaped by Congress's previous spending decisions and the needs of the economy. This resolution established binding budgetary totals for Congress. If the spring and summer spending decisions of Congress exceeded these binding totals, then budgetary discipline could be imposed through a potent *reconciliation process* that forced appropriate committees to report bills that raised revenue or reduced spending. Reconciliation "forces committees that might not want to reduce spending for the entitlements under their jurisdiction to act and report legislation." [33]

Finally, the 1974 act limited presidential use of impoundments. They are divided into two categories: *rescissions* and *deferrals*. A rescission is an executive branch recommendation to cancel congressionally approved spending for a program. Presidents propose deferrals if they want to delay temporarily the spending of certain funds.[34]

Changes in the Budget Process

Until the mid-1980s, when concern about mushrooming deficits powerfully gripped Congress, the 1974 act was amended only a few times and in relatively minor ways. Informally, it was significantly revised as the result of ad hoc actions and an "elastic clause" in the act that permits Congress to prescribe "any other procedure which is considered appropriate to carry out the purposes of this Act."

Two changes are particularly important. First, Congress dropped the fall budget resolution, leaving the first, or spring, resolution as the major vehicle for budgeting. There simply wasn't enough time to consider two major budget resolutions. Second, Congress moved the reconciliation process to the beginning of the budget timetable (in tandem with the first budget resolution) rather than to the end (see Table 13-2 for the 1989 timetable).

Reagan and the 1981 Reconciliation

The two-stage reconciliation process works this way: during stage one, Congress adopts a concurrent budget resolution giving each designated committee a dollar figure for savings and a deadline for reporting legislation to achieve the savings. During stage two, the budget panels compile the legislative recommendations of the instructed committees into an omnibus reconciliation bill.

When Reagan took office he moved quickly to cut domestic social

Table 13-2   Budget Timetable, 1989

Deadline	Action to be completed
January 9	President Reagan submits to Congress his fiscal 1990 budget, which under the Gramm-Rudman-Hollings law must include a deficit no greater than $100 billion.
February 9	President Bush outlines his own spending priorities.
April 15	Congress adopts a budget resolution, meeting the $100-billion deficit target, to guide subsequent spending and tax legislation.
June 15	Congress enacts a reconciliation bill, making any changes necessary in existing laws to achieve spending cuts and revenue increases called for in budget resolution.
August 25	OMB issues a report on the estimated fiscal 1990 deficit based on spending and tax legislation enacted up to August 15. If the deficit exceeds $110 billion, the president issues an order cutting most domestic and defense programs sufficiently to reach the $100-billion target.
October 1	Fiscal 1990 begins. If Congress still has not cut the deficit to $110 billion, automatic spending cuts take effect.
October 15	OMB issues a final report, revised to account for recent congressional action. If Congress still has not trimmed the deficit to $110 billion, the president issues a final order making the spending cuts permanent.

Source: Adapted from the *Los Angeles Times*, pt. I, January 10, 1989, 12.

programs. Skillfully he used reconciliation to package hundreds of domestic spending cuts in one bill, and he pressured Congress to pass it. In February 1981 Reagan recommended that Congress cut more than $130 billion over three years from numerous social programs outlined by David Stockman, his director of the Office of Management and Budget and a former GOP House member and congressional aide. Reagan, Stockman, and their congressional allies conceived the strategy of using the reconciliation procedure to achieve their spending goals. "Without reconciliation," said Pete V. Domenici, R-N.M., the chairman of the Senate Budget Committee, "it would be absolutely impossible to cut the budget by this dimension." [35]

Reagan's economic plan dominated the 1981 reconciliation process, and his victories were especially remarkable in the Democratic-led House. During stage one, Reagan and Stockman objected that the Democrats' cuts were not deep enough. Reps. Phil Gramm, D-Texas (now a GOP senator), and Delbert Latta, R-Ohio, developed a Reagan-endorsed substitute that the House adopted. The instruction resolution (Gramm-Latta I) passed Congress, and House and Senate panels were given three weeks to report their reconciliation bills. Working under pressure, almost every congressional committee complied, but Reagan and Stockman charged that several of the cuts made by Democratic-controlled House committees were unrealistic or even phony.

Working with Stockman, Gramm and Latta hastily drafted a substitute reconciliation package (Gramm-Latta II) the day before the vote. It was filled with penciled-in additions, crossed-out items, misnumbered pages, and even the name and phone number of a budget staff aide. This effort infuriated Democrats, especially Jim Wright, D-Texas, then the majority leader:

> There has never been an administration that has demanded to dictate so completely to the Congress, certainly not Lyndon Johnson in his heyday or Franklin Roosevelt in his. I don't know what it will take to satisfy them; I guess for the Congress to resign and give them our voting proxy cards.[36]

Despite these objections, the House agreed to the deep, multiyear reduction in domestic spending. A few days later Congress also agreed to the Economic Recovery Tax Act of 1981, which sharply cut tax rates for individuals and businesses.

Debt and Deficits

The revenue losses caused by the tax cuts, increased defense spending, and insuffficient funding reductions in other areas soon produced annual budget deficits in the $200 billion range. Never before had the nation seen such huge deficits during an economic expansion (following the 1982 recession). *Borrow* and *spend* or *debt* and *consumption* were the catchwords of this period and affected more than just the national government. As economist Lester Thurow explained:

> The federal government is not strange. The federal government is going into debt. Consumers are going into debt. Firms are going into debt. It isn't as though the federal government is being profligate and the rest of us are not. It's a consistent national pattern of behavior.[37]

As budgetary deficits mounted, so did disagreement on how to address the problem. President Reagan vigorously opposed defense cuts and tax hikes ("over my dead body," he said) and insisted on further domestic cuts. Underlying this ideological, institutional, and often sharp partisan disagreement was fundamental conflict over the appropriate role of the national government. Congress and the president each favored spending but for different priorities. Legislative-executive deadlock often characterized fiscal politics with each branch and party able to play the "blame game—blaming the other for inaction.

The Gramm-Rudman-Hollings Plan

It was this political and economic stalemate that prompted passage in late 1985 of a deficit reduction plan sponsored by Senators Phil Gramm, R-

Texas, Warren Rudman, R-N.H., and Ernest Hollings, D-S.C. The Gramm-Rudman-Hollings bill (GRH) established a statutory pathway to "zero out" the deficit and produce a balanced federal budget. The Supreme Court declared a portion of the 1985 law unconstitutional the next year because it violated the constitutional separation of powers by granting the General Accounting Office, a legislative support agency, executive functions.[38] However, Congress quickly fixed the constitutional defect by passing GRH II (the Balanced Budget and Emergency Deficit Control Reaffirmation Act of 1987). GRH II directed an executive agency, the Office of Management and Budget, to issue a report that could trigger across-the-board cuts (*sequestration*) in the domestic and defense areas. GRH II also established the budgetary timetable shown in Table 13-2.

Sequestration is the core concept of GRH. Its objective is to change the political dynamics between the legislative and executive branches. If neither branch can support a spending blueprint that meets the annual deficit reduction target ($136 billion in 1989, $100 billion in 1990, $64 billion in 1991, $28 billion in 1991, and $0 in 1993; a $10 billion "fudge factor" is built into these yearly targets), then the president must make across-the-board spending cuts evenly divided between domestic and defense programs. Nearly 70 percent of the budget is exempt from sequestration. Many domestic and defense programs are subject to automatic cuts, but popular entitlement programs, such as Social Security, are not. As Figure 13-1 shows, payments to individuals in the form of entitlements now represent the greatest share of the federal budget. Deficit reduction is difficult to achieve when so much of the federal budget is exempt from cutbacks.

Many members opposed GRH because sequestration delegates fiscal authority to unelected officials—those at OMB who prepare the sequestration report that the president is directed to submit without change to Congress. Even one of the principal sponsors, Senator Rudman, dubbed the act a "bad idea whose time has come." To avoid blame from constituents for being "soft on the deficit," most members wanted some way to address the problem, but they never expected the sequestration mechanism to be used.[39] According to Senator Hollings, the objective of the deficit reduction plan is to make certain that indiscriminate cuts in domestic and defense programs do not occur. Its real purpose, he contends, is to force Congress and the president to act responsibly in meeting the deficit targets.[40]

Despite the specter of sequestration, Congress and the president remained at loggerheads in the aftermath of GRH II. President Reagan vowed to veto any tax increases. Congress objected to further cuts in domestic discretionary programs. Neither was eager to cut defense after several years of little real growth. And neither wanted to cut entitlement programs significantly, in part because of the electoral potency of the recipients, especially the elderly.

What finally compelled the two branches to work together was the October 1987 stock market crash. "The crash did what [GRH] was

Figure 13-1   Composition of the Federal Budget, 1965 and 1990

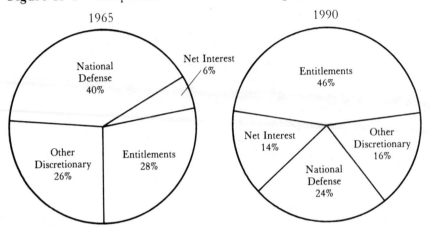

1965   1990

Source: Congressional Budget Office. Charts developed by Robert Keith, Congressional Research Service.
Note: Data based on federal budget outlays, excluding offsetting receipts.

supposed to do but never did, force everyone to negotiate," explained Rep. Barney Frank, D-Mass.[41] At a fiscal summit in November 1987, representatives of Congress and the president negotiated a two-year budget agreement. For the first time in twenty-eight years, Congress passed all thirteen general appropriations bills (which fund half of the government's programs and activities) before the start of the fiscal year on the first of October.

Assessment and Implications

What were the political, procedural, and policy consequences of Congress's revamped budget process? In this section we address this question with particular attention to effects on legislative-executive decision making.

Smoke and Mirror Budgeting

Congress's budget process is shrouded in complexities that few people, including legislators, really understand. As we have seen, Congress added budget resolution and reconciliation procedures to the authorization and appropriations processes in 1974. Then in 1987 another procedure—sequestration—was overlaid on a budget process that already was inordinately complicated. Added to all this are legislative-executive conflicts that often delay the work of shrinking the deficit and promote the use of fiscal gimmicks to give the appearance that budget targets are being met. "To show that the deficit is shrinking and to avoid triggering the automatic reduction procedures," wrote two scholars, "budgeters have sometimes used unrealistic economic assumptions, accounting gimmicks, and one-shot savings, such as loan asset sales and the shifting of pay dates." [42] Spending "cuts," then, often reflect reductions in inflated fiscal projections rather than cutbacks in the past year's actual expenditures. This type of smoke and mirror budgeting makes it hard to know whether deficits are really being reduced.

Government by Continuing Resolution

Whenever Congress cannot complete action on one or more of the thirteen regular appropriation bills by the start of the fiscal year, it provides temporary emergency funding for the affected federal agencies through a continuing resolution. Once continuing resolutions were employed to keep a few government agencies in operation for short periods (usually one to three months). In the 1980s continuing resolutions were often major policy-making instruments of massive size and scope. They authorize and appropriate money for much of the federal government and make national policy in diverse substantive areas. The surge in these omnibus packages has been attributed to Congress's inability to meet budgetary timetables, the strife engendered by rising deficits and cutback budgeting, and sharp and persistent legislative-executive conflicts over spending priorities.

In 1986 and 1987 Congress packaged all thirteen regular appropriation bills into one continuing resolution, making them the largest spending bills in Congress's history. These mega-bills, widely lambasted as a perversion of the lawmaking process, give Congress political leverage over the president. Bundling all appropriation measures into a continuing resolution undercuts the potency of the president's veto power. He is presented with a "take it or leave it" dilemma. The president could veto the continuing resolution, but that would temporarily shut down the federal government.

Budgeting and Centralized Authority

The revamped budget process has tended to centralize and integrate legislative actions. Party leaders shape the budget panels' membership, monitor their activities, and mobilize the winning coalitions needed to pass the often controversial fiscal packages. Voting on budget resolutions is along party lines. As Rep. David Price, D-N.C., put it, "The budget situation centralizes power. It affects everything we do: it affects what initiatives are viable, it affects who has power, it determines the preoccupation of the party leaders." [43] In an institution noted for its wide diffusion of power, budgetary activities are indeed centralizing forces. The members who put fiscal packages together—key committee members and party leaders—exercise potent bargaining and decision-making influence on behalf of their colleagues. Needless to say, this trend often rankles "backbench" members. Legislative-executive budget summits, as a result, are not always viewed positively by members who believe they short-circuit committee prerogatives and enhance the authority of a small group of member-negotiators at the expense of everyone else.

The "Two Congresses" Under Stress

During the 1980s, it became harder for members of Congress to initiate new programs for their constituents because of high deficits. Interest payments on the national debt (the accumulation of annual deficits) by 1989 even exceeded the annual budget deficit (around $150 billion). Along with the president and other public and private entities, Congress is responsible for the health of the national economy. Yet members must remain responsive to constituency pressures. The result is a conflict between deficit reduction and "bringing home the bacon." Here is how one conservative Republican in the House tried to resolve this conflict:

> I'm going to do everything I can to cut spending, not only in [the] Appropriations [Committee] but in the authorizing committees. But then, when it's all said and done, and money is taken from my constituents, I think it's my responsibility to get some of that money back for my constituents.[44]

The problem is that many constituents dislike deficits, oppose taxes, yet favor greater spending for popular programs. As Nobel-Prize-winning economist Paul Samuelson wrote:

> There is a fiscal impasse in American politics. But I must insist that it is not primarily an impasse between president and the Congress. The impasse is a Main Street impasse. . . . We love low tax rates. At the same time we insist on social security, health programs, defense expenditures, bank insurance, farm aids, and a safety net for the unemployed, handicapped, and aged.[45]

The arithmetic for addressing the deficit seems plain: raise revenues, cut spending, or devise an acceptable combination of the two. (To be sure, some assert that record deficits pose no immediate threat to the economy, that their high level reflects mismeasurement rather than reality, and that economic growth will produce the revenues needed to lower the deficit to an acceptable range rather than to an arbitrary and precise target specified by GRH). But the political calculus for action is more difficult to devise. The electorate appears unwilling to accept painful, belt-tightening actions. What's required, according to one analyst, is a "changed political climate: a public willing to end spending for programs that are ineffective or don't serve vital national needs, and a recognition that what's left—and any new programs—must be covered by higher taxes."[46] It is unclear whether political leadership or economic crisis will promote such a political climate.

"Zero-Sum" Policy Making

The Gramm-Rudman-Hollings deficit reduction plan has changed the procedural and political rules of legislative budget making. Procedurally, members who recommend spending more for something must suggest offsetting receipts or cutbacks in other programs. Even lobbyists, said Senator Rudman, "are forced to come up with offsetting reductions when they push their favorite causes, meaning that the budget struggle has become a 'zero sum game' that does not add to the deficit." [47] Politically, GRH has expanded the scope of interest of members and interest groups. Because of GRH, said a lobbyist for the elderly, "for the first time, we're being drawn into nonelderly matters. We even have to take positions on defense and taxes." [48]

It is difficult to promote new initiatives in a climate of fiscal austerity, yet legislators are creative politicians. They have proposed social innovations that cost little or no federal money and that create no new bureaucracies. One way to accomplish their goals and to meet pent-up public demands is to mandate that other entities—businesses or state and local governments—pay for the new programs. Another tactic of legislators is to include some major policy changes in the "must pass" reconciliation bills.

New Roles for Committees

In the contemporary climate of fiscal austerity, the authorizing committees infrequently report new programs. Instead, their primary focus is often on protecting favorite programs from drastic spending cuts. "It's no fun to be an authorization committee chairman anymore," said a House member. "They can't get new programs passed. The best they can do is preserve their most beloved programs at some level that makes sense." [49] Between the budget resolution and appropriations stages, there is little time left for debating the recommendations of the authorization committees. As a result, these panels have lost influence to the Appropriations and Budget committees.

Long regarded as protectors of the purse, the Appropriations committees have become "claimants . . . for higher spending" who are "policed by budget controls." [50] Buffeted by various changes in the 1970s and 1980s, including the right of the House Democratic Caucus to elect Appropriations sub-committee chairmen (which heightened their sensitivity to broader interests), the Appropriations committees have somewhat shifted their role from fiscal naysayers to spending advocates. Moreover, the Appropriations committees face greater challenges from rank-and-file members than in the past. Reluctant to cut entitlements or increase taxes, members now focus their deficit reduction efforts on appropriation bills.

The tax panels, long regarded as "power committees" because of their prestige, jurisdictional prerogatives, and ability to win floor enactment of their products, also changed during this period. During the 1970s, for instance, the House Ways and Means Committee was compelled to establish subcommit-tees and to conduct its meetings in public. These kinds of reforms made the panel more responsive to outside interests and to the entire House. The House and Senate tax panels adapted to the changed circumstances and began to employ a variety of effective techniques—committee party caucuses, weekend retreats, omnibus bills, strategy meetings with party leaders, discussions with noncommittee members, and closed business meetings—that produced successful legislation.[51] The landmark 1986 overhaul of the internal revenue code, accomplished despite the opposition of well-organized special interests, bears testimony to the skillful exploitation of these techniques and to the power of an idea whose time had come.[52]

Conclusion

In sum, Congress's revamped budget process has produced successes and failures. On the one hand, it has promoted budgetary coherence and coordination within the House and Senate, fostered fiscal sophistication in Congress, and strengthened the legislature's financial capabilities in dealing with presidential budgets (which now represent negotiating instruments rather than firm statements of national priorities). The Gramm-Rudman-Hollings plan has become a fiscal benchmark against which Congress's performance on deficit reduction is measured. On the other hand, members are frustrated with the budget process because fiscal matters consume so much time. The national budget is not one document but many—appropriation bills, tax bills, and reconciliation measures, for instance—that in the aggregate produce the nation's fiscal blueprint. Little surprise that budgeting has become a full-time, year-round activity.

Constrained by huge deficits, legislators operate largely in an era of fiscal subtraction rather than addition. "The process of the budget," stated House Budget Committee Chairman Leon Panetta, "has become basically a process of saying 'no.' "[53] Moreover, tight money heightens tensions among committees, between the branches, and between the parties.

Needless to say, President Bush confronts the same fiscal reality as Congress. "Drugs, education, acid rain. I talked about the same things [as Bush] in my campaign," said Rep. Stephen Neal, D-N.C. "The problem is how do you pay for it."[54] Soon after taking office President Bush reached out to Congress and urged negotiations to craft a national budget. This strategy promoted legislative-executive cooperation, but some Democrats wondered whether it was a way for Bush to share the blame with Congress for making tough decisions. As the 101st Congress got under way there was some discussion of easing deficit targets "to produce a balanced operating budget by the end of the century" rather than by 1993, the deadline set by GRH II.[55]

Many analysts see a much larger problem than the budget deficits. As one political commentator explained, "The budget deficits are ultimately a symptom of a much larger—and less manageable—weakness of the U.S. economy. We aren't getting richer as quickly as we used to."[56] Slower economic growth means fewer dollars to finance old programs or start new ones. There are no easy ways either to enhance productivity or to allocate or reallocate scarce resources among competing priorities. Governing means making choices, and, in the end, our annual national budget reflects the values, goals, and priorities that result from the clashes and accommodations that are inherent in our pluralistic policy-making system.

Notes

1. *New York Times,* January 26, 1989, D22.
2. *Wall Street Journal,* January 20, 1989, R16.
3. See David Easton, *The Political System* (New York: Alfred A. Knopf, 1963); Harold D. Lasswell, *Politics: Who Gets What, When, How* (New York: Meridian Books, 1958); and Randall B. Ripley and Grace A. Franklin, *Congress, the Bureaucracy, and Public Policy,* 4th ed. (Homewood, Ill.: Dorsey Press, 1987), 1.
4. Theodore R. Marmor, *The Politics of Medicare* (Chicago: Aldine Publishing, 1973).
5. John W. Kingdon, *Agendas, Alternatives, and Public Policies* (Boston: Little, Brown, 1984), 3.
6. Ibid, 17-19.
7. Ibid., chap. 2.
8. *Washington Post,* January 3, 1989, A5.
9. Nelson W. Polsby, "Strengthening Congress in National Policymaking," *The Yale Review* (Summer 1970): 481-497.
10. James L. Sundquist, *Politics and Policy: The Eisenhower, Kennedy, and Johnson Years* (Washington, D.C.: Brookings Institution, 1968).
11. Elizabeth Wehr, "Numerous Factors Favoring Good Relationship Between Reagan and New Congress," *Congressional Quarterly Weekly Report,* January 24, 1981, 173.
12. Kingdon, *Agendas,* 148-149.
13. American Enterprise Institute, *The State of the Congress: Tomorrow's Challenges?* (Washington, D.C.: American Enterprise Institute, 1981), 8.
14. Theodore Lowi, "American Business, Public Policy, Case Studies, and Political Theory," *World Politics* (July 1964): 677-715; Lowi, "Four Systems of Policy, Politics and Choice," *Public Administration Review* (July/August 1972): 298-310; Samuel P. Huntington, *The Common Defense* (New York: Columbia University Press, 1961); and Ripley and Franklin, *Congress, the Bureaucracy, and Public Policy.*
15. *Wall Street Journal,* May 13, 1988, 17R.
16. Mary Russell, " 'Park-Barrel Bill' Clears House Panel," *Washington Post,* June 22, 1978, A3.
17. *New York Times,* December 11, 1988, 1.
18. Marmor, *The Politics of Medicare,* 108-109.

19. *Christian Science Monitor,* April 13, 1987, 6.

20. *New York Times,* May 21, 1987, B10.

21. Lewis A. Froman, Jr., *Congressmen and Their Constituencies* (Chicago: Rand McNally, 1963).

22. Benjamin I. Page, "Cooling the Legislative Tea," in *American Politics and Public Policy,* ed. Walter Dean Burnham and Martha Wagner Weinberg (Cambridge, Mass.: MIT Press, 1978), 171-187.

23. Judy Sarasohn, "Money for Lat. 40° N., Long. 73° W," *Congressional Quarterly Weekly Report,* May 12, 1979, 916.

24. *Wall Street Journal,* July 29, 1988, 38.

25. *Washington Post,* August 30, 1988, A16.

26. Kingdon, *Agendas,* 112ff.

27. Barber Conable, "Government Is Working," *Roll Call,* April 19, 1984, 3. To be sure, there are many instances when Congress has initiated change. A classic example is the 37th Congress (1861-1863), which drafted "the blueprint for modern America" by enacting measures to finance the Civil War, build the transcontinental railroad, eradicate slavery, promote the land-grant college movement, provide homesteaded land to settlers, and create the Department of Agriculture. See James M. McPherson, *Battle Cry of Freedom: The Civil War Era* (New York: Ballantine Books, 1988), 452.

28. See Louis Fisher, "Annual Authorizations: Durable Roadblocks to Biennial Budgeting," *Public Budgeting and Finance* (Spring 1983): 23-40.

29. Robert Luce, *Legislative Problems* (Boston: Houghton Mifflin, 1935), 426. See also Louis Fisher, "The Authorization-Appropriation Process in Congress: Formal Rules and Informal Practices," *Catholic University Law Review* (Fall 1979): 51-105; and Richard F. Fenno, Jr., *The Power of the Purse* (Boston: Little, Brown, 1966).

30. Allen Schick, "Politics Through Law: Congressional Limitations on Executive Discretion," in *Both Ends of the Avenue,* ed. Anthony King (Washington D.C.: American Enterprise Institute, 1983), 173.

31. *Washington Post,* July 3, 1981, A7; and *Washington Star,* July 9, 1981, A1.

32. *Public Papers of the Presidents of the United States, Richard Nixon, Containing the Public Messages, Speeches, and Statements of the President, 1972* (Washington, D.C.: Government Printing Office, 1974), 965-966.

33. John W. Ellwood, "Budget Control in a Redistributive Environment," in *Making Economic Policy in Congress,* ed. Allen Schick (Washington, D.C.: American Enterprise Institute, 1983), 93.

34. For a thorough account of the 1974 budget act, see Allen Schick, *Congress and Money* (Washington, D.C.: Urban Institute, 1980).

35. *Wall Street Journal,* June 9, 1981, 35.

36. *New York Times,* June 17, 1981, A25.

37. Jonathan Rauch, "The Politics of Joy," *National Journal,* January 17, 1987, 130. See also Jonathan Rauch, "Is the Deficit Really So Bad?" *Atlantic Monthly,* February 1989, 36-42.

38. *Bowsher v. Synar,* 478 U.S. 714 (1986).

39. R. Kent Weaver, "The Politics of Blame," *The Brookings Review* (Spring 1987): 43.

40. *Christian Science Monitor,* March 10, 1986, 4.

41. Ibid., October 30, 1987, 6.
42. Rudolph G. Penner and Alan J. Abramson, *Broken Purse Strings: Congressional Budgeting, 1974 to 1988* (Washington, D.C.: Urban Institute Press, 1988), 78-79.
43. *New York Times,* February 11, 1988, A20.
44. Lawrence J. Haas, "Blame the Appropriators," *National Journal,* August 8, 1987, 2027.
45. *Christian Science Monitor,* December 2, 1988, 13.
46. *Washington Post,* July, 27, 1988, F1.
47. *Washington Post,* April 23, 1986, A9.
48. *Wall Street Journal,* March 28, 1986, 1.
49. *Wall Street Journal,* April 16, 1985, 1.
50. Alllen Schick, "The Three-Ring Budget Process: The Appropriations, Tax, and Budget Committees in Congress," in *The New Congress,* ed. Thomas Mann and Norman Ornstein (Washington, D.C.: American Enterprise Institute, 1981), 313.
51. See Catherine E. Rudder, "Fiscal Responsibility, Fairness, and the Revenue Committees," in *Congress Reconsidered,* 4th ed., ed. Lawrence C. Dodd and Bruce I. Oppenheimer (Washington, D.C.: CQ Press, 1989), 225-244; and M. Kenneth Bowler, "Preparing Members of Congress to Make Binary Decisions on Complex Issues: The 1986 Tax Reform Bill," *Journal of Policy Analysis and Management* 8 (Winter 1989): 35-45.
52. Timothy J. Conlan, Margaret T. Wrightson, and David R. Beam, *Taxing Choices: The Politics of Tax Reform* (Washington, D.C.: CQ Press, 1990).
53. David E. Rosenbaum, "The Budget," *New York Times,* April 20, 1989, B8.
54. *New York Times,* February 12, 1989, E1.
55. *Washington Times,* January 30, 1989, A3.
56. Robert J. Samuelson, "Beyond the Budget Fuss," *Washington Post,* November 23, 1988, A21.

House Select Hunger Chairman Mickey Leland, D-Texas, shown interviewing famine-plagued children, died when his plane crashed during a later East African tour.

CHAPTER FOURTEEN

Congress and National Security Policies

For a few weeks in the summer of 1987, the office of House Speaker Wright, D-Texas, functioned as a kind of annex of the State Department. The Nicaraguan ambassador came for lunch; the phones hummed all day with calls between Central America and Speaker Wright. The product of all this frantic diplomacy was a Wright-Reagan peace initiative for Nicaragua. "I entered into a joint declaration with the president, most of which I dictated," the Speaker boasted later.[1]

The drama began earlier in the year, when the Reagan administration dispatched an emissary to Capitol Hill to assess chances for additional aid for Nicaragua's rebel forces (known as contras). Their long-running resistance to the country's Marxist regime was one of President Ronald Reagan's favorite causes. The issue was dead on Capitol Hill, the emissary reported, unless the White House could prove its sincerity in seeking peace between the contras and the Nicaraguan government. Reagan therefore asked the Speaker to cosponsor a peace plan, and the Speaker eagerly agreed. By entering into temporary alliance the two political enemies took huge risks (as their advisers and colleagues angrily told them), but they joined forces to realize their divergent and ultimately incompatible goals: contra aid for Reagan, stability in Nicaragua for Wright.

Speaker Wright's venture quickly paid off. A few days after the Wright-Reagan package was unveiled, five Central American presidents met in Guatemala and endorsed a similar peace plan, drafted by Costa Rican president Oscar Arias, who later received the Nobel Prize for his efforts. Wright quickly endorsed the Arias plan as the most promising avenue for negotiation. This infuriated White House policy makers who felt Wright had been duplicitous. They fumed, but they could do little else: the Speaker (helped by the Central American leaders) had outmaneuvered the president. Reagan's determined opposition to the Nicaraguan government not only had failed to command majority sentiment in this country, but it also had isolated the administration from key Central American leaders, thus creating a policy vacuum. Wright, with his fluency in Spanish, thirty years of interest in

Central American affairs, and extensive information sources, was only too happy to step into the vacuum.

These incidents—only one scene in the high drama between the United States and Nicaragua in the 1980s—convey an important truth about U.S. policy making: initiative and influence in foreign and national security affairs are shared just as they are in domestic and budgetary affairs. Analysts sometimes try to contrast the foreign policy leadership of the president with the domestic policy leadership of the Congress. But such a distinction is illusory. Congress has sweeping constitutional authority to participate in making foreign and defense decisions. And despite obvious executive advantages that have been magnified in today's world of huge standing armies and high-technology weapons, it is easy for even the strongest chief executives to find themselves constrained by active, informed, and determined policy makers on Capitol Hill.

Constitutional Powers

The Constitution is "an invitation to struggle for the privilege of directing American foreign policy." [2] In other words, foreign and military powers are divided: "while the president is usually in a position to *propose,* the Senate and Congress are often in a technical position at least to *dispose.*" [3] The struggle over the proper role of each branch in shaping foreign policy typically focuses on two broad issues: conflict over policy and conflict over process.

The president's constitutional powers are formidable. He manages day-to-day relations with foreign governments, he appoints ambassadors and other emissaries, he receives other nations' representatives, and he negotiates treaties and other agreements. When duly concluded and ratified, treaties are the law of the land, but not all treaties signed by the president are accepted by the Senate. Because treaties are difficult to ratify—requiring as they do a two-thirds vote of the Senate—presidents tend to use *executive agreements* to reach accords with other nations. Although not mentioned in the Constitution, such agreements are used six times as often as treaties.

The president's leadership in conducting diplomacy leads some observers to conclude erroneously that foreign affairs are the exclusive domain of the president. Two historical sources are cited by advocates of presidential supremacy in foreign affairs. One is this statement by John Marshall in 1800, before he became chief justice: "The president is the sole organ of the nation in its external relations, and its sole representative with foreign nations." [4] But Marshall did not claim that the president could make foreign policy single-handedly; he merely noted that the president executes foreign policy that is formulated jointly.

The second source is an unfortunate statement by Justice George Sutherland in *United States v. Curtiss-Wright Export Corp.* (1936): legislation dealing with foreign affairs "must often accord to the president a degree of discretion and freedom from statutory restriction which would not be admissible were domestic affairs alone involved." [5] Because this decision dealt with a president's implementation of a congressional enactment, Justice Sutherland's expansive language was beside the point, and it certainly does not support a claim of exclusive presidential domain in foreign affairs. The most that can be said—as Justice Robert Jackson later noted in *Youngstown Sheet and Tube Co. v. Sawyer* (1952)—is that "the president might act in external affairs without congressional authority, but not that he might act contrary to an act of Congress." [6]

Congress has a sizable arsenal of explicit constitutional duties, such as the power to declare war, regulate foreign commerce, and raise and support military forces. The president's explicit international powers are to serve as commander in chief, to negotiate treaties and appoint ambassadors (shared with the Senate), and to receive ambassadors. Throughout our history, presidents have claimed not only these powers but others not spelled out in the Constitution. Whether they are called implied, inherent, or emergency powers, presidents have used them to conduct foreign policy in part because of the innate advantages of the office. As John Jay wrote in *The Federalist*, No. 64, the unity of the office, its superior information sources, and its capacity for secrecy and dispatch gave the president daily charge of foreign intercourse.[7] Moreover, Congress at that time was not in session the whole year, whereas the president was always available to make decisions.

The president's advantages are especially marked in times of warfare or crisis. The legislature's inability to manage affairs during the Revolutionary War led the Founders to champion an independent, energetic executive and to designate the president commander in chief. Wars and conflicts tend to centralize authority; presidential powers thus have been at their zenith during armed conflict. When hostilities cease, presidential powers tend to dissipate— until the midtwentieth century, that is. At the close of World War II in 1945, the power pendulum swung quickly away from the White House, but the so-called cold war between the United States and the Soviet Union and the "hot war" in Korea quickly broke the trend. Ever since, presidents have rigorously pursued their role as commander in chief—buttressed by the nation's place as a world leader and by a military and intelligence establishment that is, by historical standards, unprecedented for a period in which there are no declared wars.

Types of Foreign and National Security Policies

Foreign policy is the sum total of decisions and actions governing a nation's relations with other nations. The major foreign policy ingredients are *national goals* to be achieved and *resources* for achieving them. *Statecraft* is the art of formulating realistic goals and marshaling appropriate resources to achieve them.

Ascertaining a nation's goals is no simple matter. Many of the great congressional debates have been over divergent and even incompatible foreign policy goals—over ties to old-world powers such as England and France during our nation's first decades, over high versus low tariffs, over American expansionism and industrialization abroad, and over involvement in foreign wars. Any given issue is likely to pose a number of competing goals. Foreign policy goals are often articulated in congressional hearings or during debate on the House or Senate floor; however, linkages among goals are less frequently spelled out.

Even granting the dilemmas of identifying national goals and balancing them with national resources, it is helpful to think of several types of foreign and defense policies. *Structural policies* involve deploying resources or personnel; *strategic policies* advance the nation's interests militarily or diplomatically; and *crisis policies* protect the nation's vital interests against specific threats.

Structural Policies

Foreign and military programs require millions of employees and billions of dollars annually. Decisions about deploying these vast resources are called structural policy decisions. Examples include decisions on specific weapons systems and procurement, location of military installations, sales of weapons and surplus goods to foreign countries, and trade restrictions to protect domestic industries. Structural policy making on foreign and defense issues is virtually the same as distributive policy making in the domestic realm (see Chapter 13).

Structural decisions engage a wide variety of political groups. Defense contracts and installations, for example, are sought by business firms, labor unions, local communities, and their representatives on Capitol Hill. The Defense Department's muscle is toned by the immense volume of structural, or distributive, decisions it controls. By contrast, the State Department makes few distributive decisions.

Distributive impulses are irresistible in foreign economic policies. Distributing agricultural surpluses to needy nations not only serves humanitarian purposes, but it also provides an outlet for subsidized farm production. Trade interests, too, are well represented on Capitol Hill, where there are active voices both for protecting domestic industries by raising barriers and for aiding consumers by lowering barriers to imported goods. But when American firms and producers—from wheat growers to airplane manufacturers—encounter problems abroad, lawmakers are hard pressed to resist lobbying for trade concessions with the International Trade Commission or the Office of the U.S. Trade Representative.[8] In other words, domestic producer and consumer interests naturally project themselves, via congressional constituency politics, onto the nation's policies toward its many trading partners.

The "Congressional-Industrial Complex." As might be expected, structural decisions, like distributive ones, are typically reached in congressional subcommittees. Legislators from areas containing major military installations or defense contractors lobby with executive agencies for continued support, and subcommittee decisions are reached with local needs in mind.[9] Rarely are these issues fought out on the House or Senate floor; interested members can usually reach accommodation at the subcommittee or committee stage on how to allocate defense resources. "People used to worry about the power of the military-industrial complex," said a retired admiral. But now, he adds, the "congressional-industrial complex" often has a greater influence on boosting spending for military arms than do the armed services.[10]

Lobbying for military projects comes naturally to members of Congress who, as we have seen, are expected to champion local interests. Current budgetary shortages have only heightened pressures for widespread distribution of defense projects. "It is the last really big barrel of pork that's out there," explained Rep. Thomas J. Downey, D-N.Y. "And it's all federal money."[11]

Needless to say, Pentagon procurement officers have learned to anticipate congressional needs in planning and designing projects. The perfect weapons system, it is said, is one with a component manufactured in every congressional district in the nation. Indeed, many weapons are made up of components produced by widely scattered subcontractors. "The latest figures we're seeing show that Grumman has pieces of the F-14 [Tomcat fighter plane] being manufactured in 49 states," said Rep. George J. Hochbrueckner, D-N.Y. "If you want to develop political support, it pays to spread the work around."[12] Even when military planners agree to phase out a weapon, they may be pressured by lawmakers into keeping the item in production. The result can be both wasteful and expensive. The "military pork barrel," contended Lawrence J. Korb, former assistant secretary of defense for manpower, "costs the taxpayer at least $10 billion a year, things we don't want, things we don't need, but are in there to protect vested interests."[13]

Congress is not, however, the sole source of inefficiency and duplication in the military establishment. Within the Pentagon the three service departments—army, air force, and navy (including the Marine Corps)—are operationally separate and jealously guard their distinctive missions, programs, and traditions. In the 1983 invasion of Grenada, soldiers on the ground could not summon supporting fire from offshore ships because army and navy radio equipment were incompatible. In one instance an army officer slipped into a phone booth and used his AT&T credit card to call on a civilian line to Fort Bragg, North Carolina, so that his request could be relayed to the navy via the Pentagon.

With mounting evidence of inefficiency and interservice rivalries, the congressional armed services panels in 1986 drafted, and the president signed, a wide-ranging law to revamp the military chain of command. The

Pentagon's central management—the secretary of defense and the Joint Chiefs of Staff—was strengthened to achieve better coordination of the four services. To counter horror stories about inefficient weapons buying, a weapons "czar" was appointed to oversee procurement and to combat corruption.

Two years later Congress acted to overcome one of its own weak points: reluctance to close obsolete military installations. Under pressure from local economic interests, senators and representatives traditionally fight to keep installations open, regardless of need. By 1977 Congress had passed a law requiring expensive and time-consuming environmental impact studies before a base could be closed, making it cheaper in the short run to keep an obsolete base open than to phase it out. But the 1988 law insulated decisions on base closings from congressional pressure by creating a bipartisan commission to draw up a list of installations targeted for closure. The list would have to be accepted or rejected as a whole, a requirement that made the commission's recommendations difficult to overturn. Late in 1988, after Congress had adjourned, the first commission announced its "hit list" of eighty-three obsolete bases, and the secretary of defense subsequently accepted the recommendations.

Trade Politics.   In foreign policy the most conspicuous arena for distributive politics is foreign trade. Since the very first Congress, the power "to regulate commerce with foreign nations" has been used to protect and enhance the competitive position of domestic goods and industries—whether cotton or wheat or textiles or automobiles. After World War II these trade barriers were reduced dramatically as U.S. industries sought to extend their dominance by exporting throughout the world. By the 1980s, however, the politics of protectionism revived with a vengeance: many domestic industries had lost (or squandered) their competitive advantages, trade imbalances had soared, and pressures for protecting domestic firms had mounted. Having delegated most trade decisions to the executive in the post-World War II era, Congress now began pressing the executive branch to "get tough" with foreign competitors. Numerous trade bills were introduced that included import curbs, import surcharges, and threats to close American markets in order to open foreign markets. A new trade statute in 1988 sought to encourage presidential trade negotiators to take tougher positions with foreign countries, and as long as U.S. industries (and their workers) feel disadvantaged by foreign competitors, Congress will remain receptive to protectionist sentiment.[14]

Strategic Policies

Given the underlying need to protect the nation's interests, decision makers face the job of designing strategies toward other nations. Examples of strategic policies include overall spending levels for international and defense programs; overall military force levels; the basic mix of military forces and weapons systems; arms sales to foreign powers; trade inducements or restrictions; allocation of economic, military, and technical aid to developing nations; the extent of treaty obligations to other nations; our responses to human rights issues in other nations; and our basic stance toward international bodies such as the United Nations and world banking agencies.

Strategic policies embrace most of what are commonly thought of as major foreign policy questions; they engage not only top-level executive decision makers, but also congressional committees and middle-level executive officers. The State Department is a key agency for strategic decision making, as is the Office of the Secretary of Defense and the National Security Council. Strategic issues are generally accorded less public and media attention than are crisis situations; however, they can capture citizens' ideological, ethnic, racial, or economic interests.[15] Presidents, insofar as they can exert leadership on a strategic issue, frequently address it in broad terms of national security or national survival.

Strategic issues, while they may involve distributive benefits, typically concern broader themes. "There is a kind of reverence to strategic issues," noted former senator Gary Hart, D-Colo. "Strategic issues are of a different order, a higher order. . . . It's survival; it's the whole ball game if things go wrong." [16] The case in point was the controversial MX missile system, an advanced warhead design whose drawbacks included not only astronomical cost but a questionable basing mode (that is, how to store and launch the missiles) and the threat of escalating the arms race. Three presidents recommended the MX over an eleven-year period; scores of House and Senate votes were taken on it; and in the end only a few of the missiles were ever built with some $13 billion of public money. Congress's reluctance to say "no" to the MX was not motivated primarily by constituency politics; rather it reflected a fear of denying the president a major component of the nation's arsenal. President Reagan argued not for the system's effectiveness but rather for its use as a bargaining chip in dealing with the Soviets. His successor, Bush, pressed for funding for a railroad basing mode, offering in exchange support for Midgetman, a smaller, more mobile missile much favored by lawmakers.

The Power of the Purse. The power of the purse gives Congress the leverage to establish overall spending levels for foreign and defense purposes. Within these overall figures, priorities must be assigned—among military services, among weapons systems, between uniformed personnel and military hardware, and on economic, cultural, or military aid, to name just a few of the choices. The president exerts leadership by presenting an annual budget, lobbying for the administration's priorities, and threatening to veto options deemed unacceptable. Yet Congress is now equipped to prepare its own budgets down to the smallest detail. And the omnibus character of appropriations measures places pressure on presidents to accede to the outcome of legislative bargaining on expenditures. To get the 95 percent of the budget he needs, the president may have to swallow the 5 percent he opposes.

The portions of the federal outlays devoted to defense and international operations (that is, the money the government actually spends) are shown in Figure 14-1, which covers the years 1940 to 1994. National defense consumes a relatively large portion of the federal outlays, while funding for international affairs represents a relatively small expenditure. The notable exception occurred in the immediate post-World War II years (1947-1951), when programs to rebuild devastated Europe and Japan consumed up to 17 percent of our annual spending. In recent years such spending—for Department of State operations, the diplomatic service, and foreign aid—has represented only 1 to 2 percent of all expenditures.

More significant in dollar terms are the shifts between defense and "all other" spending—roughly speaking, the clash between "guns and butter." The year 1940 is an instructive place to start because this was a typical "peacetime" year: of the total budget of $9.5 billion, four out of every five dollars went for domestic programs. The next year, 1941, the United States plunged into a two-ocean war against Japan in the Pacific and the German-Italian axis in Europe. Federal spending soared to unprecedented heights: in the peak year of 1945, the federal budget stood at nearly $93 million—ten times the figure of five years earlier. Nine out of ten of those dollars went for the war effort.

At the end of World War II, Congress was quick to heed the public demand for demobilization and a peacetime status. Three years after the war's end, federal expenditures had been cut by two-thirds, less than one-third of which went to national defense. Military spending rose somewhat during the Korean War period (1950-1953) and then subsided, although at a higher level than ever before. Presidents Lyndon Johnson and Richard Nixon were able to conduct the Vietnam War with less than half the nation's expenditures—a declining proportion at that. Since then the ratio of domestic to defense spending has been approximately three to one—even though President Reagan was able to hike defense spending in the mid-1980s by three or four percentage points. Congress reacted to public sentiment for higher defense spending in the early 1980s and to the clamor for lower spending after that.

A related indicator of defense priorities is the size of the military forces authorized by Congress. During the first decade of the new nation, about 4,000 men were in arms. For most of the nation's history (that is, until World War II), Congress allowed the peacetime, active military to grow about as fast, or a little faster, than the general population. The pattern was a series of wartime mobilizations, followed by ever higher plateaus after the wars ended. As Christopher Deering notes, "Demobilization inevitably occurred at the close of each conflict, but rarely to prewar levels." [17] The nation's global

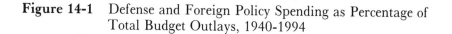

Figure 14-1 Defense and Foreign Policy Spending as Percentage of Total Budget Outlays, 1940-1994

Percentage

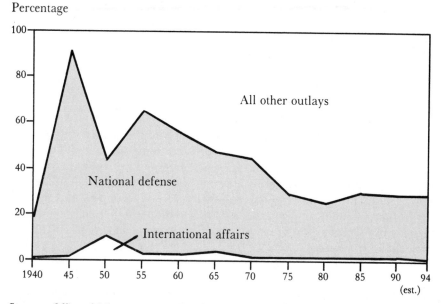

Source: Office of Management and Budget, *Budget of the United States Government, Fiscal Year 1990, Historical Tables* (Washington, D.C.: Government Printing Office, 1989), 39-45.

Note: Figures are fiscal year outlays, according to current statistical conventions for treating off-budget items. The total budget in billions of dollars was $9.5 in 1940, $42.6 in 1950, $92.2 in 1960, $195.6 in 1970, $590.9 in 1980, and an estimated $1,151.8 in 1990.

peacekeeping responsibilities following World War II shattered this pattern, resulting in a peacetime military far larger than ever before. Today about 1 percent of the U.S. population actively serves in the voluntary-based military, compared with one-tenth that proportion prior to World War II.

International operations, too, have grown in magnitude and importance as America's international leadership solidified after World War II. Until then the nation's foreign operations had required relatively little money. This changed radically after 1945, when the United States became a major provider of economic, military, and technical aid throughout the world. The United States also contributed to international and regional development banks and to various types of loan programs.

In authorizing such aid, Congress influences foreign policy for better or worse. Congress can place "strings" on foreign aid; it can restrict or prohibit funds for countries that do not conform with certain conditions, such as progress in human rights. Presidents and their aides usually deplore these strings as limiting their dealings with other countries.

In the final analysis no major foreign or military enterprise can be sustained unless Congress provides money and support. Presidents may be able to conduct an operation for a time using existing funds and supplies, as Lyndon Johnson did at first in Vietnam, but sooner or later they must ask Congress for funding. The United States' role in South Vietnam ended, belatedly, when Congress refused to provide emergency aid funds. Many of the Reagan administration's clashes with Congress took the form of fights over funding—for example, aid to the contras in Nicaragua, to the forces of Jonas Savimbi in Angola, and for arms to Saudi Arabia or Jordan.

Foreign and defense policies increasingly require economic resources. This serves to heighten Congress's leverage. It also has equalized the role of the House in comparison with the Senate. Because the House traditionally originates taxing and funding legislation, its key panels—especially Ways and Means and the Appropriations subcommittees on Defense and Foreign Operations—usually set forth the detailed specifications and dollar amounts. The Senate serves as the court of appeals, ratifying or modifying the House committees' products.

The Treaty Power.   The Constitution makes Congress a full-fledged partner with the president in one form of strategic policy: treaties with foreign powers. Although initiated by the president, treaties are made "by and with the advice and consent of the Senate." The Senate's consent is signified by the concurrence of two-thirds of the senators present and voting.

The Senate's active role in ratification was shown during its 1988 debate on the intermediate nuclear force (INF) treaty signed the previous December by President Reagan and Soviet premier Mikhail Gorbachev at the Washington summit. Selected senators served formally as "observers" during the negotiations that led to the signing. Some senators' questions about procedures for verifying the reduction in missiles sent U.S. and Soviet diplomats back to the bargaining table to work out details. Other senators, stung by what they regarded as the Reagan administration's unwarranted "reinterpretation" of an earlier treaty (the antiballistic missile treaty of 1972), sought precise agreement on the meaning of key provisions and insisted on a legislative provision that no president could later repudiate, without Senate approval, treaty interpretations presented by the administration during the ratification process. After four months of deliberation and two weeks of floor debate, the treaty was ratified, 93 to 5.

Congress may or may not be taken into the president's confidence when treaties and executive agreements are negotiated. To avoid Woodrow Wilson's humiliation when the Senate rejected the Versailles Treaty, modern chief executives usually inform key senators during the negotiation process.

The Senate may reject a treaty outright, although it rarely does. The

Senate has turned down only nineteen treaties since 1789. More often the Senate attaches reservations to a treaty, amends it, or simply postpones action. One study found that the Senate had approved without change 944 treaties, or 69 percent of those submitted to it.[18]

The hurdle of obtaining a two-thirds Senate vote has led some to suggest that the Constitution be amended to require, say, a simple Senate majority. The tendency of presidents to resort to executive agreements, which do not require ratification, has been another result. However, lawmakers have been suspicious of this practice. From time to time a constitutional amendment requiring Senate ratification of executive agreements has been pushed. Since the Vietnam War the Senate Foreign Relations Committee has shown increased vigor in reviewing executive agreements.

Crisis Policies

Self-preservation is not the only goal of foreign or military policy, but when self-preservation is directly threatened, other goals are shunted aside. One definition of an international crisis is a sudden challenge to the nation's safety and security. Examples range from Japan's attack on the U.S. naval fleet in Pearl Harbor in 1941 to Iran's seizure of American citizens at the U.S. embassy in Tehran in 1979.

Crisis policies engage decision makers at the very highest levels: the president, the secretaries of state and defense, the National Security Council, and the Joint Chiefs of Staff. Occasionally, a few congressional leaders are brought into the picture; sometimes, as in the failed 1980 attempt to rescue the American hostages in Iran, no consultation is undertaken. Even more rarely, congressional advice is sought and heeded: congressional leaders' opposition dissuaded President Dwight D. Eisenhower from intervening in Indochina in 1954.[19] Usually when executive decision makers fear congressional opposition, they simply neglect to inform Capitol Hill until the planned action is under way.

As long as the crises linger, policy makers keep a tight rein on information flowing upward from line officers. The attention of the media and public attention is riveted upon crisis events. Patriotism runs high; citizens hasten to "rally 'round the flag" and support whatever course their leaders choose.[20]

The "War Powers." International crises imply the commitment of military forces. This calls into play the so-called war powers shared by the president and Congress. The president is the commander in chief (Article II, Section 2), but Congress has the power to declare war (Article I, Section 8). Congress has declared war in only five conflicts: the War of 1812 (1812-1814), the Mexican War (1846-1848), the Spanish-American War (1898), World War I (1917-1918), and World War II (1941-45). In all but one case (the Mexican War), Congress went along enthusiastically with the president's recommendation to declare war, acknowledging in the declaration that a state of war already existed. Only once did Congress actually delve into the merits of waging war, and that was in 1812, when the vote was rather close. In two cases—the Mexican and Spanish-American conflicts—lawmakers later had reason to regret their haste.

More problematic than formal declarations of war are the more than 200 instances when U.S. military forces have been deployed on foreign soil. (The number is uncertain because of quasi-engagements involving military or intelligence "advisers.") Since the end of our last declared war, World War II, in 1945, there have been numerous hostile interventions abroad. Some of them were massive prolonged wars (Korea, 1950-1953; Vietnam, 1964-1975); others were brief actions (the Dominican Republic, 1965; the Iranian rescue mission, 1980; Grenada, 1983; Lybia, 1986); still others were "peacekeeping" missions that resulted in bloodshed (Lebanon, 1982-1983; the Persian Gulf, 1987-1988).

Most of these interventions were authorized by the president as commander in chief on the pretext of protecting American lives or property abroad; some were justified on the grounds of treaty obligations or "inherent powers" derived from a broad reading of executive prerogatives. In virtually every armed intervention in our history, constitutional provisions have generated "lively disagreement among the president, Congress, and the Supreme Court, and between the central government and the states." [21]

Members of Congress tend to support armed interventions if they come to a swift, successful conclusion with few lives lost. Actions that drag on without a satisfactory resolution or that cost many lives will eventually tax lawmakers' patience. As the sense of crisis subsides, competing information appears that may challenge the president's version of the event. As the urgency passes, congressional critics became emboldened to voice their reservations. This occurred during the undeclared wars in Korea, Vietnam, and Lebanon.

Backlash against the Vietnam War made lawmakers more skeptical of presidential initiatives abroad. In 1973 Congress passed the War Powers Resolution (P.L. 93-148) over President Nixon's veto. Under this law the president must (1) consult with Congress before introducing U.S. troops into hostilities, (2) report any commitment of forces to Congress within forty-eight hours, and (3) terminate the use of forces within sixty days if Congress does not declare war, does not extend the period by law, or is unable to meet. (The president may extend the period to ninety days, if necessary.)

The resolution is an awkward compromise of executive and legislative authority, and presidents still intervene as they see fit. In some cases members of Congress sit on the sidelines, only later questioning presidential initiatives. Other engagements, like the Lebanon mission, are debated heatedly. One action, the 1983 invasion of Grenada, proved so popular and successful that widespread misgivings were virtually silenced.

By the end of 1988, presidents had reported to Congress on a dozen occasions that troops had been deployed on foreign soil. In several other cases the military action was brief and no report was filed. In still other cases the executive branch claimed that reports were not required because U.S. personnel were not confronting hostilities or imminent hostilities. Thus, the Reagan administration failed to comply with congressional reporting requirements when it sent military advisers to El Salvador in 1981 and when it provided protection for oil tankers in the Persian Gulf in 1987.

When President Reagan committed forces to the Lebanon peacekeeping mission, he initially declined to adhere precisely to the resolution. He feared that the timetable set in motion by the resolution would limit his flexibility and might encourage hostile factions to delay coming to the bargaining table. The impasse was resolved when Congress, led by then-House Speaker Thomas P. O'Neill, Jr., D-Mass., passed a resolution authorizing troop deployment for eighteen months (extending beyond the 1984 elections). When the Lebanon mission later collapsed, both the White House and congressional leaders sought to place the blame elsewhere. In the El Salvador and Persian Gulf deployments, members of Congress opposed to the president's actions challenged them in court on the grounds that they violated the Constitution and the War Powers Resolution. The suits were rejected as the judges in essence invoked the "political questions" doctrine: if Congress wished to invoke the resolution to limit the president's actions, it should have done so directly. But in neither instance were the votes available on Capitol Hill to rein in the president; thus, the impasse stood.

With each new crisis the War Powers Resolution is attacked or defended, depending on the view held of the proposed intervention (see box on page 406). Presidents continue to insist on flexibility and to resist congressional "meddling." Lawmakers strive vainly to be consulted; they support the president as long as it is politically feasible. If the crisis persists and the president's actions backfire, however, Congress moves in and sometimes curtails the action by refusing funds.

The War Powers Resolution, it seems, satisfies no one. Presidents resist or ignore it; members of Congress are unwilling to enforce it. On the other hand, no one knows what presidential forays it may have discouraged. (Some observers suspect that President Reagan might have waged war against the government of Nicaragua had the War Powers Resolution not deterred him.) In any event by 1988 it was apparent to everyone that changes were needed; efforts were under way on Capitol Hill to reformulate the enactment.

Who Speaks for Congress?

Subjects as wide-ranging as foreign and military affairs cause huge jurisdictional entanglements among Capitol Hill committees. Foreign policy issues are considered by seventeen at least of the twenty-two standing

The War Powers Resolution in Action

Each time a president has used military forces abroad in near-combat situations or on rescue missions that might have led to combat, members of Congress have cited the resolution, if only to elicit from the executive a complete explanation of the operation. Below are the chief examples.

Indochina.   In the spring of 1975, President Ford conducted a series of rescue missions from Danang, Saigon, and Phnom Penh as U.S. involvement ceased and hostilities increased. Ford maintained he had authority as commander in chief to use troops to rescue citizens and others. But he "took note" of the resolution by informing Congress in advance of the rescue missions and submitted reports after the operations were completed.

Mayaguez.   In May 1975, Cambodian naval vessels fired on and seized the S.S. *Mayaguez,* a merchant ship in international waters that was en route to Thailand. Ford first attempted to free the ship and crew through diplomatic actions but, when that failed, ordered a military rescue involving U.S. Marines and air attacks on Cambodian vessels. The ship's crew was rescued, but 18 Marines died. Although Ford clearly complied with the resolution's requirement that a report be submitted promptly, there was considerable debate about whether he consulted members of Congress or just informed them.

Iran.   When President Carter, in April 1980, ordered an attempted rescue of the 49 hostages held in the American Embassy in Tehran, he did not consult with members of Congress beforehand or inform them of the mission until after it had been aborted. Administration officials said consultation would have taken place had the rescue effort proceeded beyond the initial phase. But congressional leaders in both parties said Carter had not complied with the resolution.

El Salvador.   In early 1981, after the Reagan administration decided to increase the number of U.S. military advisers in El Salvador, House and Senate resolutions were introduced asserting that the move required a report under the War Powers Resolution. The controversy led to an agreement between Congress and the administration that the number of advisers would be kept to 55 and that they would not be equipped for combat or placed in a hostile situation. The administration also pledged to consult with Congress if it wanted to change the status of the advisers.

Grenada.   The U.S.-led invasion of Grenada in October 1983 occurred without advance consultation with Congress: briefings for key congressional leaders took place only when the operation was imminent. But the exercise appeared to fit the resolution's definition of an emergency, in which the president was authorized to use troops. The hostilities ceased within several days, and the administration took the position that the resolution did not apply. Nevertheless, the troops were withdrawn before the 60-day period of emergency presidential authority expired.

Lebanon.   In 1983, Congress established a timetable for the withdrawal of a U.S. Marine peacekeeping force in Lebanon. However, the troops were unilaterally pulled out by President Reagan in early 1984 after more than 260 servicemen lost their lives in a terrorist attack.

Persian Gulf.   From May 1987 to August 1988 U.S. naval vessels were sent to the Persian Gulf to protect reflagged Kuwaiti oil tankers. While Congress did not invoke the resolution, it closely monitored developments.

Source: Adapted from Christopher Madison, "Despite His Complaints, Reagan Going Along with Spirit of War Powers Law," *National Journal,* May 19, 1984, 991.

committees in the House and by fourteen of the sixteen standing committees in the Senate (see Table 14-1). In each chamber Foreign Affairs/Foreign Relations, Armed Services, and Appropriations committees bear heavy duties.

The foreign affairs and national security panels are among the most visible on Capitol Hill. The Senate Foreign Relations and House Foreign Affairs committees are four times as likely to get time on the nightly television newscasts as their nearest committee rivals (the Judiciary panels).[22] The Armed Services committees ranked somewhat behind, though still relatively high in TV exposure.

The Senate Foreign Relations Committee considers treaties and many nominations of foreign policy officials. Normally, it sees itself as a working partner and adviser to the president, but during the height of dispute over the Vietnam War in the late 1960s and early 1970s, the committee became a forum for antiwar debate under the leadership of Chairman J. William Fulbright, D-Ark. Despite the committee's prestige, its subject matter is sometimes hazardous for its members. Not a few of them, Fulbright included, were defeated for reelection partly because their work was portrayed as irrelevant to constituents' concerns.

For most of its history the House Foreign Affairs Committee worked in the shadow of its Senate counterpart. This changed after World War II, when foreign aid programs thrust the House—with its special powers of the purse—into virtual parity with the Senate.[23] Today the House committee addresses nearly as wide a range of issues as does the Senate committee. It tends, however, to attract members who are more liberal and internationalist in outlook than the House as a whole. Consequently, its reports often generate fierce debate on the House floor.

The Senate and House Armed Services committees oversee the national security arena. They annually authorize Pentagon spending for research, development, and procurement of weapons systems; construction of military facilities; and civilian and uniformed personnel. In discharging these duties they duplicate, and rival, the defense subcommittees of the House and Senate Appropriations committees. While members of the Armed Services committees are interested in global strategy, it is structural policy making—force levels, military installations, and defense contracts—that rivets their attention.[24] Thus, military policy is in many ways an extension of constituency politics.

The two Armed Services panels tend to attract members favorable to military spending and home-district installations. A junior member once branded the House committee as "the Pentagon's lobby on the Hill." But in the late 1980s the committees reflected congressional skepticism over the magnitude of defense spending, and they spurred plans to reorganize the Pentagon.

Other congressional panels also get into the act. Because defense spending is the largest controllable segment of the yearly federal budget,

Table 14-1 Congressional Committees Dealing with International Affairs

Senate	House of Representatives
Agriculture, Nutrition, and Forestry Sale, donation of feed; agricultural imports, exports	Agriculture (Same as Senate Agriculture)
Appropriations Funding for foreign operations, including State, Defense, AID (foreign aid), USIA, international organizations	Appropriations (Same as Senate Appropriations)
Armed Services The common defense, including foreign military operations and assistance	Armed Services (Same as Senate Armed Services)
Banking, Housing, and Urban Affairs International monetary and banking affairs, export controls, export and foreign trade promotion	Banking, Currency, and Housing International monetary and banking affairs, international development, trade
Budget Overall budget levels for defense and international affairs	Budget (Same as Senate Budget)
Commerce, Science, and Transportation Interstate, foreign commerce; trade promotion; foreign investment; ocean policy	Education and Labor Foreign labor
Energy and Natural Resources Mineral extraction from the oceans, territories, and possessions of the U.S., including trusteeships	Energy and Commerce Interstate, foreign commerce; tourism
Environment and Public Works Ocean dumping, air pollution	Foreign Affairs Foreign policy of the U.S. generally, foreign agency authorizations
Finance Foreign trade, including tariffs and customs; reciprocal trade agreements; nontariff restrictions; taxation of foreign sales and earnings from foreign investments	Government Operations (Same as Senate Governmental Affairs)
	Interior and Insular Affairs Territorial possessions
	Judiciary (Same as Senate Judiciary)
	Merchant Marine and Fisheries Oceans, oceanography, fishing and fisheries, merchant marine, shipping regulations, international maritime conventions, navigation, Panama Canal
	Public Works and Transportation International aviation

Senate	House of Representatives
Foreign Relations Foreign policy of the U.S. generally, treaties, presidential nominations of ambassadors and other officers of U.S., foreign agency authorizations	**Science, Space, and Technology** International scientific cooperation, space exploration, technological transfer
Governmental Affairs Organization of the government, including foreign policy agencies; nuclear export policy organization and management	**Small Business** (Same as Senate Small Business)
	Veterans' Affairs (Same as Senate Veterans' Affairs)
Judiciary Immigration and naturalization, state and territorial boundaries, protection of trade and commerce against unlawful restraints	**Ways and Means** (Same as Senate Finance)
	Select Intelligence (Same as Senate Select Intelligence)
Labor and Human Resources World labor standards, regulation of foreign laborers, labor performance of U.S. firms overseas	**Select Narcotics Abuse and Control** International drug traffic
Small Business Impact of international forces on U.S. small businesses	
Veterans' Affairs Foreign battlefield cemetaries	
Select Intelligence Authorization, oversight of foreign intelligence agencies (CIA, NSA, military intelligence); covert operations	

Source: Senate, House Rules.

Appropriations subcommittees exert detailed control over foreign and defense policies. Senate and House oversight committees review intelligence activities. Tariffs and other trade regulations are the province of the taxing committees (House Ways and Means, Senate Finance). Banking committees handle international financial and monetary policies; the Commerce committees have jurisdiction over "foreign commerce generally." President Reagan's request for $100 million in aid for the Nicaraguan contras was voted on by four committees (Appropriations, Armed Services, Foreign Affairs, Select Intelligence) before it reached the House floor.

The profusion of congressional power centers leads chief executives to contend that they don't know whom to consult when crises arise and that leaks of sensitive information are inevitable with so many players. This viewpoint was expressed by retiring secretary of state George P. Shultz in a farewell address:

> What we have to fear today is not the imperial Congress but the chaotic Congress. Dialogue between the branches cannot yield productive results when, no matter what the apparent agreement, any faction, any staffer, any subcommittee, any member of Congress, can delay, and impede even the will of the majority.[25]

Congress's organization for policy making is, of course, far from tidy. But the notion that the president, key executive strategists, or even a few congressional experts "know best" is no longer an acceptable notion on Capitol Hill. As former secretary of state Dean Rusk noted, participatory decision making "has made communication between the executive and legislative branches all the more important."[26] In fact, however, chief executives have substantial freedom to consult with as few or as many lawmakers as they like—in some cases with only the joint party leaders, in others with chairmen of the relevant committees (Armed Services, Foreign Affairs/Foreign Relations, Select Intelligence).

The Ebb and Flow of Power

The Constitution, it is said, invites the president and Congress to struggle over control of foreign policy. From the beginning, initiative and influence have ebbed and flowed between the two branches; relations have been volatile since World War II. Given the United States' world leadership role, not to mention the vast resources needed to fulfill this responsibility, the stakes are higher than ever before.

The Cold War Era

The closing years of World War II and the initial postwar years (1943 to 1950) were a time of *accommodation:* "close cooperation was initiated between high-level executive officials and the committee and party leaders of Congress."[27] This cooperation fostered consistent postwar policy. It permitted speedy approval of unprecedented numbers of American treaty and aid pledges; for a time it kept foreign policy insulated from partisan politics. In this era statesmen such as Arthur H. Vandenberg, R-Mich., and Tom Connally, D-Texas, chaired the Senate Foreign Relations Committee and set an example of bipartisanship.

The next period (1950 to 1953) was characterized by *antagonism.*

Partisan squabbling broke out over the "loss" of China to the Communists, the Korean War, and President Harry S Truman's dismissal of a World War II hero, Gen. Douglas MacArthur. This period saw the meteoric rise and subsequent fall of one of the Senate's great demagogues, Republican senator Joseph R. McCarthy of Wisconsin, whose speeches were peppered with unsupported charges of Communist influence in the State Department, universities, churches, and even the U.S. Army.

Following Eisenhower's election as president, a period of *acquiescence* began in 1953. A national consensus favored the policy of containment—keeping communism within its existing borders. Congress got into the habit of ratifying the president's plans; it cut marginal amounts from program budgets but generally supported presidential initiatives. Aaron Wildavsky's "two presidencies" hypothesis captured the temper of the times: "Since World War II, presidents have had much greater success in controlling the nation's defense and foreign policies than in dominating its domestic policies." [28] This period of acquiescence lasted into the 1960s. The high-water mark occurred in 1964, when President Johnson persuaded Congress to support the Gulf of Tonkin Resolution, a vague grant of authority to act in Southeast Asia. The next year Johnson began escalating the Vietnam effort without further consultation with Congress.

Controversy over Vietnam brought a period of *ambiguity* (1969 to 1970). At first Americans supported the war as a method of containing communism. As the conflict dragged on, claiming more lives and money, public sentiment shifted—helping to drive Johnson from office in 1968. Members of Congress lagged behind the shift in public sentiment, but at last a majority of lawmakers turned against the war. The period of ambiguity decisively ended when President Nixon ordered the invasion of Cambodia in 1970 without consulting Congress. The following period of *acrimony* (1970 to 1976) was marked by disputes over Vietnam and almost every other phase of foreign policy.

The Post-Vietnam Era

In 1975 American participation in the Vietnam War was halted when Congress finally refused to appropriate more funds for the enterprise. Since then Congress has shown little desire to follow blindly wherever the president leads. I. M. Destler describes the new relationship between Congress and the president in the 1970s:

> The congressional revolution against presidential foreign policy dominance began as a revolt against the people, ideas, and institutions held responsible for the Vietnam War debacle. In terms of its objectives, this revolution was highly successful. Congress reined in the president and constrained the use of military and paramilitary power. It also elevated policy goals the executive had neglected, such as human rights and nuclear nonproliferation.[29]

This congressional activism and assertiveness survived the Reagan era, which witnessed a level of foreign intervention that had not been seen since before the Vietnam War. Reagan invaded Grenada in 1983 and attacked Libya in 1986—acts authorized swiftly by Congress after the fact. The prior consultation envisioned in the 1973 War Powers Resolution never occurred. The struggle continued over MX missile funding, research on the Strategic Defense Initiative (known as "Star Wars"), aid to anticommunist "freedom fighters" in Nicaragua and elsewhere, and Middle East arms sales. For its part, Congress pushed the president toward arms control talks, human rights activism (especially in South Africa), and trade protection for certain domestic industries.

The Iran-Contra Affair and Aftermath

In 1985 and 1986 White House staffers launched and carried out a highly secret foreign policy, apparently with President Reagan's blessing. The policy was an elaborate arms-for-hostages deal. Arms were shipped to Iran in exchange for the release by terrorists of American hostages in the Middle East and the payment of money, channeled through third parties. Some of this money eventually reached the contra forces fighting the Nicaraguan government in Central America. The vehicle for this policy was "the Enterprise," a shadowy network of private arms dealers and soldiers of fortune working under the aegis of White House operatives. Here is how Congress's Iran-contra investigating committee described this singular operation:

> The Enterprise, functioning largely at [Lt. Col. Oliver] North's direction, had its own airplanes, pilots, airfield, operatives, ship, secure communications devices, and secret Swiss bank accounts. For sixteen months, it served as the secret arm of the [National Security Council] staff, carrying out with private and non-appropriated money, and without the accountability or restrictions imposed by law on the CIA, a covert contra aid program that Congress thought it had prohibited.[30]

After a small Lebanese newspaper blew the cover off this operation in late 1986, "Iran-contra" became the biggest scandal of the Reagan administration, whose influence on foreign policy had already begun to wane. The scandal undermined the president's image of firmness in dealing with terrorists and in managing his own administration. It also eroded the trust and deference that members of Congress tend to show the president, even of the opposite party. Congress was outraged that the president had deceived it; the public was puzzled because the president had betrayed his own ideals—no duplicity in government and no concessions to terrorists. Although Reagan's personal popularity later revived, his administration never fully recovered its credibility.

For its part, Congress became more assertive on a wide range of foreign policy issues. Today Congress and the president remain locked in the ongoing struggle to guide the nation's relations with the rest of the world. "We have our [foreign policy] ideas," remarked Rep. Leon E. Panetta, D-Calif. "The administration has its ideas. And we see what happens." [31]

Conclusion

Members of Congress will not abandon their interest in foreign and national security policies. As the world grows more interdependent, these policies are increasingly important to every citizen and to every local community. As noted in Chapter 13, " 'defense pork' in the form of geographically specific military expenditures" is a key component of distributive politics today.[32] A more internationally minded electorate—sensitive to famines in Africa, deforestation in the Amazon, and foreign trade challenges—makes much less of a distinction between domestic and global matters. In such an atmosphere senators and representatives still continue to insist on playing a major role in international and defense issues.

Notes

1. Richard E. Cohen, "Full Speed Ahead," *National Journal,* January 30, 1988, 242. See also Steven V. Roberts, "The Foreign Policy Tussle," *New York Times Magazine,* January 24, 1988, 26ff.; and Tom Kenworthy, "Wright's High-Risk Strategy on Central America Pays Off," *Washington Post,* April 5, 1988, A1.
2. Edward S. Corwin, *The President: Office and Powers, 1787-1957,* 4th ed. (New York: New York University Press, 1957), 171. See also Cecil V. Crabb, Jr., and Pat M. Holt, *Invitation to Struggle: Congress, the President and Foreign Policy,* 3d ed. (Washington, D.C.: CQ Press, 1989).
3. Corwin, *The President,* 171.
4. *Annals of Congress,* 6th Cong., 1800, 613.
5. *United States v. Curtiss-Wright Export Corp.,* 299 U.S. 304 (1936).
6. *Youngstown Sheet and Tube Co. v. Sawyer,* 343 U.S. 636 (1952).
7. Edward Mead Earle, ed., *The Federalist,* No. 64 (New York: Modern Library, n.d.), 420.
8. I. M. Destler, *Making Foreign Economic Policy* (Washington, D.C.: Brookings Institution, 1980), 204ff.
9. Samuel P. Huntington, *The Common Defense* (New York: Columbia University Press, 1961), 135.
10. Kenneth H. Bacon, "The Congressional-Industrial Complex," *Wall Street Journal,* February 14, 1978, 22.
11. Jerry Hagstrom and Robert Guskind, "Lobbying the Pentagon," *National Journal,* May 31, 1986, 1316.
12. Clifford D. May, "L.I. Starts a Dogfight in Congress To Save F-14," *New York Times,* May 9, 1989, B1.

13. "Military 'Pork Barrel' Wastes Billions a Year, Official Says," *New York Times,* April 1, 1985, A17.
14. I. M. Destler, "Protecting Congress or Protecting Trade?" *Foreign Policy* 62 (Spring 1986): 96-107.
15. Charles McC. Mathias, Jr., "Ethnic Groups and Foreign Policy," *Foreign Affairs* 59 (Summer 1981): 975-998.
16. Helen Dewar, "Lawmakers Are Up on Arms," *Washington Post,* March 24, 1985, A22.
17. Christopher J. Deering, "Congress, the President, and Military Policy," *Annals of the American Academy of Political and Social Science* 499 (September 1988): 143ff.
18. Cecil V. Crabb, Jr., *American Foreign Policy in the Nuclear Age,* 4th ed. (New York: Harper & Row, 1983), 104.
19. Chalmers M. Roberts, "The Day We Didn't Go to War," *The Reporter,* September 14, 1954, 30-35.
20. John E. Mueller, *War, Presidents, and Public Opinion* (New York: John Wiley & Sons, 1973), 208-213.
21. Harold M. Hyman, *Quiet Past and Stormy Present: War Powers in American History* (Washington, D.C.: American Historical Association Bicentennial Essays on the Constitution, 1986).
22. Steven S. Smith and Christopher J. Deering, *Committees in Congress* (Washington, D.C.: CQ Press, 1984), 67.
23. Holbert N. Carroll, *The House of Representatives and Foreign Affairs,* rev. ed. (Boston, Mass.: Little, Brown, 1966), 20.
24. Huntington, *The Common Defense.*
25. *Washington Post,* January 11, 1989, A19.
26. *Miller Center Reports,* Newsletter of the White Burkett Miller Center of Public Affairs, University of Virginia, Winter 1986, 1.
27. Frans R. Bax, "The Legislative-Executive Relationship in Foreign Policy: New Partnership or New Competition?" *Orbis* 20 (Winter 1977): 881-904.
28. Aaron Wildavsky, "The Two Presidencies," in *The Presidency,* ed. Aaron Wildavsky (Boston: Little, Brown, 1969), 230.
29. I. M. Destler, "Dateline Washington: Congress as Boss?" *Foreign Policy* 42 (Spring 1981): 167-180.
30. *Report of the Congressional Committees Investigating the Iran-Contra Affair,* 100th Cong., 1st sess., 1987, 59.
31. Peter Osterlund, "Congress Moves Past Talk to Action in Foreign Policy," *Christian Science Monitor,* June 10, 1988, 6.
32. *Wall Street Journal,* May 13, 1988, 17R.

Though ambivalent about Congress, citizens flock to view the U.S. Capitol building, the focal point of governmental Washington.

CHAPTER FIFTEEN

The Two Congresses and the American People

Reacting to a bitter outburst of public opposition, the newly seated 101st Congress quickly denied itself a pay increase that had been carefully planned and orchestrated. Legislative pay has always been a sensitive issue. When the first Congress, meeting in high-cost New York City, set its pay at $6 a day, the public denounced the "high compensations and salaries." Alexis de Tocqueville complained in the 1830s that "a democratic state is most parsimonious towards its principal agents. In America, the secondary officers are much better paid and the higher functionaries much worse than elsewhere." [1]

Prospects for the pay hike hinged entirely on a "no-vote" strategy. Under the salary law both chambers would have to vote to block the pay increase within thirty days or it would take effect automatically. Thus, blame for the controversial deed would be conveniently diffused—the legislative equivalent of the young cyclist's cry "Look, Ma, no hands!"

These carefully laid plans fell apart in the face of public outrage—expressed in nationwide editorial comments, whipped up by a national alliance of radio and TV talk-show hosts, and conveyed to Capitol Hill in the form of thousands of tea bags sent by irate citizens in a modern-day analogy to the Boston Tea Party. The size of the pay hike, 51 percent, was criticized as excessive: the proposed salary, $135,000, seemed incomprehensibly high to the average voter; and members of Congress looked devious as well as greedy by trying to duck responsibility. "We became cartoon cannon fodder for trash television and talk radio," said a bitter Rep. Vic Fazio, D-Calif., who had helped develop the initial strategy for getting the pay raise. [2]

Bowing to public pressure, Senate and then House leaders agreed to schedule floor votes on the pay package, and lawmakers who privately favored the raise scurried for cover. Only six senators and forty-eight representatives voted for the pay raise to take effect. "I voted no because I think I wanted to be re-elected to Congress," Rep. Bill Richardson, D-N.M., frankly admitted. [3] Victims of the fiasco included not only legislators but also the 2,000 or so judges and senior civil servants whose salaries were linked to those of members of Congress. Also dead for the time being was an unwritten bargain that would have barred members from collecting honoraria for speeches and appearances.

Congress's image problem is as old as the Republic. Pundits and humorists from Mark Twain and Will Rogers to Johnny Carson and Jay Leno have found Congress an inexhaustible source of raw material. The other branches of government have nothing quite like the cartoon image of Congressman Bob Forehead, the shallow and silly windbag. Especially at moments like the pay raise furor, the public seems to share this disdain toward Congress.

Serious commentators' views of Congress are often scarcely more flattering than the public's. Scholarly and journalistic writing perpetuates a stereotype of the "textbook Congress": an irresponsible and slightly sleazy body of people approximating Woodrow Wilson's caustic description of the House as "a disintegrated mass of jarring elements." [4] Legislators in their home states or districts often contribute to Congress's poor image by portraying themselves as gallant warriors against the dragons back on Capitol Hill; as Richard F. Fenno, Jr., puts it, they "run *for* Congress by running *against* Congress." [5]

Citizens' ambivalent feelings toward the popular branch of government bring us back to the dual character of Congress—the theme that has provided the backlighting for our explanations of how Congress and its members work. This notion of the two Congresses reflects public perceptions and assessments: citizens view the Congress in Washington through different lenses than they do their individual senators and representatives.[6] This same dualism appears in media coverage. In fact, the two Congresses are covered by different kinds of reporters working for different kinds of media organizations.

Individual senators and representatives present themselves to their constituents mainly on their own terms—through advertising, self-promotion, and uncritical coverage by local or regional news media. Citizens tend to regard their own legislators as agents of personal or localized interests. Legislators are judged on their service to the state or district, their communication with constituents, and their *home style*—that is, the way they deal with the home folks. In one recent survey nearly two-thirds of the respondents rated their own members of Congress favorably; approval of Congress as an institution trailed by 10 percentage points.[7]

The institutional Congress, by contrast, is covered mainly by the national media—the wire services, radio and television networks, and a few prestigious newspapers. It is viewed by the public as a lawmaking instrument and judged primarily on the basis of citizens' overall attitudes about policies and the state of the nation. Such national concerns typically lead people to conclusions quite at variance with their local evaluations of their own senators and representatives.

Congress-as-Politicians

By most accounts individual members of Congress are faring rather well. The hours are long and the pay modest, but diligence and attentive home styles yield dividends at the polls. If voters think that elected officials as a class are rascals, they certainly do not feel that way about their own elected officials. Nor do they show much willingness to "throw the rascals out." As we have seen, modern-day legislators are handsomely rewarded at the polls: since World War II, 92 percent of all incumbent representatives and 75 percent of incumbent senators running for reelection have been returned to office (see Table 3-1).

This does not mean, as some have suggested, that the two chambers' membership is stagnant or unresponsive. For one thing, members of Congress view reelection rates less complacently than do scholars and reporters sitting on the sidelines. Bent on maintaining their vote margins, members see themselves as "unsafe at any margin." [8] What is more, high reelection rates do not reflect low turnover in membership. When the 101st Congress convened in January 1989, fully half of the members of both chambers had arrived during the 1980s. Voluntary retirements, including those where members seek other offices, keep turnover lively.

The impressive visibility that members of Congress enjoy in their states or districts helps explain the support they command from potential voters. A majority of citizens report contacts with their House members by receiving mail from them, reading about them in a newspaper or magazine, or seeing them on television. Incumbents, moreover, lose no opportunities to do favors for constituents. A recent National Election Study found that 14 percent of all respondents (or their families) had called upon their representative for assistance. Of those, four out of five were satisfied or very satisfied with the response they received. [9]

Another bond between members and voters is forged out of perceived mutual agreement on key issues facing the constituency and the nation. The recruitment process we described in Part II yields lawmakers who reflect local views and prejudices. Contacts with voters throughout the campaign and while in office reinforce this convergence of views, as do representational norms adopted by a large majority of members. Whatever the source, the result is that voters believe their views are shared by their representatives. In the same National Election Study, people were asked whether they generally agreed or disagreed with their representative's votes on bills. Of those who had an opinion, only 7 percent said they generally disagreed with their representative. Half the people said they agreed sometimes and disagreed sometimes, and 42 percent reported that they mainly agreed with their representative. [10]

Members and their staffs, as we pointed out in Chapter 5, devote great attention to generating publicity and local press. Most members employ one or more press aides and regularly use Capitol Hill studios, where audio or video programs or excerpts can be produced for a fraction of their commercial cost. With the advent of low-cost technology to transmit messages by tape or satellite, local outlets no longer have to rely simply on network or news service coverage of major events, especially ones with a local angle. What easier way of covering the local story than airing a statement from a senator or representative? "I am never too busy to talk to local TV," said Rep. Dan Glickman, D-Kan. "Period. Exclamation point." [11] Indeed, few lawmakers would trade exposure in the home town media for a few seconds on "CBS Evening News" or a brief mention in the *New York Times*.

Elected officials are at an advantage in impromptu interviews. Local reporters, especially for the electronic media, are usually on general assignment, which means they are ill prepared to question the lawmaker in detail about issues or events. (Sometimes they begin the interview by asking what the lawmaker wants to discuss.) Moreover, local reporters tend to treat national figures with deference and respect because of their prominence and experience. Often reporters' overriding goal is simply to get the legislator on tape or film. For politicians this is an ideal situation: it lets them express their views in their own words with a minimum of editing and no challenges from reporters.

As a result, individual members of Congress are portrayed in a favorable light by the local media, often getting a free ride from ill-prepared reporters eager for a good quote or "news bite." Or they are presented to their constituents through their own press releases, newsletters, targeted mailings, or prepared radio or television appearances. Individual members thus receive a large measure of free, uncritical publicity. Is it little wonder, then, that they have a positive public image and overwhelming reelection odds?

One looming exception to this rosy picture is the recurrence of questions about members' personal ethics (see box, page 421). The vast majority of lawmakers are dedicated and ethical in their behavior, and there is no reason to think that overall ethical standards are not as high, or higher, than at any time in history. As noted journalist David Broder wrote during Speaker Jim Wright's ethical travails, "It's politically tempting to say, based on the charges facing Jim Wright, that the House is corrupt from top to bottom. But the record shows that the House has done a whole lot more to cleanse itself than the executive branch can claim." [12]

With government cutting such a wide swath in our economic and social life, organized interests and lobbies of all kinds are eager to manipulate lawmakers and bend public policy to their wishes. Huge sums of money find their way to Capitol Hill in the form of political action committee (PAC) contributions, honoraria, and other perquisites large and small. Afraid to raise their own salaries, members all too often fall prey to the blandishments of such money.

Other ethical issues involving personal conduct and habits have height-

Congressional Ethics

Members of Congress are bound by the Constitution, federal laws, political party provisions, and House and Senate rules and conduct codes. Although many observers criticize loopholes, the panoply of regulations is quite extensive.

Constitution. Each chamber has the power to punish its members for "disorderly behavior" and, by a two-thirds vote, to expel a member. Members are immune from arrest during attendance at congressional sessions (except for treason, felony, or breach of peace); and "for any speech or debate in either house, they shall not be questioned in any other place" (Article I, Section 6). This latter provision protects lawmakers from any reprisals for expressing their views.

Criminal Laws. Federal laws make it a crime to solicit or accept a bribe; to solicit or receive "anything of value" for performing any official act, service, or for using influence in any proceeding involving the federal government; to enter into or benefit from any contracts with the government; or to commit any fraud against the United States. Defendants in the so-called Abscam affair were convicted in 1981 for violating these laws.

Ethics Codes. Adopted in 1968 and substantially tightened in 1977, the House and Senate ethics codes apply to members and key staff aides. They require extensive financial disclosure; restrict members' outside earned income (a certain percent of salaries); prohibit unofficial office accounts that many members used to supplement official allowances; and impose stricter standards for using the congressional frank. The House Committee on Standards of Official Conduct and the Senate Select Ethics Committee were created to implement the codes, hear charges against members, issue myriads of advisory opinions, and recommend disciplinary actions.

Party Rules. Congressional parties can discipline members who run afoul of ethics requirements. House Democratic rules require a committee leader who is indicted to step aside temporarily; a leader who is censured or convicted is automatically replaced.

Federal Election Campaign Act Amendments of 1974. As amended again in 1976 and 1979, FECA imposes extensive requirements on congressional incumbents as well as challengers.

ened salience because of changing standards of behavior. Sexual misconduct or substance abuse, for example, are less tolerated today than a generation ago; certainly colleagues and journalists are less inclined to look the other way. In 1989 former senator John Tower, R-Texas, Speaker Wright, and House Majority Whip Tony Coehlo, D-Calif., were among those public officials caught in the middle of changing expectations.

Congress-as-Institution

In contrast to individual legislators, Congress as a whole gets only a mediocre report card. Congress as an institution usually ranks well below the respondents' own representatives. Public approval of Congress rises or falls with economic conditions, wars and crises, scandals, and waves of satisfaction or cynicism (see Figure 15-1). Until Speaker Wright's resignation in 1989, Congress had a surprisingly positive rating (54 to 46), in contrast to the negative ratings of the late 1960s and 1970s. After Wright's resignation, a 60 to 40 negative rating was recorded.[13]

Congressional approval also often follows public approval of presidents. Perhaps people use the more visible presidency as a handle for assessing Congress and the rest of the government. More likely, people form overall impressions of how the government is doing and rate both institutions accordingly.[14] Thus, the surge in Congress's popularity in the mid-1980s occurred because people were buoyed by optimism over the government and its performance; satisfaction with President Ronald Reagan's leadership carried over into optimism and confidence in other sectors of the federal government.

As we have seen, the American public's views of Congress change over time, but its expectations of Congress remain relatively stable. The public expects Congress to exert a strong, independent policy-making role. This has been a consistent finding of surveys over a number of years, even during the "imperial presidency" period of the 1960s and the Reagan honeymoon of the early 1980s. People want Congress to check the president's initiatives and to examine the president's proposals carefully. They even support the idea of divided government: the White House controlled by one party and Capitol Hill by another. In one survey a huge majority (73 percent) rejected the view that the country would be "worse off" by having a Congress controlled by one party and the White House by another.[15] In other words, split control of the federal government was preferred to one-party control. Moreover, the voters seem increasingly to act on this preference, installing Republicans in the White House and Democrats on Capitol Hill.

Apparently, voters support the notion of divided government for much the same reason that James Madison did: they prefer that the branches of government be counterbalanced. This view, incidentally, is not shared by the majority of scholars and reformers. From Woodrow Wilson in the 1880s to the Committee on the Constitutional System in the 1980s, the intelligentsia have believed that "divided government and party disunity . . . lead to diffused accountability."[16]

Although extensively reported in the media, Congress is not well understood by the average American. Partly to blame are the size and complexity of the institution, not to mention the twists and turns of the legislative process. Despite the presence of a large press corps containing many of the nation's most skillful journalists (Capitol Hill is, after all, the

Figure 15-1 A Congressional "Fever Chart": The Ups and Downs of Congressional Popularity, 1963-1989

Percentage favorable

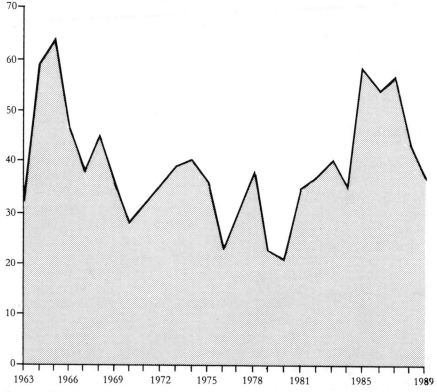

Source: The Harris Survey for 1963-1978 and 1985; NBC News-Associated Press poll for 1981; *Washington Post*-ABC News Poll for 1986-1989.

Note: Respondents were asked the following question: "How would you rate the job done this past year by Congress—excellent, pretty good, only fair, or poor?" The plotted points indicate favorable responses ("excellent" or "pretty good"); "only fair" or "poor" responses were considered unfavorable.

best beat in Washington), neither reporters nor their editors and producers can convey in the mass media the internal subtleties or the external pressures that shape lawmaking.

News about the institutional Congress is recorded and disseminated by the national press corps, a large and diverse group of journalists in the nation's capital. The inner circle of the corps includes reporters who work for the major wire services, the major radio and television networks, the national news magazines, and a few of the daily newspapers of national repute (including the *New York Times, Washington Post, Los Angeles Times,* and *Wall Street Journal*). Either they are assigned exclusively to cover Congress or one of the two chambers, or else they handle stories about a specific topic, for example, economics or foreign affairs. With many sources to choose from, they are not dependent on the goodwill of a single senator or representative. Following the canons of investigative journalism, many are on the alert for hints of scandal, wrongdoing, or corruption. Their approach is that of the suspicious adversary on the lookout for stories with good guys and bad guys, winners and losers. Ethical problems, congressional pay and perquisites, campaign war chests, and foreign junkets are frequent targets for their stories. This is perhaps as it should be, but it has the effect of reinforcing popular negative stereotypes about Congress as an institution.

A Mirror of Ourselves

If the public's views of the two Congresses—of the individual politicians and the institution—ever meet, it may well be through the telecasting of legislative sessions. Although of recent origin (1979 for the House; 1986 for the Senate), Congress's televised presence has changed the two houses in ways both subtle and obvious. Of course, television first came to Capitol Hill many years before. The Senate's 1951 investigation into organized crime riveted the nation's attention and turned its chairman, Sen. Estes Kefauver, D-Tenn., into the first presidential contender to be created by the new medium. The anticommunist juggernaut of Sen. Joseph R. McCarthy, R-Wis., came to a crashing halt with the 1954 U.S. Army-McCarthy congressional hearings that exposed his bullying tactics.

Many of TV's indelible moments in more recent years also occurred during coverage of congressional hearings. The Watergate investigations chaired by Sen. Sam Ervin, D-N.C., in the summer of 1973 hastened the end of Richard Nixon's presidency. And the collection of opportunists and zealots who perpetrated the Iran-contra fiasco and who paraded before the cameras in the summer of 1987 gave citizens a more vivid picture of a foreign policy gone haywire than all the hard-hitting reports written on the subject.

The House and Senate decided to permit live television coverage of floor proceedings to buoy their image and public support. The House panel that examined the matter concluded that TV coverage would help members and staff carry out their duties, provide a more accurate record of proceedings, and contribute to public understanding of the House. When the Senate followed suit after protracted debate, the unstated reason was the perceived need to catch up to the House in media attention.

The complete proceedings of the House and Senate are broadcast by the Cable Satellite Public Affairs Network (C-SPAN), which relays House proceedings on C-SPAN I and Senate proceedings on C-SPAN II. The House proceedings are available to cable television systems in fifty states, with some 43 million households. Senate coverage is available to approximately 17 million homes in forty-five states.

Television on Capitol Hill has been judged a success. Although it has brought few disruptions or alterations in parliamentary procedure, it has sharpened debate and made members more aware of their audience—around the nation as well as inside the chamber. In the House two longstanding customs have been adapted for television: one-minute speeches and special orders. An established informal practice, the remarks called *one minutes* are ideal vehicles for brief personal commentaries at the beginning of each day. Since television came to the House, the use of one minutes has increased threefold. At the end of the day during lulls in legislative business, members can ask unanimous consent for *special orders* to speak for up to one hour on a particular subject. Members use this procedure to vent issues they feel are being ignored in other forums.

The Senate has altered its procedures very little for the television cameras. One exception is *special-order speeches* in which senators seek unanimous consent to speak on any subject. With the advent of television, senators decided to limit these speeches to five minutes—the Senate's only formal accommodation to the cameras. Special-order speeches have soared in number.

The most enduring effect of televised proceedings will probably be enhanced public understanding of Congress. In giving citizens a window on their representatives in action, television coverage helps students learn about citizenship, law, politics, history, and journalism.

Some members have become celebrities on the tube; none are unaware of its presence. Apparently, there is a core audience of C-SPAN enthusiasts around the country, relatively small (compared with network audiences) but loyal, well informed, and politically active. In a recent study 27 percent of those surveyed reported having watched televised sessions of Congress. By a landslide the people endorsed the idea of live television coverage of congressional sessions.[17] It is not farfetched to assume that the surge in popular support for Congress in the mid-1980s was associated with televised proceedings.

Into the Third Century

The U.S. Congress recently entered upon its third century. The year 1989 marked the bicentennial of the establishment of our federal government; in 1991 we honor the historic first Congress's centerpiece achievement, the Bill of Rights.

Survival for two centuries is no mean feat. Perhaps like Dr. Johnson's dog (noted not for his skill at standing on hind legs, but for doing so at all), Congress's longevity is proof enough of its worth. Congress has withstood repeated stress and turbulence including a civil war, political assassinations, domestic scandals, and tenuous foreign involvements. It is sobering to realize that our government charter is far older than most of the world's governments. "Our present Congress was invented before canned food, the first

Wright brothers flight, refrigeration, photography, the Bessemer furnace, the typewriter and telephone; before the automobile, radio and TV; before Hiroshima and Auschwitz and computers." [18]

Mere survival, though, is not enough. Ours is an antiparliamentary age because of its staggering political, economic, and social challenges. All countries increasingly face the same or interrelated problems. With significant changes in the international arena, involving issues such as the health of the world's environment, post-Cold War defense alignments, and the spread of global enterprises that lack national identities, there is heightened discussion about the relevancy of national borders. As one scholar-diplomat put it, "A dramatic indication of the irrelevance of governments in the communication age occurred when the U.S. stock market crashed in October 1987. Direct computer and television transmissions of financial data affected markets in Tokyo, Hong Kong, London and other financial centres in ways beyond the control of any single government." [19]

The U.S. Congress struggles to maintain its autonomy by crafting its own legislation and monitoring the governmental apparatus. Yet many people question whether, realistically, Congress can retain meaningful control given the complex, interdependent character of current problems.

Also debatable is whether representative assemblies remain relevant to twenty-first century challenges. Representative assemblies rest on the principle of geographic representatation, which made sense when land was the basic productive resource. Indeed, for much of our history local and regional fissures were translated into political divisions. Today this is less true. America's divisions tend to be more economic, social, intellectual, or ideological than geographic. As we saw in Chapter 5, states and districts today tend to be microcosms of the nation as a whole in terms of the diversity of interests they embrace.

Some contend that too much is expected of members of Congress. How can elected generalists render intelligent judgments on the dizzyingly complex problems of governance? "People shouldn't expect those in office to be at the forefront of new developments," observed Rep. Barney Frank, D-Mass. "The best we can do is to be adaptors. No one has the intellectual energy to be an elected official and simultaneously break new intellectual ground." [20]

When the first Congress convened, the United States had a tiny population, mostly rural and uneducated; its social and industrial structure was simple; changes occurred slowly; and the government's tasks were few. Nothing could be farther from the contemporary situation. As one social critic put it:

> The Congress is so overloaded by conflicting demands and oceans of unsynthesized data, so many pressures and demands for instant response. The institution is creaking and overloaded and unable to churn out intelligent decisions. Government policymakers are unable to make high priority decisions or [make] them badly, while they make thousands of

small decisions. When a major problem arises, the solution is usually too late and seldom produces the desired impact.[21]

This observation about Congress applies with equal force to many other public and private institutions. Congress has responded to its overload of work by making organizational changes, primarily more division of labor and more staff assistance. It may be, however, that the challenges are so fundamental that they cannot be met with organizational tinkering.

Finally, the very concept of national policy may be unrealistic and outmoded. The foes of technology originally feared that mass production, mass communication, and other advances would create a single mass society in which individuals, brought together and exposed to the same stimuli, would march in lockstep and forfeit their individuality. If anything, the opposite has occurred: technology has "demassified" society and fostered diversity. While erasing geographical isolation, technology serves all manner of other human diversities. Far from being a single mass society, America is increasingly "sliced into dozens of different geographic, economic, social, and cultural markets." [22] According to one source, roughly 55,000 different mailing lists of citizens are available for rental by marketers, politicians, or interest groups. There are lists for gun owners, classic music lovers, biblical archeologists, physicists, and signers of petitions for the balanced-budget amendment.

Our society is being reshaped structurally by this splitting-apart process. Diversification in media is well under way: a few national magazines and journals have been supplanted by thousands of special-interest publications, and the national TV networks are waging a rearguard action against diverse cable- and satellite-based systems. The growth of voluntary associations and interest groups—always a hallmark of our nation—has been so startling in recent years that commentators speak of a "participation revolution." [23]

In light of all this buzzing profusion, a single national assembly of generalists elected by majority votes from geographical areas may seem anomalous indeed. Perhaps Congress inadequately mirrors the real-world "democracy of minorities [composed of] complex, multiple and transient minorities." [24] Perhaps we are witnessing not a retreat from participation or from civic involvement, but a movement away from older forms—mass political parties and elections—toward more varied, personal, and adaptable modes of participation.

Some commentators urge that the United States reduce its reliance upon historic representational forms—legislatures, adversarial courts, secret ballots—and move toward these more varied methods of citizen participation in decision making. Such modes, many of them already heavily used by citizens, would be given more formal recognition in political theory and practice. Benjamin R. Barber's program for "strong democracy" stresses participatory models such as neighborhood assemblies, electronic civic-communications networks, national initiative and referendum processes, and selective experiments with voucher systems for schools, public housing projects, and transportation systems.[25] Needless to say, not all of these proposals will be workable or desirable; some, like the national initiative and referendum, could yield even greater problems than the current system. More important than the content of the proposed remedies, however, is the challenge that they pose to traditional forms of representative government.

This is but the latest wave of challenges to representative assemblies. At their heart such critiques probe the dual character of legislatures that forms the *leitmotif* of this book: the demands of wise policy making versus the requirements of political representation. We have no convincing solutions to this dilemma, and so we end our discourse with questions for the uncertain future.

Are the two Congresses ultimately compatible? Or are they diverging, each detrimental to the other? The burden placed on both Congresses is vastly heavier than it was a generation ago. Congress-as-Institution is expected to resolve all manner of problems—not only by processing legislation, but also by monitoring programs and serving as an all-purpose watchdog. By all outward signs of activity—such as number of committees and subcommittees, hearings, reports, votes, and hours in session—legislators are struggling valiantly to keep abreast of these demands.

At the same moment Congress-as-Politicians is busier than ever. Partly because of the sheer scope of modern government, partly because of constituents' keener awareness, citizens are insisting that senators and representatives communicate with them more often, serve their states or districts materially, play the role of ombudsmen, and adhere to strict standards of personal behavior. Legislators have accepted and profited from these functions, but not without misgivings and not without some detriment to their legislative tasks.

The intensified demands upon the two Congresses could well lie beyond the reach of normal men and women. Reflecting on the multiplicity of presidential duties, Woodrow Wilson once remarked that we might be forced to pick our leaders from among "wise and prudent athletes"—a small class of people.[26] The same can now be said of senators and representatives. And if the job specifications exceed reasonable dimensions, can we expect even our most talented citizens to perform these tasks successfully?

In the longer view the question is whether an institution embracing so many disparate motives and careers can continue to function as a coherent whole. Can policies patched together out of many discrete interests really guide the nation on its perilous course? Ever since 1787 people have wondered about these questions. History is only mildly reassuring, and the future poses new and delicate challenges for which the margin of error may be narrower than in the past. And yet, representative democracy itself is a gamble; the proposition that representation can yield wise policy making remains a daring one. As always, it is an article of faith whose ultimate proof lies inevitably in the future.

Notes

1. Alexis de Tocqueville, *Democracy in America,* ed. Phillips Bradley (New York: Vintage Books, 1954), I, 225.
2. Tom Kenworthy, "House, Senate Reject 51% Salary Increase," *Washington Post,* February 8, 1989, A6.
3. Robin Toner, "This Was No Day for a House Party," *New York Times,* February 8, 1989, D24.
4. Woodrow Wilson, *Congressional Government* (Baltimore, Md.: Johns Hopkins University Press, 1981), 210.
5. Richard F. Fenno, Jr., *Home Style: House Members in Their Districts* (Boston, Mass.: Little, Brown, 1978), 168.
6. Glenn R. Parker and Roger H. Davidson, "Why Do Americans Love Their Congressmen So Much More than Their Congress?" *Legislative Studies Quarterly* 4 (February 1979): 53-61.
7. Louis Harris, "Overall Job Rating for Congress Nears Marks for Individual Members," *The Harris Survey,* no. 47, June 13, 1985.
8. Thomas E. Mann, *Unsafe at Any Margin: Interpreting Congressional Elections* (Washington, D.C.: American Enterprise Institute, 1978).
9. Warren E. Miller and the National Election Studies, *American National Election Study, 1982: Post-Election Survey File,* IPSR 9042 (Ann Arbor, Mich.: Inter-University Consortium for Political and Social Research, 1983), 131 (Question E-13).
10. Ibid., 136-137.
11. Bob Benenson, "Savvy 'Stars' Making Local TV a Potent Tool," *Congressional Quarterly Weekly Report,* July 18, 1987, 1551-1555.
12. David S. Broder, "Malarkey from Newt Gingrich," *Washington Post,* April 23, 1989, C7.
13. Harris, "Overall Job Rating"; Richard Morin and Dan Balz, "Majority in Poll Criticize Congress," *Washington Post,* May 26, 1989, A8.
14. Glenn R. Parker, "Some Themes in Congressional Unpopularity," *American Journal of Political Science* 21 (February 1977): 93-109; Roger H. Davidson, David M. Kovenock, and Michael J. O'Leary, *Congress in Crisis* (North Scituate, Mass.: Duxbury Press, 1966), 59-62.
15. Louis Harris, "Voters Convinced Better to Have Divided Federal Government," *The Harris Survey,* no. 59, November 3, 1986.
16. Committee on the Constitutional System, *A Bicentennial Analysis of the American Political Structure* (Washington, D.C.: Committee on the Constitutional System, 1987), 6.
17. Louis Harris, "Congress in Action Should Stay on Live TV," *The Harris Survey,* July 7, 1986.
18. Alvin Toffler, "Congress in the Year 2000," *GAO Review* (Fall 1980): 44.
19. David D. Newson, "The New Diplomatic Agenda: Are Governments Ready? " *International Affairs* (Winter 1988/1989): 33. See also Louis Uchitelle, "U.S. Businesses Loosen Link to Mother Country," *New York Times,* May 21, 1989, 1.
20. "Lessons on Opposition," interview with Barney Frank, *Working Papers*

Magazine (May/June 1982): 43.
21. Toffler, "Congress in the Year 2000," 44.
22. Robert J. Samuelson, "Cultural Salami," *National Journal,* January 28, 1984, 175.
23. Jack L. Walker, "The Origins and Maintenance of Interest Groups in America," *American Political Science Review* 77 (June 1983): 390-406.
24. Toffler, "Congress in the Year 2000," 44.
25. Benjamin R. Barber, *Strong Democracy: Participatory Politics for a New Age* (Berkeley, Calif.: University of California Press, 1984). See also Jane J. Mansbridge, *Beyond Adversary Democracy* (Chicago, Ill.: University of Chicago Press, 1983).
26. Woodrow Wilson, *Constitutional Government in the United States* (New York: Columbia University Press, 1908), 79-80.

Appendix

Table A-1 Party Control of the Presidency, Senate, House, 1901-1991

Congress	Years	President	Senate D	Senate R	Senate Other[a]	House D	House R	House Other[a]
57th	1901-1903	McKinley T. Roosevelt	31	55	4	151	197	9
58th	1903-1905	T. Roosevelt	33	57	—	178	208	—
59th	1905-1907	T. Roosevelt	33	57	—	136	250	—
60th	1907-1909	T. Roosevelt	31	61	—	164	222	—
61st	1909-1911	Taft	32	61	—	172	219	—
62d	1911-1913	Taft	41	51	—	228	161	1
63d	1913-1915	Wilson	51	44	1	291	127	17
64th	1915-1917	Wilson	56	40	—	230	196	9
65th	1917-1919	Wilson	53	42	—	216	210	6
66th	1919-1921	Wilson	47	49	—	190	240	3
67th	1921-1923	Harding	37	59	—	131	301	1
68th	1923-1925	Coolidge	43	51	2	205	225	5
69th	1925-1927	Coolidge	39	56	1	183	247	4
70th	1927-1929	Coolidge	46	49	1	195	237	3
71st	1929-1931	Hoover	39	56	1	167	267	1
72d	1931-1933	Hoover	47	48	1	220	214	1
73d	1933-1935	F. Roosevelt	60	35	1	319	117	5
74th	1935-1937	F. Roosevelt	69	25	2	319	103	10
75th	1937-1939	F. Roosevelt	76	16	4	331	89	13
76th	1939-1941	F. Roosevelt	69	23	4	261	164	4
77th	1941-1943	F. Roosevelt	66	28	2	268	162	5
78th	1943-1945	F. Roosevelt	58	37	1	218	208	4
79th	1945-1947	Truman	56	38	1	242	190	2
80th	1947-1949	Truman	45	51	—	188	245	1
81st	1949-1951	Truman	54	42	—	263	171	1
82d	1951-1953	Truman	49	47	—	234	199	1

Congress	Years	President	Senate D	Senate R	Senate Other[a]	House D	House R	House Other[a]
83d	1953-1955	Eisenhower	47	48	1	211	221	1
84th	1955-1957	Eisenhower	48	47	1	232	203	—
85th	1957-1959	Eisenhower	49	47	—	233	200	—
86th[b]	1959-1961	Eisenhower	65	35	—	284	153	—
87th[b]	1961-1963	Kennedy	65	35	—	263	174	—
88th	1963-1965	Kennedy Johnson	67	33	—	258	177	—
89th	1965-1967	Johnson	68	32	—	295	140	—
90th	1967-1969	Johnson	64	36	—	247	187	—
91st	1969-1971	Nixon	57	43	—	243	192	—
92d	1971-1973	Nixon	54	44	2	254	180	—
93d	1973-1975	Nixon Ford	56	42	2	239	192	1
94th	1975-1977	Ford	60	37	2	291	144	—
95th	1977-1979	Carter	61	38	1	292	143	—
96th	1979-1981	Carter	58	41	1	276	157	—
97th	1981-1983	Reagan	46	53	1	243	192	—
98th	1983-1985	Reagan	45	55	—	267	168	—
99th	1985-1987	Reagan	47	53	—	252	183	—
100th	1987-1989	Reagan	55	45	—	258	177	—
101st	1989-1991	Bush	55	45	—	260	175	—

☐ Republican Control   ☐ Democratic Control

Sources: Department of Commerce, Bureau of the Census, *Statistical Abstract of the United States* (Washington, D.C.: U.S. Government Printing Office, 1980), 509; and *Members of Congress Since 1789*, 2d ed. (Washington, D.C.: Congressional Quarterly, 1981) 176-177. Adapted from Barbara Hinckley, *Congressional Elections* (Washington, D.C.: CQ Press, 1981), 144-145.

[a] Excludes vacancies at beginning of each session.

[b] The 437 members of the House in the 86th and 87th Congresses is attributable to the at-large representative given to both Alaska (January 3, 1959) and Hawaii (August 21, 1959) prior to redistricting in 1962.

Suggested Readings

This list of suggested readings is not intended to be exhaustive. Journal articles, papers delivered at meetings, doctoral dissertations, and individual essays in books are not included. We have listed those books we feel are most useful and accessible to students.

Chapter 1   The Two Congresses

Bibby, John F., ed. *Congress Off the Record*. Washington, D.C.: American Enterprise Institute, 1983.

Dodd, Lawrence C., and Bruce I. Oppenheimer, eds. *Congress Reconsidered*. 4th ed. Washington, D.C.: CQ Press, 1989.

Mayhew, David R. *Congress: The Electoral Connection*. New Haven, Conn.: Yale University Press, 1974.

Miller, Clem. *Member of the House: Letters of a Congressman*. Edited by John W. Baker. New York: Charles Scribner's Sons, 1962.

Parker, Glenn R., ed. *Studies of Congress*. Washington, D.C.: CQ Press, 1984.

Chapter 2   Evolution of the Modern Congress

Cunningham, Noble, Jr., ed. *Circular Letters of Congressmen, 1789-1839*. 3 vols. Chapel Hill: University of North Carolina Press, 1978.

Foley, Michael. *The New Senate: Liberal Influence on a Conservative Institution, 1959-1972*. New Haven, Conn.: Yale University Press, 1980.

Galloway, George B. *History of the House of Representatives*. rev. ed. Edited by Sidney Wise. New York: Thomas Y. Crowell, 1976.

Haynes, George H. *The Senate of the United States: Its History and Practice*. 2 vols. Boston: Houghton Mifflin, 1938.

Josephy, Alvin M., Jr. *On the Hill: A History of the American Congress*. New York: Simon & Schuster, 1980.

MacNeil, Neil. *Forge of Democracy: The House of Representatives.* New York: David McKay, 1963.

Rothman, David J. *Politics and Power: The United States Senate, 1869-1901.* Cambridge, Mass.: Harvard University Press, 1966.

Young, James S. *The Washington Community, 1800-1828.* New York: Columbia University Press, 1966.

Chapter 3 Going for It: Recruitment Roulette

Fowler, Linda L., and Robert D. McClure. *Political Ambition: Who Decides to Run for Congress.* New Haven, Conn.: Yale University Press, 1989.

Gertzog, Irwin N. *Congressional Women: Their Recruitment, Treatment, and Behavior.* New York: Praeger, 1984.

Jacobson, Gary C., and Samuel Kernell. *Strategy and Choice in Congressional Elections.* New Haven, Conn.: Yale University Press, 1981.

Loomis, Burdett. *The New American Politician.* New York: Basic Books, 1988.

Maisel, Louis Sandy. *From Obscurity to Oblivion: Running in the Congressional Primary.* Knoxville: University of Tennessee Press, 1982.

Chapter 4 Making It: The Electoral Game

Alexander, Herbert E. *Financing Politics: Money, Elections, and Political Reform.* 3d ed. Washington, D.C.: CQ Press, 1984.

Cain, Bruce, John Ferejohn, and Morris Fiorina. *The Personal Vote: Constituency Service and Electoral Independence.* Cambridge, Mass.: Harvard University Press, 1987.

Goldenberg, Edie N., and Michael W. Traugott. *Campaigning for Congress.* Washington, D.C.: CQ Press, 1984.

Herrnson, Paul S. *Party Campaigning in the 1980s. Cambridge, Mass.: Harvard University Press, 1988.*

Jackson, Brooks. *Honest Graft: Big Money and the American Political Process.* New York: Alfred A. Knopf, 1988.

Jacobson, Gary C. *The Politics of Congressional Elections.* 2d ed. Boston: Little, Brown, 1987.

Kingdon, John W. *Candidates for Office: Beliefs and Strategies.* New York: Random House, 1966.

Mann, Thomas E. *Unsafe at Any Margin: Interpreting Congressional Elections.* Washington, D.C.: American Enterprise Institute, 1978.

Chapter 5 Being There: Hill Styles and Home Styles

Champagne, Anthony. *Congressman Sam Rayburn.* New Brunswick, N.J.: Rutgers University Press, 1984.

Davidson, Roger H. *The Role of the Congressman*. Indianapolis: Bobbs-Merrill, 1969.

Drew, Elizabeth. *Senator*. New York: Simon & Schuster, 1979.

Fenno, Richard F., Jr. *Home Style: House Members in Their Districts*. Boston: Little, Brown, 1978.

Fiorina, Morris P. *Congress: Keystone of the Washington Establishment*. New Haven, Conn.: Yale University Press, 1977.

Johannes, John R. *To Serve the People: Congress and Constituency Service*. Lincoln: University of Nebraska Press, 1984.

Miller, James A. *Running in Place: Inside the Senate*. New York: Simon & Schuster, ˙1986.

Parker, Glenn R. *Homeward Bound: Exploring Changes in Congressional Behavior*. Pittsburgh: University of Pittsburgh Press, 1986.

Chapter 6   Leaders and Parties in Congress

Bailey, Christopher J. *The Republican Party in the US Senate*. Manchester, England: Manchester University Press, 1988.

Brady, David W. *Critical Elections and Congressional Policy Making*. Stanford: Stanford University Press, 1988.

Hasbrouck, Paul D. *Party Government in the House of Representatives*. New York: Macmillan, 1927.

Mackaman, Frank H., ed. *Understanding Congressional Leadership*. Washington, D.C.: CQ Press, 1981.

Peabody, Robert L. *Leadership in Congress*. Boston: Little, Brown, 1976.

Sinclair, Barbara. *Majority Leadership in the U.S. House*. Baltimore: Johns Hopkins University Press, 1983.

Truman, David B. *The Congressional Party*. New York: John Wiley & Sons, 1959.

Chapter 7   Committees: Workshops of Congress

Fenno, Richard F., Jr. *Congressmen in Committees*. Boston: Little, Brown, 1973.

Price, David E. *Who Makes the Laws?* Cambridge, Mass.: Schenkman Publishing, 1972.

Smith, Steven S., and Christopher J. Deering. *Committees in Congress*. Washington, D.C.: CQ Press, 1984.

Wilson, Woodrow. *Congressional Government*. Reprint of 1885 ed. Baltimore: Johns Hopkins University Press, 1981.

Chapter 8   Congress and the President

Binkley, Wilfred. *President and Congress*. New York: Alfred A. Knopf, 1947.

Edwards, George C. *At the Margins: Presidential Leadership of Congress.* New Haven, Conn.: Yale University Press, 1989.

Fisher, Louis. *Constitutional Conflicts between Congress and the President.* Princeton, N.J.: Princeton University Press, 1985.

————. *The Politics of Shared Power: Congress and the Executive.* 2d ed. Washington, D.C.: CQ Press, 1987.

Jones, Charles O. *The Trusteeship Presidency: Jimmy Carter and the United States Congress.* Baton Rouge: Louisiana State University Press, 1988.

Light, Paul C. *The President's Agenda.* Baltimore: Johns Hopkins University Press, 1982.

Sundquist, James L. *Decline and Resurgence of Congress.* Washington, D.C.: Brookings Institution, 1981.

Wayne, Stephen J. *The Legislative Presidency.* New York: Harper & Row, 1978.

Chapter 9   Congress and the Bureaucracy

Aberbach, Joel D. *Keeping a Watchful Eye: The Politics of Congressional Oversight.* Washington, D.C.: Brookings Institution, 1990.

Arnold, R. Douglas. *Congress and the Bureaucracy: A Theory of Influence.* New Haven, Conn.: Yale University Press, 1979.

Dodd, Lawrence C., and Richard Schott. *Congress and the Administrative State.* New York: John Wiley & Sons, 1979.

Foreman, Christopher J., Jr. *Signals from the Hill: Congressional Oversight and the Challenge of Social Regulation.* New Haven, Conn.: Yale University Press, 1988.

Fisher, Louis. *Constitutional Dialogues: Interpretation as Political Process.* Princeton, N.J.: Princeton University Press, 1988.

Mackenzie, G. Calvin. *The Politics of Presidential Appointments.* New York: Free Press, 1981.

Ogul, Morris S. *Congress Oversees the Bureaucracy.* Pittsburgh: University of Pittsburgh Press, 1976.

Chapter 10   Congress and Organized Interests

Bauer, Raymond A., Ithiel de Sola Pool, and Lewis. Anthony Dexter. *American Business and Public Policy: The Politics of Foreign Trade.* New York: Atherton Press, 1963.

Cigler, Allan J., and Burdett A. Loomis, eds. *Interest Group Politics.* 2d ed. Washington, D.C.: CQ Press, 1986.

Freeman, J. Leiper. *The Political Process: Executive Bureau-Legislative Committee Relations.* rev. ed. New York: Random House, 1965.

Gross, Bertram M. *The Legislative Struggle: A Study in Social Combat.* New York: McGraw-Hill, 1953.

Marcuss, Stanley J. *Effective Washington Representation*. New York: Harcourt Brace Jovanovich, 1983.

Miller, Stephen. *Special Interest Groups in American Politics*. New Brunswick, N.J.: Transaction Books, 1983.

Oppenheimer, Bruce I. *Oil and the Congressional Process*. Lexington, Mass.: Lexington Books, 1974.

Sabato, Larry J. *PAC Power*. New York: W. W. Norton, 1984.

Truman, David B. *The Governmental Process, Political Interests and Public Opinion*. 2d ed. New York: Alfred A. Knopf, 1971.

Chapter 11   Congressional Rules and Procedures

Bach, Stanley, and Steven S. Smith. *Managing Uncertainty in the House of Representatives*. Washington, D.C.: Brookings Institution, 1989.

Longley, Lawrence D., and Walter J. Oleszek. *Bicameral Politics: Conference Committees in Congress*. New Haven, Conn.: Yale University Press, 1989.

Oleszek, Walter J. *Congressional Procedures and the Policy Process*. 3d ed. Washington, D.C.: CQ Press, 1988.

Redman, Eric. *The Dance of Legislation*. New York: Simon & Schuster, 1973.

Smith, Steven S. *Call to Order: Floor Politics in the House and Senate*. Washington, D.C.: Brookings Institution, 1989.

Chapter 12   Decision Making in Congress

Brady, David W. *Congressional Voting in a Partisan Era*. Lawrence: University Press of Kansas, 1973.

Clausen, Aage R. *How Congressmen Decide: A Policy Focus*. New York: St. Martin's Press, 1973.

Kingdon, John W. *Congressmen's Voting Decisions*. 2d ed. New York: Harper & Row, 1980.

Kozak, David. *Contexts of Congressional Decision Behavior*. Lanham, Md.: University Press of America, 1984.

Schneider, Jerrold E. *Ideological Coalitions in Congress*. Westport, Conn.: Greenwood Press, 1979.

Shull, Steven A. *Domestic Policy Formation: Presidential-Congressional Partnership?* Westport, Conn.: Greenwood Press, 1983.

Chapter 13   Congress, Budgets, and Domestic Policy Making

Bosso, Christopher J. *Pesticides and Politics: The Life Cycle of a Public Issue*. Pittsburgh: University of Pittsburgh Press, 1987.

Kingdon, John W. *Agendas, Alternatives, and Public Policies*. Boston: Little,

Brown, 1984.

LeLoup, Lance T. *The Fiscal Congress*. Westport, Conn.: Greenwood Press, 1980.

Light, Paul. *Artful Work: The Politics of Social Security Reform*. New York: Random House, 1985.

Polsby, Nelson W. *Political Innovation in America*. New Haven, Conn.: Yale University Press, 1984.

Reid, T. R. *Congressional Odyssey: The Saga of a Senate Bill*. San Francisco: W. H. Freeman, 1980.

Ripley, Randall B., and Grace A. Franklin. *Congress, the Bureaucracy, and Public Policy*. 4th ed. Homewood, Ill.: Dorsey Press, 1987.

Schick, Allen. *Congress and Money*. Washington, D.C.: Urban Institute. 1980.

———, ed. *Making Economic Policy in Congress*. Washington, D.C.: American Enterprise Institute, 1983.

Schuman, Howard E. *Politics and the Budget*. 2d ed. Englewood Cliffs, N.J.: Prentice-Hall, 1988.

Sundquist, James L. *Politics and Policy: The Eisenhower, Kennedy, and Johnson Years*. Washington, D.C.: Brookings Institution, 1968.

Weaver, R. Kent. *Automatic Government: The Politics of Indexation*. Washington, D.C.: Brookings Institution, 1988.

Wildavsky, Aaron. *The New Politics of the Budgetary Process*. Glenview, Ill.: Scott, Foresman/Little, Brown, 1988.

Chapter 14   Congress and National Security Policies

Crabb, Cecil V., Jr., and Pat M. Holt. *Invitation to Struggle: Congress, the President, and Foreign Policy*. 3d ed. Washington, D.C: CQ Press, 1989.

Franck, Thomas, and Edward Wiesband. *Foreign Policy by Congress*. New York: Oxford University Press, 1979.

Muskie, Edmund S., Kenneth W. Thompson, eds. *The President, the Congress, and Foreign Policy*. Lanham, Md.: University Press of America, 1986.

Waller, Douglas C. *Congress and the Nuclear Freeze*. Amherst: University of Massachusetts Press, 1987.

Whalen, Charles W., Jr. *The House and Foreign Policy: The Irony of Congressional Reform*. Chapel Hill: University of North Carolina Press, 1982.

Chapter 15   The Two Congresses and the American People

Barber, Benjamin R. *Strong Democracy: Participatory Politics for a New Age*. Berkeley: University of California Press, 1984.

Broder, David S. *Behind the Front Page: A Candid Look at How the News is Made.* New York: Simon & Schuster, 1987.

Davidson, Roger H., and Walter J. Oleszek. *Congress against Itself.* Bloomington: Indiana University Press, 1977.

Hess, Stephen. *The Ultimate Insiders: U.S. Senators in the National Media.* Washington, D.C.: Brookings Institution, 1986.

Maass, Arthur. *Congress and the Common Good.* New York: Basic Books, 1983.

Smith, Hedrick. *The Power Game: How Washington Works.* New York: Random House, 1988.

Index